THE DEATH OF THE KPD

*Communism and Anti-Communism
in West Germany,
1945–1956*

PATRICK MAJOR

CLARENDON PRESS · OXFORD

1997

Oxford University Press, Great Clarendon Street, Oxford OX2 6DP

Oxford New York
Athens Auckland Bangkok Bogota Bombay
Buenos Aires Calcutta Cape Town Dar es Salaam
Delhi Florence Hong Kong Istanbul Karachi
Kuala Lumpur Madras Madrid Melbourne
Mexico City Nairobi Paris Singapore
Taipei Tokyo Toronto Warsaw
and associated companies in
Berlin Ibadan

Oxford is a trade mark of Oxford University Press

Published in the United States by
Oxford University Press Inc., New York

© Patrick Major 1997

British Library Cataloguing in Publication Data
Data available

Library of Congress Cataloging in Publication Data
Major, Patrick.
The death of KPD : communism and anti-communism in West Germany,
1945–1956 / Patrick Major.
p. cm. — (Oxford historical monographs)
Includes bibliographical references.
1. Kommunistische Partei Deutschlands—History. 2. Communism—
Germany (West)—History. 3. Germany (West)—Politics and
government. I. Title. II. Series.
JN3971.A98K6536 1998
324.243'075'09044—dc21 97-26765
ISBN 0-19-820693-3

1 3 5 7 9 10 8 6 4 2

Typeset by Graphicraft Typesetters Ltd., Hong Kong
Printed in Great Britain by
Bookcraft Ltd., Midsomer-Norton,
Nr. Bath, Somerset

For EJW (1910–88)
whose brew was always crucial.

PREFACE

On a spring evening in East Berlin in March 1990, I emerged after a long day from a soundproofed cabin at the rear of one of the many reading-rooms frequented in the making of this book. The establishment in question belonged to what had until recently been the Institute of Marxism-Leninism, but which some pieces of black sticky tape, artfully arranged over the old name-plate, now proclaimed to be the 'Institute for the History of the Labour Movement'. (The institute underwent a second metamorphosis in 1993 to become the 'Archive Foundation of the Parties and Mass Organizations of the GDR'.) The deathly silence and almost complete darkness, culminating in an immovable door, confirmed that I had been inadvertently locked in. Looking for a means of escape, I discovered a telephone directory marked 'For the use of the comrades only'. Dialling what I thought was the porter's number, I explained my plight and was relieved to hear that he was on his way up. After twenty minutes of agitated waiting, however, I telephoned again, repeating exactly where I was—on the fifth floor—to which I received the chilling reply: 'There *is* no fifth floor.' It transpired that I had been talking to a man in a building several miles away, in another part of Berlin entirely.

My first and foremost debt is to the staff of the above-mentioned founda-tion, not only for releasing me later that evening from my Kafkaesque pre-dicament, but also for guiding me through the most important files needed in this study. In particular, Volker Lange and Ute Räuber deserve special mention. I must also thank the staffs of all the other archives consulted, especially the model service provided at the Bundesarchiv in Koblenz, and the Archiv der sozialen Demokratie in Bonn-Bad Godesberg. A special debt is also owed to Dr Ernst Schmidt for sharing his personal archive at the Ruhrland Museum in Essen, and to Dr Paul Müller for granting me early access to his recently deceased father's papers. I should also like to thank the Interior Ministry in North Rhine-Westphalia for being open-minded enough to declassify a large number of its documents and for being so generous with photocopying. Dr Horst Romeyk, of the Hauptstaatsarchiv in Düsseldorf, was also instrumental in making these files available.

The German Academic Exchange Service funded one year of research under Professor Hans Mommsen at the Ruhr University Bochum, who acted as a source of inspiration and hospitality, and opened several doors which would otherwise have remained closed. The staff of the Bochum Institute of Labour History and its excellent library were also a great support. The generosity of the Alexander von Humboldt Foundation enabled a second year of more roving research, based at the University of Mannheim's Arbeitsbereich Geschichte der DDR. There, I benefited from the considerable expertise of Dietrich Staritz, Hermann Weber, Werner Müller, Jan Foitzik, and Hermann Schwenger, who, together, provided a stimulating and congenial environment for study. Dietrich Staritz must, however, be singled out for his thoughtful suggestions and generous time, and for convincing me of the value of leaving some questions open. His precipitate departure from the university scene, following the revelations in 1994 of his involvement with the East and West German secret services in the 1960s, has saddened me for a multitude of reasons. Although such activities can under no circumstances be condoned, it would be a great pity if the scholarly corpus were to be thrown out with the Stasi bathwater.

Others who helped along the way include Dr Detlef Siegfried of Kiel; Rolf Georg Lieske of Essen; Ralf Haselow of East Berlin, as it then was, whose hospitality has always been bottomless; and fellow St Antonian, Dr Philip Murphy, who has been a great friend throughout. I am also grateful to my father, John Major, of the University of Hull, for his many useful suggestions about American sources. Last, but certainly not least, I must thank my supervisor at St Antony's, Tony Nicholls, for simply letting me get on with it and providing constant reassurance at every stage. He also kindled the initial spark by spotting a fascinating gap in the historiography at the outset of research, which proved inspired in view of the turn of events during fieldwork. Without the collapse of East German Communism in 1989, this would have been only half the book which follows.

University of Warwick   P.N.M.
1996

CONTENTS

LIST OF TABLES

ABBREVIATIONS

Abt.	Abteilung (Department)
AdsD	Archiv der sozialen Demokratie (Archive of Social Democracy)
AES	Archivsammlung-Ernst-Schmidt (Ernst Schmidt Archival Collection)
AG	*Arbeitsgemeinschaft* (Working Group)
BAK	Bundesarchiv Koblenz (Federal Archive Koblenz)
BfV	Bundesamt für Verfassungsschutz (Federal Office for the Protection of the Constitution)
BL	*Bezirksleitung* (Regional Leadership)
BzG	*Beiträge zur Geschichte der Arbeiterbewegung*
CCG (BE)	Control Commission for Germany (British Element)
CFM	Council of Foreign Ministers
DFD	Demokratischer Frauenbund Deutschlands (Democratic Women's League of Germany)
DGB	Deutscher Gewerkschaftsbund (German Trade Union Federation)
DKP	Deutsche Kommunistische Partei (German Communist Party)
ERP	European Recovery Programme [Marshall Aid]
EUCOM	European Command [US Army]
FDGB	Freier Deutscher Gewerkschaftsbund (Free German Trade Union Federation)
FDJ	Freie Deutsche Jugend (Free German Youth)
FO	Foreign Office
FRG	Federal Republic of Germany
FV	*Freies Volk*
GAP	Gruppe Arbeiterpolitik (Workers' Politics Group)
GDR	German Democratic Republic
GfDSF	Gesellschaft für Deutsch-Sowjetische Freundschaft (Society for German-Soviet Friendship)
HICOG	High Commission for Germany
HStA	Hauptstaatsarchiv (Main State Archive)
ID	Intelligence Division
IG	Industriegewerkschaft (Industrial Union)
IM	Innenministerium (Interior Ministry)
IVB	Industrieverband Bergbau (Industrial Association of Mining)
IWK	*Internationale wissenschaftliche Korrespondenz zur Geschichte der deutschen Arbeiterbewegung*
KL	*Kreisleitung* (District Leadership)

Komm.	Kommission (Commission)
KPD	Kommunistische Partei Deutschlands (Communist Party of Germany)
KPO	Kommunistische Partei Deutschlands—Opposition
KZ	*Konzentrationslager* (Concentration Camp)
LfV	Landesamt für Verfassungsschutz (*Land* Office for the Protection of the Constitution)
LL	*Landesleitung* (*Land* Leadership)
LS	*Landessekretariat* (*Land* Secretariat)
Ltg.	*Leitung* (Leadership)
Ltr.	*Leiter* (Leader)
LVors.	*Landesvorsitzende/r* (*Land* Chairman/woman)
MfS	Ministerium für Staatssicherheit (Ministry of State Security)
MRC	Modern Records Centre
NF	Nationale Front (National Front)
NKFD	Nationalkomitee Freies Deutschland (National Committee of Free Germany)
NKVD	Narodny Kommissariat Vnutrennikh Del (People's Commissariat of Internal Affairs)
NL	*Nachlaß* (Papers)
NRW	North Rhine-Westphalia
OBM	*Oberbürgermeister* (Chief Mayor)
OMGUS	Office of Military Government, United States
OSS	Office of Strategic Services
PB	Politburo
PCF	Parti Communiste Français (French Communist Party)
PCI	Partito Comunista Italiano (Italian Communist Party)
PD	Political Division
PRO	Public Record Office
PV	*Parteivorstand* (Party Executive)
RGO	Revolutionäre Gewerkschafts-Opposition (Revolutionary Trade Union Opposition)
RWIS	Rhine-Westphalia Intelligence Staff
SAPMO	Stiftung Archiv der Parteien und Massenorganisationen der DDR (Archive Foundation of the Parties and Mass Organizations of the GDR)
SBZ	Sowjetische Besatzungszone (Soviet Occupation Zone)
SED	Sozialistische Einheitspartei Deutschlands (Socialist Unity Party of Germany)
Sek.	*Sekretariat* (Secretariat)
SMAD	Sowjetische Militäradministration in Deutschland (Soviet Military Administration in Germany)
SPD	Sozialdemokratische Partei Deutschlands (Social Democratic Party of Germany)

UAPD	Unabhängige Arbeiterpartei Deutschlands (Independent Workers' Party of Germany)
VfZ	*Vierteljahreshefte für Zeitgeschichte*
VVN	Vereinigung der Verfolgten des Naziregimes (Association of Persecutees of the Nazi Regime)
WPIS	Weekly Political Intelligence Summary
WFTU	World Federation of Trade Unions
WVE	*Westdeutsches Volks-Echo*
ZL	*Zonenleitung* (Zones Leadership)
ZPA	Zentrales Parteiarchiv (Central Party Archive)
ZS	*Zentralsekretariat* (Central Secretariat)

Introduction

THE history of the Kommunistische Partei Deutschlands (KPD) in West Germany after the Second World War, banned only eleven years after it had emerged from the shadow of the Third Reich, was without doubt a political disaster. The object of this investigation is to sift through the debris and decide what combination of human error, structural failure, and adverse environmental conditions was to blame for the party's untimely end. Since this, the final chapter in the history of the KPD, has been notoriously underresearched in comparison with the Weimar party, not to mention the East German Communists, what follows is the first in-depth study of post-war West German Communism to be published in English. It is also the first general account based on the party's internal files, offering the overall contours of an almost forgotten history which, more often than not, has been further obscured and contorted in the cause of the Cold War. It is my intention, after the cessation of hostilities so to speak, to reconstruct some of the secret skirmishes fought behind the lines between Communists and anti-Communists in West Germany. Unlike the erstwhile combatants, however, I hope to generate rather more light than heat in the process.

Since this has been such a highly charged history, laden with Cold War polemic and counter-polemic, the reader may find it helpful if I first sketch out the opposing battle lines and conflicting interpretations. The most persistent preconception regarding the KPD in the western camp has been that, had the non-Communist political parties not stood up to the Communists, and had the western occupiers not stabilized the western zones economically, West Germany might well have fallen prey to Communist subversion in the late 1940s. As the American military governor of the day, Lucius D. Clay, claimed in his memoirs: 'If Germany ended in economic chaos it would be even more susceptible to Communist indoctrination.'[1] This alarmist viewpoint is echoed in more recent works, however, as, for instance, when one of the most widely read English-speaking historians of Germany described the role of the West German Social

[1] Lucius D. Clay, *Decision in Germany* (London, 1950), 123.

Democratic leader: 'Schumacher's great achievement after 1945 was to prevent the effective incursion of Communism into the Western occupation zones.'[2]

Those acquainted with the historiography of the Cold War will no doubt recognize these arguments as a main thesis of the 'traditionalist' school, which argued that the West merely reacted defensively to Communist expansionism in the immediate post-war years. The so-called 'revisionists', who challenged this explanation in the 1960s and 1970s, argued instead that the western Allies, and in particular the Americans, overreacted to the red menace and that anti-Communism was in fact little more than a cover for the restoration of capitalism in West Germany.[3] For the West German Communists themselves, in many ways revisionists before revisionism, they were simply the victims of a parasitical and long-standing anti Communist state. If the fiasco of the KPD was referred to at all, it was argued, for instance in the official East German history of the period, that the 'progressive forces' in West Germany, with the KPD in the van, 'were opposed by a front stretching from the imperialist occupation powers, to the German reactionaries, right the way to the rightist leaders of the Social Democrats and trade unions'.[4] These several enemies, if one follows this particular conspiracy theory, were in fact all pawns of a monolithic international monopoly capitalism, operating through the western occupation powers, and, at a further remove, through the Christian Democratic-led Federal government under the 'clerico-militarist', Konrad Adenauer. This reactionary oligarchy was supposedly lent a modicum of mass support by the class treachery of the Social Democratic leadership around Kurt Schumacher.

Leaving aside the intrusive political invective, the KPD could perhaps legitimately claim to have fallen victim to the same authoritarian tendencies —presided over by some of the same individuals—which had seen it banned under Hitler. Nevertheless, one must recognize even at this stage that, just as the West was capable of demonizing an exaggerated red menace, the East, too, had an interest in inflating anti-Communist persecution for the purposes of Cold War propaganda. Even less satisfactorily, the KPD's version of events massively overstated the level of popular support it enjoyed from the population at large. Despite repeated claims that it was championing the true interests of the West German people, the party was in fact

---

[2] Gordon A. Craig, *The Germans* (Harmondsworth, 1984), 37.

[3] For a recent survey of these debates see David Reynolds (ed.), *The Origins of the Cold War in Europe: International Perspectives* (New Haven and London, 1994).

[4] Institut für Marxismus-Leninismus beim Zentralkomitee der SED (ed.), *Geschichte der deutschen Arbeiterbewegung* (East Berlin, 1966), vi. 156.

shunned by an overwhelmingly hostile society with a long pedigree of anti-Communist behaviour. Clearly, therefore, one important task of this study must be to locate the experience of the KPD somewhere between the extremes of traditionalist perpetrator and revisionist victim.

More recently, since the Berlin Wall crumbled in 1989 and access to internal party documents became possible, a new victimization theory has been gaining currency, but this time of a stab in the back by the KPD's fraternal comrade in arms, the Socialist Unity Party (SED) of East Germany. As well as the West German authorities imprisoning thousands of Communist functionaries, the GDR's notorious Ministry of State Security, or Stasi, arrested and tortured an unlucky few of the KPD's leading cadres. Consequently, the blame for some of the less realistic political campaigns waged by the KPD in Bonn could more properly be laid at the door of the SED in East Berlin. Yet, whereas the KPD leadership may have been forced to yield to this tutelage, it cannot be taken for granted that the rank and file were equally accepting. As will become clearer in due course, there was a considerable gap between decision-makers safely ensconced behind closed doors in East Berlin, and the KPD's unenviable front-line troops, agitating on the shop-floors and petitioning in the streets.

As well as the intra-German context, it is also necessary to consider the KPD's international position within the global politics of the Cold War. As already noted, the western occupiers all too readily regarded the KPD as the western face of the East German SED, which in turn was dismissed as a Soviet puppet. The Anglo-Americans may also have been tempted to project the more real threat of the French and Italian Communists on to the situation in Germany. Events in the East, such as the Berlin blockade or the 1953 uprising, or, even further afield, the Prague coup of 1948, further damaged the KPD. On the other side of the world, the Korean War was also to have an indirect, but nevertheless palpable, impact on the party, turning it into a potential fifth column for those willing to believe that South Korea was a dress rehearsal for West Germany. The party's eastern chickens also came home to roost in more immediate ways, for instance with the arrival of the ten million refugees from the former eastern territories. If the expellees brought anything with them, it was a deep hatred of Communism.

The following study is based on a doctoral thesis completed at St Antony's College, Oxford, in 1993.[5] It was decided to structure the analysis

---

[5] Patrick Major, 'The German Communist Party (KPD) in the Western Zones and in Western Germany, 1945–1956', D.Phil. thesis (Oxford University, 1993).

thematically rather than chronologically in eight chapters. The first is simply designed to set the post-war KPD in its historical context. The following five examine the politics and organization of the KPD itself; the final two fall under the heading of anti-Communism and deal rather more with the KPD's enemies. Inevitably, the book as a whole is primarily a work of political history. Nevertheless, a conscious effort has been made to avoid regurgitating too many party resolutions, and to apply a pragmatic eye to the dividing line between theoretical wishful thinking and hard political reality—a notorious blindspot of the KPD leadership itself. I have also attempted, wherever possible, to give appropriate socio-historical insights into the tenacity of local KPD milieux.

As well as unearthing much original material denied earlier investigators, I was fortunate to be able to draw on a growing array of German secondary literature.[6] (There is almost literally nothing on the subject in English.[7]) As might be expected, the Weimar party has been well researched and is altogether at a more advanced stage of historical interpretation. For former GDR historians the post-war western fiasco was usually taboo, so that East German histories of the KPD are conspicuous by their almost complete absence.[8] Early West German histories are equally rare; those that were written served to justify the Federal Republic's political system, or as handbooks in the fight against Communism.[9] There are, nevertheless, a number of more recent histories, above all the pioneering work of

---

[6] Bibliographies in descending order of usefulness: Walter Völkel and Christiana Stuff (eds.), *Systematische Bibliographie von Zeitungen, Zeitschriften und Büchern zur politischen und gesellschaftlichen Entwicklung der SBZ/DDR seit 1945* (Opladen, 1986), i. 814–33; Klaus Günther and Kurt Thomas Schmitz, *SPD, KPD/DKP, DGB in den Westzonen und in der Bundesrepublik Deutschland 1945–75: Eine Bibliographie* (2nd edn.; Bonn, 1980); Institut für Gesellschaftswissenschaften beim ZK der SED (ed.), *Bibliographie zur Geschichte der kommunistischen und Arbeiterparteien (Literatur aus den Jahren 1945–1958)*, ii. *Deutschland*, pt. 2, *KPD (Mai 1946–1958)* (East Berlin, 1960); Susan K. Kinnell (ed.), *Communism in the World since 1945: An Annotated Bibliography* (Santa Barbara, Calif., and Oxford, 1987).

[7] William A. Douglas, 'The KPD against Rearmament: The Role of the West German Communist Party in the Soviet Campaign Against West German Rearmament, 1949–1953', Ph.D. thesis (Princeton University, 1964); Wallace W. Berry, 'A History and Case Study of the Communist Party of Germany (KPD) 1945–1969', Ph.D. thesis (Stanford University, Calif., 1971). Neither was able to consult primary sources.

[8] One of the few treatments is Gerhard Mannschatz and Josef Seider, *Zum Kampf der KPD im Ruhrgebiet für die Einigung der Arbeiterklasse und die Entmachtung der Monopolherren 1945–1947* (East Berlin, 1962). Less doctrinaire is Günter Benser, *Die KPD im Jahre der Befreiung: Vorbereitung und Aufbau der legalen kommunistischen Massenpartei (Jahreswende 1944/1945 bis Herbst 1945)* (East Berlin, 1985).

[9] For example, Hilmar Toppe, *Der Kommunismus in Deutschland* (Munich, 1961), 68–95. Less polemical is Hans Kluth, *Die KPD in der Bundesrepublik: Ihre politische Tätigkeit und Organisation 1945–1956* (Cologne and Opladen, 1959).

Werner Müller and Dietrich Staritz, as well as several reassessments—
some more searching than others—by writers close to the KPD's sucessor
party, the DKP.[10] This particular study only picks up the historical thread as the KPD
emerged from illegality in 1945.[11] Nevertheless, as the overview in the first
chapter is designed to show, the burden of the past weighed heavily
on the post-war party. The Communists were haunted by their share of
responsibility for the collapse of Weimar and the rise of Hitler, and in
some ways became prisoners of the mistakes they belatedly sought to
rectify. Post-war Germany was, however, not the same place as inter-
war Germany. The KPD's theory of the 'refascistization' of the Federal
Republic was consequently both an oversimplification and misrepresentation, and the belief in the inevitability of a Third World War a damaging
delusion. At the same time, the quite legitimate grievances against former
Nazi persecutors produced a form of victim mentality among Communist
survivors, who perhaps overestimated the moral capital they could subsequently expect to extract from non-Communists. Instead, as West Germany boomed under the 'economic miracle' of the 1950s, the KPD became
the ghost at the feast, an unpleasant reminder of an unpleasant past.

The real substance of the book begins with Chapter 2 and a long-
standing historical debate: was there *any* chance of a Socialist Unity Party,
based on a merger of Communists and Social Democrats, outside the
Soviet Occupation Zone? Even at the time, the Communists claimed that

---

[10] Werner Müller, *Die KPD und die 'Einheit der Arbeiterklasse'* (Frankfurt am Main
and New York, 1979); Dietrich Staritz, 'Die Kommunistische Partei Deutschlands', in Richard
Stöss (ed.), *Parteien-Handbuch: Die Parteien der Bundesrepublik Deutschland 1945–1980*
(Opladen, 1983), 1663–1809. Other recent publications worthy of mention include: Beate
Meyer and Joachim Szodrzynski (eds.), *Vom Zweifeln und Weitermachen: Fragmente der Hamburger KPD-Geschichte* (Hamburg, 1988); *KPD 1945–1968: Dokumente*, ed. Günter Judick
et al. (2 vols.; Neuss, 1989) compiled by some of those involved at the time; and Georg
Fülberth, *KPD und DKP 1945–1990: Zwei kommunistische Parteien in der vierten Periode
kapitalistischer Entwicklung* (Heilbronn, 1990), which unfortunately forgoes archival sources
for the period under consideration.

[11] The best political history of the underground KPD is still Horst Duhnke, *Die KPD
von 1933 bis 1945* (Cologne, 1972). New insights have been added by Hermann Weber,
*'Weiße Flecken' in der Geschichte: Die KPD-Opfer der Stalinschen Säuberungen und ihre
Rehabilitierung* (2nd edn.; Frankfurt am Main, 1990). Good on the practical problems of
KPD resistance are Detlev Peukert, *Die KPD im Widerstand: Verfolgung und Untergrundarbeit an Rhein und Ruhr 1933 bis 1945* (Wuppertal, 1980); and Beatrix Herlemann, *Die
Emigration als Kampfposten: Die Anleitung des kommunistischen Widerstandes in Deutschland
aus Frankreich, Belgien und den Niederlanden* (Königstein im Taunus, 1982). For KPD breakaways see Jan Foitzik, *Zwischen den Fronten: Zur Politik, Organisation und Funktion linker
politischer Kleinorganisationen im Widerstand 1933 bis 1939/40 unter besonderer Berücksichtigung des Exils* (Bonn, 1986).

only western military government and the SPD leadership stood between them and a unity party in West Germany. In turn, the KPD was accused by non-Communists of wanting unity, not so much to heal the rift in the labour movement which had existed since the First World War, but rather to gain hegemony over a united Germany as a goal of Soviet foreign policy. Certainly, the Communists campaigned hard for an SED in the western zones, but with disappointing results.

In search of the reasons for this failure, a stream of local case-studies of KPD–SPD relations has been steadily appearing since the mid-1970s.[12] In general, the reasons adduced have become more complex with deepening knowledge. As well as military government vetoes and Schumacher's intransigence, the abiding memory of internecine conflict between the reformist and revolutionary wings of the labour movement, dating back to the nineteenth century, has been cited as a cultural block to fusion. Another tendency of more recent research has been to decentralize the problem away from the respective party leaderships and to highlight the views of the rank and file. This reflects not only the clear sympathy of some authors for basis democracy, but also the anarchic conditions of post-war Germany, compartmentalized by wartime destruction and zonal division. The year 1945, in particular, has indeed been seen by some as a squandered opportunity to reconcile a divided labour movement. I do not pretend to have enlarged knowledge on spontaneous KPD–SPD merger tendencies in 1945 by undertaking the necessary micro-studies myself, but rely here on existing publications. What I have been able to do is to show the internal resignation which belied the Communists' public faith in merger. As will also become evident, if there was a window of

---

[12] Holger Christier, *Sozialdemokratie und Kommunismus: Die Politik der SPD und der KPD in Hamburg 1945–1949* (Hamburg, 1975); Lutz Niethammer *et al.* (eds.) *Arbeiterinitiative 1945: Antifaschistische Ausschüsse und Reorganisation der Arbeiterbewegung in Deutschland* (Wuppertal, 1976); Peter Brandt, *Antifaschismus und Arbeiterbewegung: Aufbau—Ausprägung —Politik in Bremen 1945/46* (Hamburg, 1976); Gerhard Fisch and Fritz Krause, *SPD und KPD 1945/46: Einheitsbestrebungen der Arbeiterparteien: Dargestellt an Beispielen aus Südhessen* (Frankfurt am Main, 1978); Ulrich Hauth, *Die Politik von KPD und SED gegenüber der westdeutschen Sozialdemokratie (1945–1948)* (Frankfurt am Main, 1978); Albrecht Lein, *Antifaschistische Aktion 1945: Die 'Stunde Null' in Braunschweig* (Göttingen, 1978); Hartmut Pietsch, *Militärregierung, Bürokratie und Sozialisierung: Zur Entwicklung des politischen Systems in den Städten des Ruhrgebietes 1945 bis 1948* (Duisburg, 1978); Inge Marßolek, *Arbeiterbewegung nach dem Krieg (1945–1948): Am Beispiel Remscheid, Solingen, Wuppertal* (Frankfurt am Main and New York, 1983); Reinhold Billstein, *Das entscheidende Jahr: Sozialdemokratie und Kommunistische Partei in Köln 1945/46* (Cologne, 1988); Detlef Siegfried, *Zwischen Einheitspartei und 'Bruderkampf': SPD und KPD in Schleswig-Holstein 1945/46* (Kiel, 1992); Udo Vorholt and Volker Zaib, *SED im Ruhrgebiet?: Einheitsfront-Politik im Nachkriegsdeutschland —eine regionale Studie* (Münster and Hamburg, 1994).

opportunity at all in 1945, the KPD was as much to blame as anyone for its premature closure.

In the light of this failure, Chapter 2 goes on to discuss the KPD's eastern connection with the SED in East Germany. This was always a taboo subject for West Germany's Communists. At most, they might have conceded sharing the same political goals, but not that they were directly controlled by the 'brother party'. From the outset of research I was sceptical about these disclaimers, in view of the two parties' almost identical political vocabulary. I was not prepared, however, for the obsessive interference by the SED in the KPD's affairs at almost every level. In the late 1940s this democratic centralist control was admittedly hampered by the after-effects of Nazi persecution and Allied zonal division, but to all intents and purposes the SED and KPD were one party, until formally separated in early 1949. This does not mean that there were not serious political differences between the two behind closed doors, yet even after the formation of separate states later that year, the long arm of East Berlin's West Commission continued to reach through the iron curtain. I was fortunate to discover some of the surviving protocols of this secret body, and also to interview its one-time director, Karl Schirdewan. However damaging the eastern connection was politically, only when one understands the intensity of the KPD's organizational and financial dependence on the SED, can one appreciate the futility of speculating about a polycentrist or 'Eurocommunist' breakaway before 1956.

Political scientists have for a long time divided Communist parties into ruling and non-ruling variants. The post-war KPD was in the dilemma of trying to be both. It is often forgotten today that in the immediate post-war years the KPD in fact held ministerial portfolios in all but one of the *Länder* of the western zones. Using a mixture of internal and published materials, Chapter 3 outlines the KPD's attempts to become a mainstream party of government in West Germany, committed to parliamentary politics. The very fact that the Communists were prepared to play the democratic game at all meant a radical departure from the rejectionist politics of Weimar. The main issues of the day—socialization of industry, denazification, and Marshall Aid—are covered, as well as the overall strategy of bloc politics, aimed at forging a popular front not only with the Social Democrats, but, more optimistically, with the Liberals and Christian Democrats too. This approach served the Communists in the Soviet Zone, as well as other eastern European ruling parties, highly effectively, but under very different circumstances. Nevertheless, what amounted to a frontist strategy was also forced upon the KPD, despite its narrowing parliamentary room for manœuvre once the anti-fascist consensus turned into an anti-Communist consensus. Moreover, there was a subtle change in the nature of the revolution being preached from the Soviet Occupation Zone (SBZ). The eastern Communists went from being a political common denominator, urging a consensual, negative programme of denazification and expropriation, to a pace-setting avant-garde bent on becoming a ruling party. Thus, from 1948 the 'anti-fascist, democratic upheaval (*Umwälzung*)' in the SBZ became less generally anti-fascist and more explicitly pro-Communist. Unsurprisingly, the western Communists were unable to keep up, and regarded this consolidation of power as a betrayal of their carefully cultivated, reformist image, which had, of course, been imposed by the East in the first place.

Despite the apparent decision to take off the parliamentary gloves and revert to the bare-knuckle politics of extra-parliamentary confrontation, symbolized by the foundation of the Cominform in September 1947, the KPD remained in an anomalous position. Unlike the French and Italian Communists, it was too weak in the trade unions to entertain serious hopes of mass resistance to the Marshall Plan, and thus delayed any calls for disruptive action until prodded from behind in late 1948. At the same time, the hopes invested by Moscow in the unification and neutralization of Germany, examined in a later chapter, demanded a brand of national, cross-class politics which acted as a constant brake upon genuinely radical action. The result was a series of ideological compromises which can at best be called verbal revolution.

This does not mean that there was not a strong movement within the rank and file to cut parliamentary losses and flex the party's extra-parliamentary muscles on the shop-floor. Echoing these frustrations, historians of the New Left in the early 1970s explicitly criticized the KPD leadership for refusing to permit direct action.[13] This censure has strong echoes of the criticisms of the left's failure to carry through a revolution after the First World War. Yet, given that most historians now accept the practical constraints operating during demobilization in 1918, when the Allied blockade was still in force, how much more compelling are these arguments when applied to occupied Germany in 1945! If one accepts that a homeless and malnourished population was on the brink of a disaster of epic proportions, the KPD leadership's responsible attitude must be acknowledged as an important contribution to the stabilization of the western zones. It is all too easy to accuse the KPD of sitting on the sidelines

---

[13] Ute Schmidt and Tilman Fichter, *Der erzwungene Kapitalismus: Klassenkämpfe in den Westzonen 1945-48* (West Berlin, 1971), 43-7.

and sabotaging the recovery, but one should not forget that many of the ministers grappling with reconstruction, health, and food supply in the western *Länder* were in fact Communists themselves.

For the occupation period, I shall focus on activities in the *Landtage* in North Rhine-Westphalia and Hessen, where, however fleetingly, mathematical possibilities of KPD–SPD majority coalitions did exist.[14] This is followed by an appreciation of the KPD's later role in the West German *Bundestag*. By then it had been ejected from all its positions in regional government, and was ostracized by the main parties to such an extent that the Leninist concept of parliament as revolutionary tribune, from which to agitate rather than legislate, had become something of a self-fulfilling prophecy. The impact of the small KPD faction was thus negligible in terms of the statute book, but it did provide a vociferous opposition to the military and economic integration of the Federal Republic into the western bloc, and many memorable interjections on the floor of the house.[15]

Although I have argued above that the KPD regarded itself as a parliamentary party after 1945, increasingly it was forced to resort to extra-parliamentary means. Chapter 4 is devoted to attempts at mass mobilization outside the *Bundestag* and *Landtage* over the issues of national unification[16] and rearmament.[17] As in other chapters, I was keen to establish the response of members, as well as leaders, to a set of policies which suspended classic socio-economic demands in favour of cross-class alliance politics. Starting with the People's Congresses in 1947–8, and then the 1949 National Front, the SED/KPD turned increasingly to experiments in plebiscitary *Sammlungspolitik*, or 'catch-all politics', wooing disaffected patriotic and pacifist support.

In the late 1940s, traumatic memories of the triumph of Weimar's 'national opposition' promised a good deal of political mileage in a nationalist strategy. The western Allies were indeed alarmed at the alacrity with

[14] See Elke Greiner-Petter, 'Antifaschistisch-demokratische Aktivitäten der KPD in den Landtagen Hessens und Nordrhein-Westfalens 1946–1948', Ph.D. thesis (Humboldt University, East Berlin, 1986).

[15] See Gottfried Hartmann, 'Die Arbeit der KPD im Parlamentarischen Rat', diploma (University of Marburg, 1978); Jens Ulrich Klocksin, *Kommunisten im Parlament: Die KPD in Regierungen und Parlamenten der westdeutschen Besatzungszonen und der Bundesrepublik Deutschland (1945–1956)* (2nd edn.; Bonn, 1994).

[16] See also Michael Klein, *Antifaschistische Demokratie und nationaler Befreiungskampf: Die nationale Politik der KPD 1945–1953* (2nd edn.; West Berlin, 1986).

[17] Arnold Sywottek, 'Die Opposition der SPD und KPD gegen die westdeutsche Aufrüstung in der Tradition sozialdemokratischer und kommunistischer Friedenspolitik seit dem ersten Weltkrieg', in Wolfgang Huber and Johannes Schwerdtfeger (eds.), *Frieden, Gewalt, Sozialismus: Studien zur Geschichte der sozialistischen Arbeiterbewegung* (Stuttgart, 1976), 496–610.

which the Communists sought to occupy the nationalist high ground. The Christian and Social Democrats, too, in spite of powerful lip-service to reunification, could not outdo the KPD in patriotic stridency. Yet it proved to be a path strewn with pitfalls for the Communists. The first stumbling-block was the question of what constituted the nation. In solidarity with their Polish comrades, the German Communists could only afford to call for the reunification of what became the Federal Republic and the German Democratic Republic, and had to maintain an embarrassed silence over the fate of the lost eastern territories beyond the Oder-Neisse. KPD arguments that Germany itself had set the precedent of ethnic cleansing in the eastern territories, and reminders of Anglo-American joint responsibility for the population transfers ordered at Potsdam, fell on deaf ears among the ten million refugees who streamed into West Germany from the East.

The inadvisability of a nationalist KPD strategy is, of course, informed by a good deal of historical hindsight, and presupposes a certain rationality in Communist decision-making which may not always have been there. With nothing to lose from their beleaguered position in the West, many KPD members may have (over)optimistically clung to a belief in a united Germany, with some limited input from the East, as the only way out of their isolation. On the other hand, they may have suspected that, for their East Berlin superiors, despite all protestations to the contrary, an East German bird in the hand was worth two in the inscrutable bush of national reunification. In other words, for East Berlin, domestic consolidation of the SBZ/GDR may have gained unspoken priority over intra-German diplomacy, leaving the West German party to go through the rhetorical motions of national unity. Bestriding the two like an uncertain colossus, with a conceivable interest in both positions, was the Soviet Union. It was with these conflicting views in mind, of a genuine and optimistic Communist *Deutschlandpolitik*[18] versus a more cynical interpretation,[19] that I approached such initiatives as the famous Stalin Notes of 1952. By

---

[18] Rolf Steininger, *The German Question: The Stalin Note of 1952 and the Problem of Reunification* (New York, 1990), and more recently Wilfried Loth, *Stalins ungeliebtes Kind: Warum Moskau die DDR nicht wollte* (Berlin, 1994); *Wilhelm Pieck—Aufzeichnungen zur Deutschlandpolitik 1945–1953*, ed. Rolf Badstübner and Wilfried Loth (Berlin, 1994).

[19] Jochen Meiners, *Die doppelte Deutschlandpolitik: Zur nationalen Politik der SED im Spiegel ihres Zentralorgans 'Neues Deutschland' 1946 bis 1952* (Frankfurt am Main, 1987); Jürgen Wendler, *Die Deutschlandpolitik der SED in den Jahren 1952 bis 1958: Publizistisches Erscheinungsbild und Hintergründe der Wiedervereinigungsrhetorik* (Cologne, Weimar, and Vienna, 1991); Heinrich Bodensieck *et al.*, *Die Deutschlandfrage von der staatlichen Teilung Deutschlands bis zum Tode Stalins* (Berlin, 1993).

examining the KPD's role in such campaigns, I hope to make a modest contribution to this long-running historical debate.

Just as with national policy, a similar ambivalence underlay campaigns against the rearmament of West Germany. Prospects for pacifism seemed good. The catastrophic consequences of the Second World War had generated a widespread antipathy to war in general across all sections of German society. As early as August 1950, however, Adenauer had controversially hinted at a West German military contingent within the NATO alliance, and in October a European Defence Community was put on the intergovernmental agenda. In May 1952 the Federal Republic duly signed up to a project which only came to grief when the French National Assembly failed to ratify the EDC in August 1954. Nevertheless, this diplomatic fiasco soon paved the way for West Germany's entry into NATO proper in May 1955.

Against this background of high *Realpolitik*, it is hardly surprising that pacifists, the so-called 'Ohne mich!' or 'Count Me Out' movement, won widespread support among West German youth, and opinion polls indicated a general aversion to rearmament. Yet KPD pacifist calls had an inevitably hollow ring to them at a time when the GDR was also building up its armed forces, beginning with the Barracked People's Police, and culminating in 1956 in a National People's Army. Indeed, the party had never been truly pacifist, advocating instead the socialist defence of the eastern bloc. The 'Ohne mich!' protestors, as their slogan suggests, had more anarchist than Communist potential, and Social Democratic and church campaigners consistently shunned the KPD. The 1950s were not the 1960s, and Korea was not yet Vietnam.

More so than the French and Italian Communist parties, the KPD remained very much a blue-collar party of industrial workers, almost devoid of intellectuals. Chapter 5 goes on to investigate the Communists' relative successes in West German industry. In so doing, I have drawn upon a growing corpus of secondary literature, as well as a wealth of new material from the archives in Berlin and London.[20] The switch after 1945 from

[20] Arnold Bettien, *Arbeitskampf im Kalten Krieg: Hessische Metallarbeiter gegen Lohndiktat und Restauration* (Marburg, 1983); Thomas Brücher, 'Die Gewerkschaftspolitik der KPD im Bergbau und in der Metallindustrie des Ruhrgebiets in den Jahren 1945–1949', diploma (Ruhr University of Bochum, 1976); Michael Clarke, 'Die Gewerkschaftspolitik der KPD 1945–1951, dargestellt am Beispiel des "Industrieverbandes Bergbau/Industriegewerkschaft Bergbau" im Ruhrgebiet', diploma (Ruhr University of Bochum, 1982); Werner Dietrich, *Sozialdemokraten und Kommunisten in den Metallgewerkschaften Nordbadens 1945–1949* (Frankfurt am Main, 1990); Michael Fichter, *Besatzungsmacht und Gewerkschaften: Zur Entwicklung und Anwendung der US-Gewerkschaftspolitik in Deutschland 1944–1948* (Opladen, 1982); Tilman

the politically and confessionally affiliated Weimar unions to the non-partisan *Einheitsgewerkschaft*, or single union, has attracted a great deal of historical interest. Yet there were various competing visions of the single union, ranging from a highly centralized federation, as emerged in the SBZ in the shape of the Free German Trade Union Federation (FDGB), to the confederation of semi-autonomous industrial unions under a central umbrella that became the German Trade Union Federation (DGB) in West Germany. What, given the Communists' initial strength, was their impact, if any, on the reorganization of the West German union system?

Institutional histories apart, the closer to the individual shop-floor, the more successful the Communists appeared to be. Above all in the works councils, those factory committees which had become a feature of the shop-floor landscape under Weimar, the KPD scored unheard-of successes compared with before 1933. This suggests that significant changes had occurred within the industrial workforce during the Third Reich. Alternatively, the reasons for KPD gains may have been located rather in the appalling socio-economic conditions of 1945–8. With an open mind, I set out to seek at least some of the answers to what promises to be a fascinating area of future research, namely the socio-cultural history of life and work in the ruins of the Third Reich. In a case-study of the KPD's chief post-war stronghold, the Ruhr coalfields, the reasons for its resurgence and decline are sought in an area which was also of more than local interest, given the West German, and for that matter western European, economy's utter dependence on Ruhr coal.

That said, undue stress on the contingencies and high politics of the Cold War could risk obscuring many of the less visible secular trends affecting Communist politics in this period. Besides overtly political interference, the Federal Republic was undergoing massive socio-economic change, in which the structure of the industrial workforce, any Communist party's natural clientele, was altering to the possible detriment of the KPD. Many of the new recruits to West German industry were drawn from the

Fichter and Eugen Eberle, *Kampf um Bosch* (West Berlin, 1974); Christoph Kleßmann, 'Betriebsräte und Gewerkschaften in Deutschland 1945–1952', in Heinrich A. Winkler (ed.), *Politische Weichenstellungen im Nachkriegsdeutschland 1945–1953* (Göttingen, 1979), 44–73; id., 'Betriebsparteigruppen und Einheitsgewerkschaft: Zur betrieblichen Arbeit der politischen Parteien in der Frühphase der westdeutschen Arbeiterbewegung 1945–1952', *VfZ*, 31 (1983), 272–307; id. and Peter Friedemann, *Streiks und Hungermärsche im Ruhrgebiet 1946–1948* (Frankfurt am Main and New York, 1977); Herbert Kuehl, *Die Gewerkschaftspolitik der KPD von 1945 bis 1956: Die Rolle der Parteimitglieder in betrieblichen Konflikten—im Schwerpunkt dargestellt anhand des Hamburger Werftarbeiterstreiks von 1955* (Hamburg, 1981); Gerald Sommer, 'Streik im Hamburger Hafen: Arbeiterprotest, Gewerkschaften und KPD', *Ergebnisse*, 13 (1981).

millions of refugees from the East, most harbouring a deep-seated anti-Communism. Although it would be counter-factual to speculate on how the West German Communists might have fared had there been no state persecution, all things being equal, their shop-floor influence would most likely have waned rather than grown in the long term. Unemployment may have reached a high of two million in 1950, but dropped steadily thereafter, so that by the middle of the decade the Federal Republic was experiencing not a final crisis of capitalism, but the beginnings of the biggest economic boom in its history. West Germany was also adopting the leisure culture of the consumer society, when even workers could aspire to a television, a car, and a package holiday. On this view, the KPD was just as much the victim of long-term modernization as of short-term persecution. This was, of course, a gradual process, and some Communist milieux, such as the Ruhr, survived to offer a sanctuary of sorts. Nevertheless, even here, countless collieries succumbed to 1958's sweeping pit closure programme, removing an important KPD recruiting ground.[21]

Like most Stalinist parties, the West German Communists sought to counter the socio-economic trends operating against them with an almost mystical faith in organization. Initially at least, this faith may not have been misplaced. In Chapter 6 I was particularly fortunate, using the meticulous records of the KPD's Organization Department, in ascertaining the quality and quantity of early membership successes. The Depression should not be viewed as the KPD's only heyday; the anti-fascist impulse after 1945 created an even larger, if similarly fragile, mass party. This was quite a feat, considering that the KPD had just come through the most violently anti-Communist regime of the century. Since the Communists were able to reorganize so quickly in 1945, this raises important questions about the extent to which the Nazis had in fact managed to atomize the labour movement. When it came to elections, however, the post-war party was patently unable to reach out very far beyond its core support. This invisible barrier to the KPD (and SPD) indicates that organization could not be an end in itself, and that the German labour movement had perhaps reached its natural limits of mobilization.

Nevertheless, early membership expansion meant a clash of cultures between *Altkommunisten* and new recruits. The majority of 'old' Communists had been socialized during their youth in the Weimar Republic, when

---

[21] See above all Axel Schildt and Arnold Sywottek (eds.), *Modernisierung und Wiederaufbau: Die westdeutsche Gesellschaft der 50er Jahre* (Bonn, 1993); also Joachim Oltmann, *Kalter Krieg und kommunale Integration: Arbeiterbewegung im Stadtteil Bremen-Vegesack 1945–1956* (Marburg, 1987).

ultra-leftism had appeared to reap political successes during the Depression. This often exhilarating experience had generated an emotional attachment to the memories of 'class against class', which survived into the post-war period and militated against the new alliance politics.[22] Older Communists were also traumatized by their defeat in 1933 and subsequent persecution, so that many felt the psychological need for compensation or even revenge after 1945. It is also my contention, and here I am hypothesizing, that the skills acquired in surviving the Third Reich created a self-reliance among the older rank and file, which posed a political challenge to democratic centralist orthodoxy.

Younger, first-time members were more likely to fit into the mould of obedient *apparatchiks*. Without the benefit of counter-experience, and possibly acclimatized by Nazi regimentation, they were far less prone to question the twists and turns of the party line. It would be equally wrong, however, to ascribe this compliance too strongly to inherently robotic, 'Communist' qualities. Using sociological models, there were strong bonding forces at work within a Communist 'in-group' surrounded by so many hostile social 'out-groups'. Just as the Third Reich had created an embattled persecution syndrome among KPD members, the Cold War brought its own special complexes. Through its spiralling dialectic of mutually reinforcing counter-ideologies, it encouraged an irrational paranoia on both sides, with the Communists' anti-Americanism mirroring McCarthyite anti-Communism. Anti-American and anti-Titoist vigilance was also quite deliberately manipulated to consolidate party organization, and, in the wake of Moscow's schism with Belgrade in 1948, all Communist parties were afflicted by internal witch-hunts. During research it was possible to provide a first overview of the extent of the purges accompanying the KPD's transformation into a 'new-type party'. The personal fate of certain leaders, early victims of the Stasi, could be documented, including a foray into the papers of the late Kurt Müller, deputy KPD chairman until his arrest in 1950.[23]

It is debatable whether organizational rigidity was a source of strength or weakness. The party of the 1940s and 1950s was very much a Stalinist entity. A great deal of the rationale for its pseudo-military democratic centralism was, of course, derived from the climate of the Cold War, so

---

[22] Dick Geary, *European Labour Protest 1848–1939* (London, 1981), 171.

[23] See also Kurt Müller, 'Ein historisches Dokument aus dem Jahre 1956: Brief an den DDR-Ministerpräsidenten Otto Grotewohl', *Aus Politik und Zeitgeschichte*, B 11/90 (9 Mar. 1990), 16–29; Karl Heinz Jahnke, 'Gegen die Allmacht der Staatssicherheit: Bericht von Fritz Sperling aus dem Gefängnis, März 1956', *BzG*, 33 (1991), 789–803.

as not to offer the class enemy a point of attack. Yet party discipline was not just a means to an end in the Marxist-Leninist parties of this period. A hypertrophic party bureaucracy and almost complete lack of internal democracy reached new heights in the early 1950s. For anyone coming to the KPD for the first time after 1945, unfamiliar with Stalinist ritual, or perhaps all too familiar with its Nazi equivalents, this oppressive culture was likely to outweigh whatever emotional anti-fascist sympathy had been attractive in the first place. My treatment of the Communists themselves ends, therefore, on this rather self-destructive note: the KPD, in part at least, organized itself to death.

This is, of course, only half the story. What finally killed off the KPD was a series of prohibitions culminating in the full-scale banning of the party. Unlike most other histories, especially former western accounts which tend to gloss over this aspect, two whole final chapters have been devoted to the phenomenon of anti-Communism in West Germany.[24] It seemed important, in the first instance, to discover whether western military government was exaggerating the threat of Communism in areas ravaged by cold and hunger. Especially so, since this fear influenced decision-making in favour of a unilateral revival of the Bizonal economy, and thus became a factor in the division of Germany.[25] Secondly, it was important to establish the level of Anglo-American interference with the KPD. Readers familiar with post-war Communist politics in France and Italy will already be aware of the controversy surrounding the PCF and PCI ministers' expulsion from government by their coalition partners in the spring of 1947. Interest has focused particularly on the Americans' role in these affairs. Since military occupation offered so many more possibilities in Germany, and McCarthyite purges coincided so closely with Federal German actions, was there in fact a transatlantic connection?

At the same time, in the final chapter, I have stressed the native exponents of anti-Communism in the infant West German state, who did not require much prompting from their senior American partners. I have also tried to show how West German society at large was receptive to a hard anti-KPD line. Thus, it may well have been the case that Federal anti-Communism was more a product 'Made in Germany' than a McCarthyite import. As well as incorporating a number of interesting recent studies on

---

[24] A rare exception is Alexander von Brünneck, *Politische Justiz gegen Kommunisten in der Bundesrepublik Deutschland 1949–1968* (Frankfurt am Main, 1978), an exhaustive study of court records.

[25] Peter Weiler, *British Labour and the Cold War* (Stanford, Calif., 1988) concentrates on Whitehall and says little on peripheral actions.

the less obvious means by which the Bonn state marginalized Communists,[26] my chief object of interest was naturally the party ban in 1956. From the outset I had found constitutional explanations of the government's indictment of the KPD in 1951 bland and unsatisfying, and discovered much evidence that this action was indeed politically motivated. The trial itself of 1954–5 is fully documented and forms the final act in the history of the legal party, before its controversial prohibition in August 1956.[27] This particular study stops there. (Strictly speaking, an underground shell lingered on,[28] until a political amnesty in 1968 permitted the formation of a successor party, the Deutsche Kommunistische Partei—DKP.[29]) Understandably, the ban has generated a substantial literature of its own, either KPD *plaidoyers*[30] or more scholarly analyses of the constitutional implications of political justice and the grey areas involved, both of which fall outside the scope of this study.[31] A number of thorny moral issues

[26] Gotthard Jasper, 'Die disqualifizierten Opfer: Der Kalte Krieg und die Entschädigung für Kommunisten', in Ludolf Herbst and Constantin Goschler (eds.), *Wiedergutmachung in der Bundesrepublik Deutschland* (Munich, 1989), 361–84; Christian Seegert, 'Betriebsfrieden im Kalten Krieg: Materialien zur Bedeutung von Betriebsverfassung und Arbeitsgerichten bei der Kommunistenverfolgung der 50er Jahre', *Marxistische Studien*, 8 (1985), 224–57.

[27] Gerd Pfeiffer and Hans-Georg Strickert (eds.), *KPD-Prozeß: Dokumentarwerk zu dem Verfahren über den Antrag der Bundesregierung zur Feststellung der Verfassungswidrigkeit der Kommunistischen Partei Deutschlands vor dem Ersten Senat des Bundesverfassungsgerichts* (3 vols.; Karlsruhe, 1955/6).

[28] Max Reimann (ed.), *Die KPD lebt und kämpft: Dokumente der Kommunistischen Partei Deutschlands 1956–1962* (East Berlin, 1963); Johannes Schneider, *KP im Untergrund: Kommunistische Untergrundarbeit in der Bundesrepublik* (Munich, 1963); Andreas Voigt, 'Nach dem Verbot: Die kommunistische Politik in Westdeutschland 1956–1961, dargestellt anhand illegaler KPD-Publizistik', MA thesis (University of Hamburg, 1989). The interested researcher, however, has a wealth of material in the Stiftung Archiv der Parteien und Massenorganisationen der DDR im Bundesarchiv in Berlin. The holdings DY 30/IV 2/10.02 and DY 30/IV A2/10.02 (Westabteilung/Westkommission), as well as DY 30/IV 2/10.03 (Arbeitsbüro), offer much material on the relationship of the illegal KPD to the SED during the 1960s.

[29] Manfred Wilke *et al.*, *Die Deutsche Kommunistische Partei (DKP): Geschichte—Organisation—Politik* (Cologne, 1990).

[30] Max Reimann *et al.* (eds.) *KPD-Verbot: Ursachen und Folgen 1956–71* (Frankfurt am Main, 1971); Erwin Gieseking and Karl Pfannenschwarz (eds.) *Urteil: KPD-Verbot aufheben: Politisches und Rechtliches zum Verbot der KPD* (Cologne, 1971); Angelika Lehndorff-Felsko and Fritz Rische, *Der KPD-Verbotsprozeß 1954 bis 1956: Wie es dazu kam—sein Verlauf—die Folgen* (Frankfurt am Main, 1981).

[31] Wolfgang Abendroth, 'Das KPD-Verbotsurteil des Bundesverfassungsgerichts: Ein Beitrag zum Problem der richterlichen Interpretation von Rechtsgrundsätzen der Verfassung im demokratischen Staat', *Zeitschrift für Politik*, 3 (1956), 305–27; Helmut Ridder, *Aktuelle Rechtsfragen des KPD-Verbots* (Neuwied und West Berlin, 1966); Wolfgang Abendroth *et al.* (eds.), *KPD-Verbot oder Mit Kommunisten leben* (Reinbek bei Hamburg, 1968); Rudolf Schuster, 'Relegalisierung der KPD oder Illegalisierung der NPD? Zur politischen und rechtlichen Problematik von Parteiverboten', *Zeitschrift für Politik*, 24 (1968), 413–29; Hartmut Mauer, 'Das Verbot politischer Parteien—Zur Problematik des Art. 21 Abs. 2 GG', *Archiv des öffentlichen Rechts* (1971), 203–36; Martin Kutscha, 'Das KPD-Verbot',

are, none the less, inevitably raised by the premature demise of the KPD. In banning the party in 1956, the Federal judiciary was laying itself open to accusations of a return to a biased system of political justice with a pedigree dating back to the Anti-Socialist Laws under Bismarck. Many Germans could still have remembered the notoriously partisan behaviour of the courts in the wake of the November 1918 revolution, when judges punished the left while turning a blind eye to the radical right. The most obvious case of political *déjà vu* was, of course, the Nazis' banning and persecution of the party after 1933, when the Communists had been the first to experience Hitler's concentration camps. Even if the 1956 ruling by the *Bundesverfassungsgericht* was constitutionally impeccable, given the suffering of the Communists at the hands of the Nazis, it was bound to strike some as politically unwise. The Federal Republic, whose Basic Law espoused freedom of speech as well as democratic probity, was thereby placing itself in the unsavoury company of a small group of authoritarian European regimes which had taken anti-Communism to its logical legal conclusion: Franco's Spain, Salazar's Portugal, and post-civil war Greece. Not even McCarthyite America went so far as an outright ban.

Some of my findings have clearly revisionist implications and, I hope, will act as a corrective to some post-revisionists[32] who may have gone too far in sanitizing anti-Communism in West Germany. Particularly since the *Wende* in 1989–90, post-war German history has focused almost exclusively on the evils of Stalinism in East Germany—a perfectly legitimate undertaking in its own right—but with hardly a reference to the blemishes on the civil rights record of the early Federal Republic. A genuine post-revisionist synthesis must, however, deal even-handedly with the rights and wrongs of *both* Cold War camps. As the title of the book suggests, I have attempted to do just that, but the reader must judge with what success.

Before turning him or her loose on the main text, a few words must be said about the archives consulted, since so much new material has recently become available on both sides of what used to be the iron curtain. Midway through research an embarrassment of archival riches was opened up with the collapse of the GDR. It was possible in the spring

in Udo Mayer and Gerhard Stuby (eds.), *Das lädierte Grundgesetz: Beiträge und Dokumente zur Verfassungsgeschichte 1949–1976* (Cologne, 1977), 42–77; Hans-Albert Lennartz, *Zur Rechtsprechung des Bundesverfassungsgerichts zu den politischen Parteien* (Munich, 1982); Axel Azzola and Jürgen Crössmann, '30 Jahre Verbot der KPD', *Demokratie und Recht*, 14 (1986), 266–81.

[32] John L. Gaddis, 'The Emerging Post-Revisionist Synthesis on the Origins of the Cold War', *Diplomatic History*, 7 (1983) 171–204.

of 1990 to consult the KPD's internal files held by the SED's Zentrales
Parteiarchiv, housed in the former Institute of Marxism-Leninism in Berlin,
now known as the Stiftung Archiv der Parteien und Massenorganisationen der DDR im Bundesarchiv (SAPMO). By far the most useful file
groups used there were those of the KPD itself (I 10 and I 11), whose
whereabouts had long been uncertain. Many files were still in flux, with
new documents being added almost daily in 1990. Unfortunately, when
SAPMO was incorporated in 1993, the custody of I 10 and I 11 appears
to have become the subject of a legal dispute between the SED's successor, the PDS, and the KPD's successor, the DKP. Only recently have they
been made available again within SAPMO, but at the time of writing they
remained closed.

For high-level decision-making I also consulted the SED executive's
minutes, West Commission protocols, as well as the Pieck and Ulbricht
papers. Since my empirical focus is on the party stronghold in the Ruhr—
although covering the national party as well—I have concentrated on
the North Rhine-Westphalian KPD, using corroborative documents in
the SPD's Archiv der sozialen Demokratie in Bonn-Bad Godesberg; the
Archivsammlung-Ernst-Schmidt in Essen; the Nordrhein-Westfälisches
Hauptstaatsarchiv, and the Innenministerium Nordrhein-Westfalen, both
in Düsseldorf. The latter were used after special permission and are not
generally accessible. I am fully aware that the Ruhr KPD was not typical
of the national party, but chose it to gauge the upper limit of the Communists' already restricted possibilities.[33]

For union activities, the Deutscher Gewerkschaftsbund-Archiv in
Düsseldorf (now Bonn), and in Bochum the Industriegewerkschaft
Bergbau und Energie's archive and the Bergbau-Archiv beim Deutschen
Bergbaumuseum proved useful, particularly for works council statistics, as
did materials collected by Michael Becker for an abortive thesis, now held
in the Zentralinstitut für sozialwissenschaftliche Forschungen at the Free
University of Berlin. The authorities' view of the KPD was divined from
British military government files in the Public Record Office, many of
which are still tantalizingly classified; and from American military government documents filmed during the OMGUS Project and held in Koblenz,
as well as recently published microfilms of State Department files. Given
the French Zone's minor importance for the KPD, I have relied on
secondary sources. The files of the Soviet Military Administration, held

---

[33] A previous early study is Gudrun Schädel, 'Die Kommunistische Partei Deutschlands
in Nordrhein-Westfalen von 1945–1956', Ph.D. thesis (Ruhr University of Bochum, 1973).

in Moscow, were not yet available at the time of research. Finally, Federal ministerial holdings in the Bundesarchiv at Koblenz proved productive, including newly released KPD documents seized in 1952 for the impending banning trial.[34] A number of questions could also be clarified in interviews with Lord Annan, deputy head of British military government's Political Division until 1946; Karl Schirdewan, responsible on the SED's West Commission for the KPD; Josef Ledwohn, leader of the Ruhr Communists throughout most of this period; and Dr Ernst Schmidt, one-time Essen functionary. Tapes of these interviews are in my possession. For reasons of time, I refrained from interviewing other surviving Communists, some of whose stories are captured already in autobiographies[35] or oral history projects.[36]

---

[34] See Bestand B 118/98–255.

[35] Analysed by Hermann Kuhn, *Bruch mit dem Kommunismus: Über autobiographische Schriften von Ex-Kommunisten im geteilten Deutschland* (Münster, 1990), especially 284–98. See also Peter Brandt *et al.*, *Karrieren eines Außenseiters: Leo Bauer zwischen Kommunismus und Sozialdemokratie 1912 bis 1972* (West Berlin and Bonn, 1983); Willi Bohn, *Einer von vielen: Ein Leben für Frieden und Freiheit* (Frankfurt am Main, 1981); Emil Carlebach, *Zensur ohne Schere: Die Gründerjahre der 'Frankfurter Rundschau' 1945/47: Ein unbekanntes Kapitel Nachkriegsgeschichte* (Frankfurt am Main, 1985); Herbert Crüger, *Verschwiegene Zeiten: Vom geheimen Apparat der KPD ins Gefängnis der Staatssicherheit* (Berlin, 1990); Willi Dickhut, *So war's damals . . . : Tatsachenbericht eines Solinger Arbeiters 1926–1948* (Stuttgart, 1979); id., *Was geschah danach?: Zweiter Tatsachenbericht eines Solinger Arbeiters ab 1949* (Stuttgart, 1990); Eugen Eberle and Peter Grohmann, *Die schlaflosen Nächte des Eugen E.: Erinnerungen eines neuen schwäbischen Jacobiners* (Stuttgart, 1982); Friedrich-Martin Balzer (ed.), *Ärgernis und Zeichen: Erwin Eckert—Sozialistischer Revolutionär aus christlichem Glauben* (Bonn, 1993); Max Faulhaber, 'Aufgegeben haben wir nie . . .': Erinnerungen aus einem Leben in der Arbeiterbewegung* (Marburg, 1988); Heiko Haumann, 'Der Fall Max Faulhaber': Gewerkschaften und Kommunisten—ein Beispiel aus Südbaden 1949–1952* (Marburg, 1987); Georg Fischer, *Vom aufrechten Gang eines Sozialisten: Ein Parteiarbeiter erzählt* (West Berlin and Bonn, 1979); Erich W. Gniffke, *Jahre mit Ulbricht* (Cologne, 1966); Paul Harig, *Arbeiter—Gewerkschafter—Kommunist* (Frankfurt am Main, 1973); Paul Meuter, *Lebenserinnerungen eines Solinger Kommunisten* (Solingen, 1992); Dieter Dowe and Friedrich-Ebert-Stiftung (eds.), *Kurt Müller (1903–1990) zum Gedenken* (Bonn, 1991); Martin Muschkau, *Entscheidende Jahre 1928–1948: Bericht eines Zeitzeugen* (Hannover, 1990); Elfriede Paul, *Ein Sprechzimmer der Roten Kapelle* (East Berlin, 1981); Willy Perk, *Besatzungsmacht gegen Pressefreiheit: Geschichte der Zeitung 'Westdeutsches Volksecho', 7. Mai 1946 bis 4. Mai 1948* (Frankfurt am Main, 1979); Käthe Popall, *Ein schwieriges politisches Leben: Erzählte Geschichte* (Fischerhude, 1985); Max Reimann, *Entscheidungen 1945–1956* (Frankfurt am Main, 1973); Franz Ahrens *et al.*, *Streiflichter aus dem Leben eines Kommunisten: Franz Ahrens über Max Reimann* (Hamburg, 1968); Richard Scheringer, *Unter Soldaten, Bauern und Rebellen: Das große Los* (reprint; Cologne, 1988); Josef Schleifstein, *Der Intellektuelle in der Partei: Gespräche* (Marburg, 1987); Valentin Senger, *Kurzer Frühling* (Frankfurt am Main, 1987); Helmuth Warnke, 'Bloß keine Fahnen': Auskünfte über schwierige Zeiten 1923–1954* (Hamburg, 1988); Klaus Weigle, 'Vom Sturmgrenadier zum KPD-Landesvorsitzenden: Eine autobiographische Skizze (1946/50)', *Demokratische Geschichte*, 7 (1992), 213–41. [*note 36 on p. 20*]

[36] Lutz Niethammer (ed.), *Lebensgeschichte und Sozialstruktur im Ruhrgebiet 1930 bis 1960*, i. *'Die Jahre weiß man nicht, wo man die heute hinsetzen soll': Faschismus-Erfahrungen im Ruhrgebiet*; ii. *'Hinterher merkt man, daß es richtig war, daß es schiefgegangen ist': Nachkriegs-Erfahrungen im Ruhrgebiet*; iii, with Alexander von Plato. *'Wir kriegen jetzt andere Zeiten': Auf der Suche nach der Erfahrung des Volkes in nachfaschistischen Ländern* (West Berlin and Bonn, 1983/1983/1985). See also Alexander von Plato, *'Der Verlierer geht nicht leer aus': Betriebsräte geben zu Protokoll* (West Berlin and Bonn, 1984). A number of interviews are also available in Bernd Sponheuer (ed.), *zeitGenossen: 17 Lebensbilder von Kommunist/inn/en* (Düsseldorf, 1988).

I

Waiting for Stunde Null
Exiled Leaders and Resistance Cadres

IT is now time to turn to the prehistory of the KPD before 1945.[1] The Weimar experience, especially the Republic's final years, had conditioned the political behaviour of the post-war KPD quite considerably. On the positive side of the balance sheet it had been a quantitative success: 5,980,614 Germans (16.9%) had voted Communist in November 1932 and party membership had reached around 350,000. Much of this growth was attributable to the radicalizing effects of the world depression, appearing to bear out the crisis of capitalism theory that Germany was on the brink of a revolutionary situation which did not merit the defence of parliamentary democracy. Nevertheless, the quality of these successes was dubious and short-lived. Many were protest votes, and the vast majority of a fluctuating mass membership was unemployed and thus notoriously difficult to integrate into a stable Communist milieu comparable to that of the SPD.

There had indeed been virtually no inroads into the Social Democratic camp, long resented as an obstacle to the KPD's perceived natural clientele, the working masses. The relationship with the SPD had deteriorated from participation in Social Democratic governments in Saxony and Thuringia in 1923, to the notorious 'social fascist' phase after 1928, when the voice of the world Communist movement, the Comintern, had ruled out any co-operation with social democracy.[2] From the mid-1920s the Comintern's hold over the KPD, the largest member party outside the

[1] Unless otherwise stated, information has been taken from the following: Siegfried Bahne, *Die KPD und das Ende von Weimar: Das Scheitern einer Politik 1932–1935* (Frankfurt am Main and New York, 1976); Werner Müller, *Lohnkampf, Massenstreik, Sowjetmacht: Ziele und Grenzen der 'Revolutionären Gewerkschafts-Opposition' (RGO) in Deutschland 1928 bis 1933* (Cologne, 1988); Hermann Weber, *Hauptfeind Sozialdemokratie: Strategie und Taktik der KPD 1929–1933* (Düsseldorf, 1982); id., *Kommunismus in Deutschland 1918–1945* (Darmstadt, 1983); Heinrich A. Winkler, *Der Weg in die Katastrophe: Arbeiter und Arbeiterbewegung in der Weimarer Republik 1930 bis 1933* (West Berlin and Bonn, 1987).

[2] Siegfried Bahne, 'Die KPD vom Sozialfaschismus zur Blockpolitik', in Winfried Becker (ed.) *Die Kapitulation von 1945 und der demokratische Neubeginn* (Cologne and Vienna, 1987), 335–51.

Soviet Union, had tightened as the German section was bolshevized by Moscow.[3] Parallel to the Soviet Union's move to 'socialism in one country', in 1928–9 the KPD launched its 'main thrust' at reformist social democracy, branding it as the left wing of a fascist movement, in which the Nazis, or 'national fascists', were allegedly a mere component. This ultra-leftist line was subsequently modified somewhat to a united front policy with three tactical variants. These ranged from offers of co-operation with the SPD leadership ('united front from above'), to attempts to bypass rightist leaders and poach grass-roots members ('united front from below'), or a combination of the two, but heavily weighted in favour of the latter.

Thus, from mid-1929 until March 1930 the SPD's leadership and rank and file were lumped together as 'social fascists'. Then, in March–April 1930, a 'united front from below' was launched to isolate the SPD leadership from its own base, but in spring 1931 the social fascist campaign was again escalated and attacks became more indiscriminate. Only at the end of April 1932, in response to Nazi gains, did tactics become more flexible, with the KPD calling on 25 May for an Anti-Fascist Action, but still insisting on 'unity from below'. From June 1932 a brief period of united front from above and below ensued, but understandably local SPD leaders remained sceptical, and in August–September the Comintern reverted to rigid unity from below. When the KPD leadership addressed its SPD opposite numbers for the first time on the day of Hitler's accession to power in January 1933, and again in March, it was clearly too late. The social fascist strategy had indeed backfired from the outset, and, instead of detaching the SPD's rank-and-file members from their rightist leadership, had only succeeded in binding them more closely.

It was only in 1934–5, in response to Soviet security needs, that a change in the world party line was instigated. The KPD leadership was notoriously slow to follow, unmoved by the French Communists' united front policy in mid-1934, and only coming around to frontism the following year under pressure from Moscow. The Comintern's 7th World Congress in the summer of 1935 conceded that Nazism could not be dismissed as simply the death throes of capitalism, and that a revised attitude to social democracy was needed. Alliance politics became the order of the day.[4] At its Brussels Conference in October, the KPD dutifully called for a proletarian 'united front of the working class', the core of a broader

---

[3] Hermann Weber, *Die Wandlung des deutschen Kommunismus: Die Stalinisierung der KPD in der Weimarer Republik* (2 vols.; Frankfurt am Main, 1969).

[4] Arnold Sywottek, *Deutsche Volksdemokratie: Studien zur politischen Konzeption der KPD 1935–1946* (Düsseldorf, 1971).

popular front to include even conservative and bourgeois opponents of the Third Reich.

The Berne Conference in early 1939 reiterated these calls, as well as making the first appeal for a unity party, although the exiled SPD leadership, the so-called *Sopade*,[5] remained guarded, if not actively hostile.

Six months later, in August 1939, Social Democratic doubts about Communist reliability seemed to be borne out by the Nazi–Soviet Non-Aggression Pact, when Hitler and Stalin appeared to settle their differences in an object lesson in *Realpolitik*. The exiled KPD leadership in Paris was clearly at a loss. For the next two years the war was to be regarded as a private conflict between capitalists, epitomized in a notorious article by Walter Ulbricht in February 1940, which attacked Anglo-French 'war plans' against the USSR and implicitly offered help against domestic opponents of the pact, in other words, fellow anti-Nazis. There was indeed active collaboration by the KPD's military and economic apparatus with the German intelligence services in her occupied territories. This is not to say that rank-and-file German Communists, especially those left inside Germany, did not continue to resist the Nazis in defiance of the official line. Yet this was anti-fascism with one hand tied behind its back, and it was only with the invasion of the Soviet Union on 22 June 1941 that KPD resistance gained a new lease of life.[6]

Dimitrov, head of the Comintern, subsequently called for broad national liberation fronts and the suppression of anti-capitalist or revolutionary vocabulary, in order not to alienate the *petite bourgeoisie*, intelligentsia, and peasantry. After the German defeat at Stalingrad, further conciliatory steps were taken. On 15 May 1943 Moscow announced the dissolution of the Comintern, transforming its sections into national parties within cross-class anti-fascist coalitions. As a gesture to the western Allies, allaying their fears of world revolution behind their lines, it signalled a shift by Stalin to the negotiating table as the means to determine post-war spheres of influence. Then, on 12–13 July 1943, the National Committee of Free Germany (NKFD) was founded, along with the League of German Officers, aimed at attracting the patriotic conservative right and rallying domestic resistance to Hitler, restricting itself to a punitive programme against Nazis and war criminals. With the patent inability of the German

---

[5] The exiled SO(zialdemokratische) PA(rtei) DE(utschlands).

[6] Werner Röder, *Die sozialistischen Exilgruppen in Großbritannien 1940–45: Ein Beitrag zur Geschichte des Widerstandes gegen den Nationalsozialismus* (Hannover, 1968), 49; Jan Foitzik, 'Die Kommunistische Partei Deutschlands und der Hitler-Stalin-Pakt: Die Erklärung des Zentralkomitees vom 25. August 1939 im Wortlaut', *VfZ*, 37 (1989), 499–514; Klaus Sator, 'Das kommunistische Exil und der deutsch-sowjetische Nichtangriffspakt', *Exilforschung*, 8 (1990), 29–45.

resistance to emulate the Italian partisan effort, and with the promise of a second front, by February 1944 Moscow had seemingly lost interest in the KPD as the focus of a national uprising, forcing it instead to accept its share of 'collective guilt'. By 1945 it was reduced to supporting the Red Army in an administrative revolution from above. To summarize, therefore, there was nothing new about the KPD's anti-fascist, democratic bloc politics, articulated in its June Appeal of 1945. Frontism had been party orthodoxy for a decade. The strategy's main flaw, however, as will become evident, lay in the fact that any anti-fascist consensus was likely to break down once its *raison d'être*—fascism—had ceased as an organized force.[7]

After thus describing the twisting path of alliance politics, I would like to turn to the post-war organizational legacy, which itself often confounded the political change of line. The twelve years of the Third Reich were a period of extreme trauma for an organism as centralized as the KPD, during which it was effectively decapitated and progressively dismembered by the Gestapo. Approximately half of the 350,000 members of 1932 did not return to the party's ranks after 1945, either because they were dead or had been permanently depoliticized by Nazi persecution. The organizational isolation of those who had remained in Germany even led to a reversion in the spring of 1945, in the absence of higher authority, to revolutionary slogans. The fundamental change in the world party line of 1935 had still not percolated down to many rank-and-file members, prompting Ulbricht's dismissive description of them as political 'stoodstills' (*Stehengebliebene*).

The party had been woefully unprepared for illegality and repression in 1933. Within months much of the central and regional leadership had been arrested, including the party chairman, Ernst Thälmann, seized in Berlin on 3 March. The rest of the Politburo, including Pieck, Ulbricht, and Dahlem, worked initially in Prague or, from autumn 1933, in Paris. By 1935, however, Pieck and Ulbricht were in Moscow, although they did not take over formal overall control until the internment in September 1939 of the entire Paris secretariat, including Dahlem, who was later extradited to Germany.[8]

Looking to the party as a whole, *in toto* perhaps 10,000 Communists fled the Third Reich. Most initially made for Czechoslovakia or France,

---

[7] Fernando Claudin, *The Communist Movement: From Comintern to Cominform* (London, 1975), 21–33 and 40–4; Röder, *Exilgruppen*, 213; Jan Foitzik, 'Revolution und Demokratie: Zu den Sofort- und Übergangsplanungen des sozialdemokratischen Exils für Deutschland 1943–1945', *IWK*, 24 (1988), 341.
[8] Allan Merson, *Communist Resistance in Nazi Germany* (London, 1985), 85.

later Spain, and finally Britain. Smaller groups settled in Switzerland, Sweden, Mexico, and the USA. Yet from 1936 ever more were seeking asylum in the USSR, which by 1940 had become the chief KPD sanctuary. Exile in the Soviet Union was none the less a mixed blessing. Of the 43 sometime members of the Weimar Politburo, 6 were murdered by Hitler and 7 by Stalin, and of the 131 Central Committee members, 18 died in Germany and 15 or 16 in the USSR. In total, of the 504 wider functionaries from the period 1924–9, Hitler claimed 86, and Stalin 43 (about 60% of those in the USSR); of the 376 of 1929–35 vintage, the Gestapo accounted for 102, and the NKVD 27. The worst chances of survival in Stalin's purges of 1936–8 were for erstwhile dissident factions, such as the Neumann Group, saddled with the social fascist débâcle discussed above.[9]

Nevertheless, assuming physical survival, exile in the Soviet Union was an important career move for KPD functionaries. Emigré German Communists continued to liaise with the Comintern under Dimitrov, and, after its dissolution in May 1943, with the CPSU's International Relations Department. From 1943–4 the party leadership also began detailed planning for post-war Germany and was able, from July 1943, through the Free Germany committee, to recruit 2,500 German POWs for training by the Red Army as close support for the Soviet occupation forces in 1945. Spearheading these operations, on 30 April 1945 ten members of the so-called Ulbricht Initiative Group flew from Moscow to Berlin, soon to be followed by the Ackermann and Sobottka Groups in Saxony and Mecklenburg. It quickly became evident that exiled Communists, particularly from Moscow, enjoyed priority over indigenous cadres who had spent the previous twelve years underground or incarcerated. Of the 16 signatories to the KPD's founding Appeal in June 1945, 13 had been in Moscow since 1940. Only 2, Jendretsky and Geschke, had spent the duration in Germany, and none featured in the later leadership of the western party.[10]

Once the Cold War escalated after 1947, it became doubly important for Communist exiles to have chosen the right host country. For simple geographical reasons, most KPD members in western Germany had headed west and became retrospectively suspect of 'imperialist' contamination, proving even less trustworthy to the Moscow exiles than the underground

---

[9] Hermann Weber, 'Ursachen und Umfang der deutschen Emigration nach 1933 unter besonderer Berücksichtigung von SPD und KPD im Exil', *IWK*, 24 (1988), 3 and 13; id., *'Weiße Flecken' in der Geschichte* (2nd edn.; Frankfurt am Main, 1990), 20–1 and 108–9.

[10] Foitzik, 'Revolution und Demokratie', 333–42; Wolfgang Leonhard, *Die Revolution entläßt ihre Kinder* (Cologne and West Berlin, 1955), ch. 7.

German cadres. Significantly, the KPD leadership in the British Zone, which came to dominate the national party, was made up mostly of Communists who had stayed in Germany; the American and French Zone leaderships, on the other hand, included a high proportion of Swiss and French exiles. As the only open forum for a *rapprochement* with the Social Democrats after 1935, foreign exile also gave an unpleasant foretaste of the insuperable obstacles to Communist alliance politics.

France had been the initial destination for most German exiles and in 1935–6 up to 5,500 German Communists were registered in Paris, outnumbering the 3,000 Social Democrats. Notwithstanding the efforts of the KPD's propaganda impresario, Willi Münzenberg, and despite the fleeting French Popular Front, the German exiles failed to achieve an alliance. Although local German Social Democrats were in favour, the Prague *Sopade* executive vetoed co-operation. During French mobilization in September 1939, the KPD Foreign Secretariat in Paris, yielding to French Communist Party pressure, disobeyed Comintern orders to flee and called on German Communists to enlist, but, rendered suspect by the Nazi–Soviet Pact, they found themselves instead interned. After the liberation, an estimated 150 'French' Communists and sympathizers returned to Germany, under the auspices of the local Free Germany committee, the Comité 'Allemagne Libre' pour l'Ouest.[11]

After the fall of France, Britain became the next major anti-Nazi refuge. Yet by 1944 it accounted for only just over 300 German Communists (still outnumbering Social Democrats by almost two to one). Of the KPD's 1942 London leadership only Becker, Zeidler, and Fladung featured in the post-war western KPD.[12] Internments were far more limited than in France, but, even so, exiled Communists in Britain failed to woo the *Sopade* executive, so that when its representative, Erich Ollenhauer, returned to Germany in 1946, he was already well versed in the anti-Communist 'Schumacher' line. Especially after the Nazi–Soviet Pact in August 1939, the Social Democrats attempted to sever all connections with the Communists. In July 1941, with Operation Barbarossa under way, the KPD proposed a loose collaborative cartel with the Union of Socialist

---

[11] Ruth Fabian and Corinna Coulmas, *Die deutsche Emigration in Frankreich nach 1933* (Munich, 1978), 54–5; Hans-Albert Walter, 'Das Pariser KPD-Sekretariat, der deutsch-sowjetische Nichtangriffsvertrag und die Internierung deutscher Emigranten in Frankreich zu Beginn des Zweiten Weltkriegs', *VfZ*, 36 (1988), 483–528; Foitzik, 'Revolution und Demokratie', 335.

[12] As a *Bezirk* secretary of IG Bergbau; in the PV's Cadre Dept.; and as head of the Cultural League respectively. Josef Schleifstein, deputy FDJ leader in Britain, joined the KPD Secretariat in 1949.

Groups, but this was unconditionally rejected on 8 August. Despite British pressure, the *Sopade* leadership held firm against sympathetic leftist Social Democrats, and throughout 1942 ignored what it saw as an unregenerate KPD. Even after the establishment in 1943 of a Free German Movement in Great Britain (FDB), a united front from above eluded the Communists, despite seriously discomfiting the Social Democratic old guard, who objected to the Moscow Communists' collaboration with *Wehrmacht* generals and other ideological compromises. The British FDB then collapsed in spring 1944 over the issues of collective guilt and territorial reparations. More successful in the unions, by 1945 Communists occupied half the ten places on the *Landesgruppe* executive of German unionists. Here too, however, discussions on a post-war single union became so acrimonious that the Communists withdrew. Nor were relations any happier among POWs, when Communists were branded as camp terrorists by fellow SPD inmates. After 1945 the British authorities were clearly in no hurry to repatriate Communists. Only two KPD leaders, Becker and Zeidler, could return to the British Zone before October 1946, but almost 80% of subsequent returnees headed in any case for the SBZ.[13]

In the United States German Communists were not permitted to function as a legal party at all, and were directed by exiles in Mexico City. After the formation of the *Sopade*-sponsored German Labor Delegation in 1939, attempts to form a united front foundered on the GLD's refusal, encouraged by the American Federation of Labor, to co-operate with Communists. Towards the end of the war, however, a Council for a Democratic Germany did decide to open its executive to the KPD, but remained fragile and far short of a Free German movement. Then, in autumn 1945, all its non-Communist members resigned in protest at Allied policy towards Germany.[14]

Sweden also proved to be of minor importance for the post-war party. The KPD there numbered only 100–20 by 1945. Although a formal Free Germany committee was never formed, the KPD cultivated unionists and leftist Social Democrats, culminating in October 1944 in its most

[13] Anthony Glees, *Exile Politics during the Second World War: The German Social Democrats in Britain* (Oxford, 1982), 99–102, 180, and 212–26; Röder, *Exilgruppen*, 47, 50, 60, and 194; Max Oppenheimer, 'Aufgaben und Tätigkeit der Landesgruppe deutscher Gewerkschafter in Großbritannien', *Exilforschung*, 5 (1987), 249 and 252; Josef Schleifstein, *Der Intellektuelle in der Partei* (Marburg, 1987), 71; Sander to Kuczynski, 24 Sept. 1943, Modern Records Centre (MRC), MSS 292/943/28; Gottfurcht to Bell, 31 Dec. 1946, MRC, MSS 292/943/4.

[14] OSS report, 10 July 1944, PA Staritz; Werner Link, 'German Political Refugees in the United States during the Second World War', in Anthony Nicholls and Erich Matthias (eds.), *German Democracy and the Triumph of Hitler* (London, 1971), 250–3.

genuine cross-party émigré success, the Working Committee of German Anti-Nazi Organizations in Sweden. Again, this occurred against the wishes of the London *Sopade*, but, as elsewhere, by the time of repatriation in 1945–6, local KPD/SPD relations had soured considerably.[15]

The Swiss leadership, as already hinted at, provided a more significant pool of KPD leaders, especially for the American Zone. From spring 1940, the Swiss, like the French, resorted to internment, and from 1942–5 the 200-strong émigré KPD was largely confined to quarters, founding an illegal Free Germany Movement in August 1943. Then, in autumn 1944, a first few 'Swiss' émigrés managed to return clandestinely to Germany, and by the capitulation approximately twenty had followed, heading mainly for Munich and South Baden.[16] A number of leftists were also parachuted or infiltrated back into Germany on intelligence missions by the American Office of Strategic Services (OSS) and British Special Operations Executive, or repatriated by the Centrale Sanitaire Suisse relief agency and former Maquis units in the French occupation army. All told, 63 Communists[17] and 77 Social Democrats have been traced. Nevertheless, these western returnees cannot be compared with the SBZ's three Initiative Groups, which enjoyed far more personnel and freedom of movement. As will also be seen in Chapter 6, the American connection was to prove politically lethal for many German Communists during the witch-hunts for 'imperialist' agents in the early 1950s, particularly contacts with Noel H. Field. As head of the Unitarian Service Committee relief agency in Geneva and an active Communist sympathizer, Field had introduced some KPD members to Allen Dulles's OSS, and was to be the pretext after 1949 for numerous interrogations, show trials, and even executions throughout the eastern bloc.[18]

The experience of the underground Communist cadres who had remained inside Germany was very different from that of the exiles and provided a further potential faction within the post-war party. Initially the illegal KPD had envisaged a centralized clandestine apparatus within Germany,

[15] Helmut Müssener, *Exil in Schweden: Politische und kulturelle Emigration nach 1933* (Munich, 1974), 119, 159–69, and 214–18.

[16] Karl Hans Bergmann, *Die Bewegung 'Freies Deutschland' in der Schweiz 1943–1945* (Munich, 1974), 23–5 and 151.

[17] 28 to the US Zone; 11 to the British; 8 to the French; 2 to Berlin; 10 to the Saar; 3 unknown.

[18] Nigel West, *Secret War: The Story of SOE, Britain's Wartime Sabotage Organisation* (London, 1992), 312–17; Peter Brandt *et al.*, *Karrieren eines Außenseiters* (West Berlin and Bonn, 1983), 120; Herbert Crüger, *Verschwiegene Zeiten* (Berlin, 1990), 123; Foitzik, 'Revolution und Demokratie', 333–42.

and during 1933 the party clung to the concept of 'mass resistance' to the Nazi regime, which, it was expected, would collapse in short order. This strategy greatly underestimated the ferocity of repression. It is believed that about half of KPD members were at some time persecuted, be it in the form of arrest, incarceration, or execution. In the Rhine-Ruhr region alone, 8,000 Communists had been arrested by April 1933, and by the outbreak of war approximately 60–70% of the KPD's remaining membership were detained in one way or another. The mass, rather than conspiratorial, approach also left the party open to widespread Gestapo infiltration. Successive illegal Ruhr leaderships rarely escaped arrest for more than a few months, and in May–June 1935 almost the entire local leadership was apprehended. Cells at certain Gelsenkirchen pits, the nuclei for rebuilding in 1945, held out longer, but were also left leaderless after October 1936.[19]

In response to Gestapo successes a peripheral strategy was adopted, and, after the Brussels Conference in October 1935, the party abandoned the Inland Leadership in Berlin and switched to an Operative Leadership. This was initially based in Prague under Ulbricht, moving to Paris in autumn 1936, then Moscow in 1940, and worked through so-called Sector Leaderships in adjacent countries. From 1939, however, successive Nazi conquests made the system unworkable. Parallel to this decentralization emerged the 'Trojan horse' plan to infiltrate Nazi organizations such as the German Labour Front, but this, too, failed to live up to leadership expectations.[20]

The exiled Central Committee subsequently claimed to have been in systematic control of illegal work in Germany throughout, but there was in fact a widening gulf between the émigré leadership and the underground cadres. Increasingly, Moscow was forced merely to sanction surviving spontaneous resistance on the ground, claiming the credit for itself.[21] Yet—in my opinion at least—the anti-fascist kudos of the KPD after 1945 must largely be ascribed to the improvised resistance of these indigenous cadres; less appealing to non-Communist target groups was the Communists' triumphal identification with the victorious Red Army as their

[19] Beatrix Herlemann, *Auf verlorenem Posten: Kommunistischer Widerstand im Zweiten Weltkrieg: Die Knöchel-Organisation* (Bonn, 1986), 26; Horst Duhnke, *Die KPD von 1933 bis 1945* (Cologne, 1972), 525; Stefan Goch, *Sozialdemokratische Arbeiterbewegung und Arbeiterkultur im Ruhrgebiet: Eine Untersuchung am Beispiel Gelsenkirchen 1848–1975* (Düsseldorf, 1990), 378 and 396–400.
[20] Duhnke, *KPD*, 193.
[21] Werner Röder, 'Zum Verhältnis von Exil und innerdeutschem Widerstand', *Exilforschung*, 5 (1987), 34–5.

power-political backer. The Moscow connection soon become a liability rather than an asset.

Recent revelations have confirmed how little control Moscow exerted over Communists in Nazi Germany. In March 1938 the Executive Committee of the Comintern's (ECCI) secretariat criticized Ulbricht and Dahlem in Moscow for the KPD's failure to achieve any form of popular front. It became clear that they had previously exaggerated the beleaguered party's potential and thus compounded ECCI's unrealistic hopes of domestic resistance to Hitler.[22] Equally unrealistically, however, ECCI called for the transfer of the Operative Leadership back to Germany. From early 1939 there was indeed a notional return to centrally co-ordinated resistance from Paris, and in the autumn a suicidal policy of resistance from inside the Reich. Yet only after 1941 and the end of the Non-Aggression Pact were minor successes registered, when the Knöchel Organization improvised an Inland Leadership, establishing contacts with Berlin and western Germany. It was nevertheless smashed by the early summer of 1943, resulting in arrest for over 200 underground Communists in the Rhine–Ruhr–Amsterdam region. Other attempts by Moscow to forge direct links with the German cadres, for instance through Anton Saefkow in Berlin, remained unsuccessful, and absurd directives, such as that broadcast in February 1942 for armed resistance and mass strikes, hindered rather than helped the struggling underground cadres.[23]

By 1945, therefore, the organized KPD was in no position to launch more than token initiatives. In August 1944 Himmler had ordered the preventive detention of *all* previous KPD, SPD, and *Zentrum* office-holders, even former local councillors. At the final collapse of Nazi Germany in spring 1945 Ruhr Communists survived only in loose self-help groups which met perhaps to listen to foreign broadcasts, or simply lay low in the surrounding countryside. It was such spontaneous groups of old acquaintances bound by common persecution, often merged in *Antifa* committees, which arranged the peaceful handovers of Oberhausen, Dortmund, and Düsseldorf to the Americans.[24] The Communists who stepped into the breach in spring 1945 were generally lower- to middle-ranking functionaries released from prison in early 1945, who bowed to returning concentration camp inmates during the early summer (some of whom were in turn replaced by émigrés). It is also worth noting that the camp cadres, who tended to be more senior, politicized during Weimar's ultra-leftist

---

[22] Hermann Wichers, 'Zur Anleitung des Widerstands der KPD: Ein Rundschreiben des ZK-Sekretariats an die Abschnittsleitungen vom 29. Juli 1938', *IWK*, 26 (1990), 526–39.
[23] Herlemann, *Auf verlorenem Posten*, 18, 110–11, and 135–55.
[24] Detlev Peukert, *Die KPD im Widerstand* (Wuppertal, 1980), 411 ff.

phase, and arrested early in the Third Reich, had remained artificially insulated against many of the social changes occurring in the intervening twelve years. This may help to explain their 'sectarian' political behaviour in 1945, which will be discussed further in Chapter 3.

As well as the functionary corps, one must also consider the experiences of the potential members and voters of a post-war KPD, in the shape of the industrial proletariat at large. The fear of the returning Moscow leadership was that working-class consciousness had been buried by twelve years of dictatorship. (It was, of course, clearly in the interests of the returning exiles to portray themselves as uncontaminated and uniquely fit to lead.) The Depression had already encouraged the defence of narrow self-interest, and the smashing of the workers' parties and trade unions in 1933 completed the organizational atomization of the proletariat. Following Mason's pioneering research, however, it is generally agreed that overt Nazi programmes to depoliticize labour with welfarist sops such as 'Beauty of Labour' and 'Strength through Joy' had no more than superficial success. Moreover, with full employment from 1936, workers had some of their bargaining power restored, if on an individual rather than a collective basis. It has also been argued by Werner that the experience of total war engendered a primitive form of survivalist solidarity, admittedly not an orthodox Marxist class consciousness, but a bonding process all the same. As will be seen in Chapter 5, industrial groups reliant on semi-skilled labour, such as mining, preserved a demonstrable measure of radicalism into the post-war years. Many of the miners' grievances could, of course, only be expressed once the war was over, but the pent-up problems of an ageing and debilitated workforce left plenty of scope for conflict.[25]

This is not to deny that German workers' class consciousness had undergone significant modifications in ways which even the Nazis had not always foreseen. As Gillingham has argued, under the regime's various vocational training schemes, many workers exchanged their blue collar for something approaching a white collar. Niethammer has also highlighted the destruction of workers' structural 'communities of solidarity'.[26] Wage

---

[25] Timothy Mason, *Arbeiterklasse und Volksgemeinschaft: Dokumente und Materialien zur deutschen Arbeiterpolitik 1936–1939* (Opladen, 1975); Wolfgang Franz Werner, *'Bleib übrig!': Deutsche Arbeiter in der nationalsozialistischen Kriegswirtschaft* (Düsseldorf, 1983); Klaus Wisotzky, *Der Ruhrbergbau im Dritten Reich: Studien zur Sozialpolitik im Ruhrbergbau und zum sozialen Verhalten der Bergleute in den Jahren 1933 bis 1939* (Düsseldorf, 1983); Detlev Peukert and Frank Bajohr, *Spuren des Widerstands: Die Bergarbeiterbewegung im Dritten Reich und im Exil* (Munich, 1987), 154–90.

[26] John Gillingham, 'The "Deproletarianization" of German Society: Vocational Training in the Third Reich', *Journal of Social History*, 19 (1986), 423–32; Lutz Niethammer, 'Rekonstruktion und Desintegration: Zum Verständnis der deutschen Arbeiterbewegung

differentials, the dilution of native workforces with foreign slave labour, and the threat of conscription had an undeniably disciplining effect on German workers. Admittedly, in the early stages of the war, with only moderate rationing and many skilled workers designated vital to the war effort, and thus protected from the draft, many of these changes did not hit home until after 1942. Yet, from 1943 the Ruhr in particular experienced intensive area bombing, physically destroying many working-class milieux. At Rheinpreußen colliery in Moers, for instance, only 60 out of 4,660 miners' dwellings remained undamaged, and by 1947 13,500 Düsseldorf and 12,000 Essen workers were still living in cellars, air-raid bunkers, or, if lucky, Nissen huts.[27] Various other effects of war became only fully felt in the hunger years of peace. The post-war barter economy, while at one level empowering works councillors assigned the task of feeding local workforces, also compelled them to learn the entrepreneurial skills of the black market, often in collusion with management. Population transfers also followed on from wartime evacuations and labour migration, in some cases causing greater heterogeneity of the working class, as first-generation workers, refugees, and *déclassés* moved into the ruins of the Weimar milieu.[28]

The post-war KPD was thus returning to a significantly different social world, but one still haunted by the political ghosts of the past. Arguably, social realities had moved too quickly for political mentalities to keep up. The process of readjustment was to last well into the 1950s. Many political conflicts within the Weimar labour movement had remained unresolved in 1933 and were still latent in 1945. Nazi persecution had kept Communist resistance cadres in a form of suspended animation, which was to put them at odds with their own returning leadership. This local attachment to radicalism and distrust of alliance politics may also help to explain the rapid post-war breakdown in relations between Social Democrats and Communists, which is the subject of the next chapter.

zwischen Krieg und Kaltem Krieg', in Heinrich A. Winkler (ed.), *Politische Weichenstellungen im Nachkriegsdeutschland 1945–1953* (Göttingen, 1979), 26–43.

    [27] Trades Union Congress, 'Report of Delegation to Germany' (17–29 Apr. 1947), MRC, MSS 292/943/65.

    [28] Ulrich Herbert, *Fremdarbeiter: Politik und Praxis des 'Ausländer-Einsatzes' in der Kriegswirtschaft des Dritten Reiches* (West Berlin and Bonn, 1985), 270; Omer Bartov, 'The Missing Years: German Workers, German Soldiers', *German History*, 8 (1990), 62–5; Hans Woller, 'Germany in Transition from Stalingrad (1943) to Currency Reform (1948)', in Michael Ermarth (ed.), *America and the Shaping of German Society, 1945–1955* (Providence, RI, and Oxford, 1993), 23–34.

Part I

Communism in West Germany

2

'Vereint sind wir alles'?

Socialist Unity in a Divided Germany

As has already been seen, from the point when the world party line changed in 1935 it was Communist policy to encourage unity of action with the Social Democrats, with a dim prospect of organizational fusion. In other western European countries this approach yielded significant, if not spectacular results. In Italy the Socialists under Pietro Nenni, although not merging, entered into a popular front with the Communist PCI in 1947, which lasted until 1956. Nenni's anti-frontist rivals under Saragat remained in a distinct minority. The Italian trade union federation, the CGIL, was also Communist-dominated in the early post-war years, and offered a powerful symbol of labour unity until Socialist and Christian Democratic breakaways between 1948–50. The French Socialists under Léon Blum were less co-operative, but, like the Italians, still tolerated a tripartite coalition with the Communists and Christian Democrats until spring 1947. French unionists went further, however, burying political and religious differences for the sake of the resistance, and reuniting the CGT in 1943 under the implicit leadership of the Communist PCF.[1]

In post-war Germany the iron curtain cut across the politics of the united front. On the one side, in the western zones, the anti-Communism of SPD leader, Kurt Schumacher, was far ahead of that of the rest of the Socialist International; on the other, in the Soviet Zone (SBZ), in April 1946 the world's first fusion of Communists and Socialists was achieved, producing the Socialist Unity Party of Germany (SED). Under the shadow of this event, one of the watersheds of the Cold War in Germany, relations not only between eastern and western Social Democrats, but also between

[1] Spencer M. Di Scala, *Renewing Italian Socialism: Nenni to Craxi* (New York and Oxford, 1988), 66–83; Daniel L. Horowitz, *The Italian Labor Movement* (Cambridge, Mass., 1963), 181–243; Wilfried Loth, 'Die französische Linke und die "Einheit der Arbeiterklasse" 1943–1947', in Dietrich Staritz and Hermann Weber (eds.), *Einheitsfront—Einheitspartei: Kommunisten und Sozialdemokraten in Ost- und Westeuropa 1944–1948* (Cologne, 1989), 355–76; George Ross, *Workers and Communists in France: From Popular Front to Eurocommunism* (Berkeley, 1982), 25–36.

Communists and Social Democrats in West Germany, reached a new low. Rather than spurring on a united front in the western zones, it appeared to stop a *rapprochement* dead in its tracks.

Subsequent East German histories published by the Institute of Marxism-Leninism claimed that there had indeed been a genuine mass will for merger in all zones, but that the historical logic of unity was only realized in the SBZ. Under the slogan 'Vereint sind wir alles' ('United, we are everything'), a romanticized official myth of unity was propagated, maintaining that a united working class could have gone on to prevent the very division of Germany. Western accounts, on the other hand, especially those appearing under the auspices of the SPD's research foundation, the Friedrich-Ebert-Stiftung, stressed the coercive aspects of the *Zwangsvereinigung* or 'forced merger', whereby Russian and German Communists in the SBZ had browbeaten the eastern SPD into joining.[2]

Only a differentiated picture can do justice to the complexities of the situation in 1945–6. Dietrich Staritz was one of the first to warn against applying too much hindsight about the outcome of 1946 to the fluid circumstances of 1945.[3] It is all too tempting to see the fusion as part of a carefully calculated Communist strategy to consolidate power, rather than as an essentially reactive and potentially risky policy. The KPD had never entertained serious hopes of going it alone and was concerned to tie itself to the SPD before the anti-fascist consensus began to unravel under the strain of electioneering. Since this opening up of the debate, as well as of the East German archives, better sources of knowledge of the intermediate levels of the eastern SPD hierarchy which did so much to facilitate merger, both wittingly and unwittingly, have become available.[4] Individual Social Democratic leaders in the SBZ had their own ulterior motives for the so-called 'eastward orientation', and were clearly at pains to break down the mistrust of the Soviet occupying power. Others patently hoped to secure hegemony over the Communists within a unity

[2] Institut für Marxismus-Leninismus beim ZK der SED (ed.), *Vereint sind wir alles: Erinnerungen an die Gründung der SED* (East Berlin, 1966); Gustav Dahrendorf, *Die Zwangsvereinigung der Kommunisten und der Sozialdemokratischen Partei in der russischen Zone* (Hamburg, n.d. [1946]); Albrecht Kaden, *Einheit oder Freiheit: Die Wiedergründung der SPD 1945/46* (Bonn, 1964); Frank Moraw, *Die Parole der 'Einheit' und die Sozialdemokratie* (2nd edn.; Bonn, 1990).

[3] Dietrich Staritz, 'Zur Gründung der SED: Forschungsstand, Kontroversen, offene Fragen', in id., *Was war: Historische Studien zu Geschichte und Politik der DDR* (Berlin, 1994), 105–36.

[4] *Auf dem Weg zur SED: Die Sozialdemokratie und die Bildung einer Einheitspartei in den Ländern der SBZ*, ed. Andreas Malycha (Bonn, 1995); also very detailed on Berlin is Harold Hurwitz, *Die Anfänge des Widerstands* (2 vols.; Cologne, 1990).

party. The SPD's traditional hierarchy and party discipline also became a liability when it came to responding to local Communist initiatives, leading as often as not to inaction. Nor should the substantial emotional support for fusion be ignored among the Social Democratic rank and file, although this may have been determined more by the practical needs of reconstruction than the dictates of high politics. Nevertheless, the grass roots tended to follow their local leaders, making it relatively easy for the Soviet authorities to concentrate their threats and cajolery upon key individuals. Ideologically, eastern Social Democratic leaders then became prisoners of their own logic: if one was for the *idea* of unity, it was very difficult to extricate oneself from the *practice* of fusion, however much one abhorred the Communists' undemocratic means.

Fusion in the Soviet Occupation Zone

In Berlin in the spring of 1945, even before the end of hostilities, Social Democrats around Max Fechner had approached surviving Communists with proposals for an immediate unity party, only to be evaded by Ulbricht and others, who apparently feared being swamped. At the end of May the decision came to rebuild a separate KPD, and SPD feelers were turned down categorically on 19 June. Whether or not the SPD was calling the KPD's bluff, it was always to hold this rejection against the Communists as proof of their duplicity. Instead of direct merger the Communists promoted the slogan 'First unity of action, then unity party!'. Intensive discussions between Communists and Social Democrats began in Berlin on 12 June 1945, upon publication of the KPD's founding Appeal, and seven days later a joint Working Committee emerged as a prototype for the united front, which was in turn to form the core of the East German bloc party system. This step-by-step pace was designed to allow time for 'ideological clarification', primarily in the KPD's own ranks, but also within the SPD, which was expected to make its peace with the Soviet Union and Marxism-Leninism. In the meantime any spontaneous moves towards actual merger were actively combatted.

Why, then, only three months later, did the KPD's Central Committee change its mind from unity of action to all-out fusion? By autumn 1945 it had become apparent that the KPD could no longer contain the SPD with unity of action alone and had lost its initial membership lead. In fact, the SPD enjoyed a larger mass base in all zones. The eastern SPD's Central Executive was also attempting to reassert its leadership of the labour movement in the SBZ, and beyond, as a 'third force'. At a rally on 14 September the eastern SPD leader, Otto Grotewohl, backed away from merger and revived the idea of a national SPD as the only feasible government party, at which, five days later, Wilhelm Pieck threw down the gauntlet for the KPD and issued the first public demand for rapid fusion. This change of course, which envisaged joint electoral lists and a national campaign, was sanctioned by the Central Committee at the end of the month and was in fact an admission of the failure of bloc politics.

October saw an intensification of grass-roots unity of action, fought out in the *Kreise* and towns of the SBZ, with the Communists badgering the Berlin Social Democrats from below via local SPD organizations. In November, after the disappointing results of the Communists in the first Hungarian and Austrian elections, the propaganda campaign moved up another gear.[5] One of the key sources of internal party pressure on the Central Executive was the new SPD factory groups, more tractable than the SPD's traditional residential groups, and accounting for most new SPD recruits, a majority of whom probably favoured fusion. Nevertheless, at a second rally on 11 November Grotewohl stated that merger must be preceded by the formation of national parties on both sides, and not 'in the least the result of external pressure or indirect coercion'—an oblique but unmistakeable criticism of the Soviet Military Administration (SMAD).[6]

Throughout, but now more so than ever, the Soviet authorities provided simultaneous pressure from above, as well as privileging the KPD with newsprint and radio air time. On 20 December 1945 the SMAD also removed Schreiber and Hermes from the Christian Democratic leadership, leaving Grotewohl in no uncertainty as to his own expendability, and Soviet officers maintained a conspicuous presence at all gatherings. Particularly after a visit by a KPD delegation under Ulbricht to Moscow on 2 February 1946, the Soviets took an ever closer interest in events. The final date of merger, 22 April, only three days before the beginning of the Paris Council of Foreign Ministers, must also have suited Molotov's foreign policy timetable. Klotzbach, however, concludes that until mid-January 1946 the SPD Central Executive was not as supine as previously thought, and was committed to preventing zonal fusion, clinging to the hope of a Reich-level merger, with the weight of the western zones' SPD behind it so as to dominate any unity party. Accordingly, the Central

---

[5] 'Danger—Austria': Pieck's notes of Karlshorst meeting, 22 Dec. 1945, in *Wilhelm Pieck*, ed. Rolf Badstübner and Wilfried Loth (Berlin, 1994), 62.

[6] Andreas Malycha, '"Hier stehe ich, ich kann nicht anders!": Rede Otto Grotewohls am 11. November 1945', *BzG*, 34 (1992), 179.

Executive's first plenary session on 4 December agreed to resist KPD overtures while sending out feelers to Kurt Schumacher in Hannover. Yet, since Schumacher, the self-appointed leader of the SPD in the western zones, had made it abundantly clear on 6 October 1945, at the Wennigsen Conference, that the western SPD regarded itself as under no obligation to its eastern comrades, this was a forlorn and perhaps irresponsible hope.

The eastern Social Democrats' mettle was further tested at one of the crucial stations on the road to amalgamation, the 'Sixty Conference' of 20–1 December 1945, where equal numbers of Communists and Social Democrats met to debate a fusion timetable. The eastern SPD acceded under duress to the KPD's principle of rapid fusion, having secured some nominal concessions, such as no joint election lists, as well as a verbal agreement to national merger only, after separate Reich conventions, in what seems to have been a bid to win time. Nevertheless, Pieck for the KPD hinted that merger *would* initially be in the SBZ only, and on 13 January Ulbricht broke the Sixty agreement by invoking unity from below. Attempts two days later by the SPD Central Executive to publicize its reservations about the conference and insist on *national* merger only, were suppressed by the SMAD, which issued a sanitized version of events. Yet, as Malycha has shown, the confused signals coming from the Sixty Conference only served to disorientate and fatally weaken local Social Democrats.[7]

Those who continued to oppose merger were either 'neutralized' by being ordered to SMAD offices while conferences were under way, or simply arrested. As well as the stick, the carrot of financial remuneration or posts in the administration was dangled before recalcitrant Social Democrats. In early February Marshal Zhukov offered Grotewohl concessions on dismantling, the withdrawal of Red Army troops from the SBZ, and a provisional central government with himself as Moscow's frontrunner for Reich Chancellor. The KPD's grass-roots campaign in the *Bezirke* and localities, fanning out from industrial Saxony, with joint party conferences and the increasingly dominant unity committees (and from late January preparatory unity bureaux), was so successful by early February 1946 that the Central Executive sensed defeat. Grotewohl and Gustav

[7] Lucio Caracciolo, 'Der Untergang der Sozialdemokratie in der sowjetischen Besatzungszone: Otto Grotewohl und die "Einheit der Arbeiterklasse" 1945/46', *VfZ*, 36 (1988), 303 and 307; *Einheitsdrang oder Zwangsvereinigung?: Die Sechziger-Konferenzen von KPD und SPD 1945 und 1946*, ed. Hans-Joachim Krusch and Andreas Malycha (Berlin, 1990), 137; Kaden, *Einheit oder Freiheit*, 228–9; *Auf dem Weg zur SED*, lxxxv ff.

Dahrendorf even confided to the British that they were being 'tickled by Russian bayonets' and 'completely undermined' in the provinces, so that resistance would only martyrize them.[8] Then, on 10–11 February, the SPD chairmen of Thuringia, Saxony, and Mecklenburg threatened to go it alone in their own areas, using the concurrent FDGB union congress as a platform. At the end of this dramatic meeting the Executive's initial anti-merger majority caved in and agreed by eight to three (with four abstentions) to fusion by 1 May. By the end of February preparatory district mergers had taken place across the SBZ, followed by *Land* amalgamations in March and April, prior to the final ritualized enactment of zonal merger on the stage of Berlin's Admiralspalast theatre on 22 April 1946.[9]

Socialist Unity Campaigns in the Western Zones

It is often forgotten that there were also vigorous socialist unity campaigns in western Germany. The object of the bulk of this chapter is therefore to explore the possibilities of co-operation and amalgamation between the SPD and KPD in the West, a subject hitherto overshadowed by the notorious merger in the SBZ. Yet this is not an issue wholly without bearing upon events in the East. Since the coercive factors in favour of fusion were absent west of the Elbe, we might be able to find some indirect answers to the extent of support for unity among German labour generally. Rank-and-file western Social Democrats were subject to the same initial euphoria for unity as in the East, but, unlike their eastern comrades, had more democratic room for manœuvre. Of course, local military government was decidedly hostile, as was the western SPD leadership, so that the western zones cannot act as a neutral control to the fusion experiment in the East. By the same token, the failure of a united front in West Germany should not be attributed solely to the intransigence of the western occupiers and their alleged protégés. There were strong tendencies within all western social democratic movements to maintain their autonomy. Thus, despite the initial willingess to co-operate in Italy and France, deriving in large part from the Communists' key role in the resistance, there was no actual merger in these areas either.

Nevertheless, given post-war German historians' agreement that there was indeed a widespread, if vague, emotional sympathy for a reconciliation of organized labour after the Nazi débâcle, were even maverick local

---

[8] Nevertheless Political Division were resolved to tell Schumacher of the 'stupidity of forcing a break at this time': Steel to FO, 7 Feb. 1946, PRO, FO 1049/323.

[9] Reiner Pommerin, 'Die Zwangsvereinigung von KPD und SPD zur SED: Eine britische Analyse vom April 1946', *VfZ*, 36 (1988), 327–30; Caracciolo, 'Untergang', 311; Moraw, *Parole der 'Einheit'*, 151–4.

mergers possible in the western zones? Although Berlin's line was to remain noncommittal on immediate fusion throughout the spring and summer of 1945, in some western areas there were indeed pressures to force the pace *before* the official acceleration in September. Many local Communists and Social Democrats, conscious of the fragility of the anti-fascist consensus, were keen to seize the moment, and, in some cases, to pre-empt the rebuilding of the Weimar workers' parties. Local initiatives were also unwittingly fostered until the autumn by the western Allies' 'bottom-up' party licensing policy, which kept the political scene in a decentralized state of limbo.

Moreover, the KPD Central Committee did not meet in Berlin until 2 July 1945, after Pieck's return from Moscow, and initially had little time for the western party formations. In the interim, concentration camp inmates released from the SBZ offered one of the only westward channels of communication, for instance Fiete Dettmann who returned to Hamburg in June, or Max Reimann who was sent to the Ruhr in August. Although a primitive courier network linked Berlin to Bremen from May, and Frankfurt and Munich from June, only from August was the Central Committee in regular contact with all western *Bezirke*. The first Berlin instructor to tour the American Zone, Bruno Fuhrmann, did not do so until August–October; and Karl Schirdewan, of the Central Committee's 'Western Germany' desk, did not visit the British Zone for himself until even later in the year.[10]

There was therefore a period of several months in 1945 in which the KPD in the western zones was operating largely on its own initiative. If one accepts that the western cadres could not be switched on and off like a tap, then the factor of spontaneity must be taken seriously. Before tackling this issue, however, the reader should also understand that there was not even a zonal, let alone a national, pattern to early KPD–SPD relations, but instead a variegated patchwork, often influenced by local personalities spared by Nazi persecution. My own view is that there can therefore be no definitive answer to the question of spontaneous merger.

1945: *Antifas* and Spontaneous Merger Tendencies

The so-called *Antifas* were the obvious nuclei for some form of cross-party *rapprochement*. Anti-fascist committees were formed all over Germany

[10] Fuhrmann, 14 Oct. 1945, SAPMO-BA, NY 4182/859; Detlef Siegfried, *Zwischen Einheitspartei und 'Bruderkampf'* (Kiel, 1992), 57; Max Reimann, *Entscheidungen 1945–1956* (Frankfurt am Main, 1973), 36–7; Dietrich Staritz, 'Die Kommunistische Partei Deutschlands', in Richard Stöss (ed.), *Parteien-Handbuch* (Opladen, 1983), 1668; Karl Schirdewan interview, 29 Aug. 1990.

in March–April 1945 and set about peaceful surrenders to the Allies, denazification, and maintaining skeleton public services. However, they were never the mass phenomenon of the councils of 1918–19, remaining local initiatives based on personal contacts, mainly between Communists and Social Democrats (a high proportion from Weimar breakaways), and a minority of the bourgeoisie. *Antifas* were regarded with suspicion by all occupiers. In the West they were viewed as Communist fronts, and Schumacher was quick to condemn them as a reincarnation of the KPD's 1932 Anti-Fascist Front. To Communist leaders they presented an opportunity to influence others, but also the risk of being swallowed up themselves, so that in the SBZ all spontaneous anti-fascist groups were dissolved by 9 May. In the West they were generally banned too, but some lingered on until the autumn, yet only rarely, as in Wiesbaden, did one lead directly to a KPD–SPD unity committee.[11]

In the Ruhr the following complex picture emerged. The Essen Fighting League against Fascism, reviving the Weimar KPD's organization of the same name, comprised German, Russian, and Polish Communists, and claimed to represent 3,000–5,000 workers, farmers, and *Mittelständler*, based on the unions and works councils. It was closed down in early May. From April an Anti-Fascist United Front, chaired by a Communist, but including Christian and Social Democrats, was co-ordinating works councils in nearby Mülheim; yet by the summer it was supplanted by the town council it had helped to inaugurate, and absorbed into the trade union. (Internally the Communists admitted appropriating 4,000 of the 7,386 Reichsmarks collected for the *Antifa*, and Berlin advised them to link up instead with the KPD's *Bezirk* Leadership.[12]) Duisburg's Anti-Fascist United Front came nearest to integrating differing political tendencies, but failed to shake up local government bureaucracy, consoling itself with union work.[13] It was in fact the Communists who backed out of its logical extension into a unity party, and from late July a separate SPD and KPD evolved, although the *Antifa* lingered on until late 1946.

[11] Lutz Niethammer *et al.*, *Arbeiterinitiative 1945* (Wuppertal, 1976), 10–13 and 642; Rebecca Boehling, 'German Municipal Self-Government and the Personnel Policies of the Local US Military Government in Three Major Cities of the Zone of Occupation: Frankfurt, Munich, Stuttgart', *Archiv für Sozialgeschichte*, 25 (1985), 333–83; Gerhard Fisch and Fritz Krause, *SPD und KPD 1945/46* (Frankfurt am Main, 1978), 90–100; Kurt Klotzbach, *Der Weg zur Staatspartei: Programmatik, praktische Politik und Organisation der deutschen Sozialdemokratie 1945 bis 1965* (Berlin and Bonn, 1982), 68.

[12] Gundelach to Ulbricht, 27 July 1945, SAPMO-BA, NY 4182/859.

[13] Gerhard Mannschatz and Josef Seider, *Zum Kampf der KPD im Ruhrgebiet* (East Berlin, 1962), 112.

Oberhausen's Anti-Fascist Action Committee was dominated by Communists, and did go as far as applying for licensing as a party in its own right. In Bochum the Anti-Fascist Freedom Movement, led by a Communist, Heinz Pöppe, was unable to win non-Communist support and collapsed after his arrest in June, with the KPD re-establishing itself separately. Similarly, in Dortmund the Anti-Fascist League could not get a foothold ahead of the two traditional workers' parties.[14] Internal evidence in fact indicates that the Ruhr KPD leadership had itself been instrumental in extinguishing the *Antifas*.[15] Everywhere it seemed that orthodox local power structures, which must include the KPD, were rendering the committees superfluous. As an American report recorded:

In the western zones the period of ANTIFA came to an end with the conclusion of the first phase of de-Nazification. Then the traditional cleavages between the Bourgeois and labor interests reappeared to divide the common front. At about the same time, the developing divergences between the Soviet and western Zones reactivated the old differences between Social Democrats and Communists. Since September 1945, with the establishment of authorized political parties, the Antifa has no longer been an active force in the western zones.[16]

Besides military government intervention, the other most often cited obstacle to merger was the personal opposition of western SPD leader, Kurt Schumacher. His attacks were characteristically vitriolic, deriding Communists as 'red-painted Nazis', 'Prussian NCOs', and 'servants of a foreign power'. In fact, ever since May 1945 he had dismissed them as simply tools of Soviet diplomacy, denying them any stake in Germany's national revival. The Soviet Union was not pursuing internationalist, world-revolutionary goals, but those of a nationalist and imperialist state. His solution to the unity party was therefore the 'social democratization' of KPD supporters and their absorption into the SPD.[17]

On 28 August 1945 Schumacher invited the re-forming western SPD *Bezirke* to a conference on 5–6 October at Wennigsen, near his political base in Hannover, enclosing his 'Political Guidelines', which advocated an autonomous mass SPD. The Social Democrats who gathered there

[14] Unless otherwise stated Hartmut Pietsch, *Militärregierung, Bürokratie und Sozialisierung* (Duisburg, 1978), 110–23.
[15] KPD-BL Ruhr, 13 Aug. 1945, SAPMO-BA, I 11/23/1; see also Schabrod, 15 Aug. 1945, SAPMO-BA, I 10/23/8.
[16] State Dept. report, 11 Jan. 1946, ZI6, Sammlung Brandt, Ordner 10/9.
[17] Lewis J. Edinger, *Kurt Schumacher: A Study in Personality and Political Behavior* (Stanford, Calif., 1965), 151; Klotzbach, *Weg zur Staatspartei*, 70–1 and 73; *KPD 1945–1968: Dokumente*, ed. Günter Judick *et al.* (2 vols.; Neuss, 1989), i. 25.

acclaimed this uncompromising stance. Schumacher also made it bluntly clear to Grotewohl, who was observing the proceedings, that, as long as there was zonal division, jurisdiction over the SPD would remain demarcated between the Büro Dr Schumacher in Hannover and the Central Executive in Berlin. Accordingly, Communists in the US Zone noted existing local co-operation from the SPD 'stiffening' after Schumacher's first rounds of the *Bezirke*.[18] The rift was deepened by a circular later that month from Schumacher to local parties, accusing the eastern SPD of political unreliability and anti-party behaviour. Despite visits from the SBZ by Grotewohl and Dahrendorf to the US Zone in November, and by Grotewohl and Gniffke to Lower Saxony in December, the drift apart continued. Then, on 3–4 January 1946, in response to the Sixty Conference, SPD leaders in the British Zone unanimously rejected past and present KPD policy, and on 6 January Schumacher repeated the exercise in the US Zone, with 144 to 6 voting against the SPD becoming a 'blood donor for the debilitated body of the KPD'. Whether Schumacher acted out of political realism or party ambition in scuppering a Reich SPD, he was withholding the only lifeline to the increasingly embattled Social Democrats in the SBZ.[19]

Nevertheless, the anti-Communist stand taken by the western SPD should not be painted as too much of a one-man operation. The exiled London Union of Socialist Organizations, embracing the *Sopade*, Socialist Workers' Party (SAP), International Socialist Combat League (ISK), and *Neubeginnen* groups, as well as the Stockholm SAP under Willy Brandt, also favoured a social democratic unity party. In September 1945 it condemned 'any sort of co-operation whatsoever with the KPD'.[20] Schumacher's militant anti-Communism also enjoyed widespread appeal among trade union officials and 'pragmatists' in the party apparatus, criticized by American observers as 'narrow-minded Party politicians, too sluggish and too set in their ways to break with the traditions of the WEIMAR Republic'.[21] In 1946 over 90% of the SPD consisted of such 'old' members, but the much-vaunted internal overhaul of the party hierarchy soon took second place to containment of the KPD.

An alternative source of support for labour unity has been sought in the SPD's rank and file, and it would indeed be wrong to equate the Social Democrats with their leaders. There is certainly evidence of a persistent

---

[18] Fuhrmann, 14 Oct. 1945, SAPMO-BA, NY 4182/859.

[19] Caracciolo, 'Untergang', 299 and 304–5; Klotzbach, *Weg zur Staatspartei*, 75; Erich W. Gniffke, *Jahre mit Ulbricht* (Cologne, 1966), 128.

[20] Anthony Glees, *Exile Politics during the Second World War* (Oxford, 1982), 235.

[21] HQ USFET, 'Weekly Intelligence Summary No. 37', 28 Mar. 1946, PA Staritz.

desire among many grass-roots Social Democrats for an immediate socialist unity party, above all in the period April–August 1945. The trauma of a divided labour movement, which it was felt had allowed Hitler into power, as well as the common experience of persecution, had caused many to reflect. It is easy, however, to overstate the bonding effects of joint incarceration. In Sachsenhausen concentration camp, for instance, Communists—admittedly as part of an SS policy of divide and rule— had used privileged posts to look after their own; in Buchenwald a *Kapo* system also operated to the advantage of the KPD.[22] Moreover, notions of the structure and programme of a unity party were vague. One Stuttgart Social Democrat scoffed at what he saw as 'a general party mush in which it [the KPD] forms the leaven'.[23] Other grass-roots calls for renewal were probably tactically motivated, for instance in October 1945 when one young Bochum SPD functionary wanted a new name, programme, and statute for the party, fearing that dominance by older colleagues would be a recipe 'to be finished off in short order' by the KPD.[24]

It is of course impossible to quantify rank-and-file SPD support for merger exactly, especially in the crucial year 1945. Schumacher seems to have consciously played sympathy down, while local leaders may have played it up. In the US Zone it was strongest in the industrial conurbations, but by March 1946 was no higher than 20%.[25] By June–July 1946 British intelligence had made the following estimates for North Rhine-Westphalia's *Regierungsbezirke* and Lower Saxony: Arnsberg 15%; Cologne 10%; Düsseldorf 7%; Münster 7%; Aachen 5–10%; Detmold 2%; and Hannover Region 3–4%.[26] Social Democrats fleeing the SBZ had reportedly helped to tip the balance against fusion, so that by January 1946 one Bremen observer could claim that:

the majority of the SPD here, of whom many were initially collaborating, are, following the reports from the East and the sharp rejection by Kurt Schumacher, now strictly against a unity party.[27]

---

[22] Reimann, Müller, Geschke, and Pointner to Ulbricht, 16 May 1945, *NL* Müller, 'Funktionäre'; Lutz Niethammer (ed.), *Der 'gesäuberte' Antifaschismus: Die SED und die roten Kapos von Buchenwald* (Berlin, 1994).
[23] Letter from 'F.E.', 20 July 1945, ZI6, Sammlung Becker, Ordner 8.5/3c.
[24] Klotzbach, *Weg zur Staatspartei*, 65.
[25] Ulrich Hauth, *Die Politik von KPD und SED* (Frankfurt am Main, 1978), 82–3 and 88.
[26] Regional Intelligence Office Münster, 3 July 1946; 11 RIS, 4 July 1946; 13 RIS, 4 July 1946, all in PRO, FO 1049/2118.
[27] I. Enderle to Szende, 20 Jan. 1946, ZI6, Sammlung Brandt, Ordner 6/5. At the turn of 1945/6 Hermann Brill, *Land* chairman of Thuringia, moved to the US Zone; Hermann Lüdemann, of Mecklenburg, went to Schleswig-Holstein; Gustav Dahrendorf fled

Although the SPD rank and file offer a shifting and complex picture, it is assumed that their KPD counterparts dutifully accepted merger. One should not assume, however, that even they were automatic converts. As the Ruhr KPD noted:

The mood of really large parts of the comrades is, as a result of the anti-unity policy of almost all upper and middle SPD echelons, currently in such a state that they would, at a sign from the *Bezirk* leadership, enthusiastically pounce on a public confrontation with the SPD.[28]

In the Saar one member of the KPD rank and file even stood up at a meeting and spouted 'to the horror of our own comrades and the SPD comrades a lot of garbled nonsense about social fascism and the like. This speech destroyed everything that we had painstakingly built up.'[29] This would suggest that lurking not very far beneath the surface of many post-war Communists was an abiding attachment to the ultra-leftism of Weimar.

What these statements also betray is the relative ease with which local party hierarchies asserted control over their grass roots. I propose therefore to spend the rest of this section looking at official KPD–SPD relations prior to the emergence in the autumn of 1945 of 'national' leaderships in the western zones. Even here, there was room for local co-operation. The most notable cases were Hamburg, the Rhine-Main and Rhine-Ruhr regions, Bremen, Braunschweig, Munich, and South Baden, mainly at a devolved level and supported by a disproportionate number of former SPD splinter groups. In general, where these moves had begun, until mid-August, it was Social Democrats who pushed for immediate union, and Communists who cautiously limited themselves to unity of action agreements with an option on future merger.[30]

In Hamburg, a unity party cum union, the Socialist Free Union, was set up in mid-May under the auspices of relatively minor functionaries on both sides, only to be banned as a political organization by the British on 20 June 1945. Immediately afterwards, the subsequent KPD *Bezirk* chairman, Dettmann, arrived from the SBZ and halted any further moves

to Hamburg in Feb. 1946; see Werner Müller, *Die KPD und die 'Einheit der Arbeiterklasse'* (Frankfurt am Main and New York, 1979), 209.

[28] KPD-BL Ruhr, 'Kaderbericht', 23 Feb. 1946, SAPMO-BA, I 11/23/1.
[29] Stötzel, 13 Dec. 1946, SAPMO-BA, NY 4036/645.
[30] Hamburg 24 July; Munich 8 Aug.; Bremen 14 Aug.; Kiel 1 Sept.; Frankfurt am Main 3 Sept.; Braunschweig 21 Sept.; see Müller, *'Einheit der Arbeiterklasse'*, 105; Hauth, *KPD und SED*, 49.

at merger beyond unity of action within an Action Committee. Nevertheless, most Social Democrats, including Dettmann's SPD opposite number, Meitmann, persisted with preparations for a unity party, even signing an agreement on 20 August pledging to form a 'Socialist Party' upon legalization of political parties. Yet in September both groups applied for separate licensing, and, although Meitmann did not definitively disown unity until 20 December, considerably irritating the Büro Dr Schumacher in the interim, the previous six months had been a progressive exercise in KPD evasion and SPD exasperation.[31]

In Frankfurt a similar pattern developed, with a joint Action Committee in July, but, when the SPD tested KPD sincerity by proposing immediate merger on 14 August, the KPD stalled. Then, from October, the Hessen SPD pursued a policy of demarcation from the Communists. In the communes of South Hessen there is stronger evidence that local SPD branches persisted longer with unity, often into 1946, and even entered into local election pacts, but ultimately they too toed the Hannover line.[32]

The Rhine-Ruhr region presented a patchwork within a patchwork. Dortmund, a bastion of the SPD's old guard, was sceptical even of unity of action with the KPD. At the other end of the Ruhr, in Duisburg, however, although the Communists decided on separate rebuilding in July, the Social Democrats only gave up on a joint Socialist Working Group in May 1946. Some Gelsenkirchen districts also continued joint SPD–KPD members' meetings into the new year. Such longevity of co-operation was, however, the exception to the rule. Close inspection of individual cases is more likely to reveal conflict than co-operation, even on the part of the Communists. At the first British zonal KPD conference, held in the Ruhr on 15 September 1945, the lack of consensus on united front tactics is striking. The Düsseldorf leaders in particular were attacked for their manipulative approach to unity. When Karl Schabrod argued for a less conciliatory line with the Social Democrats, he was shouted down with the words: 'You want to encircle the SPD—that's tacticking', to which he replied, 'We're achieving something if we encircle the SPD.'[33] Further down the Rhine, in Cologne, one will also look in vain for close KPD–SPD co-operation, let alone a spontaneous unity party. In the

---

[31] Wulf D. Hund, 'Die Sozialistische Freie Gewerkschaft', *Marxistische Studien*, 8 (1985), 165–95; Holger Christier, *Sozialdemokratie und Kommunismus* (Hamburg, 1975), 79–196; Walter Tormin, *Der Traum von der Einheit* (Hamburg, 1990); Siegfried, *Einheitspartei*, 49–109.

[32] Müller, *'Einheit der Arbeiterklasse'*, 73–94; Walter Mühlhausen, *Hessen 1945–1950: Zur politischen Geschichte eines Landes in der Besatzungszeit* (Frankfurt am Main, 1985), 74–106; Fisch and Krause, *SPD und KPD*, 101–10.

[33] Perk's notes of 29 Sept. 1945 conference, SAPMO-BA, I 10/502/1.

Bergisches Land the pattern is as disparate as in the Ruhr: Wuppertal announced its intention to form a unity party; Remscheid and Solingen did not. Confronted by this welter of local initiatives, regional SPD leaders bided their time until they felt safe to come out openly against unity. In the case of Western Westphalia, covering the eastern Ruhr, this seems to have occurred as early as April 1945; in the Lower Rhine *Bezirk*, controlling the western Ruhr, there was more caution, but a shift against unity in September.[34]

Further north, Bremen presented an initially hopeful picture with its KPD–SPD Unity of Action Contract, but again it was the Communists who applied the brakes. Also, in Braunschweig, when the former SPD-aligned splinter parties went ahead with a 'Socialist Unity Party' in 1945, the Communists were no longer involved, having sought separate licensing in late July. In Bavaria, first KPD–SPD contacts in Munich had taken place on 8 May 1945 via the unions, but the unity of action agreement of 8 August also stipulated applications to OMGUS as separate parties.[35]

South Baden, effectively sealed off from the other zones by a restrictive French occupation, offers the closest thing to a neutral test bed for fusion experiments, but still suggests that spontaneous merger was doomed to collapse under its own weight. In May 1945, before any contact with Berlin or Hannover, Swiss émigré Communists in Singen had improvised Free Germany tactics to encourage immediate amalgamated workers' parties, spreading to Konstanz and its hinterland by August. Local Social Democrats, hoping to restore pre-1914 labour unity by absorbing Communists into their 'Socialist Party, *Land* Baden', even boycotted Wennigsen and the SPD convention in May 1946, and as late as 7 March 1946 the local Socialist and Communist executives agreed on a preparatory merger committee. Yet, once the KPD, emulating the SBZ, forced the pace by issuing an appeal for fusion by 1 May, and then in June started unilaterally collecting petitions, the Baden Socialists developed cold feet and withdrew on 22 June. The KPD's own behaviour and

---

[34] Günther Högl, 'Die Reorganisation der sozialistischen Arbeiterbewegung in Dortmund unter der Britischen Besatzungsherrschaft 1945–1949', *Beiträge zur Geschichte Dortmunds und der Grafschaft Mark*, 76/7 (1984/5), 38; Pietsch, *Militärregierung*, 136–8, 159–61, and 216; Mannschatz and Seider, *Kampf der KPD*, 113–14; Reinhold Billstein, *Das entscheidende Jahr* (Cologne, 1988), 195–255; Inge Marßolek, *Arbeiterbewegung nach dem Krieg (1945–1948)* (Frankfurt am Main and New York, 1983), 134–5; SPD-BL WWf., 'Rundschreiben No. 2', 24 Aug. 1945, AdsD, *NL* Schumacher 51.

[35] Peter Brandt, *Antifaschismus und Arbeiterbewegung* (Hamburg, 1976), 184–201; Albrecht Lein, *Antifaschistische Aktion 1945* (Göttingen, 1978), 200 ff.; Walter Müller, 'Die Aktionsgemeinschaft zwischen KPD und SPD in München 1945/1946', *BzG*, 3 (1961), 121–4.

negative publicity emanating from the SBZ had thus been the deciding factors, independent of intervention by Schumacher or western military government.[36] Other crucial events prompting western Communists and Social Democrats towards separate parties had been the Potsdam declaration on imminent party licensing, and the KPD Central Committee's final contact with all western *Bezirke*, both falling in August 1945. In the Ruhr there was then only talk of collaboration, not amalgamation.[37] Over the autumn KPD instructors were busy discouraging immediate mergers in favour of a 'KPD in waiting' within an anti-fascist front. After legalization, the KPD still called for joint rallies with the SPD, which in some areas complied (Braunschweig, Osnabrück), and in others declined (Stuttgart, Hannover, Western Westphalia), but by late September 1945, precisely when merger began in earnest in the SBZ, the mass of evidence in the British Zone pointed towards SPD autonomy. Indeed, as military government noted, in the Rhineland and Westphalia the Communists' wooing of the SPD was fading noticeably.[38] SPD leaders began to back out of even unity of action agreements, so that by late September the Frankfurt SPD was refusing to put its name to the 3 September agreement; Munich's Action Group lost direction after a government was formed on 22 October; in Hamburg the last unity of action committee met on 13 October; and in the Ruhr the first *Bezirk*-level meeting between KPD and SPD on 2 November achieved merely token co-operation, after the Social Democrats had refused a permanent committee and vetoed discussions at branch level. Two more meetings in 1945 made no further headway, and the SPD refused to commit itself to paper. Consequently, in December 1945 the British could detect only isolated co-operation in vestigial *Antifas*, such as in Duisburg, but by January 1946 regarded the western SED campaign as hopeless.[39]

It would clearly be unjust to claim that there had not been genuine attempts in 1945 to heal the historical split in the German labour movement, but, for every example of innovation, one encounters at least one

---

[36] Edgar Wolfrum, ' "In der französischen Zone ist der Teufel los": Die Sozialistische Partei von 1946 und ihr überkommenes Zerrbild', *IWK*, 28 (1992), 39–51; Karl-Friedrich Müller, *Das Jahr 1945 in Südbaden* (Frankfurt am Main, 1987), 324; Peter Brandt *et al.*, *Karrieren eines Außenseiters* (West Berlin and Bonn, 1983), 127.

[37] KPD-BL Ruhr/*Sek.* to SPD-BL WWf., 6 Aug. 1945, SAPMO-BA, I 10/23/23.

[38] BAOR, 'Field Intelligence Summary No. 11', 22 Sept. 1945, PRO, FO 371/46935.

[39] Mühlhausen, *Hessen 1945–1950*, 96; Müller, 'Aktionsgemeinschaft', 129; Udo Vorholt and Volker Zaib, *SED im Ruhrgebiet?* (Münster and Hamburg, 1994), 24–5; 'Aktionseinheit im Ruhrgebiet', n.d. [late 1945], SAPMO-BA, I 10/23/8; 'Intelligence Review No. 1', 12 Dec. 1945; IR No. 3, 9 Jan. 1946, PRO, FO 1005/1700.

other of party-political restoration. Most pro-merger factions in the SPD were probably having second thoughts about an immediate unity party even *before* the heavy-handed intervention by the party leadership in Hannover, and *before* the notorious fusion campaign had begun in the SBZ in September. Ironically, the greatest allies of the SPD's restorationist old guard in the summer of 1945 had been the Communists themselves. The rapidity with which the sentiment for unity evaporated in the autumn suggests, moreover, that a solidarity, based upon anti-fascist rejectionism, had not struck particularly deep roots in the consciousness of many workers. For the mass of non-affiliated younger workers—nearly everyone below the age of 30—a united labour movement was an abstract principle rather than a personal memory. Yet, as the practical realities of the Socialist Unity Party became evident in eastern Germany, 'unity' acquired increasingly negative connotations and was portrayed by opponents as a rationale for 'totalitarian' control, analagous to the Nazis' Labour Front.

1946: The First Fusion Campaign in the Western Zones

And then came the KPD volte-face. After the switch to merger in the SBZ in September 1945, western KPD leaders suddenly found themselves officially encouraging the unofficial tendencies they had until so recently been trying to quell. Initiatives lagged considerably behind moves in the SBZ and never achieved anything like their scope, but certainly did not begin only after the final eastern fusion in April 1946, as some accounts still imply.[40] (It is admittedly difficult to detect where ailing unity of action ends, and failing merger begins.) Since one of the supposed aims of the Berlin Sixty Conference in December 1945 was for fusion in all zones, I have chosen New Year 1946 as an arbitrary and inauspicious starting-point. Inauspicious because the KPD Central Committee was clearly paying only lip-service to an all-German timetable for amalgamation, and was concentrating its energies on rapid merger in the SBZ instead. It was obvious to those on the party's 'Western Germany' desk that a full-scale western merger was a non-starter.[41] Indeed, on 6 February 1946, after returning from a trip to Moscow, Ulbricht confided that the western campaign would be nominal only. As Pieck recorded in his rather staccato notes: 'In western zone—name KPD into Socialist Unity Party.'[42]

---

[40] Vorholt and Zaib, *SED im Ruhrgebiet?*, 27.
[41] Schirdewan interview, 29 Aug. 1990.   [42] *Wilhelm Pieck*, 68.

The campaign in the West was, nevertheless, necessary to confer retrospective legitimacy on the rushed events in the East, and as a sign of goodwill to the eastern SPD. There was no real co-ordinated campaign as such, more a series of regional initiatives degenerating into local unity-from-below tactics. Firstly, forlorn attempts were made to revive or even establish *Bezirk* unity of action committees; then, in early 1946 the Communists lowered their sights to local SPD organizations, and, failing that, in the spring to individual Social Democrats; finally, there was a fresh burst of activity after the SBZ merger, which then fizzled out into a series of petitions in the early summer of 1946.

When Berlin changed its mind on fusion in September 1945, western Communists had nowhere near the same institutional purchase on their Social Democratic opposite numbers, who, as has been shown, were in the process of registering as separate parties.[43] This depressing picture was reflected at the KPD's first post-war Reich Conference, held on 8–9 January 1946 in Berlin. KPD–SPD contacts in the West were reportedly limited to joint members' meetings, communal and shop-floor unity of action committees, some rallies, evening classes, and press statements, with only a trace of co-operation at *Land* level.[44] At the same time, the KPD evidently dropped the Sixty Conference's principle of merger in all four zones, resolving on merger initially in the SBZ only. Thereafter, although there is no direct evidence to this effect, western Communists went through the unilateral motions of merger for the benefit of public consumption in the East. From late 1945 western KPD factory groups generated a paper avalanche of resolutions and petitions, publishable only in the SBZ, since a western party press did not yet exist, which were designed to document the will to unity. Behind closed doors, as may be seen, western Communists told a different story.

By February 1946—the point when the eastern SPD had cracked—the Ruhr KPD blamed its lack of progress on widespread 'Schumacherei'. The SPD hierarchy was regularly reported to be stifling local initiatives, with only Duisburg and Moers prepared to disobey their superiors. Despite acclamation for unity at public meetings, the Communists also felt hamstrung by their almost complete lack of printed matter. In

---

[43] The Ruhr, Lower Rhine, Osnabrück, Hannover, Frankfurt, and Stuttgart parties all went public in Sept. 1945.

[44] *Dokumente zur Geschichte der kommunistischen Bewegung in Deutschland: Reihe 1945/ 1946*, iii. *Protokoll der Reichsberatung der KPD 8./9. Januar 1946*, ed. Günter Benser and Hans-Joachim Krusch (Munich, 1995). A further Reich Conference on 2–3 March blamed reactionary and military government obstruction, but studiously avoided the main cause of failure in the West, namely the SPD.

Gelsenkirchen, for instance, in 'November–December of the previous year
it seemed as if the will to unity in the ranks of the SPD was strong enough
to defy the pressure from above'. Yet:

In most municipal districts no further joint sessions were achieved, since it was
pointed out by the SPD that the time was not yet ripe and the decision of their
Bezirk leadership had to be awaited.[45]

On 3 March the Western Westphalian SPD left no room for doubt when
it publicly condemned events in the SBZ and thanked Schumacher for
his defence of democracy, freedom, and socialism, pledging him its 'admira-
tion and unconditional approval'.[46] Furthermore, the famous referendum
held at the end of March by the West Berlin SPD, whose members thwarted
their executive's intention to merge, strengthened many West German
Social Democrats in their resolve to resist.[47]

KPD frustration manifested itself in increasingly personal attacks on
SPD leaders, sometimes comparing Schumacher to Hitler and Goebbels,
and prompting Hannover to step up its own counter-propaganda in
mid-February. There was also violence at some SPD meetings, and the
KPD even staged a number of rallies to coincide with appearances by
Schumacher, notably in Cologne on 31 March 1946 and Düsseldorf on
5 April. Every occasion, including memorials for victims of Nazism and
May Day celebrations, was exploited to agitate for fusion, frequently
provoking SPD boycotts. Although western Communists still doggedly
affirmed the will to unity at the SBZ's final merger convention, and sat on
the podium behind Pieck and Grotewohl, they had in fact become mere
spectators to the momentous events enacted on 22 April.[48]

It would seem to be the case that, from then on, western merger campaigns were conceived for their political rather than organizational value.
Above all, to further the USSR's *Deutschlandpolitik*. The obvious publicity target was the Paris Council of Foreign Ministers, meeting from
25 April until July 1946. According to George Kennan in Moscow, before
Zhukov's recall as head of the SMAD at the end of March, it had indeed
been decided to extend the merger campaign to the western zones as a

[45] KPD-BL Ruhr, 'Auszüge aus Kreis- und Ortsgruppenberichten über Einheitsarbeit',
n.d. [Jan.–Feb. 1946], SAPMO-BA, I 10/23/9.
[46] Resolution of SPD-BL WWf., 3 Mar. 1946, AdsD, *NL* Schumacher 77.
[47] KPD-BL Ruhr Delegates' Conference, 19–20 Jan. 1946, SAPMO-BA, I 10/23/2; Kaden,
Einheit oder Freiheit, 254–6; Müller, *'Einheit der Arbeiterklasse'*, 173 and 188.
[48] SPD-Büro der Westzonen, 'Rundschreiben Nr. 3', 17 Feb. 1946, AdsD, *NL* Schumacher 45; Müller, *'Einheit der Arbeiterklasse'*, 229; Mannschatz and Seider, *Kampf der KPD*,
129–30; Hauth, *KPD und SED*, 62–3.

prelude to Molotov's calls for a central German government. The 400,000 potential western members Berlin was counting on would reinforce the future SED's claim to be the front runner to head such an administration.[49] Staritz also perceives this diplomatic functionalization of labour unity, when he quotes Grotewohl's words in mid-1946: united Social Democratic and Communist parties 'would have become the iron corsets in the question of a united Germany'.[50]

Thus, immediately after the SBZ merger in April 1946, SED and KPD renewed the campaign in the West. On 7 May the new SED executive addressed an 'Open Letter to All Social Democrats and Communists in Germany', informing them that 'What unites you is stronger than anything dividing you!' and calling for preparatory SED foundation committees.[51] The next day the KPD sent a moderately couched letter to the SPD convention at Hannover, offering co-operation over food, denazification, elections, and unions, but received a rebuff: 'The Party Convention considers membership of the Socialist Unity Party and recruitment for the same as incompatible with membership in the SPD.'[52] At the same time western Social Democrats who had attended the last SPD convention in the SBZ before amalgamation were expelled, notably Ernst Heilmann, then on the SED executive, and Hans Venedey, briefly Interior Minister of Hessen.[53] In June the SED executive again called on SPD and KPD to form joint working committees, but to no avail.

These overtures were backed by petitions for a western SED, proving moderately successful in Middle Rhine, Baden, and Lower Saxony. Here, two Berlin Social Democrats, Erich Albrecht and Willi Buch, co-ordinated efforts in Hannover and Braunschweig respectively, the latter collecting 4,000 signatures, but only 400 of them from the SPD. Nevertheless, even the most modest results could be magnified by the SBZ press to imply widespread support for western fusion, but in only a very few local instances were figures ever published. As before the eastern merger, but now more so than ever, it would seem that the Communists were trying to detach individual Social Democrats from their leadership. Instead, they only succeeded in further isolating themselves.[54]

[49] Pommerin, 'Zwangsvereinigung', 323–4; Gniffke, *Jahre mit Ulbricht*, 164.

[50] Quoted by Staritz, 'Zur Gründung der SED', 133.

[51] *Dokumente der Sozialistischen Einheitspartei Deutschlands: Beschlüsse und Erklärungen des Zentralsekretariats und des Parteivorstandes*, ed. SED-PV (East Berlin, 1951), i. 31–3.

[52] *Westdeutsches Volks-Echo (WVE)*, 10 May 1946, 1; 14 May 1946, 1.

[53] Hauth, *KPD und SED*, 92–7.

[54] 13 RIS to Political Division, 4 July 1946, PRO, FO 1049/2118; SPD-LL Braunschweig to KPD, 5 July 1946, AdsD, *NL* Gniffke 17; Müller, 'Einheit der Arbeiterklasse', 238.

The crowning events of the 1946 campaign were the visits to the West by the SED *Prominenz* over the summer. Between June–August Gniffke and Dahlem performed reconnaissance missions to SPD *Bezirke*, but, after failing to persuade local leaders to enter into unity committees, had to content themselves with military government-vetted Socialist Mustering Committees, which were forbidden, however, to imply official SPD involvement. Rallies were only to be convened under KPD auspices, whereupon Pieck and Grotewohl addressed several crowds of up to 30,000–40,000 between 19–24 July 1946 (in Essen, Cologne, Wuppertal, Salzgitter, Braunschweig, and Hannover). A few days later Ulbricht and Fechner toured Bavaria. It is, of course, hard to gauge the impact of these events and to decide where participants' curiosity ended and commitment began. Social Democrats were nevertheless typically instructed to stay away from the Essen meeting.[55]

Once it became clear that there had been no breakthrough, either in popular consciousness or at the Paris negotiating table, the western Communists reverted to the tactics of unity of action. In August the petitions were terminated and the KPD desisted from personal abuse of the SPD leadership. In an insistent but polite letter to Schumacher, Reimann did not once mention fusion, asking instead for a united front of joint committees to discuss solving the chaos in the British Zone and denazification, as well as electoral pacts in the forthcoming local elections.[56] (There is no evidence of a reply.) Internally, it was reported that the KPD had been too weak for Schumacher, and 'developments from below not sufficiently forced'.[57] In no western *Bezirk* had it been possible to make any headway whatsoever since the merger in the SBZ, and KPD members were in a state of 'resignation'.[58] At a special review of the situation in East Berlin, several western leaders even believed it had been a mistake to promote the name SED at all after April, and Ulbricht aptly concluded that 'currently a wall exists between SPD and KPD'.[59]

1947: The Second Fusion Campaign

In 1947 a different tack was tried, that of merger between the KPD in the West and the SED in the East. On 14 February, St Valentine's Day, the two parties made their relationship public by announcing the SED–

[55] Müller, *'Einheit der Arbeiterklasse'*, 246–50 and 273 n. 250.
[56] 13 RIS to Political Division, 4 July 1946, PRO, FO 1049/2118; Reimann to Schumacher, 10 Aug. 1946, AdsD, *NL* Schumacher 78.
[57] Pieck's notes, 23 Oct. 1946, SAPMO-BA, NY 4036/643.
[58] Stötzel, 13 Dec. 1946, SAPMO-BA, NY 4036/645.
[59] SED-ZS/KPD meeting, 23–4 Oct. 1946, SAPMO-BA, DY 30/IV 2/1.01/20.

KPD Joint Working Group (*Arbeitsgemeinschaft*).[60] This had been decided upon by the SED, against the better judgement of KPD leaders in the American and especially British Zones, who did not wish to highlight the eastern connection in the run-up to *Landtag* elections.[61] At the SED executive it became clear that foreign policy considerations had again been crucial in setting the timetable. The *Arbeitsgemeinschaft* was to be a first step in a proposed referendum on German unity aimed at the Moscow Council of Foreign Ministers (CFM). This ulterior diplomatic motive is supported by later evidence, when Marshal Sokolovsky of the SMAD told US Zone Communists to continue the campaign 'from below' with a six-month deadline until the London CFM, stressing its provisional nature, and telling them to 'retain KPD until final decision taken', presumably by Moscow.[62]

For Grotewohl it was also clear that 'currently no possibility exists whatsoever of reaching a general act of union with the SPD'. Instead the KPD was to adopt the SED's programme, which Reimann, by then British Zone chairman, accepted on the understanding that SED policy in the West would in practice differ from that in the SBZ. He hoped to hive off SPD members and attract unaffiliated workers, and force the British to accept a western SED through a combination of pressure from above, in the shape of the forthcoming Moscow CFM, and shop-floor pressure from below. Fisch, US Zone chairman, was more modest:

We could win smalltime members and a large part of the non-affiliated, but we would have no representative partners from the SPD to help found the SED in the West today. This leads one to conclude that, as the Communist Party, we must unilaterally annex ourselves to the organization and political line of the SED.

Ulbricht reiterated the *Arbeitsgemeinschaft*'s dual foreign policy and domestic aims of achieving a modicum of SPD, Liberal, and even CDU/CSU co-operation for a referendum on national unity in the West, which might in turn usher in a popular front. Grotewohl echoed the view that championing unification would have political knock-on effects at home. Ackermann's was the only voice against a specifically SED–KPD joint venture, since it would only imply that the SED had been a continuation of the KPD all along.[63]

---

[60] The later leadership of the Central *Arbeitsgemeinschaft* SED-KPD had 50 members (20 SED-PV members, incl. the ZS, and 30 western members, 20 already on the SED-PV), SAPMO-BA, DY 30/IV 2/10.01/1, fo. 10.

[61] Pieck's notes, 13 Feb. 1947, SAPMO-BA, NY 4036/643.

[62] Pieck's notes, 20 May 1947, SAPMO-BA, NY 4036/643.

[63] All from 9th SED-PV, 14 Feb. 1947, SAPMO-BA, DY 30/IV 2/1/8.

In a communiqué announcing the *Arbeitsgemeinschaft*, no direct reference to a referendum was made, only to the Moscow CFM. Furthermore, as the document underlined: '*The unity of the German labour movement is not possible on the basis of the old politics of either the SPD or the KPD.*'[64] The fact that this was part of the run-up to a second merger campaign must have taken many lower western party echelons by surprise. The Ruhr KPD's convention of the preceding week seemed set for a long-term consciousness-raising drive in the factories, concentrating on building up its own strength, adding: 'We take note that because of the rigid rejection by the SPD leadership there are at present no prospects of a fusion of the two workers' parties.'[65] Even afterwards, the Ruhr Communists argued for bread-and-butter unity of action tactics, encouraging 'progressive' Social Democrats to work from within the SPD. Nor did they seem happy with criticisms of the 'old politics': 'It is thus in no way the case that the founding of the SED even in our area will mean that the policies of our party will have to be fundamentally altered.'[66]

Again it was the SED which forced the pace. On 1 March it issued an appeal for the immediate foundation of an SED in the western zones by Communists, Social Democrats, socialists, and progressives, since the KPD alone had proved incapable of decisive action. The campaign plan involved more western tours by SED leaders, which were in fact only permitted in the US Zone, with Pieck and Grotewohl beginning at Frankfurt am Main on 9 March. The SED's 'Principles and Aims' were to be adopted at forthcoming KPD *Land* conventions, as well as a commitment to fusion with the SED, the ground being prepared in joint KPD–SPD factory group meetings.[67] Despite public claims that this was not simply a name-change, Fisch conceded that a western SED would 'be based essentially on the full complement of the previous KPD membership'.[68] The Americans,

---

[64] *KPD 1945–1968*, i. 203–4.

[65] *Bericht vom Bezirksparteitag 1947 der KPD Ruhrgebiet am 8. u. 9. Februar* (n.p., n.d.), 89.

[66] 'Ein Schritt vorwärts', n.d., AES, 1947–31.

[67] 1947 *Land* conventions (with indications of the resolutions adopted: P and A = Principles and Aims of the SED; SED = merger with SED; FC = SED Foundation Com.), in Müller, *'Einheit der Arbeiterklasse'*, 328–9: 8–9 Mar. Hessen (Pieck and Grotewohl—greets *Arbeitsgemeinschaft*); 4–7 Apr. Bavaria (Pieck and Grotewohl—P and A/SED); 19–20 Apr. Württ.-Baden (Dahlem/E. Schmidt—FC); 19–20 Apr. Baden (Gniffke—SED/FC); [20 Apr. Hessen *Land* del. conf. (Ulbricht—FC)]; 26–7 Apr. Württ.-Hohenzollern (P and A/SED); 3–4 May Rhineland-Pfalz (SED); 14–16 May NRW (P and A/*Ort-Kreis* FCs); 17–18 May Saar (SED on MG approval); 30–1 May Hamburg and Schleswig-Holstein (P and A); 31 May–1 June Lower Saxony (SED).

[68] Fisch to OMGUS, 13 Mar. 1947, quoted in Müller, *'Einheit der Arbeiterklasse'*, 357 n. 111.

however, blocked the KPD's direct unilateral annexation to the SED, forcing it to go through the motions of recruiting individual Social Democrats and the non-affiliated in SED 'circles of friends' and foundation committees, before banning these in May.[69] Efforts in the British Zone were more intensive and prolonged, partly because the KPD also had *Landtag* elections to contend with. It attempted both the *fait accompli* of direct annexation and preparatory committees. On 14–15 March the Zonal Leadership welcomed the recent Frankfurt initiative. The *Arbeitsgemeinschaft*'s liaison bureau in Herne was to collect the 'friends of unity' in the British Zone for the immediate formation of the SED. At the same time, Reimann admitted that, although the new SED might attract sections of the SPD, 'we do not want to give in to any illusions'.[70] Nevertheless, at the end of March it was confidently envisaged that western parties would soon be dealing directly with the SED in Berlin.[71]

At *Land* conventions in the British Zone, the KPD was keen to display a broad spectrum of political support for unity. Individual SPD speakers such as Hans Venedey and Otto Lichtinger appeared, but were ostracized by Hannover. At the North Rhine-Westphalian convention in mid-May Reimann boasted that, in a trial of wills with military government, the SED would prevail 'from the shop-floors up', without resort to 'bayonets'.[72] The KPD would then cease to exist once the SED had been recognized at *Land* level. SED preparatory committees had been feverishly formed well before the conventions, full of hitherto political nonentities, and in early May were registering at *Kreis* level in conformity with the British bottom-up licensing policy. By the end of the month military government had received SED applications in Bochum, Dortmund, and rural Olpe, all of which were quietly filed. These local 'friends of unity'

---

[69] They continued as the Hessen Friends of Socialist Unity and elsewhere as the Circles of Friends of Unity, but failed to recruit further SPD members. In July 1948 the remaining Friends of Socialist Unity, claiming 50,000 socialists from SPD, CDU, and the unaffiliated, annexed themselves to the KPD, receiving 7 Executive seats, incl. Karl Hauser and Paul Kohlhöfer, but by 1949 all 7 had gone. See Hauth, *KPD und SED*, 182; Sozialistische Einheitsfreunde Hessens, 17 June 1948, SAPMO-BA, NY 4036/647; Hans Kluth, *Die KPD in der Bundesrepublik* (Cologne and Opladen, 1959), 25. The committees were not banned by the British until spring 1948: AG SED-KPD/ZB, 11 Mar. 1948, SAPMO-BA, DY 30/IV 2/10.01/5.

[70] Müller, '*Einheit der Arbeiterklasse*', 333.

[71] For more detail see Vorholt and Zaib, *SED im Ruhrgebiet?*, 42–63; ZL resolution, 15 Mar. 1947, AES, 1947–23; Pieck's notes, 27 Mar. 1947, SAPMO-BA, NY 4036/643.

[72] Reimann's closing speech at Solingen *Land* convention, 14–16 May 1947, SAPMO-BA, NY 4036/646.

committees then continued without either official recognition or pro-scription. By mid-June there were reportedly 138 in the Ruhr, just over half of them based in pits and factories, with Communists at pains to maintain a minority role. All told, 90,000 would-be SED members registered in the West, promising to 'join the Socialist Unity Party of Germany on the day of its authorization'.[73]

Yet these figures must be treated with caution. Even if the party was being honest that these were all non-Communists, this meant that only every fourth KPD member was able to recruit a potential SED comrade. Of Dortmund's 22,000 Social Democrats, only 50 had gone over to the incipient SED, however, although there were purportedly 8,000 SED supporters there alone (a figure suspiciously close to the local KPD membership total!).[74] Internally the SPD counselled that, without recognition of the SPD in the SBZ:

> there is no basis for discussion with the KPD/SED. No consideration will be given to local circumstances. No friendly relations. Normal treatment in parliamentary business and in the administration.[75]

Accordingly, in mid-March 1947 the SPD executive renewed its prohibition on members' participation in pro-SED activities, provoking isolated resignations. It also resorted to more direct intervention. On 11 May 900 Social Democrats even turned up at a Solingen SED recruiting rally and passed a unanimous motion of condemnation.[76] There was thus no chance for the KPD of getting beyond local initiatives, let alone of setting up *Land* SED committees.

Summarizing the abortive campaign, Berlin confirmed that committees had performed best in North Rhine-Westphalia, particularly in Dortmund,

---

[73] Rhinwest to Bercomb, 26 Apr. 1947, PRO, FO 1049/913; Reimann to SED-ZS, 9 May 1947, SAPMO-BA, NY 4036/644; Regierungsbezirk Arnsberg, 25 May 1947, PRO, FO 1049/1016; Ruhr Friends of Freedom, 7 Sept. 1947, SAPMO-BA, I 10/23/22; SAPMO-BA, I 11/401/11; AdsD, *NL* Gniffke 30; 'Stand der Organisation im Bezirk Ruhrgebiet am 31.5.1947', SAPMO-BA, I 11/401/14; Rhine-Westphalia Intelligence Staff, n.d. [Oct. 1947], PRO, FO 1049/915; SAPMO-BA, DY 30/IV 2/10.01/2.

[74] At the end of March two Social Democrats, Dielitzsch and Bennherdt, and two Communists, invoked a Dortmund SED, accompanied by extensive publicity, incl. 75,000 copies of an Open Letter signed by 68 Social Democrats. Some claimed their signatures had been forged, others stood by them and were expelled. See Vorholt and Zaib, *SED im Ruhrgebiet?*, 68–93.

[75] [Author illegible], 'Meine Eindrücke über die Vorbereitungsarbeiten der KPD zur Bildung einer S.E.D. an der Ruhr und Vorschläge für unsere Gegenmaßnahmen', n.d., AdsD, *NL* Schumacher 41.

[76] Rhine-Westphalia Intelligence Staff, 'Political Summary No. 10', 17 June 1947, PRO, FO 1005/1722.

Gelsenkirchen, and Recklinghausen. After restrictive military government measures, however:

the movement everywhere began to flag. In fact, it is already in the process of fizzling out again. Hitherto, we have not succeeded in unleashing a genuine mass movement for the SED in any area.[77]

On the eve of the second SED convention in September the *Arbeitsgemeinschaft* SED-KPD then took official stock of the 1947 campaign. Dahlem criticized signs of 'capitulation and resignation'; Gniffke tried to mitigate the failure by explaining that 'the creation of the SED in the western zones is not primarily an organizational, but a political task'; Fisch recited the stations of labour unity—the correct decision to place ideological consolidation above immediate merger in 1945; merger in the SBZ in 1946 ('Then we believed we could create the unity party in the West in one go'); and finally the *Arbeitsgemeinschaft* of 1947.[78]

In some ways KPD united front politics seemed to have come full circle from Weimar. The second western fusion campaign, in particular, had strong echoes of unity-from-below, regarding the SPD rank and file as fair game and demonizing the leadership. Clearly, some western leaders thought that this was ignoring the lessons of the past. In August 1947 the KPD's Lower Saxon chairman, Kurt Müller, criticized the SED's central organ, *Neues Deutschland*, for its attacks on Schumacher, which were only rebounding on the KPD.[79] Yet this did not change the ultra-leftist rhetoric, as a typical document from mid-1948 shows:

The old rightist SPD leaders and new bourgeois and petty-bourgeois forces streaming into the party have snatched the leadership for themselves. They are pursuing a policy which has nothing to do with socialist goals, and today they are openly sacrificing Marxism. . . . The amalgamation of the workers' parties must therefore be carried out against the leadership of the SPD.[80]

Predictably, the SPD executive of 29–30 June 1948 reacted with quarantining measures, attempting to forbid fraternization with the KPD even at local level. Frustrated local Communists sometimes even reverted to explicitly 'social fascist' slogans, so that by late 1948 it was reported in Berlin that 'the fronts between the KPD and SPD have grown even deeper'.[81]

[77] AG SED-KPD/ZB (Zilles), 4 Aug. 1947, SAPMO-BA, DY 30/IV 2/10.01/5.
[78] 251 delegates, 230 from the West, attended an AG SED-KPD Conference, 19–20 Sept. 1947, SAPMO-BA, DY 30/IV 2/10.01/2.
[79] 13th SED-PV, 20–1 Aug. 1947, SAPMO-BA, DY 30/IV 2/1/12.
[80] *KPD 1945–1968*, i. 27.
[81] SED-Westabt. on 7th KPD-PV, 20 Nov. 1948, SAPMO-BA, DY 30/IV 2/2.022/126; Hauth, *SED und KPD*, 184.

By early 1949 any pretence at co-operation had disappeared. Ulbricht no longer believed in a 'united front from above or below', but in 'oppositional groups working for the long term'.[82] A so-called Social Democratic Action (SDA) was subsequently set up under KPD auspices, as an ostensibly renegade Social Democratic group attempting to encourage leftist sympathizers within the SPD, but was rejected even by these as 'a Trojan donkey'.[83] (It was later forced to change its name to Socialist Action, and by 1952 the SPD estimated it had no more than 300 members.[84])

Over the next five years the KPD oscillated between unity-from-below and unity-from-above, though emphasizing the former.[85] Conciliatory approaches to SPD leaders followed Soviet diplomatic forays such as the 1952 Stalin Note and Khrushchev's message of 'peaceful coexistence' in 1956, yet it was demanding the impossible of KPD members to patch up relations overnight. An internal memorandum of the Lower Rhine Social Democrats after a KPD open letter of 26 January 1951 is typical of the SPD's response: 'Any dealings and any talks with the agents of totalitarian Bolshevism are not only senseless, but also politically wrong and dangerous.'[86] Their colleagues in the neighbouring *Bezirk* were in more triumphal mood, after sending a KPD deputation packing under the distinct impression:

of never before having been so badly brushed off as by us. Among other things we told them that the Communist Party is no longer a party, but a bunch of swine [Sauhaufen] with whom we will have no truck.[87]

Big Brother and Little Brother: SED and KPD

I have been perhaps a little disingenuous in omitting to explain so far that, at a senior level at least, the KPD had long been an integral part of the SED. In the light of the failure to form a legal western SED, the rest of this chapter will deal with the KPD's covert links with East Berlin. From the very outset, the Berlin Central Committee's Cadre Department under Franz Dahlem had operated a 'Western Germany' desk, initially run by a member of the Ulbricht Group, Gustav Gundelach. In July 1945

[82] Rau to Ackermann, 6 Jan. 1949, SAPMO-BA, NY 4182/867.
[83] SED-Westkomm., 29 Nov. 1949, SAPMO-BA, NY 4182/867.
[84] SPD-PV, 'Rundschreiben Nr. 35/52', 7 Apr. 1952, AdsD, *NL* Schmid 1500.
[85] Hermann Weber and Fred Oldenburg, *25 Jahre SED: Chronik einer Partei* (Cologne, 1971), 85, 87, 91, 95, 97, 101, and 107.
[86] SPD-BL Niederrhein, 'Rundschreiben Nr. 3', 9 Feb. 1951, AdsD, *NL* Schumacher 99.
[87] Wenke to Heine, 19 Feb. 1951, AdsD, *NL* Dux, Mappen 'KPD/Vertraulich'.

he was joined by Karl Schirdewan who was entrusted with British Zone liaison, while Bruno Fuhrmann dealt with the American and French Zones, aided by Hermann Zilles and Walter Hähnel, in what became the Zones Leadership (*Zonenleitung*) and later the West Commission.[88] By August 1945 contact had been established with most western cadres, and by October regular two-way communication was in place. Schirdewan made his first covert tour in late 1945 to organize four activist conferences in Hannover, Essen, Düsseldorf, and Hamburg, after being infiltrated into the British Zone through a lignite mine near Wolfsburg. Upon his return, he reported directly to Marshal Zhukov, then to Dahlem and Ulbricht.[89]

In spite of the western Communists' inability to forge their own socialist unity party, they were nevertheless represented on the SED executive. At the merger convention of 21–2 April 1946, which hosted over a thousand delegates, about 230 western Social Democrats and Communists attended, just over half from the KPD. Twelve Communists and eight Social Democrats were elected on to the SED's Party Executive,[90] but, since the western occupiers immediately objected, attendance became clandestine. At the second SED convention in September 1947, twenty western members were again co-opted, but this time anonymously. Yet western Communists were never admitted to the real centre of power, the Central Secretariat, despite repeated applications.[91]

The KPD received its more important political instructions directly from this body, which was in effect the SED's Politburo, and routine guidance from the Zones Leadership, which also functioned as a conduit

---

[88] Carola Stern, *Die SED: Ein Handbuch über Aufbau, Organisation und Funktion des Parteiapparates* (Cologne, n.d. [1954]), 184. It later became the Central Bureau of the *Arbeitsgemeinschaft* SED-KPD (Oct. 1947); Western Dept. (*Westabteilung*) (1948); West Commission (*Westkommission*) (Feb. 1949); and finally All-German Dept. (*Gesamtdeutsche Abteilung*) (1951). See below.

[89] Karl Schirdewan, *Aufstand gegen Ulbricht: Im Kampf um politische Kurskorrektur, gegen stalinistische, dogmatische Politik* (Berlin, 1994), 25–6; also Schirdewan interview, 29 Aug. 1990.

[90] The 12 Communists: Boepple*; A. Buchmann; Fisch; Gundelach; Hanna Melzer*; K. Müller; Nickolay; Paul*; Reimann; Schramm; Sperling; Zilles*. The 8 Social Democrats: Erich Braun; Hans Brede; Willi Buch; Karl Hauser; Ernst Heilmann; Gustav Müller; Yella Schaar; Gottlieb Teichert. The asterisked Communists were replaced in Sept. 1947 by: Hoffmann; Ledwohn; Niebergall; Rast; Schenk. None of the original 8 Social Democrats remained, and they were replaced by: Dielitzsch; Klupsch; Kohlhöfer; Venedey. See Martin Broszat and Hermann Weber (eds.), *SBZ-Handbuch: Staatliche Verwaltungen, Parteien, gesellschaftliche Organisationen und ihre Führungskräfte in der Sowjetischen Besatzungszone Deutschlands 1945–1949* (Munich, 1990), 503–4.

[91] Annan to Brit. Zone delegates, 23 Apr. 1946, PRO, FO 1049/327. Steel mooted putting the recalcitrant over the SBZ frontier: Steel to Annan, 24 Apr. 1946, PRO, FO 1049/327; KPD-*ZL/Sek.* to SED-ZS, n.d., SAPMO-BA, NY 4036/646.

TABLE 1. *East–West Sponsorships of the KPD by the SED, 1947*[a]

Soviet Zone	British Zone	US Zone	French Zone
Saxony	North Rhine-Westphalia	Bavaria	Saarland
Saxony-Anhalt	Lower Saxony/Bremen	—	Rhineland-Pfalz/South Baden
Thuringia	—	Hessen	Württemberg-Hohenzollern
Mecklenburg	Hamburg-Wasserkante	—	—
Brandenburg	—	Württemberg-Baden	—
Berlin	Lower Saxony	Württemberg-Baden	—

[a] 'Aufteilung der Patenschaften', 9 Jan. 1948, SAPMO-BA, NY 4182/863.

of information from the western zones. On the Secretariat itself Franz Dahlem (KPD) and Erich Gniffke (SPD) were responsible for western activities and organized monthly meetings with KPD functionaries in Berlin (usually coinciding with SED executive sessions). The Secretariat also decided on the personnel of the *Arbeitsgemeinschaft* SED-KPD and the KPD itself, and became a watchdog of party discipline.[92] Berlin also acted as a vital source of material aid. With chronic paper shortages in the western zones, printed matter from the SBZ gave the KPD a significant advantage over the other parties. The KPD in the Ruhr, Hamburg, Bremen, and Düsseldorf, for instance, was receiving several tons of newsprint from Dresden's *Sächsische Zeitung*,[93] and by late 1947 the SBZ had established a series of sponsorships with western *Länder*, as Table 1 shows.

The KPD was also heavily dependent on the SED financially. By mid-1948 the Executive in Frankfurt enjoyed a monthly budget of several hundred thousand marks. Officially the party subsisted from membership dues, collections, and donations, which before the currency reform were relatively easy to raise. Some of the more dubious 'donations' even included alleged protection payments by ex-Nazis desirous of a good word in denazification proceedings. Yet, with such high levels of expenditure

[92] Gniffke, *Jahre mit Ulbricht*, 164, 179, 186, and 219; Fuhrmann, n.d. [Mar. 1947], AdsD, *NL* Gniffke 54.

[93] Müller, *'Einheit der Arbeiterklasse'*, 264 n. 102. In 1949 the *Hamburger Volkszeitung* received a complete printing press; see Christa Hempel-Küter, *Die KPD-Presse in den Westzonen von 1945 bis 1956* (Frankfurt am Main, 1993), 62–4.

and such humble means of support, it is clear that the KPD was receiving money from outside. Indeed, from 1946 SED functionaries were occasionally apprehended by the western authorities while carrying large cash sums on their persons—Max Fechner with 53,000 RM in October 1946, for instance—presumably from the SED's *Sonderkonto West*.[94]

The currency reform of June 1948 created a problem literally overnight, turning Reichsmarks into so much worthless paper, and forcing the KPD to slim down its apparatus by dissolving the *Bezirk* leaderships. In Bavaria, for instance, the party had to dismiss 40% of its employees and raise monthly dues to 4 DM (the highest of any party), requesting members to use bicycles wherever possible! Nevertheless, Berlin's finance cadres soon developed ingenious ways around the problem. The SED even turned to black marketeering, including illicit sales of women's nylon stockings, and by late 1948 was able to provide Frankfurt with 180,000 DM per month, plus 250,000 DM from the SMAD, raised to 320,000 DM in 1949. Indeed, by 1951 KPD income was allegedly over a million Deutschmarks a month, less than half of which was covered by newspaper sales and subscriptions.[95] Political dependence on the East was thus something from which the KPD literally could not afford to free itself, when it was receiving over half its income from the SED.

To return to some of the political problems of SED–KPD relations, we can note that, from spring 1945 until a year later, most of the eastern KPD's energies had been absorbed in rebuilding the party, land reform, and the KPD–SPD fusion campaign. Nevertheless, the four-zone KPD had maintained its integrity. Yet after the creation of an SED in the SBZ only, there was a qualitative change in its relations with the western KPD.[96] The SED was becoming a ruling party; the KPD remained very much a non-ruling party, more suited to protest politics. Beneath the organizational

[94] Pieck's notes, 17 Aug. 1948, SAPMO-BA, NY 4036/643; POLAD to State Dept., 30 Dec. 1947, in *Confidential U.S. State Department Central Files: Germany—Internal Affairs 1945–1949*, ed. Paul Kesaris (Frederick, Md., 1985), 40. 18–26; Hauser to KPD-PV, 25 Dec. 1948, AdsD, *NL* Gniffke 34.

[95] Pieck's notes, 17 Aug. 1948, SAPMO-BA, NY 4036/643; Munich Consulate to State Dept., 14 Sept. 1948, in *Confidential (1945–1949)*, 14. 944; *Wilhelm Pieck*, 297; Dietrich Staritz, 'Die SED, Stalin und die Gründung der DDR', *Aus Politik und Zeitgeschichte*, B 5/91 (25 Jan. 1991), 11 and 16; HICOG to State Dept., 23 Nov. 1951—*Confidential U.S. State Department Central Files: Germany—Federal Republic of Germany. Internal Affairs 1950–1954*, ed. Paul Kesaris (Frederick, Md., 1986), 28. 192–208. With a further 720,000 DM of irregular expenditures since Mar. 1951, the monthly eastern subsidy averaged somewhat over 730,000 DM.

[96] The SBZ KPD had always outnumbered the western party—in Apr. 1946 by 624,600 to 205,000. With the merger the new SED numbered officially 1,297,600. See Broszat and Weber (eds.), *SBZ-Handbuch*, 458–9 and 510–11.

strains in the all-German apparatus discussed below, there were therefore arguably also strong political differences.

The abysmal KPD showing in local elections in the British Zone in autumn 1946 appears to have provided the spark for a minor insurrection within the western party. One leader even thought it high time to 'review our entire policies in the last 15 months'. More radically, without socialist unity, 'the creation of a central political leadership in West Germany has become a necessity'.[97] His colleague Walter Fisch, US Zone chairman, produced a catalogue of demands to combat the drift to particularism, arguing that, although a loose central party authority had continued until the creation of the SED, since then only a fraction of western SED executive members had been able to attend its meetings. The West was hardly ever discussed in Berlin, and, if it was, then only cursorily. Furthermore, 'two parties of different character' had arisen:

> The SED in the East and its Party Executive cannot speak on behalf of the KPD in the West. Its resolutions, directives, materials etc. cannot automatically be adopted by the KPD in the West.[98]

SED members had been ignorant of western conditions, reaching false conclusions on the unity party, parliamentary strategy, agitation, and organization, and nearly all senior cadres remained in any case in the SBZ. The KPD, Fisch continued, would have to adapt to its western environment and, although acknowledging the SED's programme and policy, run itself through a western 'Interzonal Secretariat' (although a full-blown Central Committee was ruled out as prejudicial to Reich unity, as well as being too expensive). Such a body would co-ordinate western policy, produce uniform information and organizational guidelines, and restore party authority over the lower and intermediate levels.

The memorandum was discussed by British and French zonal representatives the next day in Düsseldorf. Although agreeing in principle, no decision was reached, except for a cautious suggestion for an administrative KPD Liaison Committee.[99] At a conference in Frankfurt on 17–18 October, however, presumably after consulting Berlin, the idea was abandoned, ostensibly since 'until now it has proved impossible to create even workable zonal leaderships in the individual zones', let alone an inter-zonal

---

[97] Li.[chtenstein?], 25 Sept. 1946, SAPMO-BA, I 10/502/11.

[98] 'Memorandum zur Frage einer einheitlichen Partei-Organisation in den 3 Westzonen', 2 Oct. 1946, SAPMO-BA, NY 4182/862.

[99] The three 1st ZL secretaries and two or three permanent secretaries: Fisch to Buchmann/Sperling/Boepple, 4 Oct. 1946, SAPMO-BA, NY 4182/862.

leadership.[100] After being raised once more, the matter appears to have been dropped, regarded by Berlin as reflecting a 'politically incorrect attitude'.[101] Nevertheless, western resentment simmered on, as the SED's instructor reported after a tour of the US Zone: 'In all *Bezirke* a mood could be felt against Berlin.'[102]

In consolation, on 18 December 1946 a special discussion of western problems was held by the SED. Grotewohl opened by apologizing for the undue concentration on the SBZ. Sperling of Bavaria, while conceding the necessity of political leadership by the SED on national unity, warned that: 'Some comrades are saying: What is the SED? A separate party! Why are you going to Berlin?'[103] At a similar session three months later Ulbricht tried to pacify western delegates by arguing that, 'first and foremost we had to create a firm democratic order here, in order to set an example'.[104] Now, apparently, the time had come to export that example to the British Zone. Nevertheless, the exasperated tone of several western delegates indicates that they remained to be convinced.

Throughout the rest of 1947 and early 1948 there were continued discussions in Berlin, as well as meetings in the western zones, including visits by Ulbricht, but at the beginning of 1948, after the definitive failure of the second western merger campaign, and with the Cold War entering a decisive stage, the question of a separate leadership was finally conceded.[105] Nevertheless, Pieck made it clear that the SED would still be keeping a tight rein on the KPD:

Otherwise there is the danger that each faction will manœuvre off its own bat and the policies of the comrades in the West will not be sufficiently co-ordinated with those of the SED, so that the *Arbeitsgemeinschaft* SED-KPD will be left dangling in moral mid-air.[106]

The SED's Central Secretariat duly sanctioned a separate KPD leadership on 20 March 1948, approved six days later by Stalin. Berlin still insisted that there be no separate Central Committee nor Politburo and that the KPD should remain part of the SED. As for co-option of western leaders

[100] Resolution of 18 Oct. 1946, SAPMO-BA, NY 4182/862.
[101] Pieck's notes, 23 Oct. 1946, SAPMO-BA, NY 4036/643; Fuhrmann to Ulbricht, 10 Dec. 1946, SAPMO-BA, NY 4182/862.
[102] Fuhrmann to SED-ZS, 7 Dec. 1946, SAPMO-BA, DY 30/IV 2/2.022/130.
[103] SED-ZS/KPD meeting, 18 Dec. 1946, SAPMO-BA, DY 30/IV 2/1.01/30.
[104] 8th SED-PV, 22–3 Jan. 1947, SAPMO-BA, DY 30/IV 2/1/7, fos. 119–20.
[105] Pieck's notes, 13 Jan. 1948, SAPMO-BA, NY 4036/643.
[106] SED-ZS/KPD meeting, 10 Feb. 1948, SAPMO-BA, DY 30/IV 2/1.01/79.

on to the Central Secretariat, it was bluntly noted that they already sat on the SED executive.[107] The KPD's own Party Executive was elected two weeks later by over 300 delegates at the Herne Conference of 27 April 1948. Max Reimann became Chairman, and Kurt Müller and Walter Fisch his deputies. It was decided to base the Executive in Frankfurt am Main,[108] although it suffered teething problems as regional leaderships refused to surrender functionaries. Although the Convention (*Parteitag*), as the highest party instance, was supposed to be convened every two years to elect the Executive, it in fact met only twice, in March 1951 and December 1954. The Executive itself remained very much a cipher, meeting only a few times a year, while the KPD's Secretariat undertook the day-to-day running of the party. None the less, Berlin could not resist interfering even with this body, prompting it to complain—in vain as will be seen!—that since 'complete responsibility in the West was transferred to the Party Executive, this requires that all separate relations of lower party units with SED agencies must cease'.[109]

At the Herne Conference the KPD also controversially attempted to rename itself Socialist People's Party of Germany (Sozialistische Volkspartei Deutschlands—SVD). This was sprung upon the rank and file and even some *Land* representatives, leading to considerable resistance. Kurt Müller even suggested dropping the name-change altogether, and Hermann Nuding asked pointedly, 'Is this resolution born of *our* situation?'. The final vote in favour, by 251 to 18 with 19 abstentions, was overwhelming, but reportedly 'for a majority of comrades who voted for the name-change discipline, not inner conviction, was the determining factor'. Several even vented long-term dissatisfaction with the party line, above all Nuding and Leibbrand of Württemberg-Baden, but Kiel too refused to accept the name and Dettmann of Hamburg even threatened a breakaway. Needless to say, all this occurred behind closed doors, but in Berlin Pieck noted rather ominously in his papers: 'strong working-over of the party necessary—sectarianism prominent.'[110]

---

[107] Staritz, 'Gründung der DDR', 4; Herbert Mayer, 'Nur eine Wahlniederlage?: Zum Verhältnis zwischen SED und KPD in den Jahren 1948/49', *Hefte zur DDR-Geschichte*, 12 (1993), 32; *Wilhelm Pieck*, 195; Pieck's notes, 13 Apr. 1948, SAPMO-BA, NY 4036/643.
[108] In mid-1950 it moved to Düsseldorf.
[109] KPD-PV/*Sek.*, 25 Aug. 1948, SAPMO-BA, I 11/302/22.
[110] Pieck's notes, 11 May 1948, SAPMO-BA, NY 4036/643; report on Herne Conference, 7 May 1948, SAPMO-BA, NY 4036/644; Jupp Ledwohn came up with the name at a meeting with the SED-PV shortly beforehand, Ledwohn interview, 14 Sept. 1993. This dispels a popular myth that it was Stalin's personal brainchild; see Gniffke, *Jahre mit Ulbricht*, 249–51.

According to the official justification, the new *Volkspartei* was designed 'to bring the name of our party into harmony with the new policies developed since 1945 . . . and in recognition of the fact that today our party is leading the struggle not only of the working class, but also of the whole German people'.[111] By 'people' Walter Fisch meant the 'other working strata who are in danger of being ruined by the general crisis, . . . that is, the labouring peasantry, the *Mittelstand*, and the intellectual producers'.[112] Other more cynically imputed motives were a realization that the word 'Communist' alienated more West German voters than it could attract, and a rumour that the SED was also planning to rename itself SVD in order to achieve an all-German party by the back door.[113] Subsequent local conferences to approve the name-change retrospectively did not impress the occupation powers, however, and within weeks it was definitively prohibited.[114]

The final stage in official east–west disengagement was to disband the *Arbeitsgemeinschaft* SED-KPD. For reasons which are still not clear, in December 1948 Stalin advised that the KPD should 'officially dissolve [its] link with [the] SED', for the sake of national unity and the struggle against the 'colonization' of West Germany.[115] Many western Communists, facing a first *Bundestag* campaign and with mounting experience of the liability of the SED connection, must have heaved a sigh of relief. On 3 January 1949, after stressing 'full agreement' between KPD and SED policy, the KPD duly announced:

The special fighting conditions in the western zones of Germany place the KPD before the necessity of carrying out autonomous policies appropriate to these conditions. Therefore the Party Executive is passing a resolution on the organizational separation of the KPD from the SED. The Party Executive takes note that the members of the KPD who previously belonged to the party executive of the SED, have relinquished this office.[116]

The separation occurred without inner-party discussion and was announced by Pieck to the SED executive *ex post facto*, adding:

---

[111] *WVE*, 30 Apr. 1948, 1.   [112] Quoted in Müller, '*Einheit der Arbeiterklasse*', 384.
[113] Morris memo. (No. 356), 26 May 1948, BAK, Z 45 F, POLAD 798-6. Also Ledwohn interview, 14 Sept. 1993; Hamgov to Bercomb, 4 May 1948, PRO, FO 1049/1210; Morris memo. (No. 354) to State Dept., 26 May 1948, in *Confidential (1945–1949)*, 40. 157–63. Also hinted at by Paul Verner; see Herbert Crüger, *Verschwiegene Zeiten* (Berlin, 1990), 135.
[114] On 2 May the Düsseldorf, Cologne, Duisburg, and Bochum parties complained, and discussed the possibility of applying to the CCG to retain the name 'KPD': Rhinwest to Bercomb, 6 May 1948, PRO, FO 1049/1210.
[115] Pieck's notes of Stalin meeting, 18 Dec. 1948, in *Wilhelm Pieck*, 260.
[116] *FV*, 5 Jan. 1949, 1.

We do not need to advertise how we support the KPD in public, but the fact that we are obliged to do so is quite self-evident. Therefore, detachment from us does not mean a liberation from the work which we have to help perform in the West. Above all we have to take care that the internal link with the KPD is not broken off but, on the contrary, is further reinforced.[117]

The West Commission

Accordingly, the east–west connection became ever more conspiratorial. The most notorious SED body to supervise western activities, the West Commission, was formed in February 1949. Headed by Dahlem, it was responsible only to the Small Secretariat of the new Politburo, and its protocols were restricted to Ulbricht, Pieck, and Grotewohl. On the founding of separate states later that year, the Commission was significantly expanded, apparently at Stalin's behest, enjoying support from the Foreign Ministry and Ministry of Foreign Trade, as well as the Main Department of Information. By 1952 it reportedly employed 3–400 workers with six main departments, but was not limited to passive information-gathering, also deploying a so-called Operative Group. In important cases Dahlem even travelled to Frankfurt in person, for example on 16–17 November 1949 in order to reshuffle the KPD leadership,[118] and his deputy, as he told the author with a wry smile, regularly 'sat in' on KPD Executive sessions, travelling incognito to the West on a frequent basis.[119]

A relationship in which Berlin clearly regarded KPD leaders 'as politically second- and third-rate'[120] was nevertheless not without its strains. 'Political confrontations, which even took on rather acute forms' had occurred, but, as the West Commission reported, it had prevailed over sullen resistance, admitting in spring 1949 that it had 'practically intervened in the implementation of policy', helping draft resolutions and decide political, ideological, and organizational questions. KPD leaders had even complained that 'we are just the *Gauleiter* now'.[121] In order to improve

---

[117] 16th (30th) SED-PV, 24 Jan. 1949, SAPMO-BA, DY 30/IV 2/1/30. The SED had proposed to Stalin in Nov. 1948 that 'Besides the existing Western Bureau on the Party Executive a narrower systematic link is to be built up. Illegal propaganda is to be developed for the West'; see Thomas Friedrich, 'Antworten der SED-Führung auf Fragen Stalins 1948', *BzG*, 33 (1991), 373.

[118] KPD-PV/*Sek.*, 16–17 Nov. 1949, SAPMO-BA, I 11/302/24.

[119] Dahlem to Ulbricht, 28 Nov. 1949, SAPMO-BA, NY 4182/867; Staritz, 'Gründung der DDR', 10–11; 19th SED-Westkomm., 13 Oct. 1949, SAPMO-BA, NY 4182/867; SPD-PV, 'Rundschreiben Nr. 35/52', 7 Apr. 1952, AdsD, *NL* Schmid 1500; Schirdewan interview, 29 Aug. 1990.

[120] Gniffke, *Jahre mit Ulbricht*, 225.

[121] Quoted in Mayer, 'Wahlniederlage?', 38–9.

co-ordination and give the KPD some stake in western policy, the SED proposed a Western Bureau, whereby one member of the KPD Secretariat, beginning with Kurt Müller, would take up residence in Berlin. What emerged, however, was an appendage of the West Commission known as the KPD Working Bureau (*Arbeitsbüro*), which merely prepared materials on West Germany for the Politburo, and co-ordinated the various SED departments and mass organizations with the KPD.[122]

Nevertheless, at a formal level, East Germany devoted considerable resources to western activities. From the early 1950s radio programmes such as the ten-minute *Hier spricht die KPD* were broadcast by the East German networks, before the illegal KPD received its own *Freiheitssender 904* in 1956. Western Departments were set up in each of the GDR's mass organizations, including, for instance, the FDGB trade union federation. In the summer of 1950 its Bureau of Trade Union Unity employed a secretariat of five to eight members with seven departments as well as technical staff, requiring ten to twelve permanent instructors in West Germany. Furthermore, individual industrial unions were to be furnished with their own western departments.[123]

Attached to the SED's cadre section was also a Cadre Department West under Walter Hähnel, which supervised the KPD. In an attempt to deceive the West German authorities, it operated under the code-name 'xkx Jan', sending its correspondence to 'Edith Ede' in the West on easily concealed micro-thin paper. Important KPD files were none the less retained in Berlin, while working files were brought to the KPD Executive in Düsseldorf and secreted at various safe houses. With telephones tapped, communication was strictly by word of mouth or courier. The organization of illegal border-crossings and supplies of literature was overseen by the notorious Stahlmann Bureau, part of the SED's innocuous-sounding Transport Department. 'Richard Stahlmann', an alias for the rather more prosaic Arthur Illner, had conspiratorial experience stretching back to the insurrections in Germany in the early 1920s, as well as the Canton Uprising in China in 1927, and underground work in Nazi Germany and Republican Spain, where he had co-ordinated the liquidation of anarchist opponents during the civil war. From a complex in Magdeburg he ran an

---

[122] Reimann to SED-ZS, 29 Sept. 1948, SAPMO-BA, NY 4036/644; KPD-PV/*Sek.*, 23 Nov. 1948, SAPMO-BA, I 11/302/22; Mayer, 'Wahlniederlage?', 45. The KPD Working Office was, however, dissolved in Nov. 1951 and for a period western work was taken over by the All-German Department of the SED. In the 1960s the body reverted to the title Western Department (*Westabteilung*).

[123] 52nd SED-Westkomm., 7 June 1950, SAPMO-BA, NY 4182/867; Kluth, *KPD in der Bundesrepublik*, 104.

extensive courier network, using a set of illegal inter-zonal border crossings. Between the British and Soviet Zones, for instance, crossers detrained at Voelpke and walked along a railway embankment into the SBZ, before being taken by a Red Army guard to a disused flour mill. After a telephone call there, they were then whisked away by party car.[124]

Today, of course, this all sounds like something from a second-rate spy novel. At the time, however, the Communists justified their mania for conspiratorial work by the increasing surveillance to which they were subjected in West Germany, which, as will be seen in the final chapters, was all too real, if less fantastic than party vigilantes claimed. Most conspiracy theories clearly have some basis in reality, but the imagined details are nevertheless usually more revealing than the bare facts, and often more so of the friend than the foe. Mystification of a ruthless, omnipresent opponent demands radical counter-measures, and in the process creates hypocritical blind spots. Both Cold War adversaries in Germany contributed to this paranoia syndrome, and the mechanisms of mutually reinforcing Cold War *Feindbilder*, or hate figures, are something which will be returned to later. In the context of the KPD's links with the SED, what were probably fairly routine trips back and forth across the interzonal border were embroidered by the non-Communist authorities and press to paint the KPD as part of a secretive *Nacht-und-Nebel* organization, infiltrating agents through the iron curtain and routinely kidnapping political opponents.

In fact, permanent movement from West to East was far more problematic. Free two-week holidays to the Harz mountains or the Baltic, sometimes involving mild indoctrination, were offered to western workers, causing resentment among East Germans who had to pay for the privilege.[125] Moreover, the growing prosperity gap between East and West ensured a culture shock for western Communists entering a more spartan eastern environment, as attested by one SED report:

The party pupils from the West at the party school there [in Plauen] take out their white bread and American cigarettes at mealtimes and push our food aside. Our comrades at the *Kreis* party school get extremely incensed at this, and

---

[124] 'Edith Ede' schreibt an 'xkx Jan'—aus geheimen akten, ed. Kurt Zentner (Bonn, 1956), 1; Willi Dickhut, Was geschah danach? (Essen, 1990), 56; ID/EUCOM, 21 Mar. 1949, in Confidential (1945–1949), 40. 467–69; Hedwig Fischer, 21 July 1950, BAK, B 106/15890. The main routes between the British Zone and SBZ were at Voelpke, Oebisfelde, and Walkenried. US Zone crossing points were Honebach/Herringen, Hof, Eschwege, Tann, and Probstzella: ID/EUCOM, 11 Mar. 1949, BAK, Z 45 F, 7–32–3/5–6.

[125] Dok. IM-NRW Nr.: 31.

secondly it gives the impression that it really is better in the West than here with us.[126]

There were, of course, individual cases of western Communists seeking political asylum in eastern Germany, but the official line was to stand and fight in the West. As the SBZ's union leader, Jendretsky, reaffirmed in late 1947:

> Those who are afraid of Western bloc tendencies to outlaw the KPD and pro- secute KPD functionaries, and consequently flee into the Soviet Zone will be dismissed from the party and their party functions will be taken away from them. . . . Only those who can show clear evidence of persecution or probable arrest in the Western Zones will be admitted into the Soviet Zone. All others will be considered deserters and treated accordingly.[127]

The subordinate position of the KPD could not have been more clearly stated. As Herbert Mayer correctly emphasizes, the SED's formal con- trol over the KPD was absolute. In June 1950 a resolution by the SED executive decreed that, in the West, 'instructors of the SED Executive will receive a full mandate to secure the execution of party resolutions by direct intervention'.[128] Moreover, through Ulbricht's patronage of the KPD chairman, Max Reimann, who from 1954 resided permanently in East Berlin and survived all the purges described below, the SED also commanded personal loyalty. From November 1950 Reimann was obliged to report on party affairs direct to the SED Politburo, attending relevant sessions and sharing responsibility for policy in the West with Dahlem. (In his absence Schirdewan was to assume control.) During the SED leader- ship crisis of 1953, when Ulbricht came under attack from Zaisser and Herrnstadt, Reimann characteristically sided with his patron, calling for the challengers' expulsion not only from the Central Committee, but from the party too. When Herrnstadt, whose own stance offered greater KPD autonomy, taxed him on this during a break in proceedings, Reimann spelt out the depressing truth: 'I—must—believe—Walter.'[129]

Reviewing the KPD's relationship with the SED, one fundamental ques- tion still remains: why did the KPD put up with its eastern 'big brother' for so long? Conversely, one might also ask why the SED persisted so

---

[126] SED-LL Sachsen/*Sek.* to SED-ZS/Org-Abt., 21 Apr. 1948, SAPMO-BA, DY 30/IV 2/5/242, fos. 82–3.

[127] POLAD to State Dept., 30 Dec. 1947, BAK, Z 45 F, POLAD 32/12.

[128] Mayer, 'Wahlniederlage?', 44.

[129] Rudolf Herrnstadt, *Das Herrnstadt-Dokument: Das Politbüro der SED und die Geschichte des 17. Juni 1953*, ed. Nadja Stulz-Herrnstadt (Reinbek bei Hamburg, 1990), 168.

long with the KPD. The West Commission must have been more than aware that the beleaguered KPD had an in-built tendency to embellishment, in order to live up to expectations in Moscow and Berlin. As Gniffke bitterly observed, soon after defecting to the West:

And for years the situation in West Germany has been portrayed to us by the Communist reporters other than it is in reality. Indeed, it must be portrayed otherwise, since it has to be viewed through rose-tinted spectacles and since none of the reporters, be it Reimann, Müller, Ledwohn, etc., wants to fall from grace.[130]

Western Communists, torn between squaring political reality with SED ideology, were in a no-win situation. Over-optimism could lead to removal for shortcomings; over-pessimism to charges of defeatism.[131] The Stalinist reporting system tended, however, to cause functionaries to err on the side of optimism, encouraging what might be termed an 'emperor's new clothes' syndrome: observers pretended not to see the obvious deficiencies. Each level covered itself, but also, because it could not be sure how far its assessments would travel up the apparatus, covered its superiors too by accentuating the positive. Privately, the KPD and SED may have had a more realistic picture of affairs than the documents would suggest, but individuals could not afford to let the imperial hierarchy know this.

Part of the answer also lies in the Stalinist tendency to organize for organization's sake. The typical response to failure was not to do something different, but simply to do more of the same, but more systematically and intensively. More disturbingly still, it could also be argued that the SED actually needed the western Communists to fail, fulfilling a sacrificial role as the victims of western anti-Communism, and thus indirectly validating the SED's own hard line. The East German press thrived on a daily diet of reports of police brutality and anti-Communist repression in the West. As I shall also argue in the Conclusion, in dealing with Cold War politics, one must never forget that many of the propaganda salvoes ostensibly aimed at the enemy, were in fact designed to have just as much of an impact on the home audience.

It would also have been premature to expect western Communists to stage a breakaway at this time. What were the alternatives? As Chapter 6 will make clear, the few who did leave to become independent Communists were just as suspect to the general public as the KPD itself. Even the much-vaunted polycentrism of the Italian Communists was not attempted by Togliatti until 1956, after Khrushchev had signalled change

---

[130] Letter of 28 Oct. 1948, in Gniffke, *Jahre mit Ulbricht*, 371.
[131] Reimann, 'Vorschläge für die Disposition', n.d. [1950], SAPMO-BA, I 11/302/1.

and when the KPD was on the point of prohibition anyway.[132] Nevertheless, once destalinization did start to take place, and other western European Communist parties undertook modest steps towards what later became known as 'Eurocommunism', the West German Communist party, conditioned by persecution, was to remain notoriously loyal to its eastern big brother.

[132] Joan Barth Urban, *Moscow and the Italian Communist Party: From Togliatti to Berlinguer* (London, 1986), 225 ff.

3

From Coalition to Opposition
The Parliamentary Politics of the KPD

As already outlined, despite superficial similarities with the situation in 1918, revolution was very definitely off the KPD agenda in 1945. Across western Europe, Communists were primed to establish governmental bridge-heads in tripartite coalitions with Socialists and Christian Democrats. In Italy, ever since the *svolta di Salerno* in March 1944, the PCI had acted as the linchpin in a fragile anti-fascist coalition. Togliatti's 'progressive democracy' was a gradualist, some would say reformist, strategy. In the first post-war elections in 1946, the Italian Communists may have trailed third with 18.9%, but, in a pact with the Socialists, in 1948 they closed the gap behind the Christian Democrats, reaching 31%. More spectacularly still, the French PCF polled 28.8% in 1946 to become the largest single party in the National Assembly. In both cases Communists were rewarded with ministries: the Italians held as many as four portfolios, among them agriculture, finance, and justice, while at their peak the French achieved seven, including armaments, industrial production, and labour.[1]

The KPD was in a rather different position. Until September 1949 there was no central West German government, only federal *Land* governments. Moreover, the occupation regimes exerted much stronger veto powers over ministerial nominations than in France and Italy. None the less, the West German Communists achieved ministries in all but one of the *Länder*. There was a common underlying tension, however, between the interests of Communist ministers, in the French case fighting the 'battle for productivity', and the needs of their clientele, the working masses. As socio-economic conditions worsened in the post-war years, Communists across western Europe came under increasing pressure to cut loose from governmental co-operation and support wage demands and even strikes.

[1] Donald Sassoon, *The Strategy of the Italian Communist Party: From the Resistance to the Historic Compromise* (London, 1981), 8–58; Joan Barth Urban, *Moscow and the Italian Communist Party* (London, 1986), 195–200; Irwin M. Wall, *French Communism in the Era of Stalin: The Quest for Unity and Integration 1945–1962* (Westport, Conn., and London, 1983), 29–51.

PCF and PCI ministers were thus already in a half-way house between government and opposition when they were controversially ousted in May 1947. As will be seen, the KPD, too, was subject to many of the same pressures.

Anti-Fascist Democracy, 1945–1948

The Central Committee's founding Appeal (*Aufruf*) of 11 June 1945 formed the basis of KPD politics for the next three years. It was moderate in tenor. After accepting the Communist share of the blame for failing to prevent Hitler, it called for the democratization of Germany by completing the 'bourgeois-democratic reconfiguration which was begun in 1848', removing the vestiges of Prussian feudalism and militarism. A significant concession appeared in the phrase:

We are of the opinion that forcing the Soviet system on Germany would be the wrong road, since this road does not correspond to the current conditions of development in Germany.[2]

Instead, the Appeal was in favour of 'an anti-fascist, democratic regime, a parliamentary-democratic republic with all democratic rights and freedoms for the people'. In a ten-point programme it called for a purge of the Nazi administration in favour of local and *Land* self-government. Rather surprisingly for some, it encouraged the 'completely unhindered development of free trade and private entrepreneurial initiative on the basis of private property', limiting expropriations to Nazis, war criminals, large landowners, and public utilities by transferring their property to local government. Trade union provisions were defensive in nature ('protection of working people against business despotism and blatant exploitation'), but included the right of collective bargaining. The programme was to form the basis of a bloc of the anti-fascist parties—Communists, Social, Christian, and Liberal Democrats—which was duly established in the SBZ on 14 July. Thus institutionalized, the KPD aspired to an integrative and leading role, which would also prevent it from relapsing into its Weimar isolation.

The Appeal was theoretically underpinned in February 1946 in an article by Anton Ackermann, rhetorically entitled 'Is There a Special German Road to Socialism?'. With the temporary neutralization by military defeat

---

[2] *Dokumente und Materialien zur Geschichte der deutschen Arbeiterbewegung*, series III, ed. Institut für Marxismus-Leninismus beim ZK der SED (East Berlin, 1959), i. 14–20.

of the bourgeoisie's state apparatus, he held out the possibility of a 'relatively peaceful' road to socialism, not wholly dependent on the labour movement's struggle. Even so, Germany's 'special case' should not be overstated. Other Communist parties were also pursuing special roads, for instance the PCI and its *via italiana*. Besides, the article was partly designed to warm cold Social Democratic feet faltering at the prospect of merger, and although Ackermann rejected absolute dependence on the USSR at the KPD's final Reich convention, he reaffirmed the guiding principle of Marxism-Leninism.[3]

Nevertheless, the word 'socialism' in the Appeal was conspicuous by its absence, thus placing the KPD to the right of the supposedly reformist SPD on the political spectrum. Another novelty was the Communists' conversion to 'democracy', by which they did not so much mean representative parliamentarism, as a brand of direct, populist democracy, by-passing competitive electoral politics which were seen as counter-productive to reconstruction. This was not the same thing as basis democracy, however, which was stifled by the Communists' bureaucratic predilection for pre-allocated joint, or 'parity', committees. It must also be stressed that, although making political concessions to the bourgeoisie, the KPD had not abandoned socialist principles altogether, but was locked into a gradualist approach by Moscow. Dubbed by Stalin the 'zig-zag' course,[4] at one moment the SBZ appeared to be heading full-speed towards 'people's democratization' and Soviet-style socialism, only to veer off with reaffirmations of national unity and political moderation. Moscow evidently could not make up its mind on the hybrid status of the SBZ, part all-German bridgehead and part bulwark against the West.

The claim by the SED leadership that the 'anti-fascist, democratic upheaval [Umwälzung]' was feasible in *all* four zones, should be taken seriously, even if it betrayed a wild exaggeration of Communist influence. At a Munich conference in July 1946 Ulbricht pointed out that in the SBZ there had consciously been no blanket expropriations: 'We have attacked and carried out the democratic tasks which are practicable in all parts of Germany' by an anti-fascist united front of KPD, SPD, Liberals, and in some areas, even the CDU.[5] Indeed, western versions of the KPD's June 1945 Appeal hardly departed from the original. Although Hannover

---

[3] Dietrich Staritz, 'Ein "besonderer deutscher Weg" zum Sozialismus?', in id., *Was war* (Berlin 1994), 55–83.

[4] Pieck's notes of Stalin, 18 Dec. 1948, in *Wilhelm Pieck*, ed. Rolf Badstübner and Wilfried Loth (Berlin, 1994), 260.

[5] Speech notes, 28 July 1946, BAK, ZSg 1–65/44[VII].

made far fewer concessions to bourgeois addressees, concentrating on reconstruction, worker representation, and reform of local government, and Munich remained true to 'the erection of a Communist classless society', Bremen, Stuttgart, and Frankfurt conformed closely.[6]

Likewise, on 15 September 1945 the Ruhr party issued its own 12-point appeal, most of which was borrowed directly from the Central Committee. Significantly, however, the word 'parliamentary' did not feature once. Nor was the Ruhr party prepared to state its share of collective guilt for the Nazi catastrophe, conceding that the 'Ruhr and Rhine population for the most part followed these bandits' but ignored the 'warning cries of a small anti-fascist band struggling in the Ruhr, courageous unto death'. In line with an economic analysis of fascism, big business, personified by Thyssen, Krupp, and Poensgen, as well as the IG Farben and mining directors, were denounced as war criminals who had 'financed and hoisted the Nazis into the saddle'. Denazification and socialization (the German term for nationalization) were seen as part and parcel of the same problem. The steel trusts and the Langnamverein were thus to be dissolved and transferred to communal and provincial control, as were the Coal Syndicate and Mining Association: 'Mining was the basis of the armaments industry, and the handover of the pits to the provincial administration is imperative for the securing of peace.' Beyond that, water, gas, electricity, and transport were to be socialized. The Ruhr KPD was also far more specific about trade unions, calling for industrial unions at plant level under the auspices of a single union, the Free German Trade Union Federation (FDGB).[7]

If West German Communists seriously hoped that this would be the basis for a cross-party bloc, then they were to be sorely disappointed. The dire state of KPD–SPD relations has already been stressed. As for the Christian Democrats, there were undoubtedly hopes of collaboration with 'progressive' sections of the CDU, notably Karl Arnold and the later 'Ahlen' wing of the party. Elsewhere, Bavarian Communists were under orders to desist from anti-clerical propaganda and not to leave the church. Yet, as early as July 1945, Ruhr Catholics still regarded the KPD as the main enemy. While in Cologne, where Communists had sought out their Christian Democratic opposite numbers, including of course Konrad Adenauer, even before contacting the SPD, they met with indifference. And

---

[6] KPD Hannover to CCG, 8 Aug. 1945, AdsD, *NL* Schumacher 40; Dietrich Staritz, 'Die Kommunistische Partei Deutschlands', in Richard Stöss (ed.), *Parteien-Handbuch* (Opladen, 1983), 1683–85.

[7] KPD-BL Ruhr, 'Schaffendes Volk an Rhein u. Ruhr!', 15 Sept. 1945, AES, 1945–23.

although initially Martin Niemöller, a symbol of religious persecution under the Nazis, had agreed to close co-operation, the KPD was unable to recreate what it called the *Schutz und Trutz* community 'behind the electric wire'.[8] The recorded number of tripartite popular fronts which included a bourgeois element is thus tiny: Braunschweig, Dachau, Frankfurt, Stuttgart, Wanne-Eickel, and areas of South Baden. Bourgeois partners were reluctant to operate semi-legally, and, once party licensing did occur, Christian Democrats or Liberals were hardly likely to enter a bloc at a time when the SPD was pulling out of unity of action committees.[9]

What in fact was occurring, was the eclipse of the anti-fascist by an anti-Communist consensus. As Willy Boepple of Mannheim bluntly informed Ulbricht at a meeting in Berlin, the SED had persistently talked around the real obstacle to a front, since 'the central problem for the occupation forces and powers-that-be over there is not fascism and reaction, the central problem for them is Communism'.[10] According to Boepple, who resigned soon afterwards, the time had come for the KPD to distance itself from the other parties, and to develop its proletarian class consciousness.

This aversion to bloc politics and hankering after confrontation was symptomatic of a large swathe of opinion among the KPD's rank and file, known as 'sectarianism'. Sectarians deviated to the left of the party line by spurning alliances and sinking into so-called 'party-onlyism'. Because of the organizational isolation under the Nazis described above, many surviving cadres in 1945 were either ignorant of the decade-old turn to frontism, or chose to ignore it. It seems that a considerable number, especially in factory cells, clung to hopes of a Bolshevik-style revolutionary insurrection, drawing a (false) analogy with 1918–19. As Detlev Peukert has convincingly argued, especially in the light of later recurrent lapses into sectarianism, the illegal cadres had preserved a 'siege' mentality from the Weimar Republic. Berlin also noted this propensity, especially among older comrades, many of whom had spent years incarcerated, and were not as receptive to innovation as younger recruits. However, as Cold War

---

[8] 'Katholische Kameraden!', n.d. [1945], SAPMO-BA, I 10/23/6.
[9] KPD-BL Ruhr report to mid-Aug. 1945, SAPMO-BA, I 11/23/1; OSS, 'Field Intelligence Summary No. 7', 6 July 1945, AES, 1945–58; Reinhold Billstein, *Das entscheidende Jahr* (Cologne, 1988), 202; Fuhrmann, 14 Oct. 1945, SAPMO-BA, NY 4182/859; POLAD to State Dept., 10 Sept. 1948, *Confidential U.S. State Department Central Files: Germany—Internal Affairs 1945–1949*, ed. Paul Kesaris (Frederick, Md., 1985), 40. 211–22.
[10] 8th SED-PV, 22–3 Jan. 1947, SAPMO-BA, DY 30/IV 2/1/7, fo. 124.

battle lines became entrenched in 1947, this persecution reflex may also have served to acclimatize Communists to a new sacrificial role, as beleaguered outposts of the People's Democratic camp.[11]

One anonymous tract circulating in the West after the capitulation, although conceding that tactics should be frontist in the face of an American 'power factor in our area against which open challenge would be a pointless provocation', still preached a strategy 'with the end goal of the destruction of the oppressive capitalist state, proletarian dictatorship, socialism and a classless society'.[12] Berlin recorded that Ruhr Communists, ignorant of the Brussels and Berne Conferences, 'were almost everywhere in the process of resuming their work where they had left off in 1932'.[13] Much of this deviation was simply the result of ignorance, but there was also conscious resentment of dictation by 'immature Russian minds', and suspicion that the new line was merely a tactical feint.[14]

Traces of sectarianism simmered on throughout the 1940s and were always stronger in the West than the SBZ, where they had been dissipated in 1946 through a mixture of coercion and preferment. Thus, in Bremen, after defeat in the October 1947 elections, one member of the old guard contested the local leadership's evasive explanations, demanding:

the restoration of the old tradition. We should finally drop the democratic cloak and approach the public as a revolutionary movement . . . The party lacked the zest of before 1933. Now it no longer needed to become a bourgeois club [Verein], but already was one.[15]

It is impossible to quantify the extent of dissidence, since reports of it were often suppressed as embarrassments or highlighted for their scapegoat value. It was not, however, purely a German phenomenon. The Italian PCI had to control widespread insurrectionary tendencies among its own rank and file, which kept a hidden anti-capitalist agenda beyond the official

---

[11] Detlev Peukert, *Die KPD im Widerstand* (Wuppertal, 1980), 414–17; Fuhrmann to SED-ZS, 7 Dec. 1946, SAPMO-BA, DY 30/IV 2/2.022/130; Pawlowski, 17 Oct. 1946, SAPMO-BA, NY 4182/862.

[12] 'Strategie und Taktik nach dem VII. Weltkongress', n.d. [1945], AdsD, NL Schumacher 42.

[13] Stötzel report on KPD-BL Ruhr (May–June 1945), SAPMO-BA, I 10/23/8.

[14] 21 Army Gp., 'Weekly Political Intelligence Summary', 7 July 1945, PRO, FO 371/46933; Kaiser, 25 Aug. 1945, SAPMO-BA, I 10/23/8.

[15] Quoted in Werner Müller, *Die KPD und die 'Einheit der Arbeiterklasse'* (Frankfurt am Main and New York, 1979), 387.

anti-fascist line, captured in the term 'doppiezza' or 'duplicity'.[16] The crucial point in both these cases, however, is that party discipline prevailed. In one of the key documents discovered during research, the crucial role of the SED in this restraining process becomes quite evident. At a top-level meeting in Berlin in September 1946, after the first dismal election showings in the British Zone, there were signs that even the KPD leadership was pressing to abandon the parliamentary strategy in favour of radicalizing the masses. Max Reimann, not noted for questioning the party line, argued that:

Until now it was always the case that we were told in consultations: Be cautious, don't go too far! Occupying power etc.!
(Ackermann: That's the way it will stay!)
If we develop economic conflicts, a point will arrive where we come up against the occupying power. . . . At some pitheads we have had the situation of British military government deploying tanks.[17]

In the coming winter, because of the catastrophic food situation, Reimann saw strikes as inevitable, but was concerned at the low level of class consciousness. Passive resistance was then raised as a possible strategy. Kurt Lichtenstein, KPD press chief, who queried the wisdom of staying in the *Land* governments, commented that after the First World War workers had engaged in industrial conflicts to save their jobs 'even in the presence of capitalist occupying powers' (a reference to the Franco-Belgian occupation of the Ruhr in 1923 and the official policy of passive resistance). Furthermore, he wanted to follow the Italian Communists' example of strikes, pointing out the KPD's relative strength in the mining, metal, building, and transport unions: 'The question which remains open—and we are asking for your advice here—is this: how far can we go today, how far can we let a clash with the occupation power develop?' Ackermann, the SED's party theorist, dismissed the comparisons, and Ulbricht ended the session by conceding a place for passive resistance, but thought the KPD too weak to initiate strikes on its own. Instead, he advocated shop-floor united fronts with limited demands. Unilateral action and radical strike propaganda, in his opinion, would only destroy the unions and the KPD's foothold within them. Hardly the vocabulary of world revolution!

[16] Thomas Behan, ' "Riding the Tiger": The Italian Communist Party and the Working Class of the Porta Romana Area of Milan, 1943–48', *The Italianist*, 10 (1990), 111–50; Pietro Di Loreto, *Togliatti e la 'doppiezza': Il Pci tra democrazia e insurrezione (1944–49)* (Bologna, 1991).
[17] SED-ZS/KPD meeting, 25 Sept. 1946, SAPMO-BA, DY 30/IV 2/2.1/35.

The KPD's Short March through the Institutions

Before examining the electoral disappointments which had led to this discussion, it is necessary to deal first with the Communists' experience in government. Prior to the local and *Landtag* elections in 1946–7, mayors and ministers in the West were simply appointed under military government supervision. Constituent assemblies in the British and French Zones were nominated too, with seats allocated by notional party-political strength based on 1932 *Reichstag* results. Since the KPD was unable to match these in ensuing elections, its position deteriorated in the transition from nominated to elected representation. More fundamentally, the limitations of Ulbricht's étatist strategy of administrative revolution from above, without a benign occupation regime to support it, also became readily apparent.

The first handicap was the KPD's self-confessed lack of qualified personnel to take on responsible posts, exacerbated by an anti-Communist bias among some German and occupation officials.[18] Westphalia's *Oberpräsident*, Amelunxen, defended himself against such accusations by pointing out the Communists' inexpertise, although his argument for rejecting one anti-fascist was curious to say the least: '[Y]ou have engaged in armed conflict before the capitulation as a German against German troops. Your appointment in the German civil service is therefore quite obviously out of the question.'[19] In Hamburg, the British recorded how *Oberbürgermeister* Petersen, 'morbidly preoccupied with Communism', prophesied a 95% SPD/KPD landslide, and perhaps for that reason decided to appoint two Communists. It was local military government who attempted to block this, only to be overridden by its superiors in Political Division who preferred to have the two share responsibility, rather than 'sit on the touchline and jeer'.[20] Yet, as Table 2 shows, the British Control Commission's record on local government nominations in the Ruhr appears to have favoured the SPD and CDU, and distinctly disadvantaged the KPD. (Nor were the Americans any more pro-Communist.[21]) More broadly, of the

---

[18] Fuhrmann, 14 Oct. 1945, SAPMO-BA, NY 4182/859.

[19] Amelunxen to KPD-BL Ruhrgebiet, 24 Oct. 1945, NRW HStA, NW 110/434; Amelunxen to Wellensick, 15 Nov. 1945, SAPMO-BA, I 10/23/20. Typical administrative posts allotted to Communists were in public utilities, labour exchanges, and welfare offices: Kaiser, 25 Aug. 1945, SAPMO-BA, I 10/23/8.

[20] Annan to Steel, 27 Aug. 1945, PRO, FO 1049/70.

[21] Hartmut Pietsch, *Militärregierung, Bürokratie und Sozialisierung* (Duisburg, 1978), 190; Rebecca Boehling, 'German Municipal Self-Government', *Archiv für Sozialgeschichte*, 25 (1985), 333–83.

TABLE 2. *Communists in Local Government in the Ruhr, 1946–1947*[a]

Town	Oberbürgermeister	Bürgermeister	Oberstadtdirektor	Council Administrators	Councillors	
	1946	1946	1946	1947	Town 1947	District ( ) = total 1947
Bochum	SPD	Pöppe	CDU	56	1	2(45)
Bottrop	SPD	?	CDU	8	—	3(36)
Castrop–Rauxel	CDU	Göke	Ind.	8	—	1(30)
Dortmund	CDU	Kalt	SPD	52	1	2(51)
Duisburg	CDU	Ginkel	SPD	22	1	3(48)
Essen	Renner	CDU	CDU	67	1	2(54)
Gelsenkirchen	SPD	Berger	FDP	20	1	2(45)
Gladbeck	SPD	CDU	CDU	?	—	2(33)
Herne	SPD	Hülsmann	CDU	36	1	2(36)
Mülheim	CDU	Daus	Ind.	16	—	1(39)
Oberhausen	Zentrum	Wieskamp	SPD	32	—	1(42)
Recklinghausen	CDU	?	CDU	?	—	2(36)
Wanne–Eickel	Heimüller	SPD	SPD	40	—	3(33)
Wattenscheid	SPD	Jäger	Noll	39	—	1(30)
Witten	SPD	CDU	SPD	?	—	2(33)

[a] 1946: Pietsch, *Militärregierung*, 299; 1947: KPD-BL Ruhr/Abt. Land and Gemeinde, n.d., SAPMO-BA, I 11/401/14.

Oberbürgermeister (OBMs) of the 49 largest towns in the British Zone in 1946, only 4 were KPD. With 15 *Bürgermeister* they fared slightly better, but there was only one *Oberstadtdirektor*, in Wattenscheid. Yet, after the local elections in the autumn even these disappeared almost without exception.[22] Heinz Renner, a well-known name in local Weimar politics, is a case in point. Appointed OBM of Essen on 6 February 1946, the city commandant's rationale was that Renner had the necessary 'Schwung', and that if Esseners objected, they could express their disapproval at the autumn local elections, which indeed they did, after which he was replaced by the later Federal President, Gustav Heinemann.[23]

As Table 3 shows, at ministerial level the KPD received posts in all but one *Land*. Only in Württemberg-Hohenzollern was the KPD kept out, apparently at the insistence of SPD Minister President Carlo Schmid.[24] Communist ministers were invariably assigned hands-on portfolios—typically labour, reconstruction, and health—having to learn on the job and often in the teeth of engrained suspicion from civil servants. Picked specifically for their moderate views, however, some seemed in danger of being tamed by office. In Lower Saxony, for example, Labour Minister Elfriede Paul was censured by the party for her alleged 'lapse into the administrative methods of the previously ruling forces'.[25]

For reasons of space I shall limit myself to the circumstances surrounding ministers' departure from office. The first losses were self-inflicted when, in May 1946, the two KPD Senators in Bremen, Ehlers and Wolters, already rightists under Weimar, defected to the SPD. Soon afterwards Bavarian Denazification Minister, Heinrich Schmitt, resigned the party and with it his ministry. The bulk of ministerial losses occurred unspectacularly enough in reshuffles following fresh elections. Thus, in late 1946 Elfriede Paul appears not to have been reappointed, along with Rudolf Wiesener. A waning electoral mandate seems also to have been the motive for dropping Franz Heitgres in Hamburg, Emil Matthews in Schleswig-Holstein, and Albert Häusler in Bremen, and certainly was the case with Heinz Renner in NRW, who had ironically stepped down as OBM of Essen because of his nomination as Social Affairs Minister in August. In

[22] OBMs in Essen, Remscheid, Solingen, and Wanne-Eickel; see Pietsch, *Militärregierung*, 299–300. One BM survived in Bottrop, KPD-BL Ruhr/Abt. Kompol, n.d. [1946], SAPMO-BA, I 10/23/20.

[23] Renner's acceptance speech, 6 Feb. 1946; *Essener Mitteilungen*, 13 Feb. 1946, AES, 19–396, fos. 404–18.

[24] Jens Ulrich Klocksin, *Kommunisten im Parlament* (2nd edn., Bonn, 1994), 118–19.

[25] KPD-BL Niedersachsen/Sek., 2 Oct. 1946, in Martin Muschkau, *Entscheidende Jahre 1928–1948* (Hannover, 1990), 200.

Hessen the Communist Minister of Labour and Welfare, Oskar Müller, was dropped as the price for the CDU's coalition with the SPD. Erwin Eckert in South Baden was the last to succumb to 'natural causes' in July 1947.[26] By then, of course, events in France and Italy had added a new poignancy to ministerial tenure. On 4 May 1947 the French Communists had been manœuvred out of tripartite government, and on 12 May De Gasperi had also yielded to American pressure and ended the antifascist coalition in Rome.[27] It was thus unsurprising that West German Communists should consider a staged walk-out to pre-empt similar treatment. Just as in France and Italy, hanging on might even alienate support, as Fiete Dettmann ruminated in 1946:

If heavy industry is lost or remains idle, our working population will be confronted by a hitherto unknown drop in its standard of living, and be threatened by pauperization and ruin. . . . I sometimes ask myself whether it would not be better to keep out of the whole state administration business and carry no more responsibility for measures which are putting our reputation on the line.[28]

In October 1946 Pieck had advised against such drastic action, or at least not without making significant preconditions. Yet, during the following summer there were repeated calls to resign from Lower Saxony, where Karl Abel had been without a portfolio since April, and in January 1948 Kurt Müller, suspecting that the British were considering dismissals, recommended that 'our ministers march out as soon as possible' in order to form a 'healthy jumping-off point'.[29] The next month Abel apparently took the plunge. The only other case of a voluntary protest resignation appears to have been in the Saar.[30]

---

[26] Peter Brandt, *Antifaschismus und Arbeiterbewegung* (Hamburg, 1976), 207–10; Richard Scheringer, *Unter Soldaten, Bauern und Rebellen: Das große Los* (reprint; Cologne, 1988), 405 (Ludwig Ficker, state secretary in the Interior Ministry, probably committed suicide in Dec. 1947, and Alfred Kroth, Economics state secretary, had been dropped as an alleged former Nazi and replaced by Georg Fischer, who was then dismissed in 1946 for illegal border-crossing); Elke Greiner-Petter, 'Antifaschistisch-demokratische Aktivitäten', Ph.D. thesis (Humboldt University, East Berlin, 1986), 9 (Renner returned as Transport Minister in 1947 after the improved *Landtag* results in April); *WVE*, 10 Jan. 1947, 2.

[27] Ronald Tiersky, *French Communism, 1920–1972* (New York and London, 1974), 154; James E. Miller, *The United States and Italy, 1940–1950: The Politics and Diplomacy of Stabilization* (Chapel Hill, NC, and London, 1986), 223–35.

[28] Helmuth Warnke, *'Bloß keine Fahnen'* (Hamburg, 1988), 93–4.

[29] SED-ZS/KPD meeting, 13 Jan. 1948, SAPMO-BA, DY 30/IV 2/1.01/73.

[30] Pieck's notes, 23 Oct. 1946, SAPMO-BA, NY 4036/643; Muschkau, *Entscheidende Jahre*, 57–60; Klocksin, *Kommunisten im Parlament*, 199.

The last five KPD ministers were all expelled, caught up in the high politics of the Cold War. In a heated *Landtag* debate in NRW on 5 February 1948, in the wake of the Frankfurt proposals for a separate West Germany, the local KPD leader, Ledwohn, had described those involved as 'national traitors', prompting Adenauer's intervention. Two days later Minister President Arnold dismissed Renner and Paul for failing to distance themselves from Ledwohn's statement. Rhineland–Pfalz's Reconstruction Minister, Feller, went on 7 April 1948 after a vote of no confidence in his suitability to administer Marshall Aid. The last two removed were Württemberg-Baden's Minister of Labour, Kohl, who succumbed to a vote of no confidence on 27 July 1948 for refusing to support aid to blockaded West Berlin, followed the next day by Dettmann, Senator of Health in Hamburg. In no case could evidence of direct intervention by the occupation powers be found in these dismissals. In North Rhine-Westphalia the CDU appears to have been the moving force; in the others the SPD.[31]

Electoral Politics

I now propose to explore the reasons for the poor electoral performance which had undermined the Communists' position in the administration. The leadership had certainly set out, in the words of the Hessen party, to be 'no longer an ostracized opposition party as under the Weimar regime, but an acknowledged party affirming and rebuilding the new democratic Germany'.[32] There were even clumsy attempts to make the new constructive role more palatable to a suspicious membership, as in September 1945, when one Hessen leader explained that 'democracy', literally translated, meant 'people's rule' or 'proletarian dictatorship'![33] Yet there were reportedly still 'hiccups, partly because the local organizations have not correctly understood what new tasks we have as a construction party as opposed to an opposition party'.[34]

The initial hope had been to avoid at all costs an electoral confrontation with the other parties, above all the SPD. Before the first post-war

---

[31] Walter Först, *Geschichte Nordrhein-Westfalens* (Cologne and Berlin, 1970), i. 363–71; Arnold to Paul and Renner, 7 Feb. 1948, NRW HStA, NW 179/625; F. Roy Willis, *The French in Germany 1945–1949* (Stanford, Calif., 1962), 228–30; ID/EUCOM, 1 Sept. 1948, BAK, Z 45 F, 7–32–3/5–6; Ulrich-Wilhelm Heyden, 'Die Politik der KPD in Westdeutschland 1945–1948/49', MA thesis (University of Hamburg, 1990), 228–9.

[32] KPD leaflet, Nov. 1945, in Peter Brandt *et al.*, *Karrieren eines Außenseiters* (West Berlin and Bonn, 1983), 135.

[33] Oskar Müller quoted by Walter Mühlhausen, *Hessen 1945–1950* (Frankfurt am Main, 1985), 102.

[34] Fuhrmann to KPD ZK-*Sek.*, 17 Oct. 1945, SAPMO-BA, NY 4182/859.

TABLE 3. *KPD Land Ministers, 1945–1948*[a]

Land[b]	Minister	Ministry	from	until
South Baden	Erwin ECKERT	Without portfolio	19 Apr. 1946	30 Nov. 1946
Württemberg–Baden	Erwin ECKERT(S)[d]	Reconstruction	2 Dec. 1946	24 July 1947
	Max BOCK(R)	Labour	Nov. 1945	Feb. 1946
	Rudolf KOHL(E)	Labour	1 Feb. 1946	27 July 1948
Bavaria	Heinrich SCHMITT(R)	Denazification	3 Oct. 1945	1 July 1946
Bremen	Hermann WOLTERS(R)	Labour/Nutrition	6 June 1945	15 May 1946
	Adolf EHLERS(R)	Welfare	1 Aug. 1945	15 May 1946
	Albert HÄUSLER(S)	Housing/Fuel	1 Aug. 1946	28 Nov. 1946
	Käthe POPALL	Health	1 Aug. 1946	28 Nov. 1946
	Käthe POPALL(S)	Education	6 Dec. 1946	22 Jan. 1948
Hamburg	Fiete DETTMANN(E)	Health	9 Nov. 1945	28 July 1948
	Franz HEITGRES(S)	Refugees/Restitution	13 Nov. 1945	22 Nov. 1946
Hessen	Oskar MÜLLER(S)	Labour/Welfare	16 Oct. 1945	5 Jan. 1947
Lower Saxony	Elfriede PAUL(S)	Labour/Reconstruction	23 Aug. 1946	9 Dec. 1946
	Rudolf WIESENER(S)	Labour/Reconstruction	Jan. 1946	9 Dec. 1946
	Karl ABEL	Health/Welfare	9 Dec. 1946	Apr. 1947
	Karl ABEL(R)	Without portfolio	Apr. 1947	5 Feb. 1948
NRW	Hugo PAUL(E)	Reconstruction	29 Aug. 1946	7 Feb. 1948
	Heinz RENNER(S)	Social Policy	29 Aug. 1946	5 Dec. 1946
	Heinz RENNER(E)	Transport	17 June 1947	7 Feb. 1948
Rhineland–Pfalz	Willy FELLER(E)	Reconstruction	1 Dec. 1946	7 Apr. 1948
Schleswig–Holstein	Emil MATTHEWS(S)	Health	11 Apr. 1946	22 Nov. 1946
Saar[c]	Robert NEUFANG(R)	Nutrition/Agriculture	8 Oct. 1946	18 May 1947

[a] Klocksin, *Kommunisten im Parlament*, 75–120.

[b] Württemberg-Hohenzollern had no KPD minister.

[c] Frank Dingel, 'Die Kommunistische Partei Saar', in Richard Stöss (ed.), *Parteien-Handbuch: Die Parteien der Bundesrepublik Deutschland 1945–1980*, ii (Opladen, 1983), 1858 n. 32.

[d] R = resigned; S = shuffled out after new elections; E = expelled in mid-office.

polls to be held in the West, for local elections in the US Zone in early 1946, Berlin vainly urged a KPD–SPD election pact. Forced to stand separately, KPD *Rathaus* candidates played the land reform card for all it was worth, but wisely exempted church lands, and toned down official criticism of confessional education. Yet, either the SPD won in its own right, as in Hessen, or, as in Bavaria, even a combined SPD–KPD vote would have been insufficient to defeat the CSU. This did not deter Communists from arguing the moral imperative of electoral pacts to keep out the right, but they failed to impress the SPD executive in the run-up to the first local elections in the British Zone in the autumn. In Hamburg, KPD posters with the slogan 'Workers, be united, no more fraternal conflict, vote KPD' were pasted over by the SPD with the words 'We are united, vote SPD'.[35] Besides their traditional blue-collar clientele, local parties appealed to what they perceived as a new underclass of disorientated youth, single mothers, and impoverished *Mittelständler*. Yet, with Communists in Ruhr-Westphalia only able to field candidates in a quarter of constituencies, results were bound to be disappointing: in the British Zone the KPD won only 857 *Rathaus* seats, compared with the SPD's 19,671, and the CDU's 22,647.[36] In every *Land* it scored below 10%. (See Table 4 below.)

At the post-mortem in Berlin KPD leaders pointed to various scapegoats. Sperling blamed the recent boycott by the SBZ of the Bremen minister-presidents' conference; Lichtenstein criticized anti-fascist land reform as inappropriate to a food crisis; Müller accused Schumacher of dirty tricks in blowing up the Oder-Neisse and POW issues against the KPD. In the Ruhr, where the party had won about 8% of the vote, it was clear that workers who had voted KPD in factory elections were transferring their votes in local elections. It was, according to Müller, time to go on to the offensive for democracy, 'not as a party of responsibility, but as a party which confronts all reactionary forces with its positive proposals'.[37]

Such post-mortems became a regular item. The party tended to ascribe defeats to contingent political factors, rather than secular trends. Reporting on the failures in the first *Landtag* elections in the US Zone at the

[35] Pawlowski, 17 Oct. 1946, SAPMO-BA, NY 4182/862.
[36] Müller, '*Einheit der Arbeiterklasse*', 175–6 and 179; Reimann to Schumacher, 10 Aug. 1946, AdsD, *NL* Schumacher 78; KPD-KL Essen, 'Des Volkes Wille sei oberstes Gesetz', n.d., AES, 1946–30; *WVE*, 20 Sept. and 18 Oct. 1946, 1.
[37] SED-PV/KPD meeting, 23–4 Oct. 1946, SAPMO-BA, DY 30/IV 2/1.01/20; 6th SED-PV, 24–5 Oct. 1946, SAPMO-BA, DY 30/IV 2/1/5, fos. 47–56.

beginning of December 1946, Berlin repeated the victimization arguments—'rabble-rousing over Russia; deportations; prisoners-of-war; Berlin
elections'—and the inability to mobilize a mass movement through the
trade unions. Despite the KPD's exclusion from the Bavarian *Landtag* for
not clearing a unique 10% hurdle, however, its leaders resolved not to
revert to conspiratorial work, but to form an 'extra-parliamentary faction'.[38]
Indeed, the Communist press soon betrayed the defensive nature of KPD
opposition to what was seen as a reactionary plot to turn the British zonal
administration into an 'anti-bolshevist league'. After the Klöckner steelworks director, Jarres, had spoken of 'the inundation of the industrial zone
by a new red wave', Communist newspaper readers were told to brace
themselves for a 'new anti-Communist wave of rabble-rousing'.[39]

One important election defied the trend, if only temporarily, and is
thus worthy of closer consideration: the North Rhine-Westphalian
Landtag election of 20 April 1947, when the KPD won 14% (23.5% in
the Ruhr, its highest result there ever!). The election manifesto attacked
resurgent reactionaries—the 'large-scale, intricate web of sabotage by the
enemy within'—who were responsible for the lack of food and fuel and
whose power could only be broken by expropriation. Party propaganda
also called for reparations from current production, not dismantling, and
an end to the wage freeze.[40]

If you do not wish to postpone until kingdom come the transfer of the coal mines
and basic industries to the people's hands as people's property, vote KPD . . .

If you want to remove the saboteurs of our food supply, vote KPD . . .

If you aspire to social justice, vote for the KPD, which will not rest until the
war profiteers and war criminals have paid.[41]

The Communists in NRW clearly benefited from the conjuncture
of a hard winter and mismanaged food crisis. And this in spite of the
new, predominantly first-past-the-post electoral system introduced by the
British! In view of the low turn-out of 67%, the KPD's gain of about
300,000 votes over October 1946 could not have come from the SPD's
200,000 losses alone, indicating defections from the CDU also. In some
Ruhr wards the KPD had won over 25% (Bottrop 28.2%, Wanne-Eickel

[38] Fuhrmann to SED-ZS, 7 Dec. 1946, SAPMO-BA, DY 30/IV 2/2.022/130; SED-
ZS/KPD meeting, 18 Dec. 1946, SAPMO-BA, DY 30/IV 2/1.01/30.
[39] *WVE*, 8 Nov. 1946, 2; *WVE*, 20 Dec. 1946, 2.
[40] *WVE*, 22 Apr. 1947, 1; 'Es geht um Deutschland!' (1947 *Landtag* election platform),
n.d., SAPMO-BA, I 10/502/11.
[41] KPD zonal declaration, 14–15 Mar. 1947, *WVE*, 21 Mar. 1947, 5.

28.1%, Wattenscheid 26.5%), and with 25.9% in Gelsenkirchen even overtook the CDU. It had been particularly adept at channelling resentment against the German authorities, exploiting for instance corruption charges against the Dortmund SPD. The ultimate target of the protest vote may, however, have been the British occupation power, forcing it to intervene to improve conditions. This would indicate a shrewd calculation on the part of voters, rather than any ideological conversion.[42]

Still, given that the KPD had been the strongest party overall in the Ruhr between 1930–2, and given the western zones' average of only 9.4% in the first round of *Landtag* elections, the Communists were bound to be disappointed. Despite generous SED support, subsequent polls confirmed fears of a general decline. By 1954, in the third and final *Landtag* elections contested by the KPD, NRW Communists had lost 62.4% of their absolute 1947 vote. (This was even worse than the national average of 53.2%.) Yet, because the electorate had expanded considerably, in NRW from 7.9 to 9.7 millions, loyal KPD voters counted for less still—only 3.8% in NRW and 3% nationally. (See Table 4 for a complete overview.)

As the tide went out for the KPD, the bedrock of its support, perhaps more dependent on socio-economic factors than contingent politics, was laid bare. A few residual bastions stood out, notably the central Ruhr (Bottrop, Gelsenkirchen, Wanne-Eickel) and some of the outlying areas to the north (Dinslaken, Gladbeck, Marl) and south (Gevelsberg, Hattingen, Velbert), where the KPD managed to score 8% or more in 1952's local elections, against a *Land* average of 4.5%. Far more spectacular was the Bergisches Land east of Düsseldorf. Solingen, locally nicknamed 'Bergisches Moskau', with a Communist *Bürgermeister*[43] and boasting a long pedigree of skilled metalworkers, recorded 13.3% for the KPD in the same elections, and its neighbour, Remscheid, 14.4%. The only other strongholds breaking the 8% barrier at this late stage were Mannheim and nearby Weinheim in Baden-Württemberg; across the Rhine in Rhineland-Pfalz, Ludwigshafen, and the outlying district of Frankenthal, as well as Neustadt and Pirmasens; in Hessen, around Frankfurt, there was another concentration in Hanau (14.2%), Neu-Isenburg, and Rüsselsheim.[44]

It is difficult to generalize from so few cases on the reasons for this persistence. Often, these were the tail-ends of longer voting patterns. In

[42] AG SED-KPD/ZB (Zilles), 5 May 1947, SAPMO-BA, DY 30/IV 2/10.01/5; Pietsch, *Militärregierung*, 311.

[43] Arthur Schlechter, soon to be suspended by the interior ministry; see Willi Dickhut, *Was geschah danach?* (Essen, 1990), 106–27.

[44] Klocksin, *Kommunisten im Parlament*, 321–421.

TABLE 4. KPD Election Results, 1946–1956 (percentages and seats)[a]

Land	1946 Gemeinde %	1946 Kreis %	1946 Constituent %	Assembly Seats	1946–7 Landtag %	1946–7 Seats	1949 Bundestag (15 seats) %	1949–52 Landtag %	1949–52 Seats	1953 Bundestag (no seats) %	1953–6 Landtag %	1953–6 Seats
Baden-Württemberg	x	x	x	x	x	4*	x	4.4	4	2.3	3.2	—
South Baden	6.0	7.6	N[b]	4	7.4	10*	x	x	x	x	x	x
Württemberg-Baden	9.3	7.6	10.0	10	10.3	5	6.4	4.9	—	x	x	x
Württemberg-Hohenzollern	4.9	6.9	N	4	7.3	—	x	x	x	x	x	x
Bavaria	2.3	4.9	5.3	9	6.1	10	4.1	1.9	—	1.5	2.1	—
Bremen	x	x	11.5	3*[c]	8.8	4	6.7	6.4	6	3.9	5.0	4
Hamburg	x	x	N	8	10.4	10	8.5	7.4	5	3.3	3.2	—
Hessen	7.4	8.3	9.7	7	10.7	8*	6.7	4.7	—	2.5	3.4	—
Lower Saxony	4.1	5.1	N	13/4	5.6	28*	3.1	1.8	2	1.0	1.3	2
NRW	6.6	9.4	N	34/19	14.0	8*	7.6	5.5	12	2.8	3.8	—
Rhineland-Pfalz	6.5	7.4	N	9	8.7	—	6.2	4.3	—	2.3	3.2	—
Schleswig-Holstein	4.4	5.1	N	5/3	4.7	2	3.1	2.2	—	1.2	2.1	—
Saar	9.1	x	N	1	8.4		x	9.5	4	*	6.6	2
West Germany					9.4	89	5.7	3.8	33	2.2	3.0	8

[a] Heinrich Potthoff (ed.), Handbuch Politischer Institutionen und Organisationen 1945–1949 (Düsseldorf, 1983), 333–45; Gerhard A. Ritter and Merith Niehuss, Wahlen in der Bundesrepublik Deutschland: Bundestags- und Landtagswahlen 1946–1987 (Munich, 1987), 129; Klocksin, Kommunisten im Parlament, 121–202; SAPMO-BA, NY 4036/642, fos. 198–200; NY 4090/630, fo. 139.
[b] N = nominated assemblies with changes after communal elections in Sept.–Oct. 1946.
[c] * = part of ruling coalition.

the case of the Ruhr, however, it has been subtly argued by Karl Rohe that National Socialism and the effects of war (bombing, evacuation, and refugees), as well as pit-closures after 1958 and subsequent rehousing schemes, 'rationalized away' existing political, confessional, and workplace subcultures. The electorate was thus homogenized, paving the way for the SPD to take over from the more clientelist *Zentrum* and KPD. Moreover, Communists had benefited from an essentially backward-looking, proto-industrial form of protest by communities with a corporate rather than class identity, where the first industrial revolution had not been properly superseded by the second. In other words, long-term socioeconomic modernization was just as much against the KPD as the politics of the Cold War.[45]

On this view one would have to look to areas *least* touched by the effects of social dislocation to explain Communist longevity. In terms of bomb damage, the evidence is contradictory. Bottrop was about average for the Ruhr, whereas Wanne-Eickel was badly battered, and Gelsenkirchen relatively unscathed. Remscheid suffered significantly greater destruction than Solingen, as did Hanau and Pirmasens. Nevertheless, the Federal Housing Minister, Wildermuth, believed there *was* a link between homelessness and radicalism, since, allegedly, 'the number of communist voters in European countries stands in inverse proportion to the number of housing units per thousand inhabitants'.[46] In terms of population movements, however, there is clearer evidence that, with the exception of Hessen, Communist strongholds were in areas with relatively few refugees. Rhineland-Pfalz was protected by the French occupiers' restrictions, and immigrants to NRW tended to be settled in rural areas. In terms of levels of industrialization in KPD strongholds, there is a mixture of old (Ruhr mines and Solingen metallurgy) and new (chemicals in Ludwigshafen; cars in Mannheim and Rüsselsheim), as well as almost artisanal metalworkers in Rhineland-Pfalz.[47]

Confession has been cited as another classic voting indicator, with Weimar workers in predominantly Catholic areas more likely to vote KPD than SPD, provided, of course, that they first abandoned the *Zentrum*. This seems to have been less of a factor after 1945. With the possible exception

[45] Karl Rohe, *Vom Revier zum Ruhrgebiet: Wahlen, Parteien, Politische Kultur* (Essen, 1986), 29–39.

[46] Quoted in Jeffry M. Diefendorf, *In the Wake of War: The Reconstruction of German Cities after World War II* (New York, 1993), 132.

[47] Pietsch, *Militärregierung*, 298; Christoph Kleßmann, *Die doppelte Staatsgründung: Deutsche Geschichte 1945–1955* (4th edn.; Bonn, 1986), 354–6.

of Bottrop and the northern Ruhr, *all* of the other bastions were predominantly Protestant. One is left with the rather nebulous factor of 'tradition' in a close-knit community. Certainly, contemporary observers in NRW correlated surviving Communist milieux with a high degree of *Lokalpatriotismus*, nepotism, and strong ties to works with their own estates.[48] It would seem that individual personalities were also important in integrating Communist subcultures, such as Bottrop's Clemens Kraienhorst. In any case, socio-economic, as opposed to political, change, involves a marked time-lag before manifesting itself in voting behaviour, and there is a corresponding limit to how far one can pursue these factors over an eleven-year period.

Socialization

Bureaucratic stonewalling and electoral failure therefore combined to keep the KPD's government and parliamentary influence to a minimum. Consequently, any consideration of policy issues cannot ignore the fact that, without coalition partners, the KPD was unlikely to see any of its plans realized. The Communists' frustrating experience in the *Landtage* and in the administrative machinery can best be exemplified with the issues of socialization and denazification. Despite the KPD's inclusion in coalitions in Bremen, Lower Saxony, NRW, Rhineland-Pfalz, South Baden, and Württemberg-Baden, its impact was understandably modest: its number of seats was small; only in Hessen and Bremen, and very briefly in NRW, were absolute leftist majorities mathematically possible; military government enjoyed enormous veto powers over legislation; and overall strategy was dictated by East Berlin. Moreover, Communist parliamentary enthusiasm was always tempered by the belief that the *Landtage* could only represent a federal stepping-stone to a centralized Reich. Thus, it was not until the end of May 1946 that the first KPD constitutional proposals were issued in the US Zone, and these were then overtaken in November by an SED–KPD draft for an all-German constitution.

One of the most hotly contested constitutional reforms soon became that of nationalization, or 'socialization', of the economy. Hessen stands out, not only because an SPD–KPD coalition was technically possible, but also because socialization was conspicuously blocked by American intervention, even after being sanctioned by popular referendum. In some ways

---

[48] Düsseldorf Consulate to State Dept., 26 Aug. 1953, in *Confidential U.S. State Department Central Files: Germany—Federal Republic of Germany. Internal Affairs 1950–1954*, ed. Paul Kesaris (Frederick, Md., 1986), 29. 383–402.

the Hessen Communists felt that the country was too shattered for large-scale expropriations. In May 1946 they had announced that the KPD was consciously putting its socialist demands on the back burner in order to concentrate on reconstruction. The election of constituent assemblies in the US Zone in June 1946, however, forced them to start negotiating a draft constitution with the other parties. After the Americans had insisted on any socialization clause being put to a separate referendum, the KPD fought for various amendments to what became known as Article 41 of the Hessen constitution. The ultimate wording envisaged the nationalization of coal, iron and steel, energy, transport, banks, and insurance, but, on 26 September, the KPD moved to include Hessen's chemicals industry, meaning above all the Hoechst division of IG Farben. Although the SPD initially lent its support to these proposals, it withdrew it four days later after striking what became known as the 'constitutional compromise' with the CDU. Nevertheless, in the referendum of 1 December, 72% endorsed Article 41, even without IG Farben, nearly as many as the 76.8% for the constitution itself, but the Americans used their veto and suspended the socialization clause.[49]

What is striking in Hessen is the degree of consensus on socialization. The terminology may have differed somewhat between the Communists' *Verstaatlichung* and the Social Democrats' *Vergesellschaftung*, but the general goal was the same. Moreover, despite its amendments being rejected, the KPD had voted for the agreed draft. What was more alarming was that, in the process of parliamentary alignment, the Hessen SPD had opted for the CDU as a coalition partner. The 'constitutional compromise' duly became a grand coalition in December, depriving the KPD of its ministry. Similarly, the only other potential 'workers' government' failed to materialize in Bremen in 1947–8 after the KPD had refused to vote for what it saw as the SPD's watered-down socialization proposals. The Bremen SPD, preferring a centre-left coalition, chose to ally instead with the Liberal BDV, which likewise insisted on excluding the KPD.[50]

The other major area of controversy over socialization was in North Rhine-Westphalia. Here, however, the reallocation of nominated *Landtag* seats in autumn 1946 left the workers' parties without a majority. (The

[49] Mühlhausen, *Hessen 1945–1950*, 247–87; Hans-Christoffer Beyer, 'Die verfassungs-politischen Auseinandersetzungen um die Sozialisierung in Hessen 1946', Ph.D. thesis (University of Marburg, 1977), 64–5 and 139; Greiner-Petter, 'Aktivitäten', 24; *Die Ausein-andersetzung um die Länderverfassungen in Hessen und Bayern 1946—Dokumente*, ed. IMSF (Frankfurt am Main, 1978), 190–1.

[50] Brandt, *Antifaschismus*, 232–8.

Communists had their original 34 seats nearly halved to 19.) Nevertheless, as in Hessen, there was initial cross-party consensus on the need to
deconcentrate industry, partly as a means to save it from dismantling. In
Essen for instance, the works councils, unions, parties, religious leaders,
chambers of industry and commerce, labour exchange, city council, and
OBM, had all petitioned the British on 16 November 1945 to save the
recently sequestered Krupp works and permit peacetime production.[51]
The main bone of contention in NRW, however, quickly became the
mining industry. As its appeal of September 1945 showed, the Ruhr KPD
was demanding the transfer of the coal-mines to the province of Westphalia, but their seizure by the British in December of that year made
talk of expropriation a potential criticism of military government. The
KPD also remained sceptical of the SPD's plans for a socialized 'holding
company', combining the public sector, management, and unions; conversely, the Social Democrats mistrusted their rivals' strong economic
étatism, which placed great hopes in a central government. Yet, overall,
the two parties' proposals probably had more in common with each other
than either was prepared to admit.

On 12–13 November 1946 the KPD was the first *Landtag* faction in
NRW to move for the transfer of the mining industry to *Land* trustee-
ship, but its bill failed to reach the agenda. Then, at the 23–4 January
1947 *Landtag* session, the KPD moved to expropriate all collieries without compensation, accompanying this with an emergency motion to transfer coal, iron, and steel to communal hands. A Rhenish-Westphalian Mining
Corporation was to be supervised by a Coal Council of 18 unionists and
18 representatives from the NRW Economics Ministry and the *Landtag*,
pending a Reich government. When the CDU and FDP postponed a
debate, the Communists called for a referendum. This was blocked, however, by all parties, including the SPD which had proposed its own
plebiscite. A further abortive KPD motion to transfer basic industries to
state hands followed in March. Although, after its Ahlen Programme, the
CDU was also nominally reform-capitalist, on 5 March it voted down
both KPD and SPD socialization proposals. After the April *Landtag* election, however, an SPD socialization bill on coal, bearing a strong resemb-
lance to KPD plans, was finally tabled in August 1947. A year later, SPD
and KPD, with residual *Zentrum* support, approved the bill against Liberal
votes and Christian Democratic abstentions. As in Hessen, the deciding
factor in the failure of this parliamentary effort was not so much party

[51] *WVE*, 2 Aug. 1946, 2.

rivalry, since the CDU could not have stopped the socialization bill even if it had tried; it was the occupation power which stymied reform. After sustained pressure from America, the British rejected the NRW *Landtag* bill on the grounds that socialization could only be decided by a Reich and not a *Land* government, which hardly squared with their avowed policy of federalism.[52]

The New Left of the early 1970s later criticized the KPD of the late 1940s for playing too much by the parliamentary rules and accepting such defeats without a fight. To be fair, the party was not unaware of its extra-parliamentary options. As Reimann warned in May 1947, 'the entire parliamentary struggle for the future is of little use if we do not support the battle to alleviate suffering from our base in the factories, the residential areas, and the unions'.[53] The Communists did on occasion resort to direct action, for instance when they organized fifteen pithead ballots on socialization, winning over 80% support. In November 1946 the NRW faction also tried, but failed, to obtain permission for the hearing of delegations in the *Landtag*. (When in March 1947 a 300-strong deputation appeared in Düsseldorf, it was turned away.) Nevertheless, it would also be fair to say that such gestures towards popular democracy were consistently channelled into the parliamentary mainstream. This corresponded to a strategy in the SBZ which, if not parliamentary, was at least deeply étatist and mistrustful of voluntarist movements. Accordingly, the West German Communist leadership argued that true socialization was only possible in a united socialist state and consciously rejected the 1918 slogan 'Socialization on the March!'.[54]

On the related issue of land reform the party proved even less successful. On 2 September 1945 the eastern KPD had called for the punitive expropriation of war criminals and estates above 100 hectares, and over the next week a corresponding land reform was enacted in the SBZ under the slogan 'Junker Lands into Peasant Hands!'. With this in mind, on 27 March 1946 the KPD approached the British Zonal Advisory Council with similar proposals for farmers' committees to redistribute land to

---

[52] *WVE*, 21 Jan. 1947, 1; *WVE*, 28 Jan. 1947, 1; Greiner-Petter, 'Aktivitäten', 45–50; Michael Clarke, 'Die Gewerkschaftspolitik der KPD 1945–1951', diploma (Ruhr University of Bochum, 1982), 34 and 41–2; Peter Hüttenberger, *Nordrhein-Westfalen und die Entstehung seiner parlamentarischen Demokratie* (Siegburg, 1973), 410–18; Wolfgang Krieger, *General Lucius D. Clay und die amerikanische Deutschlandpolitik 1945–1949* (Stuttgart, 1987), 293–8.

[53] Reimann at Solingen convention, 14–16 May 1947, SAPMO-BA, NY 4036/646.

[54] *WVE*, 13 Sept. 1946, 1; *WVE*, 15 Nov. 1946, 1; *WVE*, 7 Mar. 1947, 2; Gudrun Schädel, 'Die Kommunistische Partei Deutschlands in Nordrhein-Westfalen von 1945–1956', Ph.D. thesis (Ruhr University of Bochum, 1973), 92.

agricultural workers, *Kleinbauern*, and refugees. In the West, however, smallholdings already predominated over large landed estates. The proposal could name only ten aristocratic landowners ripe for expropriation (admittedly huge estates ranging from 1,300–7,000 hectares), and had to include corporate holdings of industrial combines belonging to Krupp, Stinnes, and Hugenberg. Needless to say, it was not accepted, either by the British or the other parties.[55]

The impending food crisis lent urgency to KPD demands, but at the same time was given as a reason for avoiding experiments. In May 1946 the Communist press implied that food distribution was being deliberately 'disorganized' and called for the replacement of what was essentially still the Nazi Reich Food Estate, and a purge of the Economic Bureaux. In the party's newspaper columns a personal vendetta was then waged against the aristocratic Hans von Schlange-Schöningen, director of the Central Office of Nutrition and Agriculture. Junker speculators were to be charged as 'post-war criminals' and chambers of agriculture were to be set quotas instead. Using food committees with producers', consumers', party, and union representatives, the Communists thus clearly hoped to forge a political alliance with smallholders. They achieved negligible success, and in June 1947 could merely vote alongside the SPD against British proposals in the Advisory Council for land reform above 150 hectares only and including compensation. Reflecting most Communists' underlying disillusionment with the countryside, NRW's Agriculture and Nutrition desk thereafter became known simply as the 'Dung Department'.[56]

Denazification

The KPD's experience of denazification was, if anything, even more frustrating. Self-appointed removals of Nazi personnel in 1945 were not tolerated by the occupiers, despite strike threats over the retention of 'tainted' factory management. Attempts to work from within the system proved equally futile. In Bavaria, a Communist, Heinrich Schmitt, held brief office as Minister of Denazification from late 1945 until mid-1946. In Baden, too, Erwin Eckert presided over purges in 1946, but resigned when his proposed denazification law, unanimously supported by the other parties, was blocked by the French. (His Minister-President

---

[55] *WVE*, 14 June 1946, 2.
[56] *WVE*, 21 May 1946, 2; *WVE*, 26 Nov. 1946, 2; *WVE*, 13 June 1947, 1; 13th SED-PV, 20–1 Aug. 1947, SAPMO-BA, DY 30/IV 2/1/12; Heinks, 28 Jan. 1948, SAPMO-BA, DY 30/IV 2/2.022/131.

had misleadingly hinted that he might be manipulating purges for party-political purposes.) It would be unfair, however, to accuse Communist denazification schemes of being purely negative and vindictive. Punitive rubble-clearance programmes included an element of atonement, and also called on non-Nazis to pitch in. There were also constructive, long-term plans to train technically qualified anti-fascist replacements for denazified personnel.[57]

Since the KPD interpreted culpability in class as well as individual terms, denazification also provided an opportunity to attack 'monopoly capitalists'. The line between reactionary and Nazi was a correspondingly thin one for Hermann Schirmer, the KPD's Nuremberg leader, who argued that denazification was a question of 'class war', in which it was immaterial:

whether this or that [Nazi] party comrade joined before 1 May 1937 or a week later. What really matters to us is the position the man occupied then and the position he occupies today.[58]

Hermann Reusch, and any former War Economy Leader, were natural targets, as well as the Conservative Party, the Lower Saxon State Party, the Rhenish People's Party, and the right wing of the CDU. Heinrich Dinkelbach, placed in charge of decartelization, was personally confronted with his NDSAP membership by Karl Schabrod in March 1947, and Robert Pferdmenges was attacked by the NRW *Landtag* faction in June on his election to the Economic Council. The acquittal of Schacht, Papen, and Fritzsche at Nuremberg was also symptomatic for the KPD of the rehabilitation of Nazified big business.[59] This is probably what most non-Communists meant by KPD denazification policy being too 'political'.

The KPD's parliamentary experience of denazification was not a happy one. An analysis of *Landtag* factions in NRW, Lower Saxony, and Hessen shows the Communists' high hopes giving way to disillusionment and the oft-repeated accusation that 'the smallfry are being hanged while the bigshots walk away scot-free'. The floor of the house became a place to

[57] Witten report, 21 Aug. 1945, ZI6, Sammlung Becker, Ordner 3/3; KPD-BL Ruhr-Wf. to KLs/OGLs, 27 June 1946, SAPMO-BA, I 10/23/7; Klocksin, *Kommunisten im Parlament*, 85; 'Aufruf an die Bevölkerung von Groß-Essen zur Schadenstellen- und Trümmerbeseitigung', 4 Mar. 1946, AES, 19–396, fo. 301.
[58] Müller, '*Einheit der Arbeiterklasse*', 188.
[59] *WVE*, 24 Sept. 1946, 1; Chief of North German Iron and Steel Control/Schabrod meeting, 13 Mar. 1947, SAPMO-BA, NY 4036/646; *WVE*, 4 Oct. 1946, 1; Greiner-Petter, 'Aktivitäten', 100.

TABLE 5. *Affiliation of Selected Denazification Panels, 1947–1948*

Land	Number of panels	Number of members							Total	% KPD
		KPD	SPD	CDU	FDP	Independent	TU	Other		
Bavaria[a]	20									8.1
Lower Saxony[b]	110	143	398	159	82	268	—	142	1,192	12.0
NRW[c]	15	21	46	39	7	18	9	15	155	13.5
Schleswig-Holstein	26	28	71	55	9	19	11	14	207	13.5

[a] Munich Consulate to State Dept., 22 Jan. 1948, BAK, Z 45 F, POLAD 798–5.
[b] CCG/Ind. Rels. Branch to Carthy, 4 June 1947, MRC, MSS 292/943/12.
[c] Hüttenberger, *Nordrhein-Westfalen*, 403–6.

expose the opposition rather than to reach practical agreement. One KPD deputy thus taunted the opposite benches in the NRW assembly, which sat in the former Henkel washing-powder works, with the words that 'the brownified CDU cannot have its apron washed white here'.[60] His request that former NSDAP members give a show of hands was presumably a rhetorical gesture, and by the end of 1947 the KPD in NRW was dismissing parliamentary debates on denazification as a 'comedy'.

As Table 5 shows, the Communist presence on denazification panels did not offer any more scope than parliament. Responsibility for denazification was only transferred from British military government, which had dealt with it largely as a security problem, to the *Länder* in October 1947, and in the meantime the panels remained advisory. As in the ministries, a boycott had always been an option. At the beginning of 1947 Communists in NRW threatened to withdraw from the committees, and in isolated cases did so, for instance in the case of the industrialist Hugo Stinnes, who, according to the KPD, belonged before a war crimes court and not the local panel. Yet Berlin felt such a gesture premature and censured a Hessen resolution to withdraw in the summer.[61] The volte-face six months later can only be explained by changing policy in the SBZ. As an incentive to recruit former nominal Nazis into the bloc system within what became the National Democratic Party, SMAD Order No. 35 of 26 February 1948 ceased routine denazification in the eastern zone. By 11 March all US Zone Communists had also left the *Spruchkammern*, and in May a general withdrawal was ordered in NRW, leaving behind a minimal impact on the machinery of denazification by some of those who had suffered most brutally at Nazi hands.[62]

This is an instructive example of the needs of the SBZ artificially determining western policy. Berlin had become less and less interested in policies which could act as a common denominator in all four zones, and began justifying itself as a pace-setting avant-garde. It has already become clear that the KPD leadership resented the SED's failure to recognize the different prevailing conditions in the West. In practice, SED concessions

---

[60] *WVE*, 24 Jan. 1947, 2; *WVE*, 30 Aug. 1946, 1; Rudolf Billerbeck, *Die Abgeordneten der ersten Landtage (1946–1951) und der Nationalsozialismus* (Düsseldorf, 1971), 140–3 and 222–5; Hüttenberger, *Nordrhein-Westfalen*, 401.

[61] Rhine-Westphalia Intelligence Staff, 'Political Summary No. 6', 16 Feb. 1947, PRO, FO 1005/1722; in Duisburg Communists withdrew, *WVE*, 3 Jan. 1947, 1.; memo. to KPD-BL Ruhr/*Sek.*, 10 July 1947, SAPMO-BA, I 10/23/6; 13th SED-PV, 20–1 Aug. 1947, SAPMO-BA, DY 30/IV 2/1/12.

[62] Morris memo. (No. 356), 26 May 1948, BAK, Z 45 F, POLAD 798–6; KPD-LL NRW, 'Erklärung', 23 May 1948, AES, 1948–4.

to KPD autonomy were exercises in sophistry, as when Ulbricht admonished Communists in the British Zone to develop their own policies, which, he explained, would be 'the policies we are undertaking in the eastern zone applied to the British Zone'.[63] The failure of anti-fascist democracy in the West cannot, however, be attributed solely to poor tactical and strategic guidance by East Berlin and Moscow. As will be argued in more depth in Chapter 7, western military government had also played a significant role in blocking reforms. Yet, as many recent, post-revisionist histories of the Cold War have emphasized, local political conditions and cultures cannot be explained simply in terms of superpower politics. The stumbling-blocks on the Communists' all-German 'special road', in the West at least, were just as likely to be 'Made in Germany'. The KPD's concept of anti-fascist democracy failed to take into account electoral changes to the internal balance of power, as well as underestimating the fragility of a consensus based on the moral imperatives of anti-fascism and emergency reconstruction. The June 1945 Appeal was in many ways the domestic corollary to the Potsdam agreement, but a compromise between the wartime powers was not a guarantee of internal anti-fascist harmony. Admittedly, several of the KPD's demands, such as denazification, national unity, nationalization of natural resources and heavy industry, were in principle shared by other parties. Yet previous claims, that this minimal anti-fascist consensus was sabotaged chiefly by international monopoly capital and imperialist military government,[64] underrate the extent to which non-Communist politicians felt they were being forced to work, often by the same military governments, with what they regarded as a totalitarian party. By the winter of 1947–8, therefore, for all these various reasons, the KPD had reached a parliamentary dead end.

Revolution Revisited?: The KPD and the Cominform

The foundation in Poland of the Communist Information Bureau (Cominform) on 22–7 September 1947 appeared to signal the end of the western European Communists' parliamentary phase, and a move towards extra-parliamentary action. Besides encouraging the politics of confrontation, it called for a rejection of the Marshall Plan, and put forward a 'two

---

[63] Ulbricht on 19 Oct. 1947 quoted in Staritz, 'Kommunistische Partei Deutschlands', 1690.

[64] Rolf Badstübner and Siegfried Thomas, *Restauration und Spaltung: Entstehung und Entwicklung der BRD 1945–1955* (Cologne, 1975).

camp' theory with alarming implications for German unity. Of course, neither SED nor KPD was ever admitted to the organization, which was limited to the Soviet, eastern European, French, and Italian parties. When the SED later applied to Stalin for admission, it was rejected as 'not yet . . . sufficiently mature'.[65] This alone marked a great change over the Weimar KPD, which had proudly formed the second largest section of the Comintern after the Soviet Union. Yet there is sufficient circumstantial evidence to show that, at least from 1948, both SED and KPD regarded themselves as bona fide members of the world Communist movement.

Accordingly, the KPD could not afford to ignore the implications of the Cominform's founding session at Szklarska Poreba. The main Soviet delegate, Zhdanov, had taken the French and Italian Communists to task for pursuing legalistic and opportunistic parliamentarism. This conveniently ignored the fact that, in so doing, they had only been following the official party line. Instead they were to become opposition parties, using, in the words of the Yugoslav delegates, the weapons of 'demonstrations, political strike, [and] mass mobilization'.[66] In November and December brief but bitter wage strikes did indeed erupt in France and Italy, perceived by many western observers as the opening gambits in a Communist offensive against the Marshall Plan.

Leaving aside the complex motives behind these strikes, which cannot simply be ascribed to 'orders' from the Cominform, is there any evidence that the KPD, too, was being prompted to greater militancy? There are some indications that, unlike the September 1946 meeting discussed earlier, when Ulbricht had rejected strikes, the western Communists *were* being given a more confrontational lead by Berlin. At almost precisely the same time as the Cominform meeting, while addressing the *Arbeitsgemeinschaft* SED-KPD, Dahlem significantly quoted the clause of the SED's Principles and Aims which stated that:

The Socialist Unity Party strives for the *democratic road to socialism*; it will, however, resort to *revolutionary means* if the capitalist class leaves the terrain of democracy.

According to Dahlem, this permitted a dual strategy: the democratic road for the SED; revolutionary means for the KPD. Wage strikes and hunger

[65] On 18 Dec. 1948, for example, according to Dietrich Staritz, 'Die SED, Stalin und die Gründung der DDR', *Aus Politik und Zeitgeschichte*, B 5/91 (25 Jan. 1991), 8.

[66] Jan Foitzik, 'Die Bildung des Kominform-Büros 1947 im Lichte neuer Quellen', *ZfG*, 40 (1992), 1109–26; Boris Sabarko, 'Das Kominformbüro—ein Rückblick', *BzG*, 32 (1990), 454 and 457; Thomas Friedrich, 'Das Kominform und die SED', *BzG*, 33 (1991), 330; Wilfried Loth, *Stalins ungeliebtes Kind* (Berlin, 1994), 100–15.

demonstrations in the West would reinvigorate the class consciousness of a divided working class, culminating in socialist unity. If this were not enough, the 'healthy national forces against the dismembering of the country and against its colonization' by the new American 'world aggressors' would rally around an all-German SED, which was 'a German party . . . pursuing independent German politics'. For Dahlem, then, class politics and national politics were complementary.[67] It might equally well be argued, however, that national politics are by nature consensual, and class politics divisive, and thus mutually at odds. There was certainly a huge gulf between this brand of 'national revolution', and what most older KPD cadres understood by radical politics.

Yet, if one were to measure KPD militancy by actions rather than words, one might be forgiven for thinking that the western Communists were under orders to do nothing. This may have been the result of organizational weakness rather than a lack of political will. As will become clearer in Chapter 5, shop-floor Communists were in no position to launch even token political strikes in the winter of 1947–8: the Social Democrats controlled the trade unions, and hunger strikes were in any case less amenable to politicization than French or Italian wage strikes. One cannot, however, escape the impression that there was a conscious element of restraint or self-restraint at work. It was to take over a year, until October 1948, before the KPD specifically addressed the importance of the Cominform, self-critically confessing its previous neglect. There are also strong grounds, moreover, for believing that Moscow had a vested interest in not letting the Communists rock the boat too violently in Germany, for fear of jeopardizing a diplomatic solution. Although this question must for the time being remain open, further hypotheses on Soviet motives for keeping the German Communists in check will be offered in the next chapter.

Since the Cominform and the autumn strikes are very much identified with the rejection of Marshall Aid, it is worth considering the KPD's record on this issue. One reason for restraint may have been that, when Marshall Aid was announced in June 1947, three of the *Land* Ministers for Reconstruction, including the crucial North Rhine-Westphalian Minister, were in fact Communists. Moreover, until 1948, it was by no means certain that Germany would participate in the European Recovery Programme (ERP). In its first tentative responses to Marshall's speech, the KPD raised mainly economic objections, whereas the SED was more political in its condemnation of what it saw as an adjunct to the Truman

---

[67] AG SED-KPD Conference, 19–20 Sept. 1947, SAPMO-BA, DY 30/IV 2/10.01/2.

Doctrine: a quest for external markets to avert impending crisis, stifle socialization, and assume control of the Ruhr. Nevertheless, on 23 July, soon after Molotov had declined participation on behalf of the eastern bloc, the KPD issued its own rejection in the Bizonal Economic Council. The ERP, it was argued, was an attempt to 'neutralize Germany', risking perpetual division, and leading western Germany into 'political and economic dependency'.[68] Thereafter, KPD representatives were effectively frozen out of discussions on Marshall Aid.[69]

Yet there is almost no evidence of effective mass mobilization by the KPD against the Marshall Plan. Once the Social Democrats had accepted the ERP in July 1947, and the trade unions in June 1948, western Communist leaders, especially those with union posts, were unwilling to risk their already precarious positions. Whether the authorities understood this, is a different matter. It was usually assumed that the KPD was doing everything in its power to undermine the ERP. Ludwig Erhard, architect of the 'economic miracle', certainly claimed that Communists were sabotaging Ruhr coal and steel production under the slogan 'Prevent the enslavement of German industry by the Marshall Plan!'.[70] The Americans, too, received reports of SED calls for passive resistance, with the KPD supposedly under instructions to back any strike. OMGUS was correspondingly sensitive to KPD propaganda attacking the ERP. Even a newspaper cartoon, depicting American supplies being accommodated in a waiting German dustbin, earned a one-month publication ban.[71]

Nevertheless, KPD attacks remained verbal, based on theoretical predictions of a final crisis of capitalism. Propaganda played on fears for the future of the indigenous manufactured goods industry,[72] as well as dredging up memories of the fragility of the American loan system under Weimar. Transatlantic aid would mean:

destruction of the unity of Germany, re-establishment of the economic and political positions of power of big capital and structural distortion of the national

---

[68] Thomas Hartnagel and Arnold Sywottek, 'KPD, SED und der Marshall-Plan', in Othmar Haberl and Lutz Niethammer (eds.) *Der Marshall-Plan und die europäische Linke* (Frankfurt am Main, 1986), 239–40.

[69] Klaus Schwabe, 'German Policy Responses to the Marshall Plan', in Charles S. Maier (ed.), *The Marshall Plan and Germany* (New York and Oxford, 1991), 240–3.

[70] 9th Verwaltungsrat, 11 May 1948, in *Akten zur Vorgeschichte der Bundesrepublik Deutschland 1945–1949*, ed. Christoph Weisz *et al.* (Munich and Vienna, 1983), iv. 495 n. 4.

[71] POLAD to State Dept., 15 Sept. 1948, in *Confidential (1945–1949)*, 40. 230–3; Munich Consulate to State Dept., 20 July 1948, in *Confidential (1945–1949)*, 14. 935–6.

[72] KPD-BL Ruhr, 10 Mar. 1948, SAPMO-BA, I 10/23/19.

economy, which will unavoidably perpetuate misery and distress, and bring inflation, mass unemployment and economic crises of unimaginable proportions upon
our people.[73]

East Germany, on the other hand, was portrayed as immune to such problems. Yet by inviting comparisons between living standards in East and
West, the Communists were treading on very thin ice. Anything hinting
at the true state of affairs, however, was likely to invoke the wrath of
Berlin. Wilhelm Pieck was reported to have thumped the table 'like a
volcano about to erupt' and accused Reimann of 'Marshallism', after the
West German leader had made the following telling analogy to explain
the psychological effectiveness of the ERP and the currency reform:

It is a more comforting thought for the worker to stand with empty pockets
in front of full shop-windows, since in a flourishing economy he then thinks he
has only to work in order to earn money, while it has an adverse effect on the
worker's psyche if he stands with full pockets in front of empty shop-windows.[74]

As hinted at above, German Communists in both halves of Germany
did not become seriously involved with the Cominform until it turned
its attentions in on the Communist movement, following Stalin's showdown with Tito in 1948. It is thus in the area of internal consolidation,
rather than external revolution, that we should perhaps seek the real meaning of the Cominform. (The KPD's 'cadre-political' changes during the
anti-Titoist purges of 1949–51 will be dealt with in detail in Chapter 6.)
In June 1948 the voice of international Communism accused the Yugoslav
Communists of nationalist deviation, at which the SED called for a 'clear
and unambiguous pro-Soviet stance' and a Soviet-style 'new-type party'.[75]
At an important session on 15–16 September 1948, also attended by
KPD leaders, Ulbricht went further, by demanding an end to the 'special
German road to socialism' as prejudicial to the special relationship with
the Soviet Union. On 24 September in a self-critical article in *Neues Deutschland*, entitled 'On the Only Possible Road to Socialism', Ackermann duly
recanted his original theory.

In October Reimann repeated the exercise before the KPD Executive,
berating the party for neglecting the Cominform. The KPD's acceptance
of the 'special German road' was 'objectively' a 'dissociation from the
politics of the Soviet Union', encouraging those in the party who had

[73] *Hamburger Volkszeitung*, 16 Aug. 1947, in Hartnagel and Sywottek, 'Marshall-Plan',
241–2.
[74] Report, 11 Mar. 1949, AdsD, Ostbüro 0346.
[75] *Dokumente der SED*, ed. PV/ZK der SED (East Berlin, 1951), ii. 76–7.

doubted the socialist character of Soviet society and the positive contribution of its foreign policy to the German working class, especially over the Oder-Neisse and Berlin questions. The accompanying resolution renounced the 'special German road' for the USSR's Marxist–Leninist road: 'The relationship to the Soviet Union is the touchstone for every socialist.' As the 'bourgeois-bureaucratic state apparatus' had survived the Third Reich, any 'peaceful growth into socialism' was a Social Democratic illusion. Only 'revolutionary mass struggle' could dislodge it.[76] In private Reimann had nevertheless added an important rider:

Comrades! I would like to warn against the impression that this necessary observation now means a 180-degree turn in our policies, lest comrades henceforth lapse into ultra-leftist rhetoric.[77]

In the ensuing discussion there was uncertainty even among the top KPD leadership about what their strategy now should be. Was it, for instance, legitimate to continue to use the term 'democracy' at all? Nuding pointed out that many members were confusing democracy with parliamentarism; Ledwohn hedged with the formula 'revolutionary-democratic road', but wanted to ban the 'wordplay' once and for all. Clearly disorientated, the Executive reached deadlock and requested Berlin for 'a *clarification of the question of the democratic road* in the next joint session'.[78] Less surprisingly, a large part of the membership soon believed that the party had indeed performed a 180-degree about-turn away from anti-fascist democracy. As one concerned functionary noted: 'The party has to a certain extent rediscovered class struggle, and the struggle on the basis of democracy is not class struggle.'[79] It was feared members would ignore alliance tactics and veer back into radicalism.

This was not to happen, however, since the leadership kept a firm lid on the 'sectarians'. For all the rhetoric of the Cominform, it represented a fundamentally defensive strategy, which had far more in common with the Comintern's popular front phase than its revolutionary 'third period'. Only this time it was a popular front directed against perceived aggression from the Americans rather than the fascists. The KPD therefore continued its alliance politics, albeit more extra-parliamentary than parliamentary, based around a peculiarly anti-American brand of nationalism.

[76] 'Die Bedeutung der Entschließung des Informationsbüros über die Lage in der KP Jugoslawiens und die Lehren für die KPD', 6–7 Oct. 1948, SAPMO-BA, DY 30/IV 2/2.022/126.
[77] Reimann at 6th KPD-PV, 6–7 Oct. 1948, SAPMO-BA, NY 4036/644.
[78] SED-Westabt., 15 Oct. 1948, SAPMO-BA, DY 30/IV 2/2.022/126.
[79] SED-Westabt., 20 Nov. 1948, SAPMO-BA, DY 30/IV 2/2.022/126.

In France and Italy, where neither PCI nor PCF was comfortable with the direct action of 1947, both Togliatti and Thorez also seem to have made up their own minds to revert to a fundamentally parliamentary strategy as rapidly as possible.

The KPD in the *Bundestag*, 1949–1953

For the rest of this chapter I wish to return to the KPD's parliamentary politics and to trace its swansong on the national political stage in the *Bundestag*.[80] The following chapter will then go on to examine the party's extra-parliamentary attempts to mobilize the masses, in what amounted to an anti-colonial national independence struggle. The two strategies were, of course, not unrelated. Indeed, the party later claimed to have consciously used the *Bundestag* as a classic Leninist 'tribune':

The Communist *Bundestag* faction cornered Adenauer again and again, and forced the parties of the *Bundestag*, the government coalition as well as the SPD, to declare their colours and unmask themselves regarding the vital questions of the German people. At no time did it give in to parliamentary illusions. It used the tribune of the *Bundestag* in order to rally the German people to the extra-parliamentary struggle . . .[81]

This concept denied any realistic possibility of using parliament to effect change, and exploited it instead as a platform to expose to a wider audience the restorationist interests at work. KPD activities thus became ever more obstructive, and, in view of the resulting parliamentary suspensions and expulsions, some might say self-destructive. By the same token, the non-Communist parties were more than obliging in ousting the Communists from the parliamentary arena, for which treatment the tribune theory may have been little more than an *ex post facto* rationalization.

Beginning with the British Zonal Advisory Council in February 1946, the KPD had contested the legitimacy of *any* supra-regional West German executive or legislative bodies which might be seen as furthering national division. Likewise, the parliamentary council of the American *Länderrat*, established in March 1947, was derided as a 'pseudo-parliament'.[82] The first bizonal body to encompass the British and American zones was the

---

[80] Unless otherwise stated the source is Klocksin, *Kommunisten im Parlament*, 203–302.

[81] *4 Jahre Bundestag*, ed. Bundestagsfraktion der KPD (Oppau, n.d. [1953]), 54.

[82] Max Reimann and Erich Hoffmann, and later Kurt Müller, Ewald Kaiser, and Hugo Paul sat on the British Zonal Advisory Council (1946–8); Walter Fisch and Albert Buchmann on the parliamentary council of the American *Länderrat* (1947–9).

Economic Council, constituted in June 1947. In its initial configuration of fifty-two members the KPD had only three representatives, doubled in February 1948 to six.[83] The Communists criticized it for ignoring the denazification and demilitarization of the economy, and for neglecting the other two zones, describing it as an agent of political division rather than economic rehabilitation. None the less, despite their reservations, they intended to 'use the tribune of the Economic Council and the activity in its committees in the interests of the working people'.[84] It nevertheless required careful judgement not to overstep the mark by using, as Pieck put it, a 'formulation which makes it easy for the others to chuck us out'.[85] On 16 March 1948 Reimann transgressed the bounds of acceptable parliamentary discourse, however, when the Economic Council suspended him for two months for his attacks on Germans working for the Bizonal administration as 'national traitors'.

As its name suggests, the Parliamentary Council, set up on 1 September 1948 to devise the Basic Law, was a specifically proto-parliamentary body. Max Reimann and Hugo Paul (replaced by Heinz Renner) sat for the KPD. At the opening session the Communist representatives made their usual disclaimers, tabling a resolution for the Council's dissolution for contravening Yalta and Potsdam, and suggesting instead constitutional discussions with the German People's Council in the SBZ. Nevertheless, they attempted to include a whole catalogue of social legislation in the Basic Law, including the abolition of corporal punishment and absolute parental rights in schools; equality before the law for illegitimate children; the 40-hour week; equal pay for equal work; paid holidays; youth and maternal protection; the right to strike for officials; as well as the more familiar expropriation without compensation of war criminals, parity co-determination, and the transfer of basic industries and minerals to public ownership. Without exception, all of these motions were voted down.

Again, the Communists were at pains to undermine the legitimacy of the body. Max Reimann spent three months in gaol when a British court martial convicted him in January 1949 for describing Council members as 'quislings'. During the trial his defence had forced the court to concede that the term 'Allied auxiliary personnel' might equally well apply to a NAAFI lavatory attendant as to Adenauer. Reimann was paroled less

---

[83] Members with replacements in brackets: 1947: Max Reimann, Ludwig Becker (Fritz Rische), Ludwig Ficker (Fritz Sperling); 1948: Alfred Kroth, Kurt Müller, Heinrich Niebes.

[84] Klocksin, *Kommunisten im Parlament*, 213.

[85] SED-ZS/KPD meeting, 10 Feb. 1948, SAPMO-BA, DY 30/IV 2/1.01/79.

than a fortnight later, after several demonstrations and a plea from the unlikely quarter of Adenauer himself, probably to avoid making a martyr of the KPD leader. (Immediately after the Council disbanded, Reimann was rearrested by the British after a number of high-speed car-chases across their zone, and forced to sit out the rest of his sentence.) While his comrade was in gaol, Renner stressed the non-co-operative role of the KPD:

We co-operated for as long . . . as we could believe that the policy of the occupation powers here in West Germany was aiming at the implementation of the decisions of the Potsdam Agreement. I told you that on the first day. I am here to monitor you. Do you really think that I am here . . . to co-operate? I don't believe that even you are that naive.[86]

Finally, on 23 May 1949, Reimann and Renner symbolically withheld their signatures from the Basic Law, the latter explaining, 'I will not sign to the division of Germany!'.[87]

By the time of Reimann's final release the KPD was well into its first *Bundestag* campaign for the election on 14 August 1949. All the important election literature, including the manifesto, had been worked out by the SED's Politburo and the West Commission, with Franz Dahlem adding the final touches.[88] It attempted a clumsy form of *Sammlungspolitik*, appealing to the electorate to enrol in a 'national front' embracing 'all honest Germans who love their *Volk* and *Vaterland*' and wished to avoid being 'humiliated as an exploited and oppressed colonial people'. The other parties were 'freely lending their hand to the setting up of a West German colonial state under the rule of foreign finance bosses, and are prepared to take on this role against their own people in this state of bailiffs and overseers'. Berlin was clearly also banking on public receptivity to Soviet foreign policy proposals for a peace treaty and the withdrawal of occupation troops. Besides national sensibilities, the manifesto raised the economic spectre of unemployment: the 'full, brightly lit shop-windows' concealed 'distress and poverty', perpetuated by dismantling and high occupation costs. Yet some slogans, such as 'The German Economy for the German People!' and 'Democratic Rights and Freedoms for the People!', were in grave danger of rebounding on the Communists in view of their record on these issues in the SBZ.[89]

---

[86] Speech on 8 Feb. 1949 quoted by Staritz, 'Kommunistische Partei Deutschlands', 1771.
[87] Rhinwest Düsseldorf to Public Safety, 29 May 1949, PRO, FO 1030/91.
[88] Herbert Mayer, 'Nur eine Wahlniederlage?', *Hepte zur DDR-Geschichte*, 29 (1995), 39.
[89] KPD-PV, 'Einheit, Frieden, Wohlstand: Das Wahlprogramm der KPD', 24 June 1949, in *KPD 1945–1968: Dokumente*, ed. Günter Judick *et al.* (Neuss, 1989), i. 285–97.

In fact, 18% of all voters asked by American pollsters claimed that anti-Communism had been their prime motive in voting in the *Bundestag* election. The SPD capitalized on these sentiments with a particularly aggressive poster, 'A Vote for the KP is a Vote for the *KZ* [concentration camp]'. Unable to profile itself as *the* opposition party, a niche already occupied by the SPD, the KPD won a national average of only 5.7%, with a few notable exceptions in local bastions such as Solingen-Remscheid (nearly 21%), as well as Gladbeck-Bottrop and Gelsenkirchen (over 15%). (See also Table 4 above.) Under the mixed electoral system KPD candidates won no first-past-the-post constituencies, only fifteen 'reserve' seats by proportional representation from the *Land* lists, although they had been hoping for 20–5.[90]

In what can only be described as a tribunal, presided over by Pieck, Ulbricht, and five other SED leaders, Reimann and the KPD's cadre chief, Fritz Sperling, were personally dressed down by the West Commission for this poor showing. Berlin conceded some external handicaps, but attacked the KPD for keeping tactically quiet on the Soviet Union and eastern Germany, as well as Oder-Neisse, POWs, and refugees. Afterwards, Ulbricht hypocritically denied SED responsibility, claiming that 'the comrades from here only make suggestions' which Frankfurt could take or leave. The more sinister message of the *Bundestag* disaster, however, was for an internal purge of 'Titoists and Trotskyites', with Pieck concluding that expulsions were inevitable.[91]

In the KPD's own self-critical post-mortem, although Reimann blamed the 'mistaken decision' by the West German voters who had voted against their own interests, seduced by the right-wing SPD leadership, the chief culprit, echoing Berlin, was the party itself. It had spread confusion over national policy on the shop-floor, was unclear on the special relationship with the USSR and its policies in the SBZ, as well as relations with the SPD. The buck was passed on down the party hierarchy. In Bavaria, where 'personnel changes' had been announced, the leadership blamed

[90] OMGUS Report No. 191, 9 Dec. 1949, in Anna J. Merritt and Richard L. Merritt (eds.), *Public Opinion in Semisovereign Germany: The HICOG Surveys, 1949–1955* (Urbana, Ill., 1980), 316; Staritz, 'Kommunistische Partei Deutschlands', 1765; the deputies were: Agatz, NRW; Fisch, Hessen; Gundelach, Hamburg; Harig, NRW; Leibbrand*, Württ.-Baden; K. Müller*, NRW; O. Müller, Hessen; Niebergall, Rhine.-Pfalz; Nuding*, Württ.-Baden; Paul, NRW; Reimann, NRW; Renner, NRW; Rische, NRW; Thiele, NRW; Vesper*, NRW. (* replaced by Kohl, Stuttgart (1950); Niebes (1951); and Strohbach, Stuttgart (1952) respectively).

[91] 21st (35th) SED-PV, 23–4 Aug. 1949, SAPMO-BA, DY 30/IV 2/1/35; Mayer, 'Wahlniederlage?', 41–3. Yet, as will be seen in Chapter 5, a purge had been brewing for some years, and the *Bundestag* elections may simply be seen as a catalyst.

the *Kreise* for their apathy and inefficiency, who in turn blamed the church and Bavarian patriotism. Only rarely, as in Konstanz, did a local leadership challenge the wisdom of strengthening the eastern connection, pointing instead to what they knew to be the real vote-losers: POWs in the USSR; Polish and Czech party attitudes to expellees and the 'eastern territories'; as well as poor living conditions in the SBZ. The reward for such honesty was, however, only another bawling-out from on high.[92]

An in-depth analysis of the KPD's parliamentary practice in the *Bundestag* cannot be attempted here. Many of the central issues of national reunification and rearmament will in any case be dealt with in the next chapter. Needless to say, the room for manœuvre of 15 Communist deputies out of 402 was even narrower than in the *Landtage*. Initially the KPD was able to form a faction and to draft a large number of bills, all of which were thrown out. After Kurt Müller's arrest in East Germany in March 1950, however, which is discussed in Chapter 6, a letter purportedly signed by him renouncing his mandate was rejected, reducing the faction from 15 to 14. At that point a faction required 10 members, but soon the KPD was down to 9 following a string of house exclusion orders. (On 13 June 1950 Reimann was barred for thirty days for attempting to speak without the speaker's permission against a declaration in the name of the *Bundestag* condemning the Oder-Neisse border. When Renner, Müller, Vesper, and Rische tried to prevent his removal by the ushers, a scuffle ensued, and all four received twenty days.) From January 1952 the *de jure* minimum for a faction was then raised from 10 to 15, leaving the KPD *fraktionsunfähig*, stripped of important financial and secretarial privileges, as well as the right to initiate bills or gain access to parliamentary committees. Thereafter it was reduced to voicing its opinions at question time. Other procedural weapons included deprivation of the right to speak and calls to order, which were used 107 times against the KPD, out of a total of 156. Four Communist deputies also had their parliamentary immunity suspended, in Renner's case apparently for a traffic violation.

Beyond a few personal contacts, for instance with Helene Wessel of the moribund *Zentrum*, and the renegade Christian Democrat Gustav Heinemann, the Communists remained isolated. There was no question of co-operation with the SPD. Max Reimann was mostly absent from the *Bundestag*, only appearing to make speeches on major foreign policy issues such as the General Treaty, Schuman Plan, European Defence Community, and national reunification. The real driving-force behind the

[92] *FV*, 30 Aug. 1949, 4; ID/EUCOM, 9 Sept. 1949, in *Confidential (1945–1949)*, 15. 209–11; KPD-KL Konstanz, n.d., BAK, B 118/141/7939–45.

faction was Heinz Renner, master of the parliamentary aside and certainly regarded with some fondness even by his enemies. Despite the fireworks of the debates alluded to below, the KPD's parliamentary practice was, as Staritz points out, by no means revolutionary, but social reformist. In September 1951 the Communists again tried to bring in legislation to expropriate coal and steel, as well as chemicals, but nearly all KPD motions were thrown out at committee stage or in plenary session under points of order, at which the party retaliated by symbolically voting against every other party's bills. Only rarely, as during the final vote on the Works Constitution Bill in 1952, did the SPD find itself on the same side as the KPD, and only after it had voted down all prior KPD amendments to curbs on works council powers, along with the CDU and FDP. Communist attempts to refine other major pieces of legislation, such as the Equalization of Burdens Law, by banding compensation in favour of poorer refugees at the expense of the more wealthy dispossessed, also foundered.[93]

The most memorable KPD activity in the *Bundestag* centred around national issues, rearmament, and western integration, exposing alleged discrepancies between Adenauer's reunification rhetoric and separatist practice. Walter Fisch even called the Chancellor's secret diplomacy a treasonable 'breach of the constitution'.[94] Reimann's inaugural speech in September gives as good an impression as any of the love–hate relationship between Communists and non-Communists, in which banter could easily escalate into savage invective on both sides. He started by calling the Federal government a 'colonial administrative outpost', subservient to the western Allies' Occupation Statute:

The accompanying music to the formation of this government is the clatter of tanks rolling through the Ruhrgebiet and the roar of the dismantling drills destroying our peacetime industry in order to cut out German competition on the world market.

(Lively contradiction in the centre and on the right.—Many calls in the centre: Eastern Zone!)

When he talked of the Marshall Plan as a scheme to drain capital to the USA, Franz Josef Strauß of the CSU retorted: 'Better than people-export to Russia!' Reimann's son, who was a POW in the USSR, was also

[93] Staritz, 'Kommunistische Partei Deutschlands', 1772–4; *4 Jahre Bundestag*; Fritz Rische, 'Die KPD-Fraktion im 1. Deutschen Bundestag für die deutsche Einheit und den Abschluß eines Friedensvertrags', in Marx-Engels-Stiftung (ed.), *Zum deutschen Neuanfang 1945–1949: Tatsachen—Probleme—Ergebnisse—Irrwege* (Bonn, 1993), 58–73.
[94] 18th session, 24–5 Nov. 1949, in *Verhandlungen des Deutschen Bundestages: I. Wahlperiode 1949: Stenographische Berichte* (Bonn, 1950), i. 507.

frequently mentioned in heckles, but the Communist leader continued undaunted:

If I am asked the question: if you reject the West German state, is it not a matter of indifference who sits in the positions of power in that state?—then I must answer: we reject this West German state but are fighting consistently for the unity of Germany.

(Lively calls from the centre and right: For Russia!)

Yet after this West German state has been formed against our will, it cannot be of indifference to us in whose hands the positions of state power lie . . .

Then Reimann addressed Adenauer's 'magnet theory' whereby West Germany would eventually draw East Germany to it by its economic strength alone:

And if the question of magnets was raised, I can answer you today in full confidence: the magnet will not be the West German state with its Adenauer-Blücher government, but the magnet for the people will be the new democratic order in the Soviet occupation zone!

(Lively applause from the Communists. Contradiction in the centre. Prolonged commotion.—Call of: He is a good comedian!—President's bell.)

A raw nerve was touched when the KPD leader called the Oder-Neisse border the 'frontier of peace'. The house exploded:

(Continuous excited calls: Boo! Boo!—Noise.—President's bell.—Agitated interjections: Get off! Get off! . . . Dep. Strauß: Send him to Moscow! Put your uniform on! . . . Calls of: Agent of Moscow! Paid provocateur! . . .)

At this point the *Bundestag* degenerated into bad theatre:

(A spectator, by his appearance a returned prisoner-of-war from Russia, moves down the deputies' aisle towards the podium, accompanied by excited calls and pointing to his clothing and shoes. . . . The spectator is led out of the hall at the President's direction. . . . —Dep. Rische: The young man was here all yesterday evening! This provocation has been planned since yesterday evening!—Excited counter-calls from the right and centre.—Dep. Rische: You are all responsible!—Dep. Reimann: You had people gassed! You!)[95]

If my supposition is correct that proactive anti-Communism was strongest among the political élite, rather than ordinary citizens, as I shall argue in the final chapter, then such scenes can only have shortened the KPD's life expectancy. There may even have been an element of personal recrimination in the government's decision to press for a ban. At one point Reimann even drew clear parallels between Adenauer and

[95] 7th session, 22 Sept. 1949, in *Verhandlungen des Deutschen Bundestages*, i. 58–67.

Hitler, causing a rumpus and calls of 'Unerhört!'.[96] Later on, Federal Interior Minister Lehr was accused by Renner of being a 'murderer', after police had shot dead a young Communist.[97]

It required no special measures, however, to oust the KPD from parliament, since it was automatically excluded at the next polls by the new 5% hurdle. With 2.2%, the September 1953 *Bundestag* election represented an all-time post-war low. (Local parties did recover somewhat in subsequent *Landtag* elections.) One strong contingent factor must have been the extremely negative publicity surrounding the East German uprising of 17 June. The KPD's reaction was to say as little as possible and to print the SED version of events.[98] NRW's chairman, Ledwohn, thus talked of the 'fascist putsch attempt' which was:

put down by the working population and state organs. Through the intervention of the Soviet army, a bloodbath was prevented and the warmongers were denied any possibility of expanding the provocation into the outbreak of a war. The long-planned X-Day has thus become an ignominious defeat for the Adenauer government.[99]

NRW's mass agitation section did, however, attempt some more sophisticated damage limitation with a travelling exhibition on the GDR, stressing reform policy, and including displays on the Building of Socialism, New Course, but also 'The Provocation of 17 June 1953'.[100]

The bulk of the campaign had been fought on foreign policy issues, pushing socio-economic reforms on to the sidelines. The social profile of KPD voters indicates that the party was falling back on its core support. A sample of 1,000 Communist electors revealed just over 13% to be under the age of 30, but nearly 69% between 30 and 60, the remaining 18% approaching or beyond pensionable age; 64% were male (whereas the SPD and CDU scored 54% and 45% respectively), and were concentrated in towns of over 50,000. In the press the Secretariat blamed intimidation at the polls, as well as the electorate's misinterpretation of Moscow's reunification plans, but also, as in 1949, the ideological immaturity and recalcitrance of members. According to the Americans, however, the party was reportedly 'stunned' at the result, previously cocooned in a 'cult-like introversion'.[101]

[96] 24th session, 16 Dec. 1949, in *Verhandlungen des Deutschen Bundestages*, i. 739.
[97] 14 May 1952, in Klocksin, *Kommunisten im Parlament*, 262–4.
[98] *FV*, 18 June 1953, 2; *FV*, 19 June 1953, 1–2.
[99] Ledwohn at KPD-LL NRW, 12 July 1953, SAPMO-BA, I 10/28/3.
[100] *Unser Weg*, 3/12 (1953), 18–19.
[101] KPD-PV, 'Für Frieden, nationale Einheit und soziale Sicherheit!', 9 July 1953, in *KPD 1945–1968*, ii. 9–24; *FV*, 8 Sept. 1953, 1; Staritz, 'Kommunistische Partei Deutschlands', 1766; HICOG to State Dept., 10 Aug. 1954, in *Confidential (1950–1954)*, 29. 525–46.

The KPD lingered on in a number of *Landtage* and local parliaments, but in an obstructive rather than constructive role, demonstrating the Communists' fundamental opposition to the West German state. As I have argued elsewhere, and as I shall argue again, this process of marginalization was a combination of self-destruction from within and ostracism from without. The Communists' understanding of democracy was in fact deeply hostile to parliamentary norms. The treatment of the bloc parties in the SBZ, and their reduction to the status of transmission belts between the SED and East German population, could only undermine the KPD's claims to be a worthy coalition partner. The stridency of later propaganda, above all the ill-conceived National Reunification Programme of 1952, which will be discussed below, served only to alienate moderate opinion in West Germany. At the same time, the non-Communist parties had shown from very early on that they were not interested in working with the KPD. In the atmosphere of the Cold War, Communist ministers and parliamentary committee members, privy to sensitive information, were seen as a national security threat and treated accordingly. This was not just a prejudice based on concurrent events in the SBZ, however, but one based also on a long-standing hostility to Communist participation in the affairs of state, dating back to the repeated dissolution by the Weimar executive of provincial 'workers' governments'. The post-war SPD had also shown that, given the choice, it preferred a coalition with the Liberals or even the CDU, forcing the KPD ever further into the political wilderness.

4

Sammlungspolitik *in the Wilderness*

The KPD's Extra-Parliamentary Campaigns

As has been seen, the West German Communists were committed to the concept of alliance politics, but had come to grief inside the various parliaments. This does not mean, however, that they had given up on alliances *outside* parliament. Extra-parliamentary *Sammlungspolitik*, or 'catch-all politics', had a long pedigree in Germany. Ever since the late nineteenth century, leagues had existed to bypass the *Reichstag* parties by mobilizing popular grievances, using a heady mixture of anti-capitalism, anti-liberalism, anti-socialism, and anti-semitism. The politics of rejection reached their classic expression, however, after the Versailles Treaty of 1919. Above all, the conservative and radical right had identified themselves as the 'national opposition', pledged to revise or annul Allied reparations and territorial dismemberment. Since parliamentary democracy itself was seen as part of the problem, Weimar had also witnessed a huge growth of extra-parliamentary politics. The overall winner in the competition for the disaffected was, of course, the Nazi Party. Nevertheless, under pressure from the right, the Weimar KPD, too, had dabbled in the patriotic politics of 'national bolshevism', going so far as to issue a National and Social Liberation Programme in 1930. Masterminded by the ever-resourceful Willi Münzenberg, the party had also experimented with extra-parliamentary fronts, creating a whole array of Communist ancillary organizations, designed to bridge the gap between party and society.[1]

Still smarting from this inter-war defeat, the post-war Communists appear to have wished to snatch the mantle of 'national opposition' from the right once and for all. This is *not* to say that Communists after 1945 —or for that matter before 1933—were interchangeable with the radical right. Nevertheless, SED and KPD set themselves the clear task of defeating the patriotic right at its own game. Nor were they the only ones

---

[1] Louis Dupeux, *'Nationalbolschewismus' in Deutschland 1919–1933: Kommunistische Strategie und konservative Dynamik* (Munich, 1985).

on the left wishing to do so. The KPD was keenly aware that it was competing with a highly nationalistic SPD. 'Faced with Schumacher's nationalistic rabble-rousing', as one session of the KPD Executive revealed, there were 'voices calling for us to talk even more "nationally" still'.[2] It is easy with hindsight to criticize this as a form of overcompensation. The revisionists and irredentists on the maverick right conspicuously failed to convert the mainstream in Bonn to more than verbal concessions. It should not be forgotten, however, that at the time there were considerable fears of a nationalist backlash against the occupation, not least among the occupiers themselves.

The range of cross-party issues around which to focus protest in the late 1940s did indeed seem promising. National reunification was a burning issue for most West Germans, and integration into the western bloc hardly seemed the obvious strategy to achieve it; Adenauer's decision to rearm the Federal Republic so soon after the war caused widespread alarm and in some places pacifism; and, finally, the large-scale projected dismantling of industry did not endear the Allies to German workers at a time of high unemployment.[3] As may be seen in Reimann's inaugural *Bundestag* speech, however, the KPD was highly vulnerable to accusations of hypocrisy over these same issues: most West Germans wanted to believe that the Soviet Union was solely to blame for Germany's division; in June 1948, long before public talk of West German rearmament, the East Germans had set up a Barracked People's Police, which bore all the hallmarks of a military formation; and the level of dismantling in the SBZ dwarfed western confiscations. The question for the KPD, therefore, was whether it could make a *Sammlungspolitik*, based on the largely emotional issues of reunification and pacifism, attractive enough to overcome these eastern liabilities. Otherwise, it would be preaching in a Cold War wilderness.

Notwithstanding these serious handicaps, it would be no exaggeration to say that national reunification and the struggle to keep Bonn out of a western alliance became the post-war KPD's political *raison d'être*, pushing all other demands on to the margins. In 1948 the NRW party even stopped singing the *Internationale* in public, and the Bavarians dropped the hammer-and-sickle and Soviet star emblems.[4] At a more theoretical level it might be argued that any national movement would also have to

---

[2] Jungmann at 6th KPD-PV, 6–7 Oct. 1948, SAPMO-BA, DY 30/IV 2/2.022/126.
[3] Dismantling will be covered in the next chapter.
[4] Rhinwest to Bercomb, 6 May 1948, PRO, FO 1049/1210; Munich Consulate to State Dept., 20 July 1948, in *Confidential U.S. State Department Central Files: Germany—Internal Affairs 1945–1949*, ed. Paul Kesaris (Frederick, Md., 1985), 14. 935–6.

suspend the ideological battle against the class enemy. This was not always accepted by the membership. Arguments that the German *Mittelstand* should be recruited to the national cause with promises to revive intra-German trade met with objections from those preferring to remain a proletarian *Kampfpartei*, promoting social conflict.[5] One KPD works councillor in Krefeld even complained that 'We are serving as the doctor at the sick-bed of capitalism with our national policy'.[6] To prove otherwise, the leadership went through verbal acrobatics, as when in September 1949 Reimann argued that the fight for national self-determination and German reunification was simultaneously a 'struggle for the disempowerment of the most reactionary, anti-national part of the bourgeoisie—of monopoly capital. For that reason it is class struggle.'[7]

The Cominform's attacks on 'national deviation' in 1948 further narrowed the parameters of national discourse. The 'special German road to socialism' had offered West German Communists some leeway at least from traditional proletarian internationalist obligations to the Soviet Union. After 1948 even that marginal freedom was denied. Reimann's own exhortations only exposed the inherent contradictions: 'We must understand that our policy for the national interests of the German people is in no way a nationalistic policy.'[8] The KPD was expected to learn its national independence struggle from the Soviet Union 'without getting into the swamp of nationalism'.[9]

Thus denied the possibility of a 'third way' between the USA and USSR, the KPD was unable to convince the so-called 'national neutralists', who wished to see a united Germany remain equidistant from both superpower blocs. As Ackermann emphasized, however, 'No party and no individual can stand between the two camps, because there is nothing inbetween but a yawning chasm, worlds apart.'[10] Opting out of the western bloc meant opting into the eastern bloc. To all practical intents and purposes, therefore, KPD nationalism meant not so much pro-Germanism as anti-Americanism, and its neutralism was similarly compromised by its unilateral fixation with NATO, and the blind eye turned towards the GDR's 'eastern integration'.[11]

[5] Bremen Consulate to State Dept., 23 May 1949, in *Confidential (1945–1949)*, 15. 133–4.

[6] *Unser Weg*, 2/1 (1952), 33.

[7] Hans Kluth, *Die KPD in der Bundesrepublik* (Cologne and Opladen, 1959), 41.

[8] Reimann at 6th KPD-PV, 6–7 Oct. 1948, SAPMO-BA, NY 4036/644.

[9] 'Die Bedeutung der Entschließung des Informationsbüros über die Lage in der KP Jugoslawiens und die Lehren für die KPD', 6–7 Oct. 1948, SAPMO-BA, DY 30/IV 2/2.022/126.

[10] 'Wo steht und wo geht die SPD?', ed. AG SED-KPD, n.d.

[11] Dietrich Staritz, 'Die Kommunistische Partei Deutschlands', in Richard Stöss (ed.), *Parteien-Handbuch* (Opladen, 1983), 1701 and 1717.

The Paradox of Moscow's *Deutschlandpolitik*

One of the aspects of Stalin's post-war policy on Germany, which has most greatly vexed historians ever since, is that of national unity. At regular intervals Moscow and East Berlin made proposals for reunification, as well as for a peace treaty, which were all rejected without great ceremony by the western Allies and the Federal government. The sticking point was usually the East's insistence on neutrality, as well as the issue of free elections, but there is no doubt that, taken at face value, these offers represented huge concessions from the Soviet side. As the East German foreign minister, Georg Dertinger, intimated to one West German politician, Soviet policy was seriously aiming at reunification without regard to the SED: Moscow was 'ready to pay a high price for a neutralized Germany'.[12]

This poses something of a dilemma. If Stalin's avowed foreign policy were to have succeeded and reunification actually to have taken place, it would almost certainly have wiped out domestic Communist gains in the Soviet zone. (Conversely, if Sovietization of the SBZ had reached a point of no return, further all-German initiatives would have been fatally handicapped.) Perhaps Stalin was prepared to sacrifice his gains in the SBZ in return for a neutral united Germany? Or was he making offers he knew could only be refused in order to placate German nationalists? Because of this uncertainty, it is important to explore the Soviet role, which has become a little less shadowy since the end of the Cold War.

At the risk of oversimplification, one can detect in the Kremlin two main tendencies—'factions' would be too strong a term—with competing foreign policy visions. On the one hand was a 'state' group around Malenkov, Mikoyan, and secret police chief Beria. For these men, post-war diplomacy was to be reserved to conventional state institutions which would deal with the West from a pragmatic, power-political standpoint. They envisaged a Carthaginian peace with Germany, stripping the SBZ of its assets, before a relatively rapid withdrawal and eventual national reunification. In contrast was a 'party' group around Zhdanov and Voznesensky, and later Molotov, Suslov, and Yudin, which eclipsed the 'state' group in 1947. In Germany itself these frictions were to a certain extent reflected in the SMAD: Semyonov, Political Adviser and later High Commissioner,

---

[12] Lemmer to HICOG, 29 Oct. 1951, in Hermann Graml, 'Die Legende von der verpaßten Gelegenheit: Zur sowjetischen Notenkampagne des Jahres 1952', *VfZ*, 29 (1981), 311–12.

was apparently more flexible and committed to national reunification than the more dogmatic Tyulpanov, head of the Information Department and a self-confessed 'Bolshevist'.[13]

Pursuing a far more ambitious and ideologically driven foreign policy, the 'party' group appeared more interested in consolidating the SBZ as a client state under Ulbricht, while remaining far more bullish towards the West. If this is true, then reunification policy was to a great extent instrumentalized, and long-term division accepted as an unpalatable but safe alternative. What is important to recognize, however, is that *both* strategies were proclaimed in parallel, well into the 1950s, without any apparent acknowledgement of their incompatibility. East Germany could be a defensive military bulwark for the eastern bloc *and* an offensive ideological bridgehead on the West. As Tyulpanov stated in May 1948:

> The Socialist Unity Party is on the border between two worlds, where the world of capitalism meets the world of socialism. . . . [T]he party in the Zone is effectively in power and is leading the struggle for the conquest of all of Germany.[14]

Nevertheless, in this instance Tyulpanov went on to talk exclusively about internal consolidation of the SBZ. Implicitly, reunification would take place only via a policy of strength in the eastern zone. In some ways this was the Communist obverse of the 'magnet theory' in West Germany, but geared towards political rather than economic superiority. Over time, therefore, as the ratchet of SED control was tightened, particularly between 1948–52, national reunification must be viewed as more and more of a rhetorical gesture.

Stalin's death in 1953 produced a power struggle between the two groupings which promised to reverse this trend. Molotov appears to have taken over the 'party' baton from the 'Zhdanovites' (Zhdanov himself had died in 1948), and adopted an uncompromising line of defending wartime gains and negotiating from strength. This position was challenged by Beria, and probably Malenkov, who advocated a more defensive role in view of the Soviet Union's weak strategic position. The two views clashed at a session of the Soviet Presidium on 27 May 1953, when Molotov argued for the preservation of the GDR as a socialist state; Beria, manoeuvring for domestic power, suggested the unthinkable by proposing to sacrifice the

---

[13] Wladimir S. Semjonow, *Von Stalin bis Gorbatschow: Ein halbes Jahrhundert in diplomatischer Mission 1939–1991* (Berlin, 1995), 226; Wilfried Loth, *Stalins ungeliebtes Kind* (Berlin, 1994), 129–35; Vladislav Zubok and Constantine Pleshakov, *Inside the Kremlin's Cold War: From Stalin to Khrushchev* (Cambridge, Mass., and London, 1996), 48–9 and 160–4.

[14] Tyulpanov lecture, 8 May 1948, in *Wilhelm Pieck*, ed. Rolf Badstübner and Wilfried Loth (Berlin, 1994), 217.

GDR for the sake of a reunified, neutral Germany. In the end, Molotov prevailed with the support of Khrushchev, and in June Beria was arrested and, as is well known, executed later that year.[15] Nevertheless, the new Moscow leadership did agree on more flexibility in East German policy, suspending the 'Building of Socialism' (but not in time to avert the 17 June uprising!), and reminding the SED of its all-German obligations:

Since at the moment the main task is the struggle for the unification of Germany on a democratic and peaceful basis, the SED and KPD must guarantee the implementation of elastic tactics aimed at maximum fragmentation of the adversary's forces and exploitation of any oppositional currents against the venal Adenauer clique.[16]

Nevertheless, within a year priority was back with the social transformation of the GDR. Thus, throughout this period, there is ample evidence that the Kremlin and Soviet headquarters at Karlshorst repeatedly intervened in the name of national reunification, but were apparently counteracted by their own political allies in East Germany, the SED. This is still, of course, a highly contentious area requiring further research. Wilfried Loth has boldly argued the case for Stalin the *Realpolitiker*, persistently in quest of a compromise solution over Germany.[17] Others have questioned the Soviet leader's intentions and pointed to the myth-making surrounding the Stalin Notes of 1952 in particular.[18] Using East German archives alone it is probably impossible to document Stalin's authentic motives. Even if one could, intentionality and the German question are treacherous terrain. Hard- and soft-liners in the Kremlin could be equally likely advocates of offers on reunification, either as ploys to divide the West, or as tactics to achieve a compromise solution. There is also a danger, particularly among former western historians, of seeking inner-party factions where there were none. In any case, as Loth himself points out, the Stalinist hierarchy, imbued with a crude ideological mind-set, was perhaps not up to the delicate task of Stalin's new and supposedly rational foreign policy. Most important of all, eastern intentions must always be balanced against western possibilities—decision-makers in Moscow were

[15] James Richter, 'Reexamining Soviet Policy towards Germany during the Beria Interregnum', *Cold War International History Project: Working Papers*, 3 (1992).

[16] CPSU-PB resolution, n.d. [May 1953], in Rolf Stöckigt, 'Ein Dokument von großer historischer Bedeutung vom Mai 1953', *BzG*, 32 (1990), 654.

[17] Loth, *Stalins ungeliebtes Kind*.

[18] Manfred Kittel, 'Genesis einer Legende: Die Diskussion um die Stalin-Noten in der Bundesrepublik 1952–1958', *VfZ*, 41 (1993), 355–89.

often poorly informed about conditions on the ground in the West, and correspondingly unrealistic. New documentary evidence from the Moscow archives on meetings between KPD and Soviet officials bears this out. For instance, on 12 May 1949 Kurt Müller and Walter Fisch attended a meeting in East Berlin with Tyulpanov in the presence of Dahlem and Schirdewan of the West Commission. In Tyulpanov's report to Semyonov, the failure of national policy was blamed on the KPD's organizational and ideological inadequacy. The leadership was accused of party indiscipline and failing to submit its ideological review for vetting by the SED. Nor had it created peace committees across the whole of the Federal Republic. Tyulpanov even accused the West German leaders of losing touch with reality by overestimating the SPD. At a meeting a week later with Tyulpanov and Dahlem, Reimann tried to deflect criticism with a more optimistic tack, followed by Sperling who blamed other members of the KPD Secretariat. Tyulpanov berated the two West Germans for not following the shining example of Soviet policy in the SBZ, which was supposedly economically stronger than the western zones, at which Reimann admitted that this was not yet politically opportune inside, let alone outside, the KPD. In short, just like the SED, the Soviets could not see the political wood for the organizational trees. As was to happen again and again, the solution was not for something different, but simply more of the same—more efficiently and more unrelentingly wrong.[19]

While the good faith of Moscow's offers of unification is still open to speculation, the genuineness of the SED's unification propaganda is open to serious doubt. From the very outset, socio-economic transformation of the SBZ patently gained priority over national unity, and only rarely did the SED ever contemplate life without Soviet patronage.[20] The All-German Constituent Council mooted in late 1950, and the proposed all-German elections and peace treaty negotiations in September 1951, were, according to this view, consciously sabotaged by simultaneous aggressive propaganda by the SED in an attempt to neutralize Soviet initiatives. Only briefly in 1952, following the Stalin Notes, did SED–KPD language moderate, reflecting Moscow's pressure for an eleventh hour solution.[21]

[19] Gerhard Wettig, 'Die KPD als Instrument der sowjetischen Deutschland-Politik: Festlegungen 1949 und Implementierungen 1952', *Deutschland-Archiv*, 27 (1994), 818–19.

[20] Pieck's notes, 11 July 1947: 'whether to distance from SMA—towards opp. party against SMA—whether to orientate towards west. democracy', in *Wilhelm Pieck*, 128.

[21] Jochen Meiners, *Die doppelte Deutschlandpolitik* (Frankfurt am Main, 1987), 625–30; Michael Klein, *Antifaschistische Demokratie und nationaler Befreiungskampf* (2nd edn.; West Berlin, 1986), 172–4.

Nevertheless, there does seem to have been a loose grouping within the SED which favoured more flexibility over national policy. Grotewohl, who did not always see eye to eye with Ulbricht, had early on become the 'national' spokesman of the SED, chosen perhaps for his moderate Social Democratic background. Franz Dahlem, as head of the West Commission, must have been aware of the poor return on western work invested by the SED, but was marginalized from the early 1950s and purged in May 1953. Nor should one forget that Dertinger, the GDR's foreign minister from 1949–53, before being arrested by the Stasi as a western spy, was, nominally at least, a Christian Democrat. In March 1951 he even reportedly outmanœuvred Grotewohl and won support from Semyonov to place the GDR's national policy on a 'bourgeois' footing.[22] Implicit supporters of Beria's 1953 initiative, if not of Beria personally, were Rudolf Herrnstadt, editor of the SED newspaper, *Neues Deutschland*, and Wilhelm Zaisser, Minister of State Security. Herrnstadt could on occasion inject a welcome note of realism into SED leadership discussions: 'Many of us would . . . do well to free ourselves of the undialectical notion that the coming unified, democratic Germany will simply be an enlarged copy of the current German Democratic Republic.'[23] Periodically, he had attempted to raise the profile of national policy and activities in West Germany, meeting with indifference from Ulbricht. Later, when the SED leader was on the ropes during the June 1953 crisis, Herrnstadt and Zaisser had attacked him for, among other things, attempting the rapid social transformation of the GDR at the expense of national reunification.[24] Once Ulbricht had successfully counter-attacked in July, however, the Herrnstadt –Zaisser faction was silenced, and with it the western lobby.

The KPD was caught on the horns of the national dilemma, trapped between the interests of East Berlin and Moscow. At best, reunification would mean a step up for itself, but a step down for the SED; at worst, it would mean the SED sinking to the KPD's own level of isolation in a united but anti-Communist Germany. As I have argued above, in some ways the KPD was more valuable to the SED as an heroic failure (or scapegoat) than as a moderate success. Given the Soviets' more obvious interest in a compromise solution, one might have expected them to lend

---

[22] LfV Hessen to BfV, 22 Mar. 1951, AdsD, *NL* Dux, Mappen KPD.
[23] At SED-ZK, 26–7 Oct. 1950, in Loth, *Stalins ungeliebtes Kind*, 173.
[24] Elke Scherstjanoi, ' "Wollen wir den Sozialismus?": Dokumente aus der Sitzung des Politbüros des ZK der SED am 6. Juni 1953', *BzG*, 33 (1991), 662 n. 21; Herrnstadt-Zaisser 'platform' [June 1953], in Wilfriede Otto, 'Dokumente zur Auseinandersetzung in der SED 1953', *BzG*, 32 (1990), 661–2.

the KPD greater moral support. Allegedly, some East German and Soviet leaders, such as Schirdewan and Suslov, did want the West German party to detach itself somewhat from its big brother. KPD leaders were occasionally observed visiting the SMAD's Propaganda and Information Department in Karlshorst more often than the SED's Central House of Unity, and sometimes without Ulbricht or Dahlem. Yet, in the end, the Soviets preferred to deal with the KPD through the West Commission, and it was to the SED that the KPD routinely answered.[25]

The KPD's role in the East's campaigns for German unity can tell us little about the intentions behind Moscow's offers. Instead, I wish to concentrate on the functional aspects of these initiatives. Even if Stalin's intentions were honourable, could the reunification efforts have been expected to work? Analagous with tactics for labour unity, the SED and KPD were expected to provide the plebiscitary pressure from below for reunification, while the Soviets negotiated for unity from above with the western Allies on the Allied Control Council and at the Councils of Foreign Ministers (CFMs). It would appear that during the Grotewohl Letter campaign and the exchange of Stalin Notes, Moscow was seeking in the first instance to reach wavering West German political élites in order to apply pressure on the Chancellor's office and the western Allies. Failing that, the West German Communists were to promote unity from below in a series of populist petitions, rallies, and single-interest groups, to create a critical mass of public opinion to force Adenauer's hand by 'exposing' him to the electorate. Yet the accompanying aggressive language was arguably counterproductive. The West German Communists may ultimately have helped to alienate not only the undecided political élites from Moscow's conciliatory gestures, but the general public as well, just as labour unity tactics had backfired with the Social Democrats.

National but not Nationalist: KPD Reunification Policy

As early as June 1945, the KPD leadership, in consultation with Stalin, had argued for an all-German KPD as the suture to hold together a dismembered Germany. Despite the now notorious phrase, recorded in Pieck's handwritten notes, 'There will be 2 Germanys—despite all unity of the Allies', the subsequent message was to 'secure unity through [a]

---

[25] Report, 11 Mar. 1949, in AdsD, Ostbüro 0346; Gerhard Wettig, 'Die KPD als Instrument der sowjetischen Deutschland-Politik', *Deutschland-Archiv*, 27 (1994), 818–19; Karl Schirdewan, *Aufstand gegen Ulbricht* (Berlin, 1994), 32.

unitary KPD, [a] unitary Central Committee, [a] unitary party of the working people'.[26] Indeed, as has already been seen in Chapter 2, although
efforts to form an all-German SED had failed, to all intents and purposes Berlin continued to function as the KPD's national political centre.
Before looking at the campaigns for national unity, it is worth examining the nature of the disunity confronting the KPD. The British and
Americans were committed to a policy of federalizing Germany, and
the French had more sweeping separatist aspirations for some western
areas. The KPD dismissed any schemes for what it saw as particularist
'Ländchen', advocating instead a centralized Reich with a decentralized
provincial administration. Thus in July 1946 the Ruhr party opposed the
formation of North Rhine-Westphalia as the thin end of the wedge 'to
the fragmentation of Germany into federal states'.[27] Predictably, the KPD
then condemned the Bizone, formed on 1 January 1947, and later the
Trizone. Similarly, the Communists objected to the federal principle when
invoked in the cause of European integration. As an early Euro-sceptic,
Gniffke opposed curbing Germany's sovereignty for the benefit of a 'European Union', a notion he claimed was sponsored by liberal democrats in
the interests of monopoly capitalists, creating a 200 million-strong federal
superstate to freeze out the two superpowers.[28]

Alongside its general rejection of federalism as crypto-partition, the
KPD turned its guns on separatist plans for the Ruhr and Saar. As early
as March 1946 Berlin had intimated that it did not wish the Ruhr to
revert to the control of monopoly capital, and claimed PCF support
on this issue. For that very reason the British Foreign Secretary, Ernest
Bevin, suggested that, should the worst come to the worst in the shape of
a central German government under Communist control, the Ruhr at least
could be excised from a future German state.[29] Proletarian internationalism from the PCF was, however, a mixed blessing. In 1945 Thorez had
supported internationalization of the Ruhr, which amounted to forming
a new state, and separation of the Rhineland.[30] On 6 February 1947, however, he told a four-man delegation from the Saar KPD 'that we, too, are
internationalists':

---

[26] Pieck/Ulbricht/Ackermann/Sobottka meeting in Moscow, 4 June 1945; see *Wilhelm Pieck*, 50.
[27] *WVE*, 19 July 1946, 1; see also *WVE*, 4 June 1946, 2; *WVE*, 18 June 1946, 1.
[28] OMGUS on Mannheim *Land* convention of 19–20 Apr. 1947, 30 Apr. 1947, in PA Staritz.
[29] Strang to FO, 6 Mar. 1946, in *Die Ruhrfrage 1945/46 und die Entstehung des Landes Nordrhein-Westfalen: Britische, französische und amerikanische Akten*, ed. Rolf Steininger (Düsseldorf, 1988), 540; Bevin to Committee on German Industry, 11 Mar. 1946, ibid. 545–60, here 558.
[30] F. Roy Willis, *The French in Germany 1945–1949* (Stanford, Calif., 1962), 36–7.

For this reason we are taking a step backwards and are no longer calling for the internationalization of the Ruhr. We desire an international occupation to control the Ruhr and give the anti-fascist, democratic forces the possibility of carrying out a successful democratization of the Ruhr basin.[31]

The nightmare scenario for the French and German Communists would, of course, have been a repeat of the 1923 Ruhr occupation with the two on opposing sides. The KPD had indeed made some noises about passive resistance and the Schlageter Course of 1923. Yet, when the Ruhr Statute instigating the International Authority of the Ruhr was announced, the 'national resistance' invoked remained verbal, attacking the IAR as a 'direct colonial exploitation zone' within a 'protectoral zone of American monopolists'.[32]

The KPD in the Saar was in a particularly isolated position, cut off from the rest of Germany in a formal French protectorate. In respect of trade union affairs, the Saar Communists were even technically subordinate to the CGT in Paris. They were, however, the *only* local party to oppose the Mouvement pour le Rattachement de la Sarre à la France. The Saar's anomalous situation did, nevertheless, produce centrifugal forces within even the KPD. In one bizarre incident, two delegations, one breakaway, one loyalist, went simultaneously to Paris to state their cases—upon their return the separatists were expelled by the party. Under such pressures, the majority loyalists had to tread carefully, developing imaginative arguments for a bridging role for the Saar, but ultimately even these were submerged under the general struggle against western integration.[33]

The KPD's Ruhr and Saar campaigns had been undermined from the outset by its ambivalent attitude to the Oder-Neisse border and the loss of the eastern territories. The SED had hidden behind arguments that a definitive settlement was the prerogative of the Potsdam signatories. For electoral consumption it thus talked in 1946 of a 'provisional border' and possible improvements, but by late 1947 was referring to the 'peace frontier', which was fixed by treaty three years later.[34] In the West, the KPD

[31] KPD-BL Saar to SED-PV, 19 Feb. 1947, SAPMO-BA, DY 30/IV 2/2.022/129.

[32] 'SVD'-BL Ruhr, 11 June 1948, ZI6, Sammlung Becker, Ordner 19/10. Schlageter had become a folk hero of the patriotic right when he blew up a railway bridge during the Ruhr occupation of 1923 and was subsequenty executed by the French; see *WVE*, 7 May 1946, 2.

[33] Frank Dingel, 'Die Kommunistische Partei Saar', in Richard Stöss, *Parteien-Handbuch* (Opladen, 1983), ii. 1852–79; Strasbourg Consulate to State Dept., 17 Nov. 1950, in *Confidential U.S. State Department Central Files: Germany—Federal Republic of Germany. Internal Affairs 1950–1954*, ed. Paul Kesaris (Frederick, Md., 1986), 29. 682–711; KPD-BL Saar to SED-PV, 19 Feb. 1947, SAPMO-BA, DY 30/IV 2/2.022/129.

[34] Frank Thomas Stößel, *Positionen und Strömungen in der KPD/SED 1945–1954* (Cologne, 1985), i. 241–6 and 317.

was particularly vulnerable to accusations by other parties of *de facto* support for the settlement. At one of the first public Communist meetings in Hamburg, Dettmann made a point of distancing himself from the loss of the eastern territories. In March 1947 Reimann formally announced that the KPD had agreed to differ with the Poles over the eastern border, which he found unacceptable. In private he also reportedly criticized Ackermann's recent statement disowning Germany east of the Oder-Neisse, since it 'was pulling KPD policy off its hinges'.[35]

Berlin was in fact prepared to make considerable tactical concessions, and on 10 March 1947 Pieck, Grotewohl, Dahlem, and Gniffke appeared on a rostrum in Frankfurt am Main before a backcloth of the Reich within the borders of 1937! Two days later, at a pro-merger rally in Munich, Pieck explicitly stated that the SED was against Oder-Neisse, but was forced to accept it as an Allied *fait accompli*, which at best could be revised by later negotiation, but not by chauvinist or nationalist protest. After the deadlock at the Moscow Council of Foreign Ministers soon afterwards, however, attitudes appear to have hardened. When the Ruhr leader, Ledwohn, requested more leeway for the KPD, he was reputedly carpeted by Pieck before the entire SED executive. Thereafter the eastern frontier was justified as anti-imperialist.[36] Nevertheless, as the following anguished plea from the Party Executive shows, the Oder-Neisse issue continued to generate only confusion in the KPD, and typifies the West German Communists' dilemma:

How can one reconcile Comrade Stalin saying, 'Follow a good national policy and help the Soviet Union', and on the other hand the Warsaw Conference declaration that any infringement of the Oder-Neisse border means war?[37]

The People's Congress Movement

1946 witnessed a familiar pattern emerge to the German Communist drive for national unity. Just as campaigns for proletarian unity, in the shape of the SED, had followed the rhythm of the Councils of Foreign Ministers, national moves were closely synchronized with Soviet diplomatic initiatives. Whenever a round of inter-Allied negotiations was looming, the German Communists were expected to orchestrate a chorus of national approval. In fact, national and labour unity were inextricably bound up

---

[35] Report on meeting of 16 Oct. 1945, PRO, FO 1014/547; *WVE*, 4 Mar. 1947, 1; report, 8 Mar. 1947, AdsD, Ostbüro 0346.
[36] Stößel, *Positionen und Strömungen*, i. 243; Munich Consulate to State Dept., 20 Mar. 1947, in *Confidential (1945–1949)*, 14. 842–5; Report, 11 Mar. 1949, AdsD, Ostbüro 0346.
[37] 6th KPD-PV, 6–7 Oct. 1948, SAPMO-BA, DY 30/IV 2/2.022/126.

with one another in Communist thinking. The creation of the SED in 1946, ahead of the Paris CFM, was thus justified by Stalin as the first step to unification, rather than as the first stage of division.[38]

Although the unstated purpose of the resultant unity party may have been to neutralize the eastern SPD, its public function was to provide the core of a future all-German administration. In this vein, on 20–2 June 1946, echoing Molotov at the Paris CFM, the SED executive called for the realization of the five all-German state secretariats promised at Potsdam. At the same time, in order to forestall western Allied criticism that the SED was still unrepresentative of the national will, the new party also proposed an all-party conference on unity. Analagous to domestic bloc tactics, the SED was keen to draw bourgeois parties, including those from the western zones, into an institutional dialogue. Later, prompted by Byrnes's September 1946 Stuttgart speech promising to keep US troops on German soil, Grotewohl went on to demand a referendum on national unity in all four zones. In the same month the SED published its basic rights of the German people and in November a draft constitution for a 'German Democratic Republic', with Grotewohl repeating the call for a referendum.[39] As with labour unity overtures, however, nothing came of the 1946 initiatives on national unity.

At a meeting in Moscow in January 1947 the pre-emptive nature of Communist unification proposals became more evident: if nothing were done, a creeping form of economic unification might occur under American auspices. Although the alternative of a separate East German government was discussed, it was seen as something to be avoided rather than aspired to, and firmly rejected.[40] Accordingly, on 14 February 1947, closely linked with the formation of the *Arbeitsgemeinschaft* SED-KPD and the forthcoming Moscow CFM, the SED executive produced a draft policy document on national strategy. Preventing unity were, in the first instance, monopoly capitalists and Junkers, followed by British and American finance capital fearful of German competition, and, lastly, the SPD leadership. The only consistent defender of national unity was the SED. A referendum (*Volksentscheid*) on a democratic united state—*not* a federation of states or a federal state—with a decentralized administration, so the draft argued, would appeal to the other bloc parties, but also to significant numbers of ex-NSDAP supporters from the countryside and

[38] Loth, *Stalins ungeliebtes Kind*, 53.

[39] Werner Müller, *Die KPD und die 'Einheit der Arbeiterklasse'* (Frankfurt am Main and New York, 1979), 277–8.

[40] Pieck's notes of Stalin meeting, 31 Jan. 1947, in *Wilhelm Pieck*, 111–14.

Mittelstand. In addition to the five departments of finance, transport, post, foreign trade, and industry, provided for by Potsdam, a further eight were to be added to a central administration, which would organize a referendum in conjunction with the Allied Control Council (ACC). (Privately, Grotewohl hoped for a majority in such a plebiscite of 30 out of 50 million Germans.[41]) Moreover, a western SED would be the political expression of the labour solidarity necessary for national unity and reconstruction, and would force the bourgeoisie into co-operation. The document was not published, but on 1 March the SED formally demanded a referendum.[42]

Unsurprisingly, nothing came of this initiative. It foundered on western Allied resistance at the Moscow CFM, but, in the run-up to the London CFM in November, SMAD and SED stepped up their efforts quite dramatically. The announcement of Marshall Aid and the Economic Council, as well as the refusal of the Munich minister-presidents' conference to discuss national unity—all falling in June 1947—appear to have prompted the SMAD to act. On 20 June it called for a high-profile campaign for German unity, which would lead to some form of referendum to put pressure on the Allied Control Council.[43] The chosen forum was the People's Congress (*Volkskongreß*).[44]

Accordingly, on 13 November 1947 the SED called on all democratic parties, trade unions, and mass organizations for a common stance on the forthcoming London CFM. When the western parties, and more significantly the eastern CDUD, declined, the SED was forced to appeal over their heads to the public. On 26 November the SED executive duly sent out invitations to an inaugural People's Congress for Unity and a Just Peace in Berlin. The eastern Liberal Democratic executive agreed under duress after resistance from the local parties; the CDUD refused point-blank, precipitating the removal of its leaders, Kaiser and Lemmer, by the SMAD.

The first Congress thus gathered inauspiciously on 6–7 December 1947 in the Berlin Admiralspalast. Despite partial bans by military government,

[41] Loth, *Stalins ungeliebtes Kind*, 81.
[42] 'Thesen über die Lage und die Aufgaben der SED', SAPMO-BA, DY 30/IV 2/1/8, fos. 97–105; *Dokumente der SED*, ed. PVIZK der SED (East Berlin, 1951) i. 162–7.
[43] Gerhard Wettig, 'All-German Unity and East German Separation in Soviet Policy, 1947–1949' (unpublished paper delivered at CWIHP conference, 28–30 June 1994), 11.
[44] Klaus Bender, *Deutschland, einig Vaterland?: Die Volkskongreßbewegung für deutsche Einheit und einen gerechten Frieden in der Deutschlandpolitik der Sozialistischen Einheitspartei Deutschlands* (Frankfurt am Main, 1992); Manfred Koch, 'Volkskongreßbewegung und Volksrat', in Martin Broszat and Hermann Weber (eds.), *SBZ-Handbuch* (Munich, 1989) 345–57.

462 of the 2,215 delegates were from the western zones, but only 242 officially from the KPD, although internal reports admitted that 80% of Ruhr emissaries were Communists. A resolution was carried, calling for a peace treaty, an all-German government, and German unity, but an intended seventeen-person delegation to the London CFM, including Reimann and Ficker for the KPD, never left Germany. The British government refused entry visas for what it regarded as a 'Communist stunt'.[45]

The Berlin Congress was intended to spark off a chain of regional congresses in the West. Indeed the idea had originated with the Lower Saxon KPD's Congress for Bread, Coal, Justice, and Peace, planned for November 1947, but transferred to Bremen in the US enclave after a British ban. The SBZ provided all the main speakers, including Nuschke and Grotewohl, but the congress itself, held on 17–18 January 1948, was boycotted by the major western parties. Despite its momentous claims, it was a discreet affair, banished to Bremen's Vegesack suburb after losing out to a rabbit show in a double-booking of the sports hall. Further substitute rallies in the British Zone were disbanded by the police, although a second local People's Congress was allegedly held in Rendsburg in Schleswig-Holstein on 13 March 1948, but, it seems, as a closed gathering.[46]

Nevertheless, at national level the unity campaign continued apace. The second Berlin People's Congress of 17–18 March 1948 was timed to celebrate the centenary of the 1848 revolution, with 512 of the 1,989 delegates (144 KPD) defying western military government restrictions to be there. Its final resolution repeated December's demands, adding calls for the expropriation of war criminals, land reform in the West, and the dissolution of the Economic Council. As planned, a 400-strong German People's Council was elected, with 100 anonymous western representatives scattered among its committees, including the propagandistically important Peace Committee.[47] Since the referendum which Grotewohl had desired since late 1946 was legally inadmissible, a petition (*Volksbegehren*) was to be organized to force the ACC to legislate the necessary machinery 'for the implementation of a referendum for a unitary German democratic republic with the rights of the *Länder* according to the principles of the

[45] *Wilhelm Pieck*, 192; ZB/AG SED-KPD, 11 Dec. 1947, SAPMO-BA, DY 30/IV 2.10.01/5; FO to Robertson, 11 Dec. 1947, PRO, FO 1049/916.

[46] The 1,037 Bremen delegates included: 306 KPD, 32 SED, 48 SPD, 332 non-party, 107 Ind., and only 5 CDU, 3 LDP, 3 FDP, and 1 *Zentrum*; see *WVE*, 20 Jan. 1948, 1; Bremen Consulate to Garran, 21 Jan. 1948, PRO, FO 1049/1206; Klein, *Antifaschistische Demokratie*, 74 and 78.

[47] Koch, 'Volkskongreßbewegung', 351; Klein, *Antifaschistische Demokratie*, 80.

Weimar constitution'.[48] In June 1948 12.9 million signatures in favour were recorded in the SBZ and Berlin, but fewer than a million and a quarter in the British Zone.[49] (The petition was prohibited in the US and French Zones.)

The failure of the People's Congress signalled the end of the phase of national unity from above, predicated upon a serious hope of agreement between the wartime Allies. The London CFM had ignored the first congress and broken up in disarray; within two days of the second congress the Soviets had walked out of the Allied Control Council. Endeavours for national unity were entering a critical phase by mid-1948, demonstrably impotent against the unilateral steps towards division by the London six-power conferences, and seemingly redundant after the onset of the Berlin Blockade. Behind closed doors SED leaders were already pressing to cut their losses and take reciprocal separatist action.[50] On 30 June Grotewohl was possibly acting under duress when he described the division of Germany as complete, denying a bridging function for the SBZ between East and West, and publicly calling for people's democratization and an orientation 'unambiguously and without reservation towards the East'.[51] The crucial retarding factor, perhaps unsurprisingly, proved to be Moscow. In May–June 1948 the SMAD did indeed discuss the anticipated integration of the SBZ into the eastern bloc, but on 26 June refused to give the green light for a separate East German state.[52]

Again, a clear decision between eastern integration and reunification had been agonizingly deferred. At the same time, a new anomalous factor was added to the national paradox. The Cominform had just launched its offensive against 'national deviationism' in Yugoslavia. How are we to explain the decision to continue at all with German campaigns for national unity? Zhdanov's 'two camp' theory sounded for all the world like the acceptance of division. Yet as Reimann argued, 'the cut does not

[48] BAK, B 118/3, fo. 3.
[49] NRW 830,000; Hamburg 100,000; Lower Saxony 200,000; Schles.-Hol. 100,000: Pieck's notes, 28 June 1948, SAPMO-BA, NY 4036/643. 100,000 were supposed to have signed in Hessen; see Klein, *Antifaschistische Demokratie*, 86. Noble/Schmidt meeting, 28 Apr. 1948, BAK, B 118/3; Daniel E. Rogers, *Politics after Hitler: The Western Allies and the German Party System* (Basingstoke, 1995), 95–6.
[50] Oelßner and Dahlem at 10th (24th) SED-PV, 12 May 1948; see Dietrich Staritz, 'Die SED, Stalin und der "Aufbau des Sozialismus" in der DDR', *Deutschland-Archiv*, 24 (1991), 690–1.
[51] *Parteiensystem zwischen Demokratie und Volksdemokratie*, ed. Hermann Weber (Cologne, 1982), 96–7; Loth, *Stalins ungeliebtes Kind*, 138–9.
[52] Dietrich Staritz, 'Zur Gründung der DDR', in id., *Was War: Historische Studien zu Geschichte und Politik der DDR* (Berlin, 1994), 5.

go, as the USA imperialists and their reactionary allies in the various countries desire, through Germany, but runs, as Comrade Zhdanov correctly said, across the whole capitalist world'.[53] Nor should it be forgotten that, according to the Cominform's original declaration, 'Communists will form the spearhead of the resistance against plans for imperialist expansion in the political, economic, and ideological fields, and rally all the democratic and patriotic forces of the nations to which they belong.'[54]

The National Front

As I have already suggested, the connotations of national unity became ever more negative and anti-American—a political guerrilla campaign to disrupt the economic and military integration of the Federal Republic into the western bloc. The main aim was to delegitimize the FRG, or, as the SED later explained national strategy to Moscow: 'The western government is to be unmasked as the organ of the western powers.'[55] There is also considerable evidence that Stalin was a crucial factor in holding the SED to the struggle for peace and unity.[56] Thus, in June 1948, at the same time as the decision to postpone a separate East German state, as well as the Cominform offensive, Semyonov requested the SED leadership to draft a manifesto for a 'National Front' to intensify the 'national liberation struggle'. Since he was concerned that it be accessible to former Nazis and *Wehrmacht* members too, one important function of such an organization must have been to integrate a potential internal opposition inside the GDR.[57]

Yet the project hung fire for the duration of the Berlin Blockade. The reasons why are not fully clear. The renunciation of the 'special German road' in September and discussions with Moscow on a separate East Germany in November–December seemed to make the 'people's democratization' of the SBZ more likely and national reunification more remote. Yet again Moscow appears to have applied the brakes. In December 1948 the Kremlin required the SED to lend the KPD additional aid in the 'reinforcement of the struggle for the unity of Germany and against the colonization of West Germany', and the SBZ was explicitly designated to be 'not a people's democratic order'.[58]

[53] Reimann, 2nd KPD-PV, 3–4 June 1948, SAPMO-BA, I 10/301/1.
[54] Julius Braunthal, *History of the International* (London, 1980), iii. 550.
[55] SED-ZS to Stalin, 19 Sept. 1949, in *Wilhelm Pieck*, 296.
[56] Loth, *Stalins ungeliebtes Kind*, 142–8.   [57] 10 June 1948, in *Wilhelm Pieck*, 233.
[58] Thomas Friedrich, 'Antworten der SED-Führing auf Fragen Stalins 1948', *BzG*, 33 (1991), 367 and 373.

Furthermore, on 6 May 1949 Semyonov revived the request for a National Front (NF), adding that Stalin desired it to be taken a step beyond the People's Congresses. Once again, it would appear that the timetable had been determined by Soviet diplomatic needs and the forthcoming Paris CFM. Ulbricht duly raised the call in mid-May, prior to the third and final People's Congress in Berlin on 29–30 May.[59] At the next SED executive in July an NF was officially instituted, with Dahlem making analogies to the French resistance's concessions to the Gaullists and the 1943 National Committee for a Free Germany in Moscow, as well as hopelessly misguided prognostications on refugee support:

I see no danger in working together with those circles which are still standing on the sidelines. The danger for the national movement is if the working class does not seize the leadership, since a national movement is arising in Germany. It will drift into nationalist and chauvinist waters if the working class does not get it firmly in its grasp.[60]

Although the NF had less significance for the SBZ until the founding of the GDR, when it became the framework for its notorious single-list election system, in the West it formed the KPD's platform in the first *Bundestag* election. Indeed, its whole campaign was turned into a plebiscite on national unity. Already, at the campaign launch during the Solingen Conference of 5–6 March 1949, Reimann had talked of the burgeoning West German administration as a colonial 'marionette government', part of a 'twin yoke of exploitation by German and foreign monopoly capital', sustained by a 'crust' of German collaborators including the CDU, SPD, and trade unions. West Germany was being turned into an 'arsenal of Anglo-American imperialism against the East' and an 'operational base in a new world war', using 'the German people as cannon fodder'. The KPD, on the other hand, counted itself as part of a worldwide national liberation struggle, following the example of the Chinese, but at the head of a '*Sammlung* of all good Germans'.[61] In a subsequent analysis Fisch explained who the 'natives' were to be in this anti-colonial 'national front':

with the exception of a paper-thin upper crust of German junior partners of foreign monopoly capital, all strata of our people, workers and peasants, *Mittelstand* and small industry, as well as the intelligentsia.[62]

---

[59] Dietrich Staritz, 'The SED, Stalin, and the German Question: Interests and Decision-Making in the Light of New Sources', *German History*, 10 (1992), 283–4; Pieck's notes of meeting with Semyonov, 19 July 1949, in *Wilhelm Pieck*, 287–90.

[60] 20th (34th) SED-PV, 21 July 1949, SAPMO-BA, DY 30/IV 2/1/34.

[61] 'Entschließung der Solinger Delegiertenkonferenz der KPD', in *KPD 1945–1968: Dokumente*, ed. Günter Judick et al. (Neuss, 1989), i. 266–84.

[62] Quoted in Staritz, 'Kommunistische Partei Deutschlands', 1704–5.

Less clear was the fact that the NF was also angling for capitalists, former officers, and even nominal ex-Nazis. When it was unveiled in mid-June to local Bavarian Communists by their chairman, Hermann Schirmer, he tried to play it down as a tactical manœuvre, conscious of the resistance from *Altkommunisten* in outlying rural districts. One member of the Munich secretariat, Karl Feuerer, refused point-blank, unable to stomach electoral pacts with ex-Nazis. Party members with strong Soviet links and those incarcerated during the Third Reich were reportedly most hostile to the national line. Yet the party was under strict orders to desist from disruptive or violent *Bundestag* electioneering for fear of alienating 'bourgeois elements'.[63]

This blurring of anti-fascist politics later reached schizophrenic heights, when the KPD was attacking the FRG as neo-fascist while attempting to recruit ex-Nazi *Mitläufer*. The culmination of years of attacks on recrudescent imperialism was the theory of West Germany's 're-fascistization'. In 1951 Reimann even spoke of Bonn's move 'to the use of fascist government methods' and of the 'modern Görings and Heydrichs, the *Reichstag* fire-raisers of today'.[64] Yet, in Lower Saxony's May 1951 *Landtag* election, the neo-Nazi Socialist Reich Party (SRP) won over six times as many votes as the KPD and could no longer be ignored. By the autumn the British believed there had indeed been isolated 'non-aggression pacts' between the KPD and SRP, and that the neo-Nazis were receiving some money from the Communists. There was also limited KPD–SRP co-operation (and competition) in unemployment committees, as well as sporadic cases of 'born-again' Hitler Youths seeing the Communist light, although, on the whole, contact seems to have been slight.[65]

Somewhat later, but only marginally more successfully, the Communists tried to forge a front with the 'national neutralists', those conservatives who espoused an independent third way between the superpowers. Out of a Working Circle for German Understanding and a whole raft of associated peace organizations, on 29 June 1952, in Dortmund, there emerged the Deutsche Sammlung under the auspices of one-time Reich Chancellor Josef Wirth, of Rapallo fame, and Wilhelm Elfes, ex-*Oberbürgermeister* of Mönchengladbach. The Deutsche Sammlung was initially circumspect about association with the USSR and GDR, but in late 1952 Wirth

---

[63] Munich Consulate to State Dept., 26 July 1949, in *Confidential (1945–1949)*, 15. 169–72; POLAD to State Dept., 16 Aug. 1948, in *Confidential (1945–1949)*, 40. 177–83; ID/EUCOM, 5 Aug. 1949, in *Confidential (1945–1949)*, 40. 546–9.
[64] 2nd KPD-PV, 9 Nov. 1951, quoted by Staritz, 'Kommunistische Partei Deutschlands', 1722; Klein, *Antifaschistische Demokratie*, 114–15.
[65] Young minute, 3 Sept. 1951, PRO, FO 371/93361.

and Elfes were seen increasingly often in East Berlin. During the second *Bundestag* campaign, the movement spawned a party, the League of Germans for Unity, Peace, and Freedom (Bund der Deutschen für Einheit, Frieden und Freiheit—BdD) on 10 May 1953. This was soon making overtures towards Heinemann's Gesamtdeutsche Volkspartei (GVP), which represented disaffected Christian Democrats unhappy with Adenauer's rearmament policy, as well as towards the vestigial *Zentrum*, Föderalistische Union, and the KPD. The BdD ultimately concluded an electoral pact with the GVP in July, whereby it fielded no candidates of its own and, at GVP insistence, Communist members of its executive were forced to step down. Unable to rid itself of accusations of pro-Communism, however, the GVP–BdD list won only 1.2% of the 1953 *Bundestag* vote, although overall the BdD was far from simply a KPD front.[66]

The internal controversy over pacts with the patriotic and even neo-Nazi right had proved rather academic. Unless the KPD could demonstrate its independent credentials, it stood almost no chance of a true *Sammlung* of a nationalist protest vote. Although the SED and KPD had publicly severed their links in January 1949 in deference to the 'special conditions' in western Germany, the precarious position of the KPD was repeatedly undermined by inept reminders that it owed its ultimate allegiance to the Soviet Union. This was typified by a telegram sent by the SED to the 1949 Solingen Conference, in which, in line with the French, Italian, and British parties, the KPD was urged 'in the event of aggression . . . to fight against the aggressors and support the Soviet army to bring about peace'.[67] Hardly a reassuring statement while the Berlin Blockade continued! Some members of the KPD's Secretariat, particularly Müller and Nuding, would have preferred to ignore the telegram altogether, but Müller eventually took it upon himself to read it out with the rather feeble qualification that the KPD could not be held responsible for the views of other parties.[68]

As another example of psychological ineptitude, in July 1950, a month after the outbreak of the Korean War, Grotewohl introduced the slogan of 'national resistance':

The National Front is entering a new phase of its struggle; if it was the period of simple national protest at the beginning, this became national self-help in the second period, only to rise up today in the third phase as national resistance in

---

[66] Klein, *Antifaschistische Demokratie*, 188–200.   [67] *Dokumente der SED*, ii. 221–3.
[68] *FV*, 1 Mar. 1951 (Thesis 52), 3 and 7–10.

the face of the policy of division, colonization, and war by Anglo-American imperialism and its German lackeys.[69]

The eastern 'peace camp' would eventually prevail but was not to become pacifist nor neutralist, mobilizing instead against the 'feudal rule of the High Commissars' and for the 'disempowering of . . . the finance hyenas and Junkers and the scattering of their political lackeys, the Heusses, Adenauers, Schumachers, Reuters and Co.'. Pieck also admonished KPD delegates to 'shout less and work more among the masses', conceding that many SED members were forgetting their all-German obligations and restricting their horizons to the GDR. The Convention's resolution in fact combined a curious mixture of defiance and despondence:

The apparent consent of the West German population to occupation policy, achieved by means of trickery and terror, can easily deceive as to the true mood of the masses. Beneath the surface glow the embers of growing national resistance.[70]

In fact, the National Front was being organized to death, as an institution to legitimate the new East German state, rather than as a focus of popular will. The KPD, too, was safely worked into the national edifice. In the summer of 1950 a third of seats were reserved for West Germans on the NF's recently formed National Council. In June 1950 a special commission was also at work co-ordinating the West Commission, the KPD Secretariat in Frankfurt, and the National Council's western department, whose instructors were to consolidate the western NF with reference to particular target groups. On 25–6 August 1950 around 1,000 West Germans appeared at the first NF National Congress in Berlin, after which a West German Working Committee was founded. Walter Vesper in particular, seconded from his duties as a *Bundestag* deputy, co-ordinated the western departments of the GDR bloc parties in a bid to win over commercial and intellectual fellow travellers in the West. Yet, if the public opinion surveys discussed below are anything to go by, by trying to be all things to all Germans, the National Front probably ended by attracting almost nobody.[71]

---

[69] *Protokoll der Verhandlungen des III. Parteitages der Sozialistischen Einheitspartei Deutschlands 20. bis 24. Juli 1950 in der Werner-Seelenbinder-Halle zu Berlin* (East Berlin, 1951), i. 211–12; also i. 46–7; ii. 240.

[70] Ibid., ii. 238.

[71] Siegfried Suckut, 'Die Entscheidung zur Gründung der DDR', *VfZ*, 39 (1991), 143; 54th Westkomm., 7 June 1950, SAPMO-BA, NY 4182/867; Klein, *Antifaschistische Demokratie*, 98–9; William A. Douglas, 'The KPD against Rearmament', Ph.D. thesis 59.

Grotewohl Letters and Stalin Notes

Interest in subsequent Communist unification initiatives has long become fixated with the Stalin Notes of March and April 1952. There were, however, earlier diplomatic forays by the East German government, which deserve some mention. On 30 November 1950, prompted by Moscow and the Prague ministers' conference of the previous month, Grotewohl wrote to Adenauer suggesting an All-German Constituent Council with equal representation from East and West to negotiate on a central government. In late January 1951 he added the prospect of all-German elections, but without the United Nations observers demanded by the West, under the slogan 'Germans around One Table!'. Nevertheless, Bonn continued to insist on its formula of free elections first, negotiations second. Grotewohl's initial thrust appears to have been genuinely directed at Adenauer, with the KPD little in evidence.[72] When the Chancellor showed only lukewarm interest, however, the western Communists were then called upon to launch a wrecking campaign to expose the Bonn leadership. This, at least, is how I understand the 57 KPD Theses presented with great pomp at the Munich Convention of March 1951, which gave great prominence to the Grotewohl Letters.

According to the theses, a 'popular movement' was to be unleashed by the NF. Thousands of propaganda groups were to mobilize patriotic support, agitating among various social groups in West Germany for the resignation of Adenauer and his 'marionette government', which was portrayed as the antithesis of Grotewohl's Constituent Council (Theses 21 and 23). The theses also called for a peace treaty and the withdrawal of occupation troops, directing members 'to work in all other—even reactionary—organizations, if these include masses of workers, peasants and intellectuals' (34). Thesis 42 hoped to involve the patriotic bourgeoisie, symbolized by Gerecke, Heinemann, and Niemöller, in the 'national liberation struggle'. Thesis 43 explicitly angled for patriotic nominal ex-Nazis and *Wehrmacht* officers, even redefining a war criminal as one who 'actively participates in the preparation and execution of the remilitarization of West Germany and its inclusion in preparations for a new war', independent of any previous wartime record. The GDR was to be popularized, although its achievements could not be 'schematically'

---

[72] Meiners, *Doppelte Deutschlandpolitik*, 187; Michael Lemke, 'Eine deutsche Chance?', (unpublished paper delivered at CWIHP conference, 28–30 June 1994), 9–12.

applied to the FRG (46), and the peace-loving Soviet Union was to be defended against anti-Communist propaganda (47).[73] The high point of Soviet diplomatic initiatives, however, came with the Stalin Note of 10 March 1952. As is well known, it proposed a neutral, united Germany in the borders of 1945 with its own defence forces, and a peace treaty followed by free elections. Controversy has raged ever since as to the sincerity of the offer, coinciding as it did suspiciously closely with the final negotiations for the European Defence Community treaty. Rolf Steininger has argued on the basis of British and American documents that Adenauer's behaviour in ignoring the initiative was a 'wasted chance'.[74] The western Allies were somewhat keener to test the offer, but ultimately refused to delay German EDC membership, thus effectively killing off the proposals with the signing of the treaty on 27 May. (The scheme was, of course, never ratified by the French.) New evidence from Soviet archives has nevertheless placed the Steininger thesis in considerable doubt.[75] The SED only learned of the contents of the first Stalin Note a day in advance, but did not seem unduly perturbed. In a meeting with Pieck, Grotewohl, and Ulbricht on 1 April, Stalin did not even discuss the March Note, concentrating instead on arming the GDR as a bulwark against the West. Six days later he was predicting a negative response to his second note.[76]

More about Moscow's thinking on the KPD's role during the 'battle of the notes' is now known. On 18 February 1952 Bakulin, head of the Department of All-German Affairs at the Soviet Control Commission, which had replaced the SMAD in October 1949, issued guidelines to Semyonov for use with the KPD. It was to play on West Germans' desire for a peace treaty, as a prelude to a 'unitary, independent and democratic' state on the basis of Potsdam, conditional upon the dissolution of all treaties with the West and the withdrawal of occupation troops. The aim was 'to attack the Bonn government and the Bonn parliament with such a quantity of resolutions and demands that both parliament and government

---

[73] *FV*, 1 Mar. 1951, 3 and 7–10. The theses on remilitarization and unions are dealt with separately.

[74] Rolf Steininger, *The German Question* (New York, 1990).

[75] Gerhard Wettig, 'Die Deutschland-Note vom 10. März 1952 auf der Basis der diplomatischen Akten des russischen Außenministeriums', *Deutschland-Archiv*, 26 (1993), 786–805.

[76] Staritz, ' "Aufbau des Sozialismus" ', 694; see also Pieck's notes for Stalin meeting, 25 Mar. 1952, in Wilfriede Otto, 'Sowjetische Deutschlandnote 1952. Stalin und die DDR: Bisher unveröffentlichte handschriftliche Notizen Wilhelm Piecks', *BzG*, 33 (1991), 382.

experience strong pressure from the people'. The KPD would launch a campaign against national service in West Germany, lodging an appeal with the *Bundesverfassungsgericht* and writing to leftist politicians abroad and maverick bourgeois politicians in the FRG, including Martin Niemöller, Gustav Heinemann, and Helene Wessel. The SPD leadership was to receive an open letter, in conjunction with approaches to grass-roots Social Democrats, in support of the recent appeal from the *Volkskammer* to the *Bundestag*. Following the note itself, the KPD was to unleash mass demonstrations and protest strikes[77] against the envisaged General Treaty (which stipulated the Allies' reserved rights after the almost complete restoration of sovereignty to the FRG). Yet, when reporting back to the Soviets a few days later, Fritz Rische of the KPD leadership had to admit that the East German government's *Volkskammer* initiative was still largely unknown in West Germany. Characteristically, on 15 March Pushkin, head of the Soviet Diplomatic Mission in East Berlin, reported to Moscow that ideological and organizational weaknesses had prevented the KPD from 'winning the sympathies of the masses'.[78] Just as defeat in the 1949 *Bundestag* election was misdiagnosed as an internal failure of ideology and discipline, the KPD again became the scapegoat for the overambitiousness of its superiors.

The Programme for the National Reunification of Germany

After this renewed failure, the KPD's national line experienced an aggressive turn, intelligible only in connection with the concurrent radicalization of domestic policy in the GDR. Ulbricht had long since desired to make the final push to people's democratization, but had been checked by Soviet gradualism. Moscow appears to have relented, however, after Adenauer's signing of the EDC and the failure of the Stalin Notes. On 2 July 1952 the SED leadership requested permission from Stalin for formal people's democracy status for the GDR, which was finally granted by the CPSU Politburo on 8 July, one day before the second SED Party Conference which announced the 'Building of Socialism'.[79] Such official blessing for the consolidation of the GDR spelled doom for any realistic national policy, and not surprisingly many western Communists felt 'written off'.[80] Herrnstadt certainly interpreted the 'Building of Socialism' in this light:

---

[77] An SED 'Ruf an die Nation' of 16 Apr. 1952 did call for strikes; see *Dokumente der SED*, iv. 22–7.
[78] Wettig, 'KPD als Instrument', 822–8.
[79] Staritz, ' "Aufbau des Sozialismus" ', 698–9.
[80] A KPD propagandist in Aug. 1952, quoted by Klein, *Antifaschistische Demokratie*, 177.

Moscow's 'agreement to this solution means at the same time . . . an extremely negative judgement on the work of the KPD and SED with regard to the decisive question, the German question'.[81] Furthermore, the conference appeared to be burning its West German boats by its incitement to what amounted to treason:

The national liberation struggle against the American, English and French occupiers in West Germany, and for the overthrow of their vassal government in Bonn, is the task of all peace-loving and patriotic forces in Germany.[82]

Following this lead, in September the KPD Executive dutifully resolved to devise a 'national liberation programme' to rally patriotic Germans, regardless of their political or social standpoint, culminating on 2 November 1952 in the Programme for the National Reunification of Germany. (It had in fact been masterminded by the SED Politburo in Berlin.[83]) It represents KPD national hyperbole at its melodramatic peak, farthest detached from political reality. According to the Programme, West Germany was in a state of Allied 'slavery', suffering 10 billion DM of annual occupation and rearmament costs to finance the West's bid for world domination and an offensive war against the eastern bloc, functioning as America's 'drill square' in the EDC. Large sections of the population were below the breadline, and farmers' land was being ruined by military manœuvres. The authors became almost Spenglerian in their condemnation of American imperialism as the killer of German 'national culture', replacing it with its own 'superficial and primitive "culture" '. The clichés did not end there: 'German women and girls count as fair game for the occupiers.'

The real target of the Programme was the Adenauer government, a front for revanchist 'monopoly bosses and estate owners' supported by rightist SPD leaders—a 'regime of national treason'—signing away Germany's coal and steel under the Schuman Plan and gambling away the Saar. European integration was thus undermining German sovereignty. Adenauer himself was an interchangeable figurehead, resorting to terroristic methods to hold down the West German population, prior to a military dictatorship: 'That is why the Adenauer regime must be overthrown, and a free, unitary, democratic, and peace-loving Germany created on the rubble of this regime.' Another gift for government lawyers

---

[81] At SED-PB, 6 June 1953; see Loth, *Stalins ungeliebtes Kind*, 191.

[82] *Protokoll der Verhandlungen der II. Parteikonferenz der Sozialistischen Einheitspartei Deutschlands 9. bis 12. Juli 1952* (East Berlin, 1952), 490.

[83] Kluth, *KPD in der Bundesrepublik*, 42; SED-PB, 10 June 1952, in Staritz, ' "Aufbau des Sozialismus" ', 697; see also *Wilhelm Pieck*, 407.

working on the case pending before the *Bundesverfassungsgericht* were the words: 'Undoubtedly our struggle will demand sacrifices. But for every patriot who falls or is torn from the struggle, thousands of others will arise.' The patriotic forces, with the working class and farmers in the van, leading the bourgeoisie and intelligentsia, would form up in the National Front and create a bilateral commission (a precursor to a 'Government of National Reunification'). This would discuss all–German elections to a National Assembly, a peace treaty, and the withdrawal of occupation troops, ensuring no military bases on German soil, but permitting an independent German force, in accordance with Stalin's March Note.[84]

The Programme had a clear antecedent in the 'Programmatic Declaration on the National and Social Liberation of the German People' of 24 August 1930, when the Weimar Communists had attempted to steal some of the Nazis' thunder. In fact, it was the first KPD programme since then. Yet, unlike its predecessor, the 1952 document was not competing with anything like the same degree of organized revisionist nationalism. It was clearly an embarrassment to many KPD functionaries, who did not take the trouble to verse themselves in its demands. Ledwohn recollects 'considerable doubts about the reality or usefulness' of the more extreme language, but that Reimann browbeat the Programme Commission into acceptance by invoking the will of Stalin.[85]

This may just have been bluff. At any rate, the Soviet Control Commission also appears to have had serious reservations about the Programme, although it is difficult to believe that such an important document could have been published without its approval. As has been seen above, however, with the advent of a new leadership in Moscow after Stalin's death in 1953, more realism crept back into SED–KPD national tactics. The Beria interlude and the New Course appeared to place the star of unity back in the ascendant, only for it to fall rapidly back into obscurity. In March 1954 Ulbricht returned to the 'road to socialism' and the Soviet Union granted the GDR sovereignty. At once the SED adopted a more conciliatory tone towards Bonn, in a bid to elicit diplomatic recognition. The KPD thereafter echoed a negotiated approach through all-German economic and cultural commissions, implicitly shelving all hopes of altering the FRG from within. The final nail in the coffin of national unity in this period came with the breakdown of four-power talks in Geneva in

---

[84] *KPD 1945–1968*, i. 396–415.

[85] Josef Ledwohn, 'Nichts in der Geschichte ist wichtiger als Tatsachen: Erkenntnisse aus dem Neubeginn 1945/1946', in Marx-Engels-Stiftung (ed.), *Zum deutschen Neuanfang 1945–1949: Tatsachen—Probleme—Ergebnisse—Irrwege* (Bonn, 1993), 133.

July 1955. Immediately afterwards, Khrushchev publicly elaborated his 'two-state theory', whereby the socio-economic achievements of the GDR were not to be sacrificed for the sake of national unification.[86] In the final analysis, the KPD was unable to convince very many non-Communists at all that it was a credible exponent of nationalist ideas, shooting itself in the foot with its concurrent championing of the USSR and GDR. Opinion polls indicate public apathy and even hostility. When quizzed on the People's Congresses, only 51% of those in Darmstadt had ever heard of them, but 87% said they would not sign any petition which they knew came from a Communist organization. When asked in September 1949 which was more important, reunification or checking the spread of Communism, only 25% in the US Zone chose the former, while 71% elected anti-Communism. The public was more open to the Grotewohl Letter, with 67% wishing Adenauer to respond, but this receptivity was tempered by the fact that over three-quarters rejected unification under Communism. As to the Stalin Notes, 67% of West German respondents felt they were only propaganda, and 62% were content to see them rejected.[87] This is not to say that the decision between western integration and reunification was not a highly complex one, with many intermediary stations. Reunification continued to figure as the West Germans' prime concern for years to come. Yet the fears generated by the Korean War and the emotional attachment to the eastern territories were always going to count against the KPD.

A substantial number of the party's own members also remained sceptical. Nationalism and class conflict were ultimately irreconcilable. Attempts to appropriate the romantic language of the revolutionary independence struggles of China, Vietnam, and other post-colonial developing countries, jarred with memories of Hitler's expansionist, racial hyper-nationalism. The mystification of the party by identifying it with the 'Volk'—as evidenced in the following passage—did not ring true:

Our party is boldly and courageously carrying ahead of our *Volk* the banner of national sovereignty and independence which the German big capitalists are trampling under their feet. . . . Our party embodies everything noble and good,

[86] Alexei Filitov, 'The Soviet Policy and Early Years of Two German States, 1949–1961' (unpublished paper delivered at CWIHP conference, 28–30 June 1994), 19.

[87] OMGUS Report No. 123, 23 May 1948, in Anna J. Merritt and Richard L. Merritt (eds.), *Public Opinion in Occupied Germany: The OMGUS Surveys, 1945–1949* (Urbana, Ill., 1970), 241; HICOG Report No. 1, 30 Dec. 1949; HICOG Report No. 55, 28 Dec. 1950; HICOG Report No. 137, 21 May 1952, all in Anna J. Merritt and Richard L. Merritt (eds.), *Public Opinion in Semisovereign Germany: The HICOG Surveys, 1949–1955* (Urbana, Ill., 1980), 53–5, 98–9 and 167–8.

everything progressive and revolutionary in our nation. The party is the future, the conscience, and honour of our *Volk*.[88]

At the risk of repetition, the brand of nationalism being championed by the KPD was not so much Germanocentric, as *anti*-American and *pro*-Soviet. National reunification had soon become a very obvious Cold War football, used by the East to discredit the western Allies, but also as a convenient rearguard cover for its own separatist moves. The Communists had also overestimated the non-Communists' national conscience. For instance, dangling a patriotic carrot in front of western Social Democrats unsusceptible to the stick of a forced merger, in the belief that the SPD would sacrifice party independence for national unity, was a gross miscalculation. Schumacher's slogan for the party, 'Freedom not Unity!', soon became the justification for splitting not just the labour movement, but Germany itself. Similarly, if East Berlin thought it was forestalling the resurgence of revanchist nationalism in the CDU/ CSU, of the order of the inter-war years, it was punching into space. Although many conservatives may have shared hopes of long-term reunification, they rejected a short-term solution in which East Berlin could dictate *any* of the terms. What the Americans said of the 1952 Programme is probably true of the KPD's national line generally—for most West Germans the KPD was not part of the solution, but part of the problem:

Non-Communists in Western Germany are becoming increasingly immune to 'all-German' blandishments identifiable as Communist ventures. The more openly the call comes from the SED or the Communist Party, the more it seems doomed from the very outset, and since the current project has now received the most official SED/KPD blessing, it has probably received the kiss of death unless, of course, Moscow should follow it up with more serious and ostensibly sincere offers.[89]

Peace without Pacifism: The KPD against Remilitarization

As will already have become clear, the Communist concept of neutrality was inextricably entwined with that of national unity, as part of a two-pronged strategy. If a separate West German state could not be prevented, at least a rearmed West Germany could; and if West Germans valued reunification sufficiently, they might be prepared to sacrifice a western alliance to achieve it. The potential for pacifism after Germany's most

---

[88] *FV*, 30 Dec. 1953, 1.
[89] HICOG to State Dept., 2 Dec. 1952, in *Confidential (1950–1954)*, 29. 314–25.

catastrophic war seemed high, but, as with reunification, disarmament was a complex issue. The West German peace movement in the early 1950s covered a much broader spectrum than simply Communists, and included Social Democrats, trade union youth associations, as well as ex-*Wehrmacht* members opposed to rearmament, embraced from late 1950 by the Ohne mich! or Count Me Out! movement. Early opinion polls showed a clear majority against German rearmament. In December 1949 opponents of a revived military outweighed supporters by 62% to 26%, leaving a few waverers. Yet, by the time of the Korean War support was much more evenly divided: 45% to 43%. Moreover, the issue was more differentiated than a simple yes or no: 63% were prepared to countenance a German army if it were tied to a western European alliance, which was in itself a reflection of the fear of Soviet expansionism.[90]

Moreover, the KPD was swimming against the tide in claiming that America, not Russia, was the real threat. The party could nevertheless always comfort itself that it had played the role of Cassandra once before, in the 1930s, when its early warnings about Hitler's ambitions had gone unheeded, before seeing them horrifically borne out. The longer the much-prophesied American offensive failed to materialize, however, the more the party seemed to be crying wolf. Much of its peace propaganda was also psychologically inept, stressing the invulnerability of the Soviet Union once it had exploded its own atom bomb in August 1949. To most observers, however, if KPD pacifism were limited to attacks on remilitarization in the West alone, but remained silent on the creation in East Germany of institutions such as the Barracked People's Police, and later the National People's Army, it was patently guilty of hypocrisy.

For reasons of space, I shall consider KPD peace-campaigning under the Federal Republic only. The party received two important pacifist impeti in late 1949. In November the Cominform launched its so-called 'peace offensive', to be fought with the weapons of committees, petitions, protests, and opinion polls. The following month Adenauer also let it be known that under certain circumstances he would favour a West German defence contingent in a western alliance. This, in conjunction with ambivalent statements in the *Bundestag* on the 'liberation' of the East, provided ammunition for such East German headlines as: 'Adenauer demands war against East—Rearmament and fascist restoration.'[91] The outbreak of the Korean War in June 1950 further raised the temperature

---

[90] HICOG Report No. 36, 15 Sept. 1950, in Merritt and Merritt, *HICOG Surveys*, 82–3.
[91] See *Neues Deutschland*, 10 May 1950, in Meiners, *Doppelte Deutschlandpolitik*, 215–17.

in Germany, but although the threat of a ground war seemed closer, by analogy, the Communists and not the Americans appeared the likely aggressors. Precipitated by Korea, there also emerged, in the guise of the French Pleven Plan of October 1950, a much-contested scheme for a European Defence Community with German membership. This was to become one of the chief targets of KPD peace propaganda over the next four years.

Given the hostile political environment in the FRG, the KPD increasingly turned to less immediately recognizable Communist initiatives, retreating instead behind a battery of auxiliary bodies and single-issue lobby groups. Its peace drive was no exception. The West Commission thus set about expanding westwards the activities of the GDR's German Committee of Peace Fighters, under the auspices of Hans Fladung, leader of the western branch of the Cultural League. It was to collaborate with the existing Hatzfeld Peace Committee, to which the KPD was to attach its own office and staff, co-ordinated by Erich Jungmann of the KPD's Secretariat. Although this effort was centrally directed, with the aim of a national West German Peace Congress, it was clearly designed to garner grass-roots support too, through a series of *Land* delegates' conferences.[92]

The KPD's main weapon in its peace-campaigning proved to be the petition. In spring 1950 the party had joined the World Peace Council's Stockholm Appeal, a petition deploring the atom bomb. A signature collection initiated in its name by the Committee of Peace Fighters in West Germany in April was continued by the KPD, reaching a creditable interim result of 2.5 million by September. In December the Communists then formed a Committee against Remilitarization, picking up on the residue of an abortive Protestant initiative by Niemöller, Heinemann, and Noack, of the Nauheim Circle, to appeal to the Allies for a plebiscite (*Volksbefragung*) on German unity and rearmament. On 28 January 1951 a KPD-led conference against remilitarization in Essen duly called on Bonn for a plebiscite with the somewhat leading two-pronged question: 'Are you against the remilitarization of Germany and for a German peace treaty in 1951?'[93]

The demand was repeated in the Munich Theses of the KPD Convention in March, the top priority of which was to combat remilitarization in an FRG portrayed as the Allied jumping-off point for a third world war. Under the 'revanchist politician Adenauer', the West German economy was moving on to a war footing, its people 'cannon fodder'. The

---

[92] SED-Westkomm., 1 Dec. 1949, SAPMO-BA, NY 4182/867; 58th SED-Westkomm., 15 June 1950, SAPMO-BA, NY 4182/867.
[93] Fritz Krause, *Antimilitaristische Opposition in der BRD 1949–55* (Frankfurt am Main, 1971), 44.

Ohne mich! movement was to be elevated to a 'resistance movement', labour service boycotted, and arms production monitored on the shop-floors, since the consequences of remilitarization would be lower living standards, the bankruptcy of industries not vital to rearmament, and increased unemployment. (This failed, of course, to recognize the large spin-offs of rearmament for the West German economy.) National unity and anti-remilitarization were also notionally linked in Thesis 14:

The unification of the German people in the framework of a democratic, peace-loving, unitary German state will strengthen the democratic and patriotic forces, isolate the militarists and revanchist politicians and thereby render impossible the misuse of the population of West Germany for the . . . imperialists' goals.[94]

Constitutionally, only the Federal government was empowered to call a plebiscite and the KPD was hardly surprised when it refused. Undaunted, on 14 April 1951 a Main Committee for *Volksbefragung* was set up by the party to carry out an independent referendum, banned by the government ten days later. It nevertheless continued clandestinely to poll an alleged 9 million citizens in the FRG, almost 95% of whom claimed to be against remilitarization and for a peace treaty. By the end of July 1951 1.7 million signatures had supposedly been recorded, and a final tally was given in March 1952 of 5,917,683, to which were added about 3 million collective votes derived from resolutions, meetings, and newspaper questionnaires, including a 900,000 bloc vote representing the Bavarian unions. No allowance was made for duplications, however, and the real total may have been somewhere nearer 500,000.[95]

Polling methods had been unorthodox, to say the least. At a cinema in Celle, for instance, moments before the final credits rolled, one pollster asked all those against remilitarization to stand up in their seats, instantly registering 800 positive votes. At Christmas 1951 two festive Reutlingen pollsters even disguised themselves in suitably red Santa costumes and white beards, using their sacks as ballot boxes while evading their police pursuers in the shopping crowds![96] Nevertheless, despite irregularities, the *Volksbefragung* was still a considerable feat in view of the official sanctions meted out (pollsters in fact suffered 7,331 arrests and over a thousand prosecutions).[97] Moreover, independent surveys confirmed that

---

[94] *FV*, 1 Mar. 1951, 3 and 7–10.
[95] The poll held in the GDR from 3–5 June 1951 yielded 95.8% in favour; see Klein, *Antifaschistische Demokratie*, 158–9.
[96] Report on 'Linksradikale', 10 Dec. 1951, AdsD, *NL* Dux, Mappen 'KPD/Vertraulich'; *FV*, 24 Dec. 1951, 2.
[97] *KPD 1945–1968*, i. 36.

76% favoured the principle of a plebiscite on rearmament, so that support cannot be written off simply as a Communist conspiracy, as Adenauer was wont to do.[98] On the contrary, as one official British observer reported: 'These protests are not confined to KP members and sympathisers but are, I think, the genuine expression of the vast majority of the people.'[99] The KPD's peace struggle entered a critical phase in 1952, when in February the *Bundestag* approved Adenauer's plans for a German contingent within the European Defence Community (EDC), against only SPD and KPD votes. A corresponding treaty was signed in Paris in May and ratified in Bonn on 19 March 1953. Although it finally came to grief in August 1954 when the French National Assembly refused to do likewise, by the end of October of that year an alternative Paris treaty had paved the Federal Republic's way into NATO. In spite of a last-ditch Soviet diplomatic foray in December, which held out the prospect of national unity if West Germany stayed out of a western alliance, in February 1955 the *Bundestag* ratified the October treaty and in May Bonn joined NATO. Thus perished all hopes of accomplishing the KPD's second great preventive mission.

Although, by the time of these momentous events in the mid-1950s, the SPD and trade unions had taken a lead in mobilizing public opinion against German inclusion in NATO, in the earlier years the Communists had been very much out on a limb. Yet, although Berlin recognized that the KPD needed allies, it refused to acknowledge leaders of rival labour organizations, which in turn shunned the Communists. In addition, religious leaders such as the Catholic Rossaint and the Protestant Niemöller, as well as other 'bourgeois' pacifists, declined to share platforms with well-known Communists.[100] Ostensibly cross-party fronts were only partially successful. On 17 May 1952 a Working Circle for German Understanding —for a Just Peace Treaty, formed on 30 March from the remnants of the 1951 Main Committee for *Volksbefragung*, called for a referendum to reject the pending General Treaty and demand a peace treaty. In their bid to register mass votes, Communist pollsters 'appropriated' other demonstrations, for instance against the curbing of works council powers, to arrive at wholly artificial results. By January 1953 bloc votes of sympathetic

---

[98] HICOG Report No. 80, 28 May 1951, in Merritt and Merritt, *HICOG Surveys*, 119–20; Rob Burns and Wilfried van der Will, *Protest and Democracy in West Germany: Extra-Parliamentary Opposition and the Democratic Agenda* (Basingstoke, 1988), 79.

[99] Acting British Resident's Monthly Report, Jan. 1952 (western Ruhr), PRO, FO 1013/1284.

[100] 58th SED-Westkomm., 15 June 1950, SAPMO-BA, NY 4182/867; Helmuth Warnke, *'Bloß keine Fahnen'* (Hamburg, 1988), 127.

organizations, electoral registers of whole areas affected by NATO manœuvres, as well as cinema audiences, yielded a fantastic 15,002,126 positive
responses—almost half the West German electorate![101]
Once national armed forces for the GDR were announced in July 1952,
the KPD's fight against the EDC and NATO lost much of its moral
force. Western party members and even some leaders voiced their dis-
quiet, and failed to be placated by arguments that the GDR was creating a non-militaristic, 'socialist' defence force comparable to the peasant
militias of the sixteenth century or the Red Ruhr Army of 1920. In
fact, the SED leadership had always insisted on a 'clear stance against
pacifism'.[102] By the time compulsory military service was introduced in
the FRG in spring 1956, the KPD's youth wing, the Free German Youth
(FDJ), was unable to recruit significant numbers of potential draftees,
and was reduced instead to proclamations and declarations. Its pacifist
message was, in any case, blunted by its unqualified support for the GDR's
armed forces, symbolized by the presentation by one West German FDJ
delegation of 1,350 DM for the purchase of small-calibre rifles to train
young East Germans in the art of shooting.[103]

By the time a concerted non-Communist opposition to West German
membership of NATO emerged in spring 1955, it was too late for the
KPD to be accepted into the extra-parliamentary mainstream. The
Paulskirche Movement, headed by Ollenhauer of the SPD, Reuter of the
DGB, as well as church and civil rights campaigners such as Gollwitzer,
Heinemann, and Niemöller, actively shunned the Communists, as its
slogan made plain: 'Save Unity, Peace and Freedom! Against Communism
and Nationalism!' The organizers also consciously excluded the Communists from their 'German Manifesto', recognizing that KPD involvement
would alienate many more supporters than could be gained by at most
80,000 Communists.[104]

Indeed, the authorities and the political right did not hesitate to discredit even patriotic neutralists such as the Nauheim Circle, or Helene
Wessel's Emergency Committee for Peace in Europe, as Communist fifth
columns.[105] The classic exponent of such smear tactics was the anti-
Communist vigilante group, Save Freedom!, which in 1960 even published

[101] Klein, *Antifaschistische Demokratie*, 162–7.
[102] Pieck's notes, n.d. [Mar. 1952], in Staritz, ' "Aufbau des Sozialismus" ', 695.
[103] Klein, *Antifaschistische Demokratie*, 178–9; Michael Herms, 'Zur Stalinisierung der
West-FDJ 1949 bis 1952', in Helga Gotschlich (ed.), *'Links und links und Schritt gehalten . . .':
Die FDJ: Konzepte—Abläufe—Grenzen* (Berlin, 1994), 112–13.
[104] *Unser Weg*, 5/1 (1955), 7.
[105] Burns and van der Will, *Protest and Democracy*, 80.

a rather sinister Red Book with a list of hundreds of pacifist academics and artists accused of Communist contamination.[106] Thus, just as the issue of national reunification had been polarized by the larger East–West conflict, so the West German peace movement was dragged willy-nilly into a cold civil war. As in most civil wars, however, the victims were all too often non-combatants, neither Communist nor anti-Communist.

It has been argued by one author that, given the finely balanced nature of the rearmament issue, the KPD was in a position to tip the scales of West German opinion in favour of neutrality.[107] Taking the 1953 *Bundestag* election as a potential turning-point, however, there is little evidence that the KPD had been able to use the single issue of remilitarization to alter the political allegiance of voters. The CDU/CSU in fact increased their share of the vote by a staggering 14.2 percentage points. Yet, despite the instrumentalization of the KPD leadership's peace initiatives in the interests of the Cold War, there were undoubtedly sincere pacifists among the party's campaigners. Its ubiquitous daubed slogans and precariously positioned peace flags on top of factory chimneys and public buildings may have contributed in some small way to the consciousness-raising of an otherwise passive West German public. The SPD's experimentation with extra-parliamentary opposition, beginning in the mid-1950s, was no doubt partly prompted by a desire to deny this ground to the Communists. Yet it was never prepared to go as far as the KPD, which in May 1955, at the moment of West Germany's entry into NATO, asserted the citizen's right of resistance and civil disobedience, encouraging farmers to protest against military manœuvres and the requisitioning of land for runways. The Communists also played a path-breaking role in campaigns against the stationing of atomic artillery in the FRG, an issue which only really gained mass appeal in the Fight Atomic Death movement after the party had been banned.[108] Posthumously, therefore, the KPD may have gone some way to preparing the way for West Germany's explosion of pacifism a generation later in the 1970s and 1980s.

---

[106] Hans Karl Rupp, *Außerparlamentarische Opposition in der Ära Adenauer* (Cologne, 1970), 297–301.
[107] Douglas, 'KPD against Rearmament', 318 ff.
[108] HICOG to State Dept., 10 Aug. 1954, in *Confidential (1950–1954)*, 29. 525–46.

5

The 'Battlefield on the Shop-Floor'
Factory Groups, Works Councils,
and Trade Unions

IF there were a post-war KPD success story, then it must surely be in the workplace. After 1945 the KPD transformed itself from the classic Weimar party of the unemployed into a force to be reckoned with on the shop-floor, sweeping works councils in many of West Germany's household industrial names. This was as much a protest at the appalling socio-economic conditions of 1945–8, as it was a political reaction to the fascism which had gone before. Inevitably, however, the high politics of the Cold War also began to make themselves felt even at the workplace. One should, however, beware of seeking to explain the low politics of the shop-floor too strongly in terms of the global, national, or even regional political landscape. It was quite possible, in the Ruhr, for instance, to vote for a Communist works councillor, only to transfer one's allegiance at the next municipal election to a Social or Christian Democratic town councillor.

Indeed, each shop-floor presented a complex family tree. In surprisingly many plants a core of *Stammarbeiter*, too old for war service, had survived from Weimar, or even the Kaiserreich, permeated by private networks and rivalries based on religious, ethnic, or kinship ties. At the same time, a younger generation of workers had arisen in the factories, socialized, and some would say depoliticized, by Depression, Nazism, and war. Nevertheless, all these various groups had a common interest in the preservation of their livelihood. Faced with the possibility of economic extinction, be it through rationalization, bombing, dismantling, or starvation, the German workplace in the 1940s had become a *Schicksalsgemeinschaft*, a 'community of fate' based upon survival. In the process, class consciousness of the type preached by the pre-1933 labour movement had often been reduced to a more primitive form of plant patriotism. It could also be argued that, within this community, functional loyalties had developed which often transcended classic party-political allegiances.

Post-war Communists, by definition some of the Third Reich's arch-survivors, often enjoyed a head start over less inspiring SPD old hands. As one despondent Social Democrat observed:

The KPD is putting its best functionaries into factory work—the factory is its political base. We are short of young trade unionists. In the mines there are many young colleagues who were released during the war and acquired good skills. They lived through the misery of the bombing, and then in many cases joined the Communists in the food catastrophe.[1]

Three pillars of the shop-floor community will be examined—factory groups, works councils, and trade unions—in an attempt to discover where the KPD's strengths and weaknesses lay. In the process, the reader will, it is hoped, gain an insight into the complex relationship between high and low politics in the factory, and the limitations of political activism in an economy paralysed by cold and hunger.

In theory the Weimar KPD had been structured around its factory cells, but most members were in practice attached to street cells. Mass unemployment had further undermined the party's weak position on the shop-floor. Generally, it had proved weakest in larger concerns, the so-called *Großbetriebe*, with a cell in only every fifth factory employing over 500. For example, at Krupp with a workforce of 21,000, there were only 90 KPD cell members in 1931. This changed after 1945. After the capitulation, factory cells re-emerged spontaneously as the nuclei for the party's rebuilding, but were soon renamed 'factory groups' (*Betriebsgruppen*) so as to sound less conspiratorial. By August, in some areas of the Ruhr they ranged up to 50 in strength, strongest in the mines and steelworks and weakest in the public utilities and railways. By the year's end Krupp boasted a 240-strong group, and in May 1947 there were 1,908 groups in the western zones, higher than anything comparable under Weimar. Moreover, they were now concentrated in *Großbetriebe* with over 1,000 workers.[2]

One task of the factory groups, once paper became available in any quantity, was to produce factory broadsheets (*Betriebszeitungen*), aimed at the local workforce. These were usually mimeographed amateur affairs,

[1] [Author illegible], 'Meine Eindrücke über die Vorbereitungsarbeiten der KPD zur Bildung einer S.E.D. an der Ruhr und Vorschläge für unsere Gegenmassnahmen', n.d. [Mar. 1947], AdsD, *NL* Schumacher 41.

[2] Christoph Kleßmann, 'Betriebsparteigruppen und Einheitsgewerkschaft', *VfZ*, 31 (1983), 274 n. 5; Heinrich August Winkler, *Der Weg in die Katastrophe* (West Berlin and Bonn, 1987), 596; KPD-UBL Oberhausen, 15 Aug. 1945, SAPMO-BA, I 10/28/17; SAPMO-BA, I 10/23/19, fo. 14; KPD-PV/Org.-Abt., 7 Aug. 1947, SAPMO-BA, I 10/401/1; KPD-PV/LL NRW session, 6–7 Dec. 1949, SAPMO-BA, I 11/302/24.

peppered with caricatures of top-hatted capitalists, and most often found in the metal and mining industries around Hamburg and the Ruhr, as well as in public utilities, docks, and shipyards. Titles were suitably graphic and often in dialect: 'Hammer Blow', 'Spark', 'Davy Lamp', 'Winding Tower', 'Rivet Hammer', and 'Searchlight' were recurring choices. Rising in number from about 100 in 1951 to over 600 in 1956, with an alleged circulation of 1.5 million, they nevertheless remained sporadic affairs. Indeed, their proliferation in the KPD's declining years hardly reflected actual shop-floor support, but rather the semi-legal status of a party facing prohibition. Nevertheless, they are evidence that some sort of Communist subculture persisted.[3]

The SPD, on the other hand, had never had factory groups and at first viewed them as an affront to union neutrality. Characteristically, however, it decided to fight fire with fire and create its own. The earliest rival groups were seen in 1946 in Berlin, Lower Rhine, and Bremen, becoming more widespread in 1947. In Dortmund, in mid-March 1947 local union and SPD leaders argued that the Communists had started the rift, but skirted around the obvious objection that SPD factory groups were simply replacing one form of party-political interference with another. The solution was to be greater discipline and co-ordination of SPD shop-floor policy. By the end of the year SPD groups in some areas had actually overtaken the Communists. After 1948 they were centrally co-ordinated by Siggi Neumann, an ex-Weimar Communist poacher-turned-gamekeeper, who went on to establish a factory group desk on the SPD executive, by which time several thousand groups existed, mainly in medium to large factories. Although clearly a response to the KPD, the factionalization of shop-floor politics was to make a farce of the neutral *Einheitsgewerkschaft* and goes a long way to explaining the demise of Communists on works councils, although in some cases it took many years to break their hold.[4]

At the same time, the KPD's factory groups experienced an internal decline. Unwillingness to leave residential groups, chronic in Weimar, continued, although a majority of party members were now industrial workers. According to the 1951 party statute, factory groups belonged in

[3] Dok. IM-NRW No. 15, 14 Jan. 1954; Christa Hempel-Küter, *Die KPD-Presse in den Westzonen von 1945 bis 1956* (Frankfurt am Main, 1993), 34–6. For a selection of facsimiles see Willi Dickhut, *Was geschah danach?* (Essen, 1990), 189–231.

[4] Smektala/Henßler correspondence, Aug. 1945, in *Der Freiheit eine Straße: Dortmund 1945*, ed. IG Metall, Verwaltungsstelle Dortmund (Kösching, 1985), 74–9; SAPMO-BA, I 11/401/14; Kleßmann, 'Betriebsparteigruppen', 278–81; Christoph Kleßmann and Peter Friedemann, *Streiks und Hungermärsche im Ruhrgebiet 1946–1948* (Frankfurt am Main and New York, 1977), 111–15 and 122–3.

all enterprises with three or more Communists, but the proportion of members in them had dropped by 1950 to 16.5% (22% in NRW), despite 57% of members being classified as 'workers'. This meant that only one in three of rightful factory group members was joining. In plants with as many as 45 Communists there were allegedly no groups at all, and by December 1954 the total number in West Germany had dropped to 755, of which many existed only on paper. Previous schemes to entrust each *Bezirk* leadership with its own token group had conspicuously failed to activate the membership. Reading between the lines, many armchair members probably feared losing their jobs as a result of open Communist activity at the workplace, and so joined residential groups instead.[5]

Works councils (*Betriebsräte*) were bodies outside the party, originating in the workers' councils of 1918–19. These had been viewed by the Weimar unions, especially the SPD-affiliated ADGB, as an unwelcome attempt by the Communists and Independent Social Democrats to usurp them with an autonomous 'council movement'. The 1920 Works Council Law was therefore a successful bid to legislate them into a more tractable position. Its provision for the delegation of two shop-floor representatives on to a company's supervisory council fell well short of more radical demands for economic democracy or co-determination. Moreover, Social Democrats succeeded in controlling the vast majority of works councils in late Weimar. Despite local KPD successes in 1931 (25.8% of Ruhr miners; 12.0% of metalworkers in the Rhine-Ruhr region and 26.5% in Kiel; as well as good results at IG Farben), nationally the party won only 3.4% of seats to the SPD's 83.6%.[6] It is against this background that one must measure the relative success of post-war Communist works councillors.

In the first few weeks after the Nazi collapse councils were usually self-appointed, offering a *fait accompli* by the time the occupiers turned their attention to industrial relations. In Hagen, for example, on 23 April 1945 Communists 'certified' 36 shop-stewards with rubber stamps found at the local police station, before organizing tripartite works councils with Social and Christian Democrats. Such bodies were regarded by military government as transitional, however, until the phased rebuilding of the trade unions. From April–May 1945 they were thus permitted only limited rights of consultation at the workplace, and not the right to strike or dismiss personnel. Unilateral attempts to remove Nazified management were quashed as a threat to continued production. Nor could councils amalgamate and

[5] Report, 31 Dec. 1954, SAPMO-BA, I 11/401/12; Topf, *Kommunistische Betriebs- und Gewerkschaftsarbeit: Eine Abhandlung* (Düsseldorf, n.d. [1958]), 14–48.
[6] Winkler, *Weg in die Katastrophe*, 598 and 956–9.

threaten to become a 'movement' comparable with 1918–19. In Essen, for example, they were permitted by the British in July 1945, but were forbidden to engage in politics or collective bargaining.[7] In the absence of proper trade union representation, and even of political parties in the early months, the councils nevertheless gained significance by default. Later, the western Allies appear to have realized that it had been a mistake to permit works councils while restraining the unions. In 1947, reports were reaching the American military governor that the Communists commanded anything up to 50% of shop-floor support. At the same time, a rift developed in OMGUS's Manpower Division between the defenders of bottom-up democracy—former New Dealers and officials from the Congress of Industrial Organizations (CIO)—and conservatives, especially those from the American Federation of Labor (AFL). In the end, however, the latter prevailed with a scheme for top-down union rebuilding as a means to install reliable Social Democrats to counterbalance the works councils.[8]

The average British officer also equated works councillors with the 'reds' (often confusing works councils with workers' councils), and in July 1947 Steel described them as the Communists' 'most dangerous weapon'.[9] In spite of worries that too strong a Communist influence would prompt a Christian Unionist breakaway, open British intervention was nevertheless rejected in favour of encouragement of SPD/CDU co-operation and explicit discouragement of union-sponsored co-determination. Policy was to strengthen the unions and avoid dealing with the works councils as separate organizations outside the union movement, a relationship enshrined in the Allied Control Council's Law No. 22 of April 1946, which effectively tamed the works councils, allowing the unions to 'put their foot in the door'.[10]

Although military government had no clear overall picture of Communist strength in the councils until extensive surveys in 1948, its concern seems to have been in part justified. In autumn 1945 the KPD was reported to be outstripping the SPD at all the Nuremberg *Großbetriebe*. In Frankfurt

[7] Paul Harig, *Arbeiter—Gewerkschafter—Kommunist* (Frankfurt am Main, 1973), 23; Hartmut Pietsch, *Militärregierung Bürokratie und Sozialisierung* (Duisburg, 1978), 86; NGCC/ No. 4 District, 20 July 1945, ZI6, Sammlung Becker, Ordner 3/2.

[8] Report to Clay, 27 Sept. 1947, ZI6, Sammlung Becker, Ordner 13/1; Carolyn Eisenberg, 'Working-Class Politics and the Cold War: American Intervention in the German Labor Movement, 1945–49', *Diplomatic History*, 7 (1983), 284–9.

[9] Quoted by Gloria Müller, *Mitbestimmung in der Nachkriegszeit: Britische Besatzungsmacht —Unternehmer—Gewerkschaften* (Düsseldorf, 1987), 207–8.

[10] Luce to Gottfurcht, 26 June 1947, MRC, MSS 292/943/12; CCG/HQ ID, 'Trend Report No. 3', 14 Mar. 1948, PRO, FO 1051/424.

TABLE 6. *Works Councils at the KPD's Schwerpunkt Factories 1945–1947*[a]

Industry	KPD	SPD	CDU	Independent	Total
Steelworks[b]					
Bochumer Verein, Bochum 1946	9	10	1	—	20
Hasper Hütte, Hagen-Haspe 1947	8	2	1	2	13
Krupp, Essen 1946	8	—	2	1	11
Reichswerke, Salzgitter 1946	3	2	—	—	5
Engineering[c]					
Bosch, Stuttgart-Feuerbach 1947	12	3	—	1	16
Büssing, Braunschweig 1947	2	12	—	—	14
Henschel, Kassel	no figures				
Coal Mines[d]					
Friedrich-Heinrich, Lintfort 1947	4	9	—	1	14
Nordstern, Gelsenkirchen 1946	10	2	1	—	13
Westfalen, Dortmund 1947	9	4	—	2	15
Chemicals[e]					
BASF, Ludwigshafen 1947	4	23	3	—	30
Continental, Hannover 1947	7	5	—	—	12

[a] According to 1951 *nomenklatura*; see Hans Kluth, *Die KPD in der Bundesrepublik* (Cologne and Opladen, 1959), 63.

[b] *Neubeginn bei Eisen und Stahl in Ruhrgebiet*, ed. Gabriele Müller-List (Düsseldorf, 1990), 30–1; SAPMO-BA, I 10/23/19, fo. 14; Kleßmann, 'Betriebsparteigruppen', 303; Archiv der Stadt Salzgitter, *Demontage*, 160.

[c] SED conf., 19–20 June 1947, SAPMO-BA, DY 30/IV 2/1.01/50; NSIS to PD, 27 Oct. 1948, PRO, FO 1049/1348.

[d] RWIS, 3 Dec. 1948, PRO, FO 1013/247; ZI6, Sammlung Becker, Ordner 23.2/2.

[e] Kleßmann, 'Betriebsparteigruppen', 304; NSIS to PD, 27 Oct. 1948, PRO, FO 1049/1348.

the picture was more balanced, but in general the KPD was far stronger in southern Germany than it had ever been before 1933. Particularly successful in larger plants, by 1946 Communists also had a majority on about 25% of councils at the Ruhr pits. A notorious firebrand in Bottrop, Clemens Kraienhorst, even became collective works council chairman of the eighteen Hibernia mines, clearly relishing the discomfort this caused management. Communists also chaired the works councils of all Hamburg's big shipyards, and were almost unchallenged at the docks. An examination of the KPD's so-called *Schwerpunkt* factories, as in Table 6, shows several startling breakthroughs at some of West Germany's household industrial names.

Such individual successes must, of course, be balanced against the broader picture. Before giving perhaps more meaningful regional statistics, however, a word of warning about sources. Since works councils were officially neutral, party affiliations were not published and so one is reliant on

Industry	KPD	SPD	CDU	Independent	Total
Cars [f]					
Borgward, Bremen 1946	5	5	—	1	11
Daimler-Benz, Mannheim 1946	9	2	—	—	11
MAN, Augsburg 1947	5	13	1	1	20
MAN, Nuremberg 1947	9	7	—	—	16
Opel, Rüsselsheim 1946	12	6	2	—	20
Volkswagen, Wolfsburg 1946	10	6	—	2	18
Shipyards/Docks [g]					
Deutsche Werft, Hamburg 1947	9	2	—	2	13
Howaldt-Werft, Kiel 1945	6	6	—	1	13
Bremerhaven Docks, 1947	9	3	—	3	15
Hamburg Docks, 1947	18	1	—	—	19
Port of Duisburg	no figures				
Railway repair shops [h]					
RAW Freimann, Munich 1945	8	2	—	—	10

[f] OMG Bremen, 9 July 1947, ZI6, Sammlung Becker, Ordner 19/5b; SAPMO-BA, NY 4182/1169, fo. 39; SAPMO-BA, I 10/401/1, fo. 7; *Sopade*/396, 11 Feb. 1948; ID/EUCOM, 8 June 1949, in *Confidential (1945–1949)*, 4. 503–9; SED-PV/KPD meeting, 18 Dec. 1946, SAPMO-BA, DY 30/IV 2/1.01/30.

[g] HHIO, 16 July 1948, PRO, FO 1013/1347; Detlef Siegfried, *Zwischen Einheitspartei und 'Bruderkampf'* (Kiel, 1992), 346; NSIS to HQ/ID, 8 Sept. 1948, PRO, FO 1049/1348.

[h] SAPMO-BA, NY 4182/859, fo. 170.

secret headcounts, which may vary according to source. If collected at all, they tended to be from larger plants only, where the KPD was relatively stronger anyway. (See, for instance, the dramatic effect on the Bremen Communists in 1948, when more comprehensive figures were gathered.) Moreover, later on, state agencies were liable to include even breakaway Communists who had resigned from the party, under the rubric of the KPD. With these qualifications, the figures in Table 7 still represent the most complete overview so far.

What were the reasons for the Communists' success? Of course, not everywhere had the KPD appeared from out of the blue. In some cases Weimar tradition undoubtedly played a role. As mentioned above, in 1931 Communists had scored over 25% in the Ruhr mines and done particularly well at IG Farben. Although unable to repeat the latter successes,[11] there is evident continuity between mining results in late Weimar and

[11] 1947 results (1931 in brackets): BASF—13.3% (24.0%); Hoechst—9.5% (27.6%); Leverkusen—11.4% (32.6%), all in Kleßmann, 'Betriebsparteigruppen', 304; SAPMO-BA, DY 30/IV 2/10.01/2, fo. 118; OMG Hessen/Manpower, 1 Nov. 1947, BAK, Z 45 F, POLAD 816–58.

TABLE 7. *Affiliation of Works Councils in West Germany, 1945–1955*

Year	Number of plants	KPD		SPD		CDU		Independent		Other		Total
		No.	%	No.	%	No.	%	No.	%	No.	%	
Württemberg-Baden[a]												
Baden, 1945	42	136	47.4	78	27.2	11	3.8	62	21.6	—		287
1947	?	678	48.5	613	43.9	106	7.6	—		—		1,397
Bavaria												
1947	?	571	34.1	503	30.0	54	3.2	547	32.7	—		1,675
Bremen[b]												
1946	42	94	34.9	104	38.7	—		71	26.4	—		269
1947	25	65	39.6	52	31.7	—		47	28.7	—		164
1948	560	215	9.5	682	30.2	11	0.5	1338	59.3	9	0.4	2,255
1950	9	25	21.3	71	60.7	1	0.9	20	17.1	—		117
1953	11	45	21.4	118	56.2	2	1.0	45	21.4	—		210
Hamburg: General[c]												
1946	234	538	52.4	329	32.0	—		160	15.6	—		1,027
1947	196	245	18.4	688	51.6	—		392	29.4	8	0.6	1,333
1948	196	192	13.4	834	58.1	—		396	27.6	13	0.9	1,435
1949	?	126	10.6	751	63.1	—		307	25.8	7	0.6	1,191
Hamburg: Shipyards												
1947	9	28	43.1	22	33.8	—		15	23.1	—		65
1948	9	28	42.4	23	34.8	—		15	22.7	—		66
Hamburg: Engineering/Metal												
1947	49	67	21.7	147	47.6	—		95	30.7	—		309
1948	49	54	16.9	164	51.3	—		101	31.6	1	0.3	320

Hessen[d]												
1945	57	98	*36.7*	65	24.3	24	9.0	80	30.0	—		267
1946	121	265	*33.8*	221	28.2	23	2.9	275	35.1	—		784
1947	303	566	*27.8*	613	30.1	73	3.6	755	37.1	29	1.4	2,036
1948	112	108	*11.8*	472	51.6	28	3.1	306	33.5	—		914
Lower Saxony[e]												
1946	45	55	*27.6*	114	57.3	—		30	15.1	—		199
1947	34	84	*14.8*	326	57.5	34	6.0	106	18.7	17	3.0	567
1948	34	96	*14.8*	355	54.9	42	6.5	140	21.6	14	2.2	647
NRW: Mining[f]												
1945	126	239	*45.5*	145	27.6	95	18.1	45	8.6	—		525
1946	?	655	*37.3*	691	39.3	234	13.3	177	10.1	—		1,757
1947	225	676	*29.3*	933	40.5	344	14.9	315	13.7	36	1.6	2,304
1948	226	660	*27.2*	993	41.0	393	16.2	349	14.4	30	1.2	2,424
1949	?	618	*25.8*	885	37.0	403	16.8	447	18.7	39	1.6	2,392
1950	215	420	*19.9*	844	39.9	360	17.0	470	22.2	17	0.8	2,116
1951	?	?	*19.6*	?	37.3	?	16.5	?	26.6	—		?
1953	137	349	*18.5*	727	38.5	358	18.9	456	24.1	—		1,890
1955	137	345	*18.0*	721	37.7	309	16.1	539	28.2	—		1,914
NRW: Metal[g]												
1947	82	288	*36.1*	305	38.3	66	8.3	136	17.1	2	0.3	797
1948	126	273	*22.8*	513	42.9	130	10.9	274	22.9	6	0.5	1,196
1949	154	?	*20.2*	?	50.7	?	15.1	?	13.0	?	1.0	?
1953	52	120	*17.0*	270	38.3	88	12.5	227	32.2	—		705
1955	52	145	*20.1*	243	33.6	68	9.4	267	36.9	—		723
NRW: Chemicals[h]												
1947	11	21	*17.6*	44	37.0	20	16.8	33	27.7	1	0.8	119
1948	16	30	*18.0*	51	30.5	41	24.6	43	25.7	2	1.2	167

TABLE 7. (cont'd)

Year	Number of plants	KPD		SPD		CDU		Independent		Other		Total
		No.	%	No.	%	No.	%	No.	%	No.	%	
NRW: Public Utilities[i]												
1947	23	37	20.8	72	40.4	34	19.1	35	19.7	—		178
1948	41	29	8.8	118	38.3	77	25.0	83	26.9	1	0.3	308
Rhineland-Pfalz[j]												
Rhineland, 1947	544	?	8.5	?	18.5	?	4.0	?	69.0	—		2,053
Pfalz, 1947	?	?	14.0	?	32.0	?	3.0	?	49.0	—		1,135
1948	?	140	5.8	440	18.3	128	5.3	1188	49.3	513	21.3	2,409
Schleswig-Holstein[k]												
1946	127	234	47.6	209	42.5	—		47	9.6	2	0.4	492
1948	94	75	14.1	328	61.5	—		130	24.4	—		533

a *Protokolle des Sekretariats des ZK der KPD*, 477; KPD-BL W-B, 8 July 1947, SAPMO-BA, I 10/401/1.

b SAPMO-BA, NY 4090/630, fo. 127; SAPMO-BA, I 10/401/1, fo. 7; NSIS to PD, 25 Mar. 1948, PRO, FO 1049/1347; Bremen Consulate to State Dept., 18 May 1953, in *Confidential (1950–1954)*, 29. 344–52.

c SAPMO-BA, NY 4090/630, fo. 127; HIO to PD, 16 July 1948, PRO, FO 1049/1347; Kleßmann, 'Betriebsparteigruppen', 305.

d *Protokolle des Sekretariats des ZK der KPD*, 480; SAPMO-BA, NY 4090/630, fo. 127; Angelika Jacobi-Bettien, *Metallgewerkschaft Hessen 1945 bis 1948* (Marburg, 1982), 376; Kleßmann and Friedemann, *Streiks*, 88–9 n. 72.

e OMG Bremen, 9 July 1947, ZI6, Sammlung Becker, Ordner 19/5b; NSIS to PD, 27 Oct. 1948, PRO, FO 1049/1348.

f SAPMO-BA, I 10/23/19, fos. 11–20; CCG/ID, 10 Feb. 1949, PRO, FO 1013/750; DKBL report, 2 Jan. 1950, PRO, FO 1013/750; SPD-PV cited by Pietsch, *Militärregierung*, 312; Kleßmann, 'Betriebsparteigruppen', 301; Arbeitsbüro, 11 Aug. 1955, SAPMO-BA, DY 30/IV 2/10.02/75, fos. 45–52.

g RWIS to HQ/ID, 22 Sept. 1948, PRO, FO 1013/247; report, 9 May 1949, PRO, FO 1013/751; Arbeitsbüro, 11 Aug. 1955, SAPMO-BA, DY 30/IV 2/10.02/75, fos. 45–52.

h RWIS to HQ/ID, 22 Sept. 1948, PRO, FO 1013/247.

i RWIS to HQ/ID, 22 Sept. 1948, PRO, FO 1013/247.

j Baden Consulate to State Dept., 24 Jan. 1948, BAK, Z 45 F, POLAD 852–42; Kleßmann, 'Betriebsparteigruppen', 305.

k Siegfried, *Einheitspartei*, 354; S-HIO to PD, 14 June 1948, PRO, FO 1049/1347.

those after 1945, although more will be said on the pits below. As British intelligence joked, another traditional KPD clientele was the dockers, whose 'old school neckerchief is red'.[12] What was new, however, was the breakthrough in the metal industry, where in 1946–7 the Communists appeared to score much higher results than before 1933, breaking an SPD monopoly. Support there was to erode correspondingly quickly, however, particularly in the south, so that after 1948 the KPD was defending only isolated metalworking bastions.

At the so-called *Stunde Null* in 1945, the KPD's illegal Third Reich network had undoubtedly given it a small head start on the shop-floor. Its councillors would, in addition, appear to have been slightly younger than the SPD's. As noted, the SPD had no factory groups of its own until 1947, so that many early works council elections, pending legal unions, were organized by default by the KPD's groups. Yet this alone does not fully explain their success. Turn-out is also a poor indicator. At the Hamburg docks, low turn-outs of just over 3% of the 1,900 stevedores were interpreted as beneficial to the Communists, but so too were high turn-outs in the Ruhr, of over 75% among Recklinghausen miners.[13] At the risk of speculation, one specifically post-war factor, which may have aided the Communists, was the disguised unemployment and temporary deskilling occurring at plants standing idle or under-capacity as a result of war damage or fuel shortages. Nordstern colliery, for example, did not reopen until 1948, and was a KPD works council stronghold. In many steelworks, skilled metalworkers often spent years performing the unskilled labour of clearing up, and may have temporarily abandoned the SPD. What seems certain, however, is that the Third Reich had created an unusually large pool of unaffiliated workers for the KPD to tap into. In Frankfurt, according to American observers, it was thus strongest in plants with few veteran unionists, where most workers were 'declassed and uprooted elements hired during or after the war'.[14]

Although regulations prohibiting party-political lists in works council elections soon became a farce, with some candidates almost coming to blows, local personality rather than high politics probably played a significant role. Undisguised personal patronage thus led 75% of workers

---

[12] S-HIO to Pol. Div., 14 June 1948, PRO, FO 1049/1347; Fuhrmann, 14 Oct. 1945, SAPMO-BA, NY 4182/859; Erika Runge (ed.), *Bottroper Protokolle* (Frankfurt am Main, 1968), 25.

[13] HHIO to Regional Commissioner, 11 Mar. 1948, PRO, FO 1049/1208; SAPMO-BA, NY 4182/859, fo. 245.

[14] OMGUS report, 21 July 1947, in *Gewerkschaften in Politik, Wirtschaft und Gesellschaft 1945–1949*, ed. Siegfried Mielke and Peter Rütters (Cologne, 1991), 433–4.

at one plant in Hessen to join the local KPD factory group. During short-ages the works council office at any factory often acted as a semi-official distribution point for black market goods. The Americans soon noted KPD attempts to recruit 'non-political' workers by providing work cloth-ing and shoes. Mining works councils were often in a position to allocate pit-owned housing, and the 'red' Hasper Hütte works council even went so far as to build its own works accommodation. Ultimately, however, the Communists could not compete with the dense Social Democratic network of patronage, and in no sense could they exploit the sort of insti-tutionalized clientelism aiding the Italian PCF. In Germany the state con-tinued to take care of individual welfare needs, and in 1948 the currency reform largely eradicated the barter economy. One should in any case not overrate the militancy of workforces often forced into a common front with management against the occupation authorities. Military government's rationing of raw materials and threats of dismantling had clearly perpetu-ated the 'community of fate' established between workers and employers during the war, designed to ward off the worst effects of total mobiliza-tion by the Nazi state.[15]

Although the decline of the Communists' shop-floor power base was symptomatic of longer-term socio-economic changes, short-term losses were attributable to tactical SPD–CDU works council coalitions. Anti-Communist pacts were often a means for local Social Democrats to bind wayward Christian unionists, threatening breakaways, to the union, and at the same time to eliminate KPD influence. As Michael Fichter has shown in the Stuttgart metal plants, the Social Democrats consciously politicized the avowedly non-partisan works council elections and suc-cessfully isolated the KPD. Later, at Bremen's AG Weser shipyard in 1953, it was ironically the Communists who doggedly fielded a Works Unity List against an anti-Communist IG Metall/SPD coalition.[16]

The party's position in the works councils was not only undermined by its political enemies. In 1948, when the councils in the SBZ were subordinated to the local works union, and thus effectively dissolved,

[15] ICD Hessen, 13 Aug. 1947, ZI6, Sammlung Becker, Ordner 19/5b; James A. Diskant, 'Scarcity, Survival and Local Activism: Miners and Steelworkers, Dortmund 1945–8', *Journal of Contemporary History*, 24 (1989), 547–73; Alexander von Plato, '*Der Verlierer geht nicht leer aus*' (West Berlin and Bonn, 1984), 101; Lutz Niethammer (ed.), *Lebensgeschichte und Sozialstruktur im Ruhrgebiet 1930 bis 1960* (West Berlin and Bonn, 1983), ii. 301; Harig, *Arbeiter*, 94–6.
[16] Michael Fichter, 'Aufbau und Neuordnung: Betriebsräte zwischen Klassensolidarität und Betriebsloyalität', in Martin Broszat et al. (eds.), *Von Stalingrad zur Währungsreform* (Munich, 1988), 504; Heinz-Gerd Hofschen, 'Werftarbeiterstreik, Gewerkschaftsausschlüsse und die Absetzung des Betriebsrates der AG "Weser" 1953', *1999*, 2 (1990), 36–59.

ammunition was handed to critics on a plate.[17] The party compounded the damage with the Thesis 37 fiasco in 1951, which will be discussed below, and was increasingly confronted by ex-Communists standing as independents, some sympathetic, some hostile. Thus, in 1955, renegades reportedly accounted for 72 seats at 51 Ruhr pits, and, at one of the *Schwerpunkt* factories, Daimler-Benz in Mannheim, five Communists were confronted by four former comrades. The last surprise result for the Communist works council in West Germany was in November 1955, when, at Dortmund's Westfalenhütte, the KPD won an impressive 16 of the 25 seats. Yet such isolated victories were the result of SPD complacency and KPD voting discipline, not increased support. By 1954 the party commanded only 8–10% of all the Federal Republic's shop-floor mandates, and, after the Works Constitution Law of 1952, works council powers were in any case severely curtailed.[18]

The KPD's relationship with the unions themselves had always been highly ambivalent, oscillating between collaboration from within and confrontation from without. Under Weimar, inside influence had remained slight—a combination of members' apathy in joining and expulsions for disruptive behaviour. Concurrent with the party's 'social fascist' line, at the end of 1929, a breakaway union, the Revolutionary Trade Union Opposition (RGO), was founded, reaching some 255,000 members by 1932, although many disappeared as suddenly as they had arrived. They tended to come from low-paid, semi-skilled workers in more recently unionized industries, for instance in the mines in Lower Rhine and the northern and eastern Ruhr, articulating a protest vote. Nevertheless, the high proportion of unemployed among Communist supporters ruled out anything other than small-scale wildcat strikes, which Social Democratic unionists were quick to disavow. Yet in January 1931 the RGO could mark up a minor victory when it successfully called out 14.5% of Ruhr miners.[19]

With the RGO the Communists had therefore contributed significantly to Weimar's system of partisan unions, or *Richtungsgewerkschaften*. Divided in 1933, the unions fell notoriously quickly to the Nazi onslaught, adding

---

[17] Neumann radio address, 5 Mar. 1949, DGB-Archiv, *NL* Böckler, Kasten 10/29.
[18] HICOG to SD, 10 Aug. 1954, in *Confidential U.S. State Department Central Files: Germany—Federal Republic of Germany. Internal Affairs* 1950–1954, ed. Paul Kesaris (Frederick, Md., 1986), 29. 525–46; Karl Lauschke, ' "Der Dicke muß weg!". Betriebsratswahlen 1955 auf der Westfalenhütte', in Peter Grafe *et al.* (eds.), *Der Lokomotive in voller Fahrt die Räder wechseln* (West Berlin and Bonn, 1987), 87 and 92; Dietrich Staritz, 'Die Kommunistische Partei Deutschlands', in Richard Stöss (ed.), *Parteien-Handbuch* (Opladen, 1983), 1740.
[19] Freya Eisner, *Das Verhältnis der KPD zu den Gewerkschaften in der Weimarer Republik* (Cologne and Frankfurt am Main, 1977), 215–16; Werner Müller, *Lohnkampf, Massenstreik, Sowjetmacht* (Cologne, 1988), 148 and 337–59.

fuel to calls after 1945 for a single union or *Einheitsgewerkschaft*. For the Communists the *Einheitsgewerkschaft* became the syndical corollary of the missing socialist unity party, and thus warranted strong support. Despite the general consensus, however, there were serious disagreements over the modalities of a single union. Some wanted a federation of autonomous industrial unions, others a centralized super-*Einheitsgewerkschaft*, in which the industrial unions were in practice appendages; a few advocated a hybrid party cum union. In principle the Communists favoured the second option, criticizing the ultimate West German arrangement of autonomous industrial unions under the umbrella of the German Trade Union Federation (DGB) as a federated compromise, and identified—unsurprisingly—with the Free German Trade Union Federation (FDGB) in the SBZ.[20]

Nevertheless, the issue of a centralized or federated *Einheitsgewerkschaft* was not a simple Communist versus non-Communist issue. Hans Böckler, for instance, the leading Social Democratic unionist in North Rhine Province and later chairman of the DGB, had also been an early proponent of centralization. After British intervention in late 1945, however, he was converted to the principle of autonomous industrial unions. Armed with this decision, on 14 December the SPD leadership in Dortmund managed to sidestep a KPD delegation seeking a commitment to a centralized Ruhr union, whose provisional title was not insignificantly 'FDGB'.[21] Nevertheless, this was still not the end of the tug of war between the centralists and federalists. When a British zonal union conference convened in August 1946, still under the provisional designation FDGB, the Communists were calling for it to be the 'tightest possible combination of all industrial associations'.[22] The British forbade the title, but only in May 1947 was the 'F' definitively dropped, leaving the more familiar 'DGB'.[23]

What motivated the British was not just a belief in grass-roots democracy, but a fear that an over-centralized West German *Einheitsgewerkschaft* could amalgamate with the FDGB in the SBZ. Concern only abated slowly over the course of the unions' nine Interzonal Conferences, which brought together unionists from all four zones from November 1946– August 1948, although none of the western delegates appears to have been a Communist. Sponsored by the World Federation of Trade Unions, the conferences debated strategies for socio-economic change, but became

---

[20] Michael Fichter, *Einheit und Organisation: Der Deutsche Gewerkschaftsbund im Aufbau 1945 bis 1949* (Cologne, 1990).
[21] Lichtenstein, 28 Dec. 1945, SAPMO-BA, NY 4182/859.
[22] *WVE*, 25 Aug. 1946, 2.   [23] *WVE*, 9 May 1947, 2.

bogged down over the main agendum of an all-German trade union move-ment. By the time of the sixth conference at Bad Pyrmont in October 1947, which passed a resolution permitting union federations to amalgam-ate between individual zones, there was considerable opposition among western delegates to the plan for an all-German union congress the fol-lowing spring. The only inter-zonal merger was thus between the British and American federations in the Bizone. The Americans had also intro-duced obstacles, making economic unity a precondition for a united trade union beyond the Bizone, and the French barred delegates from their zone from attending the seventh conference in Dresden in February 1948. At that meeting the leading unionist in the American Zone, Fritz Tarnow, came out unambiguously for autonomous industrial unions, and the penul-timate conference fell apart when the western leaders attempted to force the FDGB to accept the Marshall Plan. When an Independent Trade Union Opposition (UGO), sponsored by the Americans as a West Berlin break-away from the FDGB, insisted on recognition at the ninth conference, proceedings were suspended, indefinitely as it transpired.[24]

Even in the West, therefore, union-rebuilding had been closely super-vised by military government, and it would indeed be hard to ignore the occupiers' impact on the German labour movement. At the beginning of May 1945 military government in the Ruhr announced that unions would be permitted, but only at local level, and without bargaining rights on wages and working hours. In July–August 1945 the British elaborated a three-phase union plan which envisaged, firstly, founding meetings and executive elections; then the establishment of offices and recruitment; and finally regional amalgamations. This cumbersome process was only com-pleted in the second half of 1946, when a zonal leadership was established in the British Zone, to form the core of a Bizonal union structure in 1947. Although fears of a Communist-dominated union movement may not have been the fundamental cause of this gradualism, they certainly served to justify it.[25]

The slow pace of reorganization also allowed Social Democratic union-ists from the former Weimar ADGB, who had resisted becoming involved in the semi-legal works councils, to establish themselves as local union nominees. This left the KPD with very few top posts, even in the regional industrial unions. Only one Communist, Konrad Skrentny, made it on

[24] Peter Weiler, *British Labour and the Cold War* (Stanford, Calif., 1988), 176–7; Albert Behrendt, *Die Interzonenkonferenzen der deutschen Gewerkschaften* (East Berlin, 1959), *passim*; Eisenberg, 'Working-Class Politics', 297–9.
[25] Pietsch, *Militärregierung*, 96–7.

TABLE 8. *Communists on Trade Union Executives in the Bizone, 1947*[a]

Union	DGB	Mining	Building	Metal	Textiles	Food	Chemicals	Printing	Transport	DAG (White Collar)	Timber	Horticulture	Railways
British Zone	1/12	8/26	1/10	3/15	0/15	0/12	0/15	1/16	6/41	0/17	0/15	0/11	0/12
Hessen	0/14	1/8	2/18	4/11	1/7	?	1/9	1/5	2/10	?	1/12	3/9	?
Württemberg-Baden	1/13	—	4/9	5/10	3/10	3/10	1/6	2/3	5/24	0/13	1/3	1/1	3/13
Bavaria	2/14												

[a] KPD on left / total on right: CCG/Manpower Div., 23 Jan. 1948, PRO, FO 1051/427; ICD/Hessen, 13 Aug. 1947, Zl6, Sammlung Becker, Ordner 19/5b; KPD-BL W-B, Sept. 1946, SAPMO-BA, NY 4182/861, fos. 228–9.

to the British zonal executive of the DGB, and he resigned from the party in February 1948. Of course, this was in part the price paid for neglect of union work under Weimar, but also, as discussed above, the result of deliberate military government policy. An overview of union leadership posts in the British Zone, and in Hessen and Württemberg-Baden in the American Zone (Table 8), demonstrates the KPD's resultant thin representation, particularly glaring outside the mining, metal, and transport unions. By way of comparison, Table 9, showing political affiliations at branch level in NRW, indicates that the Communists did somewhat better in the intermediate union hierarchy, particularly in the building industry, as well as at local strongholds such as Remscheid.

Apart from the miners, who will be discussed below, IG Metall was the only other union to score over 30% in NRW. It is clear, however, that even here the Communists were in a minority position, contrary to some American reports. Moreover, while the metalworking industry was operating at less than capacity, its leverage was slight and the relatively impressive KPD representation in 1947–8 in the middle hierarchy correspondingly tenuous. The KPD never reached the full-time IG Metall executive in the British Zone, although three Communists served on an honorific basis. As Table 9 shows, of the twenty-eight district chairmen in NRW in 1948, seven were Communists, but in only four branches did they dominate the local committee. In fact, of the 200,000 metalworkers in the Ruhr, only 5,000 were reckoned to be KPD members, but this did not stop IG Metall from later abolishing plant-level representation in order to deny the Communists a supposed platform. Prospects looked a little better for the KPD in the US Zone. In Hessen's IG Metall, the SPD, with six executive members, held sway over four Communists and one Christian Democrat, but in Württemberg-Baden SPD and KPD were balanced at five apiece. At *Bezirk* level the Communists were generally relatively stronger but rarely able to challenge the SPD, except in isolated towns such as Heilbronn. In Bavaria the party was reported to occupy only 15% of posts. Details from the French Zone are sketchier still, and certainly deserve further research. In both Rhineland-Pfalz and Württemberg-Hohenzollern, however, the KPD headed the local IG Metall, and in South Baden held an impressive 8 out of 22 DGB posts. Whether the Communists had been assisted by the strong position of the PCF in the French CGT, remains unclear.[26]

---

[26] Heath to State Dept., 14 Apr. 1947, in *Foreign Relations of the United States, 1947,* ii (Washington, DC, 1972), 861–3; Denis MacShane, *International Labour and the Origins of the Cold War* (Oxford, 1992), 214–25; *Organisatorischer Aufbau der Gewerkschaften 1945–*

TABLE 9. *Communists on Local Trade Union Committees in NRW, 1948*[a]

Branch	DGB	Mining	Building	Metal	Textiles	Food	Chemicals	Printing	Transport	DAG (White Collar)
Aachen	1/10	—	K/20	K/33	I/15	K/20	I/25	S/—	S/10	I/ 3
Bielefeld	0/ 4	—	K/20	S/ 5	S/—	S/—	S/ ?	K/10	S/—	—
Bochum	2/ 8	S/22	K/100	K/55	—	K/33	S/—	—	C/ 7	—
Bonn	1/ 7	—	C/—	S/18	S/—	I/—	S/—	S/—	S/—	S/—
Bottrop	2/ 6	K/60	S/33	S/25	—	K/33	K/16	C/—	—	C/25
Cologne	2/16	S/—	K/50	S/—	I/—	S/22	S/—	S/—	S/13	C/14
Dinslaken	3/ 4	K/70	S/80	S/ 8	—	—	—	—	S/25	—
Dortmund	3/17	S/20	I/36	S/26	—	S/—	S/11	K/14	K/20	S/11
Düsseldorf	6/24	—	K/40	K/50	S/37	S/36	S/—	S/—	S/12	S/12
Duisburg	2/17	C/20	K/100	K/69	I/ 6	K/25	S/20	S/18	S/—	C/—
Essen	2/11	S/25	S/—	S/50	—	S/—	K/43	—	S/15	F/—
Gelsenkirchen	2/11	K/14	S/—	S/50	—	I/—	S/—	—	S/ 7	S/—
Gladbeck	2/ 7	S/17	S/17	S/—	—	S/—	—	—	S/ 8	C/—
Hagen	2/ 8	—	S/—	K/25	S/14	S/33	S/17	S/—	S/10	—
Hamm	0/ 4	S/36	S/16	C/12	—	S/—	S/—	—	S/20	—
Krefeld	1/13	S/22	K/45	S/22	S/21	K/22	C/10	K/14	S/—	—
Mettmann	7/14	—	K/25	I/43	S/—	K/57	S/—	C/—	C/—	—
Mönchengladbach	1/12	—	C/33	C/ 8	C/ 8	—	—	—	S/14	—
Moers	7/12	S/14	K/50	S/37	—	S/12	—	—	—	C/—
Mülheim	5/13	—	S/20	S/40	S/33	—	—	—	S/14	—
Münster	3/13	—	S/10	C/—	—	C/—	K/16	I/20	S/10	—
Oberhausen	2/11	C/10	S/11	S/16	—	S/—	—	—	S/11	—
Recklinghausen	2/11	S/25	K/86	S/28	—	S/—	—	S/—	C/ 9	—
Remscheid	8/11	—	C/20	K/79	I/43	K/70	—	K/33	S/37	S/—
Siegen	1/ 5	?/50	S/25	S/28	C/—	—	K/25	S/20	C/20	K/75
Solingen	4/ 8	—	S/—	K/65	K/55	S/25	I/50	I/20	S/25	S/10
Unna	2/12	K/100	—	—	—	S/—	—	K/25	S/—	S/25
Wuppertal	7/16	—	K/44	S/40	S/43	S/15	S/13	S/20	S/10	I/25
NRW	26%	34%	31%	29%	17%	17%	13%	11%	11%	11%

[a] RWIS to PD, 30 June 1948, PRO, FO 1049/1347. Left-hand letter indicates affiliation of chair; right-hand figure percentage KPD.

Pithead Politics: The KPD in the Ruhr Coalfields

Since the KPD performed so well in the Ruhr coal industry, which achieved the status of a Communist bastion, it is worth dwelling at some length on the reasons for this success. In the miners' union the Communists almost achieved the very top leadership, and in the first pithead works council elections in 1945 the KPD was the strongest party overall. Moreover, since the Ruhr coalmines were so crucial to the economic recovery of West Germany, and, for that matter, of western Europe too, the Anglo-Americans kept a particularly close eye on Communist activity at the pits. The British tried again and again, without obvious success, to raise mining productivity. The export of German coal as reparations from current production to France and the Benelux countries meant that the disruption of Ruhr production could also have international ramifications. Control of the Ruhrgebiet was, in addition, the subject of intense diplomatic wrangling between the former wartime allies, making it arguably the most sensitive industrial region in the world, with a high potential for politicization from outside.

The Ruhr pits also had a high internal potential for conflict. In Chapter 1 it was argued that one of the reasons for miners' militancy was the many grievances accumulated under the Nazis' coercive system of production drives, which had bequeathed an ageing, sick, underfed, and overworked workforce. With collieries chronically undermanned, especially after the repatriation of foreign slave labour, and replacements in short supply, miners were in a uniquely strong bargaining position. This is to say nothing of the miners' long-standing corporate identity, in certain respects continuing pre-industrial patterns of conflict from the nineteenth century. The Communists had already successfully adapted grievances against rationalization under the Weimar Republic to their own cause. They also cultivated the traditional sense of comradely exclusivity among miners, known to each other simply as the *Kumpels*.

More specifically, the Ruhr KPD was also able to build on its anti-fascist resistance network, focused on the pits in and around Gelsenkirchen. Under Walter Jarreck and Hans Schiwon a small but intact group of Communists had survived in this town in the heart of the Ruhr. (The SPD's support was centred in Dortmund under the Weimar miners' leader,

1949, ed. Siegfried Mielke *et al.* (Cologne, 1987), 65; Pietsch, *Militärregierung*, 277; HQ ID/ CCG, 'Trend Report No. 3', 14 Mar. 1948, PRO, FO 1051/424; ID/EUCOM, 21 Feb. 1949, BAK, Z 45 F, 7–32–3/5–6.

August Schmidt.) The sacrifices endured during resistance soon repaid themselves in works council successes, however, and it was to be here, rather than in the union, that the Communists established their real power base. As early as 30 March 1945, the day the Americans liberated Gelsenkirchen, 7 Communists and 3 Social Democrats, led by Jarreck, agreed to take matters into their own hands and remove Nazi Labour Front shop stewards, as well as to organize provisional works council elections. At eleven Gelsenkirchen pits, 31 Communists, 14 Social Democrats, 8 Catholics, and 1 white-collar representative were thus elected by a simple show of hands.[27]

The first balloted works council elections were held in the autumn at British insistence. Despite the KPD's desire for single lists, they were fought along party-political lines in closed pit communities by miners in the 35–55 age bracket, veterans of Weimar elections who had in the main avoided evacuation or conscription. In fact, some pithead elections, at Rheinbaben, for example, were almost straight re-runs between Weimar *Richtungsgewerkschaften*. The results show that the Communists did not win an absolute majority, but a strong plurality of the vote (see Table 6 above). Whether the undermanning of pits distorted results in the KPD's favour is open to question. In May 1945 there had been only about 70,000 miners, and by August 160,000, but still only half the normal complement. Results were certainly unevenly spread, often reflecting pithead landslides for a local personality—at Dannenbaum colliery, for instance, an 89% turn-out of around 800 miners apparently voted by 725 votes for the KPD, to the SPD's 3![28]

The problem facing Communists was to translate this apparent works council strength into union posts. (After 1949 mining works councils were in fact formally subordinated to the local union, underlining the real power structure.) At a first works council conference, held secretly on 15 April in Gelsenkirchen-Buer, with 120 representatives from over 25 plants, including 22 pits, Jarreck pleaded on behalf of the Communists for a single union and not craft unions. A committee, chaired by Schiwon, of 4 Communists, 2 Social, and 2 Christian Democrats, was then elected to prepare the way for *Einheitsgewerkschaften* at all pitheads. A second conference of 360

[27] Walter Jarreck, 'Vom Neubeginn der Kommunisten 1945 an der Ruhr' (copy of *c.*1966 typescript in possession of the author), 4–5 and 10; UB Gelsenkirchen-Buer, n.d., SAPMO-BA, I 11/401/14, fo. 157.

[28] KPD-UBL Recklinghausen, mid-Nov. 1945, SAPMO-BA, NY 4182/859; Schabrod, 13 Aug. 1945, SAPMO-BA, I 11/23/1; 'Intelligence Review No. 6', 20 Feb. 1946, PRO, FO 1005/1700; report on Ruhr, Sept. 1945, SAPMO-BA, I 10/23/18.

delegates from 56 pits, as well as chemicals and metal plants, met on 29 April, drawing up a blueprint for a more ambitious Ruhr-wide Free German Trade Union Federation (FDGB), including a subordinate Mining Industrial Group, to be followed by other industrial groups. The British monitored these developments with trepidation, and when the FDGB Mining Industrial Group came out into the open on 7 October 1945, they promptly disbanded it and impounded its funds.[29]

Ratcheting union-building back to *Bezirk* level was not the wisest way for the British of containing the Communists. In Essen, on 2 February 1946, the KPD won an impressive 52% of the constituent *Bezirk I* vote and 65 delegates; the SPD 15% and 19; the CDU 22% and 28; and the Independents 11% but no delegates respectively. Four Ruhr *Bezirke* were founded, which in March created the provisional Ruhr executive of an Industrial Association of Mining (IVB), under the chairmanship of the Social Democrat August Schmidt (probably on Communist sufferance), with the KPD's Schiwon acting as deputy, responsible for works councils. Finally, in December 1946, a zonal IVB executive was elected at Herne. Immediately beforehand there had been a tussle within the KPD for the main candidature between Schiwon, the man of 1945, who claimed to have the backing of all salaried employees, many Christian and some Social Democrats, and even renegade Communists, and the leadership's nominee, Willi Agatz, recently released from a Soviet POW camp. Schiwon, conducting his nomination campaign from a hospital bed, was nevertheless forced, for reasons which are still not clear, to stand down on pain of party expulsion. Moreover, at the conference itself on 8–9 December, the Communist delegates appear not to have maintained full voting discipline, allowing Schmidt to be elected chairman over Agatz by a narrow margin of 168 to 155.[30] Nevertheless, this still left the Communists in their strongest position of any West German union, as Table 10 shows.

The Communists' presence may have been impressive on paper, but they were still in a minority. With this in mind it is time to turn to the KPD's pit politics. Given the relative strength of the Communists and the sensitivity of Ruhr coal production, whenever the authorities encountered resistance to higher productivity, KPD saboteurs were often

---

[29] Jarreck, 'Neubeginn', 16; Taylor to CCG Münster/Ruhr Gp., 4 Sept. 1945, PRO, FO 1051/943; Annan, 15–17 Oct. 1945, PRO, FO 371/46935.

[30] Report, 23 Feb. 1946, SAPMO-BA, I 10/23/9; KPD-BL Ruhr/*Sek.*, 27 Nov. 1946, SAPMO-BA, I 11/23/1. Jarreck was marginalized, see ibid., 29 Jan. 1947; IVB meeting of 3 Dec. 1946, in *Gewerkschaften*, 270; Michael Clarke, 'Die Gewerkschaftspolitik der KPD 1945–1951', diploma (Ruhr University of Bochum, 1982), 28.

TABLE 10. *Affiliation of the Miners' Union Leadership, 1946–1948*[a]

(a)

Main Executive	KPD	SPD	CDU	Independent
Full-time	4[b]	6	—	1
Coopted	4	8	2	1
Total of 26	8	14	2	2

(b)

Bezirk	I Essen	II Aachen	III Cologne	IV Bochum	V Gelsenkirchen	VI Dortmund
Chairmen[c]	KPD	CDU	SPD	KPD	KPD	SPD
Sub-chairmen	1 KPD 3 SPD	?	?	2 KPD 2 SPD	3 KPD 2 SPD	1 KPD 1 SPD 1 CDU

[a] CCG/Manpower Div., 23 Jan. 1948, PRO, FO 1051/427; KPD-BL Ruhr/Abt. A and S, 15 Sept. 1947, SAPMO-BA, I 10/23/19; Pietsch, *Militärregierung*, 276; Bremen Consulate to State Dept., 18 June 1948, BAK, Z 45 F, POLAD 785–6.

[b] Willi Agatz, Karl Becker, Alfred Mattern, Karl Herzfeld—the latter later expelled for agreeing to the points system; see *WVE*, 19 Sept. 1947, 2.

[c] Schneider (I); Freischläger (IV); Schiwon (V).

assumed to be the cause. The reality was, however, far more complex. More often than not, in 1945 it had been Communist *Kumpels* who had prevented the dynamiting or flooding of mines by the retreating *Wehrmacht*. (Even the most ardent subsequent advocates of socialization did not wish to destroy their own livelihood!) In fact, the earliest proponents of strikes tended to be Social Democrats, whereas, like their French comrades, the German Communists placed national reconstruction before wage increases or even denazification of management. Only as socialization attempts foundered in 1947–8, and it became clear that the Soviet Union was going to be denied a stake in the control of the Ruhr, could it be argued that the KPD had an interest in undermining production.

Nevertheless, the dire socio-economic state of the collieries in the wake of the Nazi defeat created conditions which transcended political alignments. To a certain extent, therefore, no agency controlled the actions of the Ruhr miners. The issue which soon took on almost existential importance for the *Kumpels*, rendered more acute by the worsening food crisis, was that of raised productivity, and, more particularly, overtime.

On 14 November 1945 over 200 works councillors and unionists from the Ruhr pits met at a first so-called *Ruhrrevierkonferenz* in Bochum, together with Westphalia's three *Regierungspräsidenten* and the former Prussian minister, Carl Severing, to debate a British overtime scheme. The KPD's Schiwon caught the mood of the meeting, however, and carried a motion of rejection, adding political demands for increased works council powers, including consultation over management appointments and dismissals, as well as union recognition.[31] Faced with this opposition to their policies designed to raise coal production, one response for the British would have been to use force. At one pit in Dortmund soon afterwards, military government did indeed carry out an exercise to deal with the scenario of a stone-throwing crowd of angry miners attacking the director's office. Under some pressure from the British commander, the colliery was even conspicuously occupied by British troops and German police. Whether this was for the benefit of the Communist works council chairman, who dutifully reported back to Berlin, is not known. Yet, in the end, the British-run North German Coal Control (NGCC) could not afford the political costs of what might so easily be decried as Nazi-style production drives at the coalface.[32]

Throughout 1946 the miners were dogged by low calorie intake, high levels of sickness, and absenteeism rates of over 20%, leading to serious shortfalls in production. The solution for Agatz, soon to be Schiwon's successor as deputy miners' leader, was also political rather than economic: only socialization, denazification, and co-determination would raise miners' morale, and thus productivity. In September, however, NGCC persuaded his superior and Social Democratic rival, August Schmidt, to accept a scheme for monthly Sunday shifts to provide household fuel for the populace. The KPD leadership conceded the need in principle, but made overtime dependent on more food and a 25% pay increase, as well as co-determination and union/works council control of coke distribution. In the meantime it also became evident that not all the coal under this scheme was destined for German homes, and that some was for export to western Europe as reparations from current production. In Bochum, at another *Ruhrrevierkonferenz* on 18 October 1946, delegates from over 200 pits flatly rejected the IVB leadership's recommendation to accept Sunday shifts, despite last-minute concessions by the British and the personal intervention of Böckler, who was heckled with the words 'He's

[31] Gorisek, 20 Nov. 1945, ZI6, Sammlung Becker, Ordner 3/5.

[32] 'Sonderbericht Dortmund', 22 Nov. 1945, SAPMO-BA, I 10/502/10; Mark Roseman, *Recasting the Ruhr, 1945–1958: Manpower, Economic Recovery and Labour Relations* (New York and Oxford, 1992), 23–58.

talking like Bevin!'. After what was by all accounts a stormy meeting, delegates voted by 500 to 8 against the motion, demanding instead socialization and co-determination. A Ruhr-wide pithead referendum on 16 November acclaimed the conference's rejection by 86.9%, and the following month the occupation authorities gave up on overtime plans permanently.[33]

In January 1947, the NGCC, with crucial backing from the Americans, now with a vested interest in the new Bizone, devised instead the points system. In theory, this was a simple incentive scheme of material rewards to increase mining productivity with food and luxury goods coupons. The party clearly found such a plan more difficult to reject than overtime, except as a veiled form of coercion. Nevertheless, for the KPD co-determination and expropriation remained the only long-term solutions.[34] As Agatz again argued in the press:

> The points system must therefore be firmly linked to the demand for socialization of the mines . . . Bacon, sugar, coffee, schnapps, cigarettes, and other things are doubtless very necessary for the miner, yet it is far more important that the miner should now heed the historical call which is going out to him.[35]

The faulty working of the system, which was supposed to penalize absenteeism, but literally failed to deliver the goods, led to a 24-hour strike by 300,000 miners on 3 April 1947. In front of 600 IVB delegates on the eve of the stoppage, including many local militants, Agatz defended his position as deputy leader of a union which had accepted points, but also pressed for action, rejecting privileges for miners denied to the rest of the population. Nevertheless, it would be highly misleading to see Agatz as some sort of rabble-rousing demagogue, since he added that 'Today we believe that it would be irresponsible to talk of strikes rather than protest actions'.[36] Moreover, local Communists were careful 'not to carry it too far', fearful of military government intervention.[37]

The next year, however, when they *were* prepared to be more disruptive, perhaps under the influence of the Cominform or the example of the French and Italians, it was too late. When the IVB's local leaders

[33] Ulrich Borsdorf, 'Speck oder Sozialisierung?: Produktionskampagnen im Ruhrbergbau 1945–1947', in Hans Mommsen et al. (eds.), *Glück auf, Kameraden!: Die Bergarbeiter und ihre Organisation in Deutschland* (Cologne, 1979), 345–66; *WVE*, 30 Aug. 1946, 2; *WVE*, 1 Oct. 1946, 2; 'Bericht der Betriebsräte und Schachtgruppenleiter des Industrieverbandes Bergbau am 18.10.1946 im Parkhaus in Bochum', n.d., SAPMO-BA, I 10/502/7; Gerhard Mannschatz and Josef Seider, *Zum Kampf der KPD im Ruhrgebiet* (East Berlin, 1962), 202.
[34] KPD-BL Ruhr/*Sek.*, 6 Jan. 1947, SAPMO-BA, I 11/23/1; *WVE*, 21 Jan. 1947, 2.
[35] *WVE*, 25 Feb. 1947, 2.   [36] Ruhrrevierkonferenz, 2 Apr. 1947, IGBE, DIV. 4.
[37] Gerber at Ruhrrevierkonferenz, 10 May 1947, IGBE, DIV. 4.

met on 12 January 1948, Agatz conspicuously failed to circumvent the executive's no-strike policy.[38] It would be unfair to say that the confrontations of the previous two years had been *only* about food and overtime, since clearly socialization had been a popular demand at the pits, and, as was seen in Chapter 3, was not simply limited to the Communists. Yet clearly the successful delivery in the interim of the now famous Care Packets by the Americans, containing necessities as well as luxuries of life, was important in taking the edge off the miners' specific grievances. It was fatal for the Communists to reject this humanitarian aid, however correct they were about its underlying political nature.[39] Another important factor which was beginning to isolate the Communists from their clientele among the *Kumpels* was the burgeoning Cold War. From the turn of 1947–8, KPD agitators found themselves fighting a losing battle to link superpower high politics to pit politics. Whereas non-Communist workmates had been ready to go along with socialization, they were not prepared to entertain the KPD's theories about the rejection of Marshall Aid or the paramountcy of the national struggle outlined in earlier chapters. Nevertheless, Communist miners' leaders came to insist that *all* other demands be subordinated to what were essentially foreign policy issues. Yet when they stepped up on to the bench of the colliery washroom, the traditional platform for pithead agitation, and argued the primacy of the national line, they met with irritated disapproval.[40]

The KPD's main political target at the pits from 1948 on became the German Coalmining Leadership (DKBL), founded as a German trustee body in the previous November to prepare the way for Marshall Aid. Its head, Heinrich Kost, was denounced as a Nazi War Economy Leader, although Agatz continued to sit on its advisory council.[41] When, in mid-1948, the DKBL introduced a productivity-related ration system to achieve 290,000 tonnes of coal per day, a leaflet war ensued. The KPD then came out strongly against the scheme, prompting the IVB executive to accuse it in turn of misrepresentation and sabotage of the Marshall Plan, and allege that the 'KPD is not a German party', but one working 'in the interests of Bolshevist victory'.[42] In August Agatz then retaliated by denouncing the rest of the miners' union leadership as the 'the long arm of the DKBL', further isolating himself.[43]

---

[38] Borsdorf, 'Speck oder Sozialisierung?', 359–64; Kleßmann and Friedemann, *Streiks*, 61–2.
[39] *WVE*, 16 Jan. 1948, 2.   [40] Schmidt interview, 9 Aug. 1989.
[41] Clarke, 'Gewerkschaftspolitik', 53.
[42] IVB exec., leaflet, Aug. 1948, IGBE, DIV. 3.
[43] Agatz to Schmidt, 19 Aug. 1948, IGBE, DIV. 12, Mappe 5.

The subsequent decline of Communist influence at the pits was surprisingly rapid, a product of short-term political intervention and medium-term socio-economic change, hastened by the self-defeating political campaigns just elaborated. The existing core clientele proved remarkably loyal—at Sachsen colliery in Hamm, for example, from 1948–55 the Communists' below-ground representative consistently polled the highest vote in an otherwise SPD-dominated works council. The Communists were indeed renowned for their unstinting efforts on the miners' behalf, often putting in a 12–15-hour day. The problem was their inability to make inroads into changing and expanding workforces. 'New miners', perhaps only half of whom were previously unionized, without proper training and sometimes even work clothing, and who were often confined to hostels, seemed to offer fertile recruiting ground. Yet since many were refugees or expellees from the East, from a predominantly agrarian or handicraft background, they harboured a natural antipathy to Communism. None the less, the KPD attempted to mobilize them as works council candidates, and in 1951 established a Committee to Defend the Interests of Young and New Miners, but to no visible effect. According to Roseman, although new miners were only one depoliticizing factor among many, the net loser was the KPD.[44]

Soon the party began to suffer significant losses even in mining works councils. Although recorded results vary, it seems the SPD had already overtaken the KPD by 1946, and stabilized at around 40%, while the KPD dropped steadily to about 18% by the time of the ban in 1956. Those who gained were the Independents, some of them undoubtedly ex-KPD and often outnumbering the Communists themselves by the 1950s. It is still guesswork whether contingent Cold War events, such as the June 1953 uprising, weakened support, as slight recoveries at some pits in 1955 would suggest. Certainly, mining works council elections, like those elsewhere, were consciously politicized. An ex-KPD poacher turned SPD gamekeeper, named Meyer, even began a party whipping system to co-ordinate the SPD's pithead factory groups, works councillors, and local party chairmen. In 1947 Lower Rhine Social Democrats began to attack Communists as anti-unionists,[45] explicitly canvassing an SPD vote, and

---

[44] Bergbau-Archiv, 54/499–500; Peter Clark, n.d. [1950–1], NRW HStA, *NL* Clark, RWN 134/1; Roseman, *Recasting the Ruhr*, 281–6 and 303.

[45] 'Die Betriebsrätewahlen im Ruhrgebiet', n.d., SAPMO-BA, NY 4182/865; SPD-BL Niederrhein, Oct. 1947, in *Gewerkschaften*, 275–7. The KPD had been equally guilty! See *WVE*, 25 Aug. 1946, 2.

in the Ruhr ran cinema advertising and anti-Soviet posters, signing off circulars with the words 'Attack is the best form of defence'.[46] SPD black propaganda even compared KPD methods with those of the Third Reich and claimed that '[m]any German women are slaving in the mines of Siberia and the heavy industry of Russia!'[47] The Social Democrats also started entering into pacts with Christian Democrats, although the rules explicitly forbade this. Thus, on 20 September 1947, one SPD member of the IVB executive held a secret conference of 600 Ruhr miners to agree tactics to oust the Communists. At the same time Catholic bishops called on miners to elect only God-fearing candidates.[48]

Besides works council losses, in 1948 the Communists were man-œuvred out of the IVB hierarchy, which gave up any pretence at being an *Einheitsgewerkschaft*. In January one of its Social Democratic executive members confided to Schumacher that the ageing August Schmidt was not up to the job of containing the Communists, who were supposedly running riot in the union hierarchy. Schumacher allegedly responded by instructing SPD union officials to remove their KPD counterparts, although Schmidt denied this. Nevertheless, in the spring local Social and Christian Democrats, in collusion with some executive members, tried, but failed, to vote Schiwon out as *Bezirk* leader of Gelsenkirchen. The real showdown, however, came at the end of 1948 with the creation of a Bizonal miners' leadership, the elections for which became a Cold War battlefield. The SPD majority on the executive prevented a 200-strong East German delegation from attending, as well as a KPD motion to with-draw from the DKBL as 'simply the red flower in the buttonhole of man-agement'.[49] Although Agatz still received 232 votes to Schmidt's 349, SPD and CDU tactical voting almost completely wiped out the Communists: the new executive of the renamed 'IG Bergbau' consisted of 7 Social and 4 Christian Democrats; the advisory council contained a further 13 SPD, 4 CDU, but only 1 Communist. Two years later the KPD was elimin-ated completely. More significantly perhaps, local strongholds were also beginning to crumble by 1950. At Bottrop, the party lost its majority on the local branch committee for the first time since the war, retaining only

[46] SPD-UBL Dortmund, 9 Sept. 1947, in Kleßmann and Friedemann, *Streiks*, 118.

[47] SPD-LL NRW leaflet, Jan. 1948, in *Gewerkschaften*, 445–7.

[48] Kleßmann and Friedemann, *Streiks*, 71–2 and 120; DPD press release, 24 Oct. 1947, BAK, Z 45 F, ODI 7/23–1/21.

[49] The conference of 28 Nov.–1 Dec. 1948 had elected 282 Social Democratic, 163 Communist, 59 CDU, and 13 Independent delegates: Ind. Rels. Sec./Manpower Adviser, 7 Dec. 1948, MRC, MSS 292/943/14.

9 of the 32 seats, and by 1956 the KPD held only 8 of IG Bergbau's total of 107 local mandates.[50]

In retrospect, the Communists' position at the pits was probably more fragile than it seemed at the time. Of course, the occupation authorities' fear of upsetting the apple cart of coal production meant that they were prepared to tolerate perhaps more radicalism than elsewhere. The miners were also partially sheltered from the food crisis, which in other sectors absorbed surplus energy which might otherwise have been devoted to politics. This in turn reduced whatever illicit patronage might have been gained from feeding and clothing workforces through the black market. Yet in the final analysis, the KPD could not compete with the prospect of regular aid (the points system, Care Packets, and Marshall Aid) to which the authorities soon learned to attach political strings. Socialization and co-determination, the KPD's political staples, were thus effectively bought off with material incentives, until the onset of economic recovery in the 1950s. More importantly, and what is often overlooked, is that, from as early as 1946, the SPD was clearly predominant in both the miners' union and the works councils, seriously limiting the KPD's room for manoeuvre. Moreover, the restructuring of the Ruhr workforce did not work to the long-term advantage of the KPD, so that in both the mining union and the works councils it was facing terminal decline. Both political contingency and socio-economic circumstance had conspired, therefore, to undermine the Communists' Ruhr bastion.

The Politics of Hunger and KPD Strike Policy

> Are worries about food weighing on us so heavily that the brain of the West German is no longer capable of any other thought than potatoes, bread, and fat!
>
> (*Westdeutsches Volks-Echo*, 4 October 1946)

What was true of the Communists' position at the pits, was doubly so in other areas of the West German economy. Unlike post-war France and Italy, where wage strikes lent themselves relatively easily to politicization, early strikes in the western zones of Germany were largely economistic, or, more often, primitive hunger strikes for higher rations. (Overtly political strikes were, of course, banned by the military government.) Indeed,

[50] Jochem to Schumacher, 2 Jan. 1948, ZI6, Sammlung Becker, Ordner 3/3; Frese to Schmidt, 16 Jan. 1948, IGBE, A (Org) 14, Mappe 2; Schmidt to KPD, 27 Jan. 1948, ZI6, Sammlung Becker, Ordner 8.6/7; Clarke, 'Gewerkschaftspolitik', 65–6 and 68–71; Peter Clark, n.d. [1950/1], NRW HStA, NL Clark, RWN 134/1; KRO Bottrop/Gladbeck, Apr. 1950, PRO, FO 1013/1398; Dok. IM-NRW Nr.: 79, 13 Mar. 1956.

popular misery, particularly in the industrial conurbations, was at its most acute since the Thirty Years War, and was certainly more debilitating than the Allied blockade of 1918–19. In the spring of 1947 calorie intake in some Ruhr towns dropped to a third or half of the official ration, and food distribution often degenerated into simple black marketeering. It is therefore no surprise that spontaneous protest strikes of around a million participants occurred early in 1947, followed by 4 million in January–February 1948.[51]

At first sight, this catastrophic situation would seem to have been highly propitious for the Communists. In fact, the KPD used its shop-floor positions between 1946–8 cautiously, attempting to politicize protests only by highlighting the connections between food supply and perceived political restoration.[52] As the US Zone leader, Walter Fisch, pointed out at a session in East Berlin, although 'the food situation can reach critical proportions', the state would 'break the tip off any strike movement'.[53] The SED, for its part, seems to have been alarmed by the implications of a protest movement in the West spilling over into the SBZ. At the same meeting Pieck underlined this fact in his notes, querying the possible 'effect on [the] *eastern zone*'.[54] The SED was in fact required to defend the rationing policy of the Soviet authorities. Pieck later raised the contradiction between the KPD slogan 'We want to eat so that we can work!', and SMAD Order No. 234, which offered food in return for higher productivity. Reimann responded uncharacteristically brusquely:

Comrade Wilhelm Pieck, we have a completely different situation. (W. Pieck: I realize that!) The people would think we were all idiots if we said: work more so that we can eat. For us it is the other way around: first eat and then work! (Walter Ulbricht: By that token you are working much too much.—Laughter.)[55]

Hunger was thus probably more of a retardant than a radicalizer. The 'save-as-save-can' mentality of those scavenging for food reduced West Germans to the status of latter-day hunter-gatherers, and was not conducive to class solidarity. It was also clear to most, including the Communist leadership, that a strike would not solve distribution overnight and could even be counterproductive. On 3 February 1947, for example, about 17,000 orderly demonstrators protested at the bread shortage in Essen,

[51] Günter J. Trittel, *Hunger und Politik: Die Ernährungskrise in der Bizone (1945–1949)* (Frankfurt am Main and New York, 1990), 254–61.
[52] SED/KPD conference at Frankfurt am Main, 21 Apr. 1947, BAK, B 118/1.
[53] SED-ZS/KPD meeting, 23–4 Oct. 1946, SAPMO-BA, DY 30/IV 2/1.01/20.
[54] Pieck's notes, 23 Oct. 1946, SAPMO-BA, NY 4036/643.
[55] SED-ZS/KPD meeting, 13 Jan. 1948, SAPMO-BA, DY 30/IV 2/1.01/73.

during which the Communist ex-mayor, Heinz Renner, exercised a moderating influence, much to the relief of his successor, Gustav Heinemann, and a visibly rattled British commandant. In front of the *Rathaus* Renner applauded the miners' solidarity, but told them to go back to work. The KPD could thus hardly be held responsible when, a few minutes later, the entire Krupp workforce spontaneously downed tools and marched on military government headquarters.[56]

The pattern was the same in ensuing hunger strikes, which peaked in March–April 1947. Works councils or local union branches channelled spontaneous stoppages into orderly demonstrations and rallies. If the KPD appeared at all, it was as an intermediary in a brief protest strike, which was usually contained by the unions and, if necessary, by military government itself. Only rarely were demands for the purge of Schlange-Schöningen's Nutrition Office, or land reform, politicized into calls for nationalization of the mines and expropriation of basic industries. In fact, by April the Americans could find no positive evidence of KPD strike control in the Bizone, although Social Democrats thought Communists had inspired early strikes in Essen, Duisburg, and Oberhausen, before losing control to the unions and SPD. US intelligence distinguished between high-level KPD leaders who recognized open strike agitation as futile in improving the food situation, and local hotheads. The British also tended to ascribe unrest to Communists at local and regional level, although Steel and Strang were convinced that most hunger marches were spontaneous. As one report of December 1946 put it, the prime motivator was 'a starvation level ration scale' whereby the KPD was 'lifted into prominence after its defeat at the elections, not by the agitation but by the tidal wave of distress'.[57]

In the winter of 1947–8 hunger strikes were back on the agenda, in response to renewed ration cuts. In early January 1948 about 100,000 Ruhr metalworkers and 12,000 Hamburg dockworkers started a series of peaceful protests, which eventually encompassed about 4 million West Germans. Unlike the French and Italian strikes of November and December 1947, made possible by inflation and aimed at the Marshall Plan, the politicization of German actions was unfocused and secondary. This is not to say that union leaders and political opponents did not play the

---

[56] RWIS to Dep. Regional Commissioner, 8 Feb. 1947, PRO, FO 1013/42; Schmidt interview, 9 Aug. 1989.
[57] RWIS, 'Political Summary No. 4', 16 Dec. 1946, PRO, FO 1005/1722; ODDI/ EUCOM, 10 Sept. 1947, BAK, Z 45 F/POLAD 32/12; Werner Müller, *Die KPD und die 'Einheit der Arbeiterklasse'* (Frankfurt am Main and New York, 1979), 355 n. 84; Müller, *Mitbestimmung*, 201.

Communist conspiracy card for all it was worth, partly to prompt the western Allies to give humanitarian aid.[58] Although the 1948 strikes were ultimately bigger than 1947's, the unions appear to have been in greater control. Admittedly, Böckler was given a bumpy ride by local unionists when he forbade strike calls by works councillors or unionists at two Ruhr conferences in Mülheim on 14 and 30 January 1948, but a KPD plan for a 24-hour strike on 2 February never materialized.[59] It was next to impossible for the KPD to attach political demands—by which it meant 'national' rather than 'socio-economic'—to the general unrest:

We have switched the initiative down to the local [union] cartels and shop-floors, and thus taken much of the wind out of Böckler's sails [but] it is still the case in the factories that we cannot get the workers out with slogans for the unity of Germany and against Frankfurt.[60]

By May Reimann's message was even blunter: 'All preconditions for a general strike are missing.'[61] When it came to a managed 24-hour general strike on 12 November 1948, arranged by the DGB to protest at price rises, the party appeared to have learned the lesson of the spring and did not attempt to nationalize the dispute.[62]

This is not to say that workers and Communists were otherwise totally quiescent. The miners were prepared to fight for socialization, which was hardly an economistic issue. Ever since Weimar the labour movement had also been seeking greater co-determination (*Mitbestimmung*), both of the economy and industrial management. In the immediate after-shock of defeat some Communists had even attempted to enforce unilateral shop-floor co-determination. In 1945 Paul Harig, Communist works council chairman at Klöckner's Hasper Hütte, convened all the conglomerate's directors and works councillors, securing the removal of several managers and demanding parity representation on each supervisory council and board of directors.[63] Predictably enough, however, the British refused to sanction such moves.

The relationship between industrial workers and management was formalized in the ACC's Law No. 22 on works councils of April 1946. It ruled out collective bargaining, providing instead for individual works agreements, but in practice these proved enforceable only by strikes. The

[58] Trittel, *Hunger und Politik*, 261.
[59] Kleßmann and Friedemann, *Streiks*, 63–4; KPD-BL Ruhr/*Sek.*, 27 Jan. 1948, SAPMO-BA, I 11/23/1.
[60] Reimann at SED-ZS/KPD meeting, 10 Feb. 1948, SAPMO-BA, DY 30/IV 2/1.01/79.
[61] Pieck's notes, 11 May 1948, SAPMO-BA, NY 4036/643.
[62] KPD-LL NRW, 28 Oct. 1948, in *Gewerkschaften*, 450–2.
[63] Harig, *Arbeiter*, 74–6.

test case for shop-floor co-determination occurred at Hannover's Bode-Panzer plant in November–December 1946 (the first German strike since Hitler), when works councillors, led by the KPD factory group, created a *fait accompli* for IG Metall and successfully forced the hands of the employers' association. For British military government's part, Manpower Division clearly feared that the floodgates were being opened to a wave of political strikes by the KPD the following spring. Yet in 1947 the DGB successfully managed the disputes by enforcing a model works agreement, thus effectively taking the initiative from the works councils. By 1948, plant-level co-determination strikes were becoming a thing of the past. At the same time, attempts to legislate co-determination from above, to include, for instance, consultation over personnel policy and protection against mass lay-offs, also failed. Consequently, a bill along these lines by Württemberg-Baden's Communist Labour Minister, Rudolf Kohl, was diluted by the *Land* government and later nullified by the 1952 Works Council Law.[64]

Decartelization—the break-up of Germany's notorious industrial monopolies—offered a less confrontational but perhaps more effective avenue of co-determination. The party was at first uncertain about how to respond to the new post of labour director, offered as a sweetener on the board of some decartelized industries. To hard-liners, the lure of a company car smelled of the gravy train (*Bonzifizierung*), and soon decartelization was being attacked as a masquerade for the regrouping of German industrialists under American auspices. In March 1947 the NRW *Landtag* faction came out against parity representation on the supervisory councils of decartelized concerns as throwing 'sand in the eyes of the workers again',[65] and in September Reimann announced the withdrawal of all KPD labour directors. The crisis of loyalty, for Willy Wagner at Bochumer Verein for instance, was nearly always decided in favour of the seat on the board, resulting in party expulsion. Subsequently, none of 32 labour directors in the NRW metal industry, nor some 63 at the pits, was Communist, the post becoming a mainly Social Democratic preserve.[66]

[64] SED-PV/KPD meeting, 18 Dec. 1946, SAPMO-BA, DY 30/IV 2/1.01/30; POLAD to State Dept., 19 Nov. 1948, in *Confidential U.S. State Department Central Files: Germany —Internal Affairs 1945–1949*, ed. Paul Kesaris (Frederick, Md., 1985), 15. 11–16; Müller, *Mitbestimmung*, 207.

[65] Elke Greiner-Petter, 'Antifaschistisch-demokratische Aktivitäten', Ph.D. thesis (Humboldt University, East Berlin, 1986), 48.

[66] Pieck's notes, 19–20 Sept. 1947, SAPMO-BA, NY 4036/643; SED-ZK/Westabt. on 7th KPD-PV, 20 Nov. 1948, SAPMO-BA, DY 30/IV 2/2.022/126; ZI6, Sammlung Becker, Ordner 4/2.

A new round of co-determination disputes surrounded two bills before the *Bundestag* in the early 1950s, the 1951 Law on Co-Determination in Heavy Industry (*Montanmitbestimmungsgesetz*) and the 1952 Works Constitution Law (*Betriebverfassungsgesetz*). Regarding the first, after massive strike threats from IG Bergbau and IG Metall, in 1950–1 the Federal government conceded joint supervisory councils between workers and management, as well as labour directors across the whole of the coal and steel industry. In return the unions tacitly acquiesced in Adenauer's foreign and defence policies, thus securing the acceptance of the Schuman Plan to pool the industrial resources of the Ruhr. Although the KPD abstained from the *Bundestag* vote on the bill, on the floor of the house the Communists denounced it as an instrument of rearmament and corporatist diversion. The unions, however, attempted to portray it as a victory for collective action and the beginning of the revival of the post-war labour movement. Far more controversy surrounded the proposed Works Constitution bill, which threatened to remove many of the works council powers accorded by the Allies in 1946. In the spring of 1952 the unions went so far as to organize demonstrations and warning strikes. The KPD, intent on the national issues described in the last chapter, was still directing its main fire at Adenauer's foreign policy towards the European Defence Treaty and the General Treaty. Thus, despite subsequent claims to have led resistance to the bill, which was nevertheless passed in July, the Communists did little to avert what has been seen as a turning-point in the taming of the West German labour movement.[67]

Dismantling, because of its plant-by-plant nature, offered perhaps better prospects of Communist-led industrial action than what were essentially parliamentary disputes over co-determination. 'Factory patriotism', as outlined above, also seemed the perfect link between the shop-floor and the national struggle. This failed to take account, however, of the resentment among German workers at Moscow's massive programme of dismantling and reparations from the SBZ. Internally, the German Communists themselves admitted that their support, or at least silence, over what ultimately meant the disappearance of nearly a third of East German industry, was casting them as an 'appendage of pro-Russian foreign policy'.[68] Moral condemnations by the KPD of later 'competitive dismantling' by western capitalists were thus undermined from the outset. Moreover, while eastern dismantling was still in full swing, the KPD was

---

[67] Eberhard Schmidt, *Die verhinderte Neuordnung 1945–1952* (Frankfurt am Main, 1970), 193–220.

[68] SAPMO-BA, DY 30/IV 2/10.01/2, fo. 103.

forbidden by Berlin from protesting, keeping quiet, for instance, over the fate of the Siemens-Martin blast furnaces at Krupp. These, like a quarter of all western removals, were destined for Soviet hands and thus politically taboo. The party also remained painfully ambivalent over other threatened works, such as Hamburg's Blohm and Voß shipyard. When the first dismantling list was issued in October 1947, the furthest the KPD seemed willing to go was to publish the names inside a symbolic black border.[69]

In fact, western dismantling did not reach significant proportions until 1949, by which time the Cold War had saved many of the factories slated for destruction. Nor was the selective nature of the programme conducive to solidarity. This partly explains the poor results of concerted attempts by the North Rhine-Westphalian KPD, over the summer of 1949, to organize protest strikes in support of conscientious objectors, put on trial for refusing to dismantle their own livelihoods. The party succeeded in achieving token stoppages at only five pits, despite strong KPD influence at forty. In Bochum there were even mutterings from party members who refused 'to be harnessed before the cart of private enterprise which is only interested in the preservation of its factories'.[70] When in April 1950 a KPD-inspired Committee against the Dismantling of Peace Industries called on the inhabitants of Essen to occupy the Krupp works, there was no response. Nor was the party able to avert the destruction of Europe's largest and most modern steelworks, the Reichswerke at Salzgitter. On 8 November 1949 the Lower Saxon party called in vain for a general strike to save the plant. The British responded by sentencing the *Land* chairman, August Holländer, and KPD journalist Werner Sterzenbach to eighteen and twelve months' imprisonment respectively for this act of incitement. At the same time, East Berlin tried to appropriate the dismantling issue for the cause of national unity. Demonstrators against the Salzgitter convictions swathed themselves in the patriotic black, red, and gold, condemning British policy as the continuation of wartime bombing by other means. Throughout 1949 the West Commission had also encouraged delegations from western plants to visit the German Economic Commission, the East German version of the Economic Council, to negotiate 'export' orders to keep alive internal German trade. The Reichswerke

---

[69] KPD-BL Ruhr/*Sek.*, 21 Oct. 1947, SAPMO-BA, I 11/23/1; *WVE*, 17 Oct. 1947, 1; Peter Grafe, 'Der Kommunist im Ost-West-Konflikt: Erinnerungen von Ernst Schmidt', in id. *et al.* (eds.), *Der Lokomotive in voller Fahrt die Räder wechseln* (West Berlin and Bonn, 1987), 98; Ulrich-Wilhelm Heyden, 'Die Politik der KPD', MA Thesis 242–6.
[70] 'Konkrete Formen der nationalen Politik', 10 Aug. 1949, SAPMO-BA, DY 30/IV 2/2.022/126.

was tempted in this way with a 20 million DM contract, in what seems to have been little more than an SED propaganda exercise.[71] In turn, subsequent KPD strike policy also became subsumed under the high politics of the Cold War, above all the struggle against remilitarization described earlier. In 1950, for instance, the party attempted to organize a boycott of American arms shipments to Bremerhaven. It also denounced fortnightly overtime in the mines as 'panzer shifts' for Korea, reminiscent of Nazi productivity drives, but pithead strikes fell flat. During the four-week Hessen metalworkers' strike in September 1951, KPD strike committees also tried in vain to turn a wage dispute into a campaign against rearmament. Only following the general ideological wind-down after 1953 did KPD industrial action became less overtly political. When Hamburg's Howaldt shipyard defied its works council and IG Metall to begin a spontaneous wage strike in August 1955, the KPD factory group and local leaders were caught unawares, and perhaps for that reason managed to keep to bread-and-butter issues.[72]

In the final analysis, did KPD strike involvement make any difference? Perhaps, unwittingly, only to discredit the weapon of the strike in the eyes of the rest of the West German labour movement. Genuine grievances could all too easily be dismissed by the unions, employers, state authorities, and press as part of a Communist conspiracy. KPD involvement thus often spelled the kiss of death for a strike. For instance, when, during a dockers' dispute in Hamburg and Bremen in October 1951, autonomous strike committees with KPD chairmen accepted 300,000 DM from the GDR's IG Transport, the West German Transport and General Workers' Union (ÖTV) disowned what it claimed was a Communist wildcat action. More significantly, the state authorities became involved, seizing food donations, while the Federal government warned of a 'Bolshevist inundation'.[73] IG Metall and ÖTV thereafter routinely denounced *all* wildcat strikes as Communist inspired, so as to cover their backs at wage negotiations with employers. Of course, the major long-term factor

---

[71] Dok. IM-NRW Nr.: 64, 27 June 1950; HICOG to State Dept., 18 Mar. 1950, in *Confidential (1950–1954)*, 28. 504–8; Archiv der Stadt Salzgitter (ed.), *Die Demontage der Reichswerke (1945–1951)* (Salzgitter, 1990), 169 and 184.

[72] White to State Dept., 18 July 1950, in *Confidential (1950–1954)*, 28. 580–1; Leaflet (Agatz), n.d. [Nov. 1950], IGBE, T3, Mappe 2; Arnold Bettien, *Arbeitskampf im Kalten Krieg* (Marburg, 1983), 317–35; Herbert Kuehl, *Die Gewerkschaftspolitik der KPD von 1945 bis 1956* (Hamburg, 1981), 145–200.

[73] Gerald Sommer, 'Streik im Hamburger Hafen', *Ergebnisse*, 13 (1981) 55–96; Rainer Kalbitz, *Aussperrungen in der Bundesrepublik: Die vergessenen Konflikte* (Cologne and Frankfurt am Main, 1979), 101–15.

explaining the quiescence of the West German unions, in comparison with their western European neighbours, was the huge rise in the standard of living from the mid-1950s. Nevertheless, in the early 1950s the 'economic miracle' was still on the horizon for most West German workers, and in the meantime the Communist spectre arguably played an important bridging role in maintaining industrial discipline.

The Ejection of the Communists from the Unions

As has been seen in the mining industry, from late 1947 the KPD had been fighting a losing battle within the unions against the SPD. The party's response was a partial reversion to the separatist tactics of the Weimar RGO. Para-union Metal Commissions were thus set up in October 1947, followed in 1948 by Coal Commissions in the Ruhr and its five *Bezirke*, mirroring IG Bergbau structures even down to individual pit-heads. Local Communist unionists daring to criticize such moves as inherently sectarian, were attacked by the leadership with the party's other stock deviation, 'opportunism', which implied making too many revolutionary concessions to the reformist enemy. In 1949 the shop-floor was further polarized along Cold War lines after the American AFL and British TUC walked out of what they saw as an increasingly Communist-dominated World Federation of Trade Unions (WFTU). Instead, they founded the International Confederation of Free Trade Unions, to be joined by the West German DGB not long afterwards. In November the Cominform then went on to vilify rightist Social Democratic and union leaders—views echoed in the KPD's policy statement of March 1950, 'The Trade Union Movement and the Communists'. With its own heady mixture of sectarianism and opportunism, it fantasized about the shop-floor as a militant springboard to bypass reformist union leaders, while insisting that wage demands, job security, and co-determination should remain subordinate to the pacifist and nationalist issues discussed in the previous chapter.[74]

In March 1951 the party signed what amounted to its own union death warrant in the shape of the Munich Convention's notorious Thesis 37. This accused rightist union leaders of selling out to foreign and domestic monopoly capitalists, by accepting seats on supervisory councils in a latter-day Stinnes-Legien pact, analogous to the deal struck between Weimar

---

[74] KPD-LL NRW/Abt. A and S to Ortsgruppen, 9 Oct. 1947, AdsD, BL WWf. 69; DKBL report, Bremen Consulate to State Dept., 27 June 1949, in *Confidential (1945–1949)*, 15. 146–56; Gee to Carthy, 13 Aug. 1949, MRC, MSS 292/943/6; Sonderbeilage to *Wissen und Tat*, 1950/2.

industry and the unions in November 1918. The Thesis continued in this aggressive tone: 'They are doing this so that domestic and foreign monopolists can prepare the third world war.' Communists, with a particular eye on non-unionized workers, were 'to unleash militant action against the will of rightist union leaders', turning the unions into syndicalist 'fighting organizations'.[75] At the same time the party took the idea of para-union commissions one step further, by convening whole conferences timed to coincide with union gatherings. In 1951 a WFTU-affiliated European Workers' Committee against the Remilitarization of West Germany led to an SED/KPD German Workers' Committee in April, and in January 1952 to an All-German Miners' Conference in Oberhausen, a West German Metalworkers' Conference in Duisburg, and a Hamburg Harbour Workers' Conference. Boycotted by the mainstream West German unions, these events only ever reached a small audience.[76] This was, nevertheless, reminiscent of previous RGO tactics and, as will be seen below, was to backfire similarly badly, fostering greater solidarity among non-Communist trade unionists and catapulting Communists out of their residual union posts.

As early as June 1947, the SPD leadership had also begun to take a more interventionist line on the shop-floor, when Schumacher called for an end to the 'fools' licence' (*Narrenfreiheit*) enjoyed by Communists in the unions.[77] This was allegedly only increasing the risk of the unions' other main fear, a threatened breakaway Catholic union. A few weeks later the SPD executive applied more direct pressure on union leaders, including Böckler and Tarnow, suggesting that hitherto passive Social Democrats be activated through factory groups in order to ward off the dual encroachments of Communist and Christian unionists. Henßler, the SPD's Ruhr leader, advocated open campaigning in works council and union elections, and Schumacher demanded a showdown, arguing that '[w]e cannot circumvent the battlefield on the shop-floor'.[78]

Böckler, true to the *Einheitsgewerkschaft*, was still keen to preserve nominal independence from *any* political party. Yet during 1948 the single

[75] *FV*, 1 Mar. 1951, 3 and 7–10.

[76] Michael Klein, *Antifaschistische Demokratie* (2nd edn.; West Berlin, 1986), 134; Rainer Kalbitz, 'Gewerkschaftsausschlüsse in den 50er Jahren', in Otto Jacobi *et al.* (eds.), *Gewerkschaftspolitik in der Krise—Kritisches Gewerkschaftsjahrbuch 1977/78* (Berlin, 1978), 159.

[77] *Protokoll der Verhandlungen des Parteitages der Sozialdemokratischen Partei Deutschlands vom 29. Juni bis 2. Juli 1947 in Nürnberg* (reprint, West Berlin and Bonn-Bad Godesberg, 1976), 48.

[78] SPD-PV/union meeting, 30 July 1947, in *Gewerkschaften*, 438–44.

union was threatening to collapse into its constituent parts. At the 1948 May Day parade in Duisburg, for instance, Christian Democrats literally stepped out of line, refusing to march behind the red flag.[79] The Social Democratic majority thus increasingly found itself being forced to decide between an *Einheitsgewerkschaft* that was either politically or confessionally inclusive. At the end of September 1948 Böckler seemed to have made up his mind in favour of the latter, even before a disciplinary DGB meeting to which he had summoned Christian Democratic troublemakers, while rather disingenuously claiming that an invitation to the KPD would have been 'pointless'. Albers of the CDU made it clear that the price of his members' co-operation was the isolation of the Communists. Böckler then took the decisive step of warning that 'all members, especially full-time officials who engage in Communist agitation within the unions, are to be removed from their posts'.[80]

As yet, however, little occurred except in the miners' union, and the unions appeared content to use the weapon of election pacts to remove Communists. A more proactive policy emerged in 1950–1, however, starting on 6 March 1950 when the DGB executive discussed methods of combatting KPD and FDGB infiltration. This led in October to a brochure, 'Enemies of the Unions, Enemies of Democracy', which pressed member unions for instant dismissals of Communist subversives. Already, in June, Paul Harig, First Plenipotentiary of IG Metall at Hagen-Haspe, as well as being a *Bundestag* deputy, had been suspended for an alleged wildcat strike. A week later he was dismissed without notice, causing an overnight stoppage. Then, on 18 September Willi Agatz, former deputy miners' leader, was expelled from IG Bergbau.[81]

Nevertheless, the blame for these ruptures in the *Einheitsgewerkschaft* cannot be attributed solely to infighting within the German labour movement. The Cold War soon brought outside agencies into the conflict on the West German factory-floor. Thus, in November 1948 the British Trade Union Congress had urged the DGB to 'make short shrift of the instigators of this sabotage campaign', meaning the Communists.[82] US military government's Manpower Division also believed it necessary to

[79] Letter to Föcher, 20 May 1948, DGB-Archiv, *NL* Föcher, Kasten 1/4.

[80] DGB exec., 27 Sept. 1948, DGB-Archiv, Bestand 11/13. A repeat was held in 1949: DGB exec., 21 Mar. 1949, DGB-Archiv, Bestand 11/11.

[81] DGB (Karl), n.d. [1950], MRC, MSS 292/943/17; Harig, n.d., [1950], ZI6, Sammlung Becker, Ordner 14/14; IGB expulsions, IGBE, V4, Mappe 1; Sommer, 'Streik im Hamburger Hafen', 40.

[82] TUC's letter of 10 Nov. 1948, referred to in Böckler to Tewson, 15 Nov. 1948, DGB-Archiv, *NL* Gottfurcht, Kasten 17/66.

'minimize and eliminate Communist influence in the whole of the trade union field'.[83] Later, after the American CIO had begun expelling Communists at home, Harvey Brown, Director of Labor Affairs in the US High Commission, played an important role in co-ordinating the individual German unions and prodding them into action against their Communist members in 1950.[84]

The West German state was also an actor. Marking the cards of Communists at the labour exchange was a venerable practice dating back to Weimar, and continued after the war. The Bremerhaven exchange thus connived in the dismissal of 70 KPD dockers, including works councillors, when the port authority secretly passed on a blacklist, although its director was apparently notorious for describing any troublemakers as Communists. In certain cases the security services, the *Verfassungsschutz*, informally notified employers of Communist job applicants, sometimes leading to forfeiture of a job or company housing. Many works regulations were unrevised since the Third Reich and continued by default. Some labour tribunals upheld Communist dismissals in the interests of a corporatist works peace (*Betriebsfrieden*); others gave priority to freedom of speech and insisted on reinstatement. In April 1951, however, the Munich labour tribunal ruled that, in the conflict between the 'Christian-occidental cultural conception' and the 'Communist-Bolshevist world and state conception', and in the interests of shop-floor harmony, workers in the public sector (including works councillors) might be dismissed for simple KPD membership. A year later this principle was extended to the private sector. The July 1952 Works Constitution bill further depoliticized the workplace. In its name, three KPD works councillors at AG Weser were removed by court order for disrupting the works peace, after they had condemned in the plant's name a *Stahlhelm* veterans' procession as militaristic.[85]

There were, of course, other semi-private agencies, such as the Community for the Protection of German Industry, founded in 1952 to combat Communist infiltration; the Federal Association of German Industry's

[83] Quoted by Weiler, *British Labour*, 180.

[84] Harvey Brown, HICOG's leading labour official, at a meeting with IG leaders, 14 Aug. 1950; see Michael Fichter, 'HICOG and the Unions in West Germany', in Jeffry M. Diefendorf *et al.* (eds.), *American Policy and the Reconstruction of West Germany, 1945–1955* (Cambridge, 1993), 267.

[85] Bremerhaven Vice-Consul to State Dept., 21 Dec. 1948, BAK, Z 45 F, POLAD 798–8; Alexander von Brünneck, *Politische Justiz gegen Kommunisten* (Frankfurt am Main, 1978), 300–4; Christian Seegert, 'Betriebsfrieden in Kalten Krieg', *Marxistische Studien: Jahrbuch des IMSF*, 8 (1985), 233–4 and 241; Hofschen, 'Werftarbeiterstreik', 36–59.

Consultancy for Works Protection, which used former *Wehrmacht* counter-intelligence officers to advise on purging vital concerns of workers with eastern contacts; and the Industrial Warning Service, which published newsletters on Communist subversion. The American-inspired missionary organization, Moral Rearmament (Moralische Aufrüstung), also organized two-week coach trips to Caux in Switzerland, where workers listened to company directors extolling the virtues of Christian harmony based on the principles of 'good will' and 'loving kindness'.[86]

A closer study of one well-documented case of shop-floor anti-Communism, at the Opel works in Rüsselsheim, reveals a complex relationship between Communists, Social, and Christian Democrats on the one hand, and management, military government, and the state on the other. The 9,300-strong car plant, the largest factory in Hessen, became a testing ground between the Americans and the KPD factory group, centred around a six-man anti-Nazi resistance cell. In autumn 1947 the Communists lost their absolute majority on the works council, partly because of management intervention and food parcels from the parent company, General Motors, but in October 1948 regained it in collaboration with leftist Social Democrats. Aided by the failure of the SPD and CDU to agree an election pact, the Communists had scored highest in the repair shops and cutting and pressing sections. Here they attracted about ten times as many votes as they had members, and were strong enough to influence hiring policy and thus exert a primitive form of patronage. SPD tactics of homing in on national issues such as the Berlin Blockade made little impression. Then, in early 1949 General Motors plant supervisors tried direct intervention at Opel, attempting to reinstate a denazified shop steward, but reached deadlock when the Communists threatened a stoppage. When a 15 pfennig/an hour wage rise was demanded, the German manager, who privately admitted no difficulty in paying, approached the Americans. They urged him to hold out, and enlisted IG Metall and AFL support. The KPD majority was then successfully reversed in 1949, but the Communists were still seen as the best hope of realizing the plant-level economic co-determination which the recent Hessen Works Council Law had so conspicuously failed to deliver. With this in mind, the fragile new SPD-led works council lobbied the Hessen interior ministry, always receptive to arguments about Communist subversion, to pressurise an intransigent Opel management into making concessions over shop-floor

---

[86] Werner Hofmann, *Stalinismus und Antikommunismus: Zur Soziologie des Ost-West-Konflikts* (Frankfurt am Main, 1967), 164; *Arbeit und Freiheit: Informationsblätter der SPD* (Nov. 1952), 8–9.

co-determination. It failed, but the Ministry of All-German Affairs still agreed in 1951 to spend 7,500 DM for the express purpose of combatting the Opel Communists.[87]

The radicalization of KPD union policy described above, in the shape of Thesis 37 and the para-union conferences, must thus be seen in the context of this creeping persecution. Given the Communists' precarious position, however, Thesis 37, with its below-the-belt attacks on SPD and union leaders, proved suicidal. The SPD reacted swiftly. On 20 April 1951, little more than a month after the theses were published, Siggi Neumann informed various union leaders that:

We believe it is time for the DGB as well as the individual industrial unions . . . to put an end to Communist subversion within the unions. It is absolutely intolerable that Communists are being employed in some cases full-time and are thereby given an opportunity to operate beneath the mask of the 'neutral unionist' and engage in subversion. We believe that this is a good opportunity for a general purge of the trade union movement.[88]

The relevant passage of Thesis 37 was included as well as a proposed 'disavowal' (*Revers*) which suspects would have to sign, distancing themselves from the Munich Theses, and which the individual industrial unions duly adopted. A device dating back to Weimar, the Communists had nevertheless signed declarations on the Leninist principle of remaining in the unions at all costs. The KPD Executive now decided, however, to forbid their members to sign, placing many Communists in the dilemma of signature or party expulsion. Probably the majority refused to sign, and thus lost their union posts.[89]

The DGB co-ordinated expulsions, collating blacklists of members exhibiting 'anti-union behaviour', of whom 654, mainly senior and middle-ranking union officials, had been expelled by 1955.[90] Jarreck and Schiwon, the founding Gelsenkirchen mining unionists, went in September 1951; in early 1952 five other Communist miners' leaders followed, linked with Thesis 37 or the All-German Miners' Conference; Max Faulhaber, chairman of

---

[87] OMGUS, 29 Oct. 1948, BAK, Z 45 F, POLAD 822–43; OMGUS, 3 Dec. 1948, BAK, Z 45 F, POLAD 822–43; ID/EUCOM, 8 June 1949, in *Confidential (1945–1949)*, 40. 503–9; Wynn to Werts, 8 Apr. 1949, ZI6, Sammlung Becker, Ordner 13/1; Bettien, *Arbeitskampf*, 335–46.

[88] *KPD 1945–1968: Dokumente*, ed. Günter Judick *et al.* (Neuss, 1989), i. 48.

[89] For instance Leonhard Mahlein (later chairman of IG Druck und Papier), Fritz Strothmann (on the IG Metall exec.), and Willi Bleicher (a later *Bezirk* leader of IG Metall); see *KPD 1945–1968*, i. 48; Eisner, *Verhältnis*, 217.

[90] Metal 349, mining 60, chemicals 42, ÖTV 40, railwaymen 40, building 34, food 27, textiles 24, timber 20, others 18; see Kalbitz, 'Gewerkschaftsausschlüsse', 162.

IG Chemie in Baden, was removed in October 1951; Eugen Eberle, works council chairman at Bosch, was expelled from IG Metall in January 1952. Local bastions were also broken up. IG Metall dissolved its Solingen branch, expelling eight Communists, including the First Plenipotentiary, Leupold, and the works council secretary, for protests at arms production. The most notorious case of executive action occurred on 16 January 1956, however, when the building union, IG Bau, dissolved its entire North Rhine *Bezirk* —along with all 49,000 members!—and expelled sixteen officials accused of KPD subversion.[91]

It was only in December 1954, at the KPD's Hamburg Convention, that the party relaxed its ruling on the signing of disavowals. The Convention also rescinded an earlier resolution condemning involvement in supervisory councils. Nevertheless there were still 42 votes against these changes from hard-liners. By then, the KPD enjoyed very few residual positions at local level in any case, and only half of its members were in fact still unionized. For the part of the unions themselves, the energy devoted to such purges can only have weakened their efforts during other, arguably more worthwhile campaigns, such as the grand co-determination disputes of 1951–2 discussed above.[92]

To conclude with some more general observations. The end of the Second World War has been seen by many social historians as a watershed in the development of organized German labour—the beginning of the end. In West Germany it was the iconoclastic Theo Pirker who became especially identified with this pessimistic interpretation.[93] The social history of post-war German labour is still largely *terra incognita* compared with the Third Reich, but a few trends have been discerned by Christoph Kleßmann. For the older generation, socialized before the world depression, the memory of organized labour under the Weimar Republic remained an attractive one. This partly explains the deceptive organizational renaissance after 1945. What probably suffered more obviously were the penumbral organizations which had formed the subculture of the Weimar milieu. For younger workers—those under 30 in 1945—there was a much more positive attitude to Nazi labour policies. Life in the army or as an

---

[91] IGB exec., 24 Sept. 1951, IGBE, V4, Mappe 1; Schädel, 'KPD', 164–5; Heiko Haumann, *'Der Fall Max Faulhaber'* (Marburg, 1987), 11; Tilman Fichter and Eugen Eberle, *Kampf um Bosch* (Berlin, 1974), 187; Dickhut, *Was geschah danach?*, 99; Dok. IM-NRW Nr.: 10; Georg Leber, *Vom Frieden* (Stuttgart, 1979), 36–56.

[92] *KPD 1945–1968*, i. 61 and 65–6.

[93] Theo Pirker, 'Das Ende der Arbeiterbewegung', in Rolf Ebbighausen *et al.* (eds.), *Das Ende der Arbeiterbewegung in Deutschland? Ein Diskussionsband zum 60. Geburtstag von Theo Pirker* (Opladen, 1984), 5–20.

overseer of foreign slave labour may have been experienced as a form of empowerment. Furthermore, the division of Germany and the Cold War accelerated the decomposition of the labour movement. In particular, the behaviour of the SED in East Germany went a long way to discrediting the name of socialism for many western workers. Finally, the material successes of the 'economic miracle' after the currency reform of 1948, admittedly often more mythical than real, lent themselves to a pragmatism at odds with Marxist theory. The social market economy, embodied by co-determination in heavy industry and the partial redistribution of wealth under the equalization of burdens law, also encouraged a widespread faith in reformism.[94]

The organizational question raised by Kleßmann will be discussed in the next chapter, but clearly quantitative success was no substitute for qualitative success. Yet what of the other three criteria—generation, Cold War, and economic miracle? Undoubtedly, the Communists themselves believed that the Nazis had depoliticized the younger generation. One Communist works councillor bemoaned the fact that many older colleagues had been worn out ('verschlissen') by the Third Reich, but were receiving little support from politically inactive younger workmates who 'have been strongly influenced by Nazi ideology':

Most young people equate the works council with the [Nazi] council of trust, treating it as an object of respect in the Nazi sense and accepting its directives without criticism. On top of this comes the fact that for most young people all *joie de vivre* was forcibly repressed during the war and is now forcibly resurfacing. The dance-floor is the first item on the agenda for most [followed by] black-marketeering.[95]

The political impact of the Cold War, besides the numerous examples cited above, is also corroborated by a 1952 report on the Ruhr by a young Christian Democratic observer—but, significantly, only in so far as it fitted into a larger socio-economic pattern. He reported that Communist longevity was thus most marked at older plants with higher accident rates and few welfare provisions. Waning shop-floor influence was particularly noticeable in the metal industry, and could only be countered by personal loyalty to Communist works councillors successful in wage negotiations. Some factories had sought to accelerate the process by dismissing

---

[94] Christoph Kleßmann, 'Elemente der ideologischen und sozialpolitischen Integration der westdeutschen Arbeiterbewegung', in Ludolf Herbst (ed.), *Westdeutschland 1945–1955: Unterwerfung, Kontrolle, Integration* (Munich, 1986), 107–16.

[95] Wilhelm K. to FDGB's Works Council Dept., 24 Feb. 1947, SAPMO-BA/FDGB-HaVo, A 800.

KPD workers at the first excuse; other managements preferred pre-
vention rather than cure, enquiring of local police if job applicants had
a Communist record. Overt anti-Communist activity on the shop-floor
centred around expellees, refugees from the GDR, and returning POWs
from the Soviet Union, sometimes even culminating in punch-ups at the
factory gates.[96]

The advent of the conflict-free social market economy, reliant on
ordered rounds of tariff negotiations, was probably less of a factor in the
KPD's demise, for the simple reason that it came too late to make a difference. Despite the subsequent corporatist claims made for the social
market economy, its architect, Ludwig Erhard, was in many ways an orthodox liberal economist. In any case, the so-called 'economic miracle' did
not begin to make itself felt until the mid-1950s, when the Communists
were on the point of being banned anyway. In the interim, it was arguably
as much the persecution of the Communists in the early 1950s which had
contributed to the works peace, as the reformist aspirations of West German
workers following the currency reform.

In conclusion therefore, from 1945-8, when the KPD enjoyed most
political leverage on the shop-floor in the works councils, it was effectively boxed in by Allied legislation. In the early years the party sought
to alter that legislation primarily by parliamentary means, not militant
industrial action. Shop-floor solidarity was expressed by the resolution, not
the strike. The party's relative quiescence was thereby self-imposed. In
any event, in the hunger years of 1945-8 it proved impossible to mobilize
long-term support outside the party's traditional clientele or to politicize
issues in the name of national unity. The chaotic nature of the crisis in
fact precluded co-ordination, and communization was not the first instinct
of most West Germans, who probably harked back instead to the relative order and plenty of National Socialism.

KPD works councillors and union officials earned their colours in the
struggle for survival, and to some extent lost the basis of their patronage
after the currency reform and incipient stabilization of 1948. At the same
time, the high politics of the Cold War were transferred to the shop-
floor, rapidly eating away the Communists' socio-economic kudos. Indeed,
it would be pointless to try to disentangle social from political factors
completely, in explaining the KPD's industrial decline. Even the changing structure of the factory workforce, with the influx of new labour from
the East, was a product of the Cold War. The party itself was, of course,

---

[96] Junge Union Deutschlands, Mar. 1952, BAK, B 106/15419.

also partly responsible for this politicization of union affairs after the *Einheitsgewerkschaft*'s brief post-fascist honeymoon. Thesis 37 was typical of the attempt to import the national and pacifist struggle into local disputes. Yet this self-marginalization cannot be divorced from the process of deliberate ostracism by non-Communist rivals, notably the SPD, but also the CDU. Explanations for the continued stability of the *Einheitsgewerkschaft* are therefore to be found just as much in the anti-Communist consensus of the 1950s as in the anti-fascist consensus which had gone before.

6

From Mass Party to Cadre Party
The Organization of the KPD

ANY non-ruling Communist party must decide between organization as
a conspiratorial élite of professional revolutionary cadres, or as a broad
protest movement. Under the exceptional circumstances of late Weimar
the KPD appeared to have opted for the latter, but was unable to preserve its mass base under the Nazis and was indeed forced into an ultra-
conspiratorial role. Upon emerging from illegality, it was therefore keen
to break out of its isolation and become not only a proletarian mass party,
but a *Volkspartei* with national appeal. It has been suggested that the preconditions for such a quantum leap in post-war western Europe depended
largely on the host political culture: the larger the vacuum of detached,
non-affiliated workers, the greater the scope for Communist expansion.[1]
Thus, in France with a reasonably mature labour movement, the PCF
stabilized at roughly its pre-war level; in Italy, where the workforce was
notoriously underorganized, the PCI made spectacular breakthroughs (num-
bering only 5,000–6,000 in 1943, by 1945 it had soared to 1,770,000[2]).
Germany was in an anomalous position: until 1929/33 it had enjoyed the
world's most highly organized labour movement, with well-established
Social Democratic, Communist, and Catholic wings; yet from 1933–45
organized labour had been atomized into its constituent parts by Nazi
dictatorship.

One of the paradoxes of post-fascist Germany is therefore the rapid
but fragile organizational recovery of the workers' parties. To be sure, compared with the recruiting successes of the French and Italian Communists,
the post-war KPD's expansion seems modest indeed. At the same time,
however briefly, it surpassed anything achieved under Weimar, reaching
over 300,000 members in half the previous recruitment area. Consequently,
the post-war KPD seemed predestined to continue as a popular protest

---

[1] Karl Rohe, *Vom Revier zum Ruhrgebiet* (Essen, 1986), 30.
[2] Donald Sassoon, *The Strategy of the Italian Communist Party: From the Resistance to
the Historic Compromise* (London, 1981), 24.

party, attempting to mobilize the West German masses. Three factors militated against this: first, by 1949 it had lost so many of its new-found supporters that it could no longer pretend to be a mass party; second, in the paranoid atmosphere of the Cold War, it consciously emulated the ideological retrenchment of the SED to become a Stalinized new-type party; finally, in response to official persecution, it was forced back into conspiratorialism.

The Post-Fascist Surge: The KPD as Mass Party, 1945–1948

Without doubt, the Third Reich had decimated the KPD's cadres. Of the original 350,000 KPD members in 1932 only around 150,000 remained active after 1945; about half of these—roughly 75,000—were situated in western Germany.[3] Thus, it was often up to émigrés to stop the gap. In fact, of the then fifteen *Bezirke* in the western zones, six were initially led by returned émigrés.[4] Notably, the British Zone was run almost exclusively by indigenous German Communists, returning neither from Moscow nor western exile. Reorganization was further hampered in the West by later party-licensing than in the SBZ, where the KPD was rebuilt from the top down, whereas the western KPD existed in a semi-legal state until late in 1945, officially emerging in three stages (*Kreis—Bezirk—Land*). Nevertheless, military government regulations could not deter clandestine rebuilding from the middle down, with *Bezirk* leaderships, often based on anti-Nazi networks at the seat of the old Weimar headquarters, orchestrating the officially vetted local and district organizations.

The Ruhr provided the focus for the other re-emerging *Bezirke* in the British Zone, despite an early leadership challenge from Hamburg. Party couriers soon improvised a primitive zonal communications network as stowaways on goods trains, and early contact was also established with Berlin, although travel was still dangerous. One courier 'had the bad luck to be shot by the Tommies while swimming the Elbe and went to the bottom', but recovered in a field hospital and later made it through.[5] In the case of the Ruhr, in August 1945 Ewald Kaiser was dispatched to the Central Committee to report on the sectarian difficulties with the new

---

[3] 30,000–40,000 had been executed; 60,000 had been incarcerated; 50,000 had died in the war; 100,000 had been conscripted; see Pieck, 'Sitzungsnotizen', 1946–7, SAPMO-BA, NY 4036/739, fo. 13.

[4] North West—Knigge (France); Hessen—Fisch (Switz.); South Bavaria—Ficker (Switz.); Württemberg-Hohenzollern—P. Acker (Switz.); Rhineland-Pfalz—H. Müller (France); Saar —Nickolay (France).

[5] Report by E.K., 30 June 1945, SAPMO-BA, I 10/502/3.

TABLE II. *KPD Membership in West Germany (registered members), 1945–1954*[a]

Land	October 1945	March 1946	May 1947	May 1948	September 1949	March 1951	August 1953	December 1954
Baden-Württemberg	x	x	x	x	x	x	10,271	8,957
South Baden	?	?	6,178	5,086	3,461	2,200	x	x
Württemberg-Baden	6,200	13,647	20,887	19,762	15,685	12,300	x	x
Württemberg-Hohenzollern	x	3,353	3,140	2,802	2,508	2,100	x	x
Bavaria	5,110	25,067	37,418	30,042	23,539	16,830	10,541	10,089
Bremen	6,000	7,000	?	4,110	3,164	2,422	1,894	1,807
Hamburg	12,000	26,000	21,080	20,280	14,749	11,403	8,457	6,731
Hessen	7,000	17,774	27,800	20,906	17,125	11,044	7,719	7,087
Lower Saxony	5,400	16,215	41,213	26,746	18,000	12,489	7,530	6,351
NRW	35,593	61,127	120,310	114,388	76,134	56,599	36,171	33,853
Rhineland-Pfalz	2,187	6,133	20,282	16,919	12,340	6,534	3,765	4,152
Schleswig-Holstein	x	x	20,423	17,324	9,303	5,593	2,915	?
Saar	1,000	4,356	5,483	5,146	3,253	3,066	2,402	?
West Germany	74,490	180,672	324,214	283,511	199,261	142,580	91,665	79,027

[a] 1945: Hans-Joachim Krusch, 'Neuansatz und widersprüchliches Erbe: Zur KPD 1945/1946', *BzG*, 33 (1991), 624; later figures collated from SAPMO-BA, NY 4182/860, I 10/401/1 and I 11/401/11; AdsD, *NL* Gniffke 17.

party line among local Communists, prompting Berlin to send back Max Reimann and Willy Perk as 'reinforcements'. A centrally approved Ruhr leadership was subsequently elected on 15 September 1945, followed two weeks later by a secret zonal conference.[6] The western KPD's loyalties to Berlin meant that it was slow to adapt to the federal logic of western Germany. There was political resistance to zonal leaderships, for instance, because of their separatist implications. Nevertheless, by the end of 1948 the old Weimar *Bezirke* had been replaced by *Land* leaderships. The hole left between *Kreise* and *Länder* by the defunct *Bezirke* was filled by sets of roving instructors, transmitting and monitoring resolutions, and reporting back to the centre on local conditions. They were often shunned by local parties, however, or blamed for their high-handed interference, and in many ways the early KPD was not a model of democratic centralist control.[7]

As early as July 1945 the national Cadre Chief, Franz Dahlem, had talked of the KPD becoming 'in the truest sense of the word a *Volkspartei*', fighting for national integrity and made up of anti-fascists from all social strata, the doors open to peasants, white-collar workers, artists, and the technical intelligentsia, as well as workers. The true state of affairs in most local parties in late 1945, however, was far different. In Hessen, for instance, the party was 'still trapped in the isolation of the old, narrow party circle', with 80–90% of members of Weimar vintage. The story was similar elsewhere. On 1 January 1946 two-thirds of members in Württemberg had belonged to the KPD before 1933. Recruiting drives succeeded, however, in decreasing the proportion of *Altkommunisten*, so that by 1949 the national percentage of pre-1933 KPD members was down to 31.8%.[8]

More surprising, perhaps, is that the post-war KPD so quickly surpassed its Weimar strength. There was clearly a wave of support in 1946, reaching its zenith in May 1947 with 324,214 registered members, around 90% of them paid-up. (Table 11 gives comprehensive figures.) In spring 1946 over 60% of members were classified as workers, and in 1954 it was

[6] BAOR, 'Field Intelligence Summary No. 11', 22 Sept. 1945, PRO, FO 371/46935; Walter Jarreck, 'Vom Neubeginn der Kommunisten 1945 an der Ruhr' (copy of *c.*1966 typescript in possession of the author), 54; KPD-ZK/*Sek.*, 25 Aug. 1945, *Protokolle des Sekretariats des ZK der KPD*, 75; Perk's notes of 29 Sept. 1945 conference, SAPMO-BA, I 10/502/1.

[7] ID/EUCOM, 25 Aug. 1949, in *Confidential U.S. State Department Central Files: Germany —Internal Affairs 1945–1949*, ed. Paul Kesaris (Frederick, Md., 1985), 15. 198–203.

[8] Werner Müller, *Die KPD und die 'Einheit der Arbeiterklasse'* (Frankfurt am Main and New York, 1979), 82, 129, and 132.

still over 50%. The KPD thus remained more proletarian than the SED, whose proportion of industrial workers dropped below 50% as early as 1947. The distinction between skilled and unskilled workers is harder to trace, but in South Baden in August 1947 35% of members were officially skilled and 28.1% unskilled. There does appear to be something in the argument, moreover, that the KPD was breaking into politically virgin territory. In southern Bavaria in spring 1946, 68% were first-time members in any political party, whereas only 2% came from the SPD; of 10,500 new recruits in NRW in spring 1948, over a third of whom were miners, 89% were listed as politically 'indifferent', and less than 2% had defected from the SPD. Mass pretensions also implied, of course, a willingness to accept ex-NSDAP members, or at least fellow travellers. There was, however, strong local resistance to taking even nominal ex-Nazis, despite leadership encouragement. The party also found it difficult to recruit women (17.5% in the western zones in 1947), as well as youths, *Mittelständler*, and farmers, as Table 12 shows. What the party called the 'intelligentsia' also proved resistant. In a survey of 3,000 Germans in the British Zone in 1947–8, only 9% of Communist men and 14% of women supporters had graduated beyond elementary school, whereas in the SPD the figures were 28% and 20% respectively. Yet what the Communists lacked in intellect, they made up for in commitment: of the KPD's supporters, 69% of men and 39% of women in the NRW sample were also party members, over double the levels in other parties.[9]

Given the crucial factor of unemployment in the late Weimar party, when as many as 85% of members had been on the dole, it is perhaps also surprising that the post-war KPD did not capitalize on redundancies after 1948's currency reform. In September 1949 only 3.9% of members were unemployed; in February 1950 (the very peak of unemployment at almost 2 million) only 4.3%; and in December 1954 4.5%. This was apparently not for want of trying. In 1949 the party set up unemployment committees to agitate for increased benefits and soup kitchens, but to little avail. The fact that over a quarter of registered unemployed were women, and about a third expellees, may help to explain this lack of success. The problem may, however, be partly one of categorization. In 1945 there had indeed been huge *hidden* unemployment, of the order of 60–70% in Düsseldorf and 90% in Solingen. In the Hagen-Haspe area it was

[9] KPD-BL Südbaden, 7 Aug. 1947, BAK, B 118/24/75–84; report, 28 Mar. 1946, SAPMO-BA, NY 4182/860; SAPMO-BA, I 10/23/9; 'Organisationsbericht der KPD', n.d., SAPMO-BA, I 11/401/1; Public Opinion Research Office (PORO) Report No. 111, n.d. [summer–autumn 1947] and Report No. 5, 22 June 1948, PRO, FO 1005/1868.

TABLE 12. *Social Composition of KPD Members, 1949 and 1954*[a]

Composition	1949 %	1954 %
Occupation		
Worker	52.9	51.5
White-collar	6.2	6.7
Self-employed	1.3	6.0
Artisan	8.6	—
Farmer	0.6	0.5
Housewife	14.9	11.1
Other	15.6	24.2
Age		
Under 25	6.4	6.7
25–35	13.5	13.6
36–50	46.5	33.7
Over 50	33.7	46.0
Party vintage		
Pre-1933	31.8	—
Post-1945	68.2	—

[a] 'Ergebnisse der Mitgliederkontrolle', 12 July 1949, SAPMO-BA, NY 4036/644; 'Statistischer Überblick zu den Ergebnissen des Umtausches', 27 Dec. 1954, SAPMO-BA, I 11/401/12.

estimated by party instructors in August 1945 that only 260 out of 700 enterprises were working as a result of fuel shortages. Early on, the KPD may well have been attractive to these ghost workforces, although it complained at the time of their general passivity.[10]

Many newcomers were probably motivated to join out of moral and emotional empathy—in the words of one university graduate, since 'this was the only party which did something [against the Nazis]. Ideological considerations did not play a role at the time.'[11] This was perhaps not

[10] Report, 30 Feb. 1950, SAPMO-BA, I 11/401/11; report, 31 Dec. 1954, SAPMO-BA, I 11/401/12; Gee to Bell, 2 May 1949, MRC, MSS 292.943/5; HICOG to State Dept., 30 Jan. 1951, in *Confidential U.S. State Department Central Files: Germany—Federal Republic of Germany. Internal Affairs 1950–1954*, ed. Paul Kesaris (Frederick, Md., 1986), 28. 890–908; *Statistisches Jahrbuch für die Bundesrepublik Deutschland*, ed. Statistisches Bundesamt (Stuttgart and Cologne, 1952), 91; *Protokolle des Sekretariats des ZK der KPD*, 285–309.

[11] Hans Z. (Fragebogen), a *Diplom-Volkswirt* who joined the KPD in 1945 aged 26, leaving in 1946, put off by party formalities, but who rejoined in 1951; see BAK, B 118/172/13195.

the most solid basis upon which to build a mass party. Early resignations indicate that opportunism or misplaced careerism must also have played a part for many, or at least the need for reinsurance against a possible Soviet encroachment westwards. An early signal that the wrong horse had been backed came with the elections of late 1946, when the French noted opportunists jumping back off the bandwagon. On the principle of last-in, first-out, Staritz ascribes most departures to the middle generation who had joined up to 1947 during the 'post-fascist impulse', leaving a core of *Altkommunisten*.[12]

The majority of resignations were probably for such universally banal reasons as apathy or unpaid subscriptions, a tendency accelerated by the currency reform in June 1948 and shared by *all* parties. Immediately after the introduction of the Deutschmark, only 56% of the KPD's 300,000 members were paid-up. Nevertheless, there were also a limited number of principled resignations, even by 1918–19 foundation members in some areas of NRW. At the beginning of 1947 the deputy *Bürgermeister* of Cologne, Dr Louis Napoleon Gymnich, and almost the entire editorial staff of *Volksstimme*, walked out, appalled at 'Stalin's criminal policy towards Germany'. They pledged instead to build a revolutionary party. Elsewhere, Karl Hoppe, *Landtag* deputy in the Saar, cited Oder-Neisse, the Berlin Blockade, and the camps in the SBZ, in his letter of resignation.[13]

Despite American speculation that disappearances were part of a calculated policy to lay down a dormant underground membership, this cannot account for the mass exodus beginning in 1948.[14] By 1949 the rot had set in everywhere, when the average national net loss each month was 2,524, rising to 3,695 in 1950. The number of workers leaving was above average, and the share of post-1945 members involved ranged from 75% in Bremen, to 85% in Württemberg-Baden, to 93.5% in South Baden. Age did not appear to be a consistent factor. Moreover, unlike late Weimar's constantly fluctuating membership, as the party Organization Department glumly noted in 1951:

[12] Baden-Baden Consulate to State Dept., 23 Jan. 1948, BAK, Z 45 F, POLAD 825–14; Hamburg's cadreman talked of 'Konjunkturrittern': Liebenwalde conference, 1 Feb. 1948, SAPMO-BA, DY 30/IV 2/1.01/76; Dietrich Staritz, 'Die Kommunistische Partei Deutschlands', in Richard Stöss (ed.), *Parteien-Handbuch* (Opladen, 1983), 1787.

[13] Pieck's notes, 17 Aug. 1948, SAPMO-BA, NY 4036/643; Dok. IM-NRW Nr.: 25, 3 Mar. 1950; Müller, '*Einheit der Arbeiterklasse*', 388 and 401 n. 170; Bremen Consulate to State Dept., 10 Mar. 1948, in *Confidential (1945–1949)*, 14. 900–1; Hoppe to KPD-LL Saar, 12 Oct. 1948, SAPMO-BA, DY 30/IV 2/2.022/129.

[14] Morris memo. (No. 326), 16 Feb. 1948, BAK, Z 45 F, POLAD 798–5.

the obviously strong reverse trend in membership has nothing in common with a membership fluctuation, with an ebbing and flowing of members, but signifies a much more far-reaching and continuous crumbling away of the party organization.[15]

The KPD's *Gleichschaltung* to a New-Type Party, 1948–1951

After the Yugoslavs' excommunication from world Communism in 1948, a wave of show trials engulfed the eastern bloc, accusing various party leaders of betrayal to the Titoists, Nazis, Anglo-Americans, and, for good measure, Trotskyites. The focus of espionage allegations was Noel H. Field, an American Communist sympathizer, who, while head of a wartime religious relief agency in Switzerland, had aided exiled Communists by securing backing from the OSS under Allen Dulles and allegedly infiltrating them into eastern European Communist parties after 1945. Field was arrested as an American agent in Prague in May 1949 and only released in 1954, when the accusations were declared 'groundless'. At the trial of Laszlo Rajk in September 1949, however, the Hungarian foreign minister and former interior minister 'confessed' to Trotskyism, Gestapo collaboration, and connections with American and Yugoslav intelligence. Traicho Kostov, Bulgarian deputy premier, was also put on trial in December, but, unlike Rajk, refused to co-operate. Both were nevertheless sentenced to death and hanged. Despite the gamut of crimes cited, the chief motive was to curb any national Communist tendencies threatening the special relationship with the USSR.[16]

Between mid-1948 and early 1949, against the background of the anti-Titoist consolidation of the eastern bloc, the SED underwent the transformation to a Soviet-style new-type party. This involved the creation of a Central Party Control Commission (ZPKK) in September 1948, and a Soviet-style Politburo in January 1949. At the same time, former Social Democrats within the party were marginalized and the principle of parity between former Communists and Social Democrats was abandoned. Since SED and KPD were formally still one party in 1948, it was not long before western Communists were being forced to follow suit. Objections that this might be inappropriate, in an opposition party geared to mass mobilization, were discounted in the interests of disciplining maverick leaders and a sectarian rank and file—all in the name of anti-Titoism.

---

[15] 'Bericht zur Mitgliederbewegung im Jahre 1950', 12 Mar. 1951, SAPMO-BA, I 11/401/12.

[16] See Georg H. Hodos, *Show Trials: Stalinist Purges in Eastern Europe 1948–1954* (New York, 1987).

At the end of August 1948 Frankfurt informed all party organizations that a 'membership review' would take place to reactivate the party, raise the ideological level of the membership, and improve the leadership. As well as tightening control over the rank and file, the KPD Executive was expected to make an issue of the Moscow/Belgrade crisis, and the overhaul was in fact a proto-purge, in Pieck's words an 'ideological workover' to discipline wayward western *Länder* such as Rhineland-Pfalz, and to 'create authority' for SED directives. The review's results became known in April 1949, but it seems that the KPD received a stay of execution until after the *Bundestag* elections in August.[17]

Then, in September 1949, General Serov, head of Soviet security in the SBZ, directed the SED to investigate all Field's connections with German Communists in Swiss or French emigration, furnishing the Interior Administration's K5 desk, the forerunner of the notorious Ministry of State Security (MfS) or Stasi, with the pertinent dossiers. It is clear that the West Commission was also closely involved in co-ordinating the purges. Immediately after the SED Politburo had decided on 14 November to start recalling western party members to Berlin for three-monthly investigations, Dahlem went in person to Frankfurt to install a KPD Party Control Commission. Back in Berlin he then set up a commission for the 'ideological clarification of the KPD'. Dossiers were to be prepared on the Frankfurt Executive and all *Land* leaderships by the Cadre Department West. Nevertheless, the ultimate authority behind the scenes appears to have remained the MfS. In early 1951 Ulbricht even wrote to its then head, Wilhelm Zaisser, asking him to speed up the vetting of the KPD leadership.[18]

Kurt Müller issued the opening anti-Titoist shots on behalf of the KPD in mid-September 1949, in an article rhetorically entitled 'Is there a danger of Titoism in our party?'. Within days a series of closed sessions of Stalinist 'critique and self-critique' were begun with the regional KPD leaderships. Georg Fischer, ex-chairman of Bavaria, stormed out of the Munich meeting and resigned on the spot, apparently after emptying

[17] KPD-PV to all Grundeinheiten, 30 Aug. 1948, SAPMO-BA, I 10/401/1; Pieck's notes, 14 Sept. 1948, SAPMO-BA, NY 4036/643.

[18] Jochen von Lang, *Erich Mielke: Eine deutsche Karriere* (Berlin, 1991), 74; Hermann Weber, 'Schauprozeßvorbereitungen in der DDR', in id. and Dietrich Staritz (eds.), *Kommunisten verfolgen Kommunisten: Stalinistischer Terror und 'Säuberungen' in den kommunistischen Parteien Europas seit den dreißiger Jahren* (Berlin, 1993), 439; KPD-PV/*Sek.*, 16–17 Nov. 1949, SAPMO-BA, I 11/302/24; 24th Westkomm., 24 Nov. 1949, SAPMO-BA, NY 4182/867; Herbert Mayer, 'Nur eine Wahlniederlage?', *Hefte zur DDR-Geschichte*, 12 (1993), 45.

the contents of an ink-pot over his accusers. He was soon followed in Rhineland-Pfalz by Herbert Müller. Hamburg and Schleswig-Holstein were treated as particularly prone to revived KPO influences —Kurt Müller and the new Hamburg leader, Willi Prinz, even accused the local party of harbouring a 'party-hostile faction'. Kiel was attacked for its laxity with 'party enemies' and its *Kreis* chairman, Fritz Latzke, expelled along with most of the local leadership. On 23 November Walter Fisch, advocate of limited autonomy in 1946, was 'neutralized' on the national secretariat for permitting an article querying the Titoist threat in *Freies Volk*. Jupp Schappe, its deputy editor, was removed in December and expelled on 6 February 1950, accused of disseminating Yugoslav literature. In connection with Schappe, in a ritual worthy of Brecht's *Der Jasager und Der Neinsager*, Ewald Kaiser and Rudi Treiber (the latter ex-KPO), were dropped from the NRW secretariat, and its chairman, Hugo Paul, deposed for negligence, prompting the words: 'Twice I stood before the [Nazi] *Volksgericht* which had demanded the death penalty for me. This evening—this is worse for me.'[19]

This first round of purges culminated on 28–30 December 1949 in a highly critical Ideological Resolution, which took the entire western party to task. Events did not stop there, however. After the SED's Field Declaration of 24 August 1950, cadre talks were held in East Berlin with all KPD functionaries who had emigrated to the West during the Third Reich. KPD leaders deemed to be security risks were relieved of their functions and transferred to the GDR. Many assumed desk jobs in publishing or academia, although some returned to West Germany after 1956. Later on, the Party Control Commission also demanded comprehensive lists of former dissidents (Communist Party Opposition, Lenin League, and International Socialist Fighting League), as well as POWs at western and Yugoslav camps who had attended training courses. Ex-POWs often automatically lost their functions, since western moles had supposedly been planted in the camps. Even members working for military government on party orders were debarred from party functions. Local parties despaired of finding replacements, but only a few dared to complain at the Executive's high-handed interventions.[20]

[19] *FV*, 14 Sept. 1949, 5; Ulrich Heyden, 'Säuberungen in der KPD 1948 bis 1951', in Wolfgang Maderthaner *et al.* (eds.), *'Ich habe den Tod verdient': Schauprozesse und politische Verfolgung in Mittel- und Osteuropa 1945–1956* (Vienna, 1991), 139–58; Wilfried Reckert, 'Die "Zerschlagung des Titoismus" in der KPD', *LILI Korrespondenz*, 1 (1991), 33–51; KPD-PV/LL NRW session, 6–7 Dec. 1949, SAPMO-BA, I 11/302/24.

[20] *KPD 1945–1968: Dokumente*, ed. Günter Judick *et al.* (Neuss, 1989), i. 298–334; Willi Dickhut, *Was geschah danach?* (Essen, 1990), 67; KPD-PKK, 4 Apr. 1951, BAK,

In fact, the Executive and its Secretariat were among the hardest hit. In 1949–50, besides Kurt Müller and Fritz Sperling, Hermann Nuding, Hugo Ehrlich, Walter Fisch, Jupp Schleifstein, Erich Jungmann, and Rudi Singer were all demoted or transferred, leaving only Reimann and Ledwohn. Nuding, the KPD Secretariat's trade union secretary, was expelled in May 1950 for 'opportunism', that is, hindering KPD–SED collaboration and the popularization of the Soviet Union, and opposing the use of the unions for the peace struggle. In April 1951 he was ordered to renounce his *Bundestag* seat for 'health reasons' and report to Berlin. He declined a post in the GDR, however, and died a rather pathetic figure in 1966, wracked by ill health. Ehrlich and Fisch were also accused of 'opportunism'; Jungmann and Singer confessed to Field connections. Kurt Lichtenstein, Executive member and editor of the Ruhr's *Neue Volkszeitung*, was also stripped of all functions, purportedly for failing to reproduce in full the KPD's telegram to Stalin on his seventieth birthday.[21] Table 13 gives some idea of the turn-over in the top KPD leadership in this period.

In a few spectacular cases, KPD leaders were even arrested by the East German Stasi. Because many had necessarily been western émigrés during the Third Reich and had come into regular contact with western military government, often at the party's bidding, they offered particularly fertile ground for those in Berlin fabricating evidence for a show trial. Kurt Müller, deputy chairman of the KPD, was the first high-ranking German Communist from either SED or KPD to be arrested. While on a routine visit to East Berlin, he was apprehended on 22 March 1950 in Richard Stahlmann's apartment by Stasi officers posing as Russians. Under Soviet supervision, his nocturnal interrogations were personally handled by Erich Mielke, deputy head of the MfS, which he went on to run until the collapse of the SED in 1989. The first interrogation belies subsequent accusations of espionage, since Mielke focused on Müller's 1932 involvement with Heinz Neumann, saddled with the 'social fascism' débâcle and later shot in Stalin's purges. Müller was informed that a show trial à la Rajk was being prepared for later that year, at which he was to be accused of plotting the assassination of Voroshilov and Molotov in 1934

B 118/137/7165; SAPMO-BA, DY 30/IV 2/10.02/247; Hamburg cadre conf., 29 June 1952, BAK, B 118/125/4867–913; KPD-KL Bremerhaven to KPD-LL Bremen, 29 Feb. 1952, BAK, B 118/210/102123; KPD-LL R-P/*Sek.* to KPD-PV/Kaderabt., 13 Mar. 1952, BAK, B 118/214/102354.

[21] KPD-PV/*Sek.*, 5 Apr. 1951, BAK, B 118/137/7115; Nuding to KPD-PV/*Sek.*, 28 June 1956, SAPMO-BA, NY 4142/4; Rainer Zunder, *Erschossen in Zicherie: Vom Leben und Sterben des Journalisten Kurt Lichtenstein* (Berlin, 1994), 77–91.

on behalf of Trotsky; Gestapo collaboration; complicity with Yugoslav, American, and British intelligence, including Reimann's arrest in January 1949; as well as refusing to read out the Solingen Conference telegram (see Chapter 4). Indeed an entire dossier of rather inept incriminating forgeries was compiled by Mielke. Despite a 'confession' on 3–4 October 1950, the torture lasted several more years, including sleep deprivation, 'water' cells, 'standing' cells, and a bout in the Soviets' notorious Karlshorst Coal-Hole. Finally, in 1953, Müller was deported for 25 years to a Siberian labour camp, although he was released in October 1955, along with the last batch of German POWs secured by Adenauer's Moscow negotiations.[22]

Müller's replacement as deputy chairman in May 1950 was Fritz Sperling. At the end of August, however, he was ominously required by the SED to report in detail on his Swiss exile. On 26 February 1951, while in the GDR for genuine health reasons, he was arrested in hospital by the MfS and interrogated first by Mielke, then periodically at night by Soviet and MfS officers. He, too, confessed to party crimes he had never committed and was forced into incriminating fellow KPD leaders as western agents. Accused of the usual collaboration with American and British intelligence in Switzerland, as well as Trotskyism, he was sentenced in March 1954 by the GDR's Supreme Court to seven years penal servitude, until pardoned in March 1956. Sperling remained in the GDR and was rehabilitated internally by the KPD in August, but any further exoneration by the SED was obstructed. In April 1958 he succumbed to a chronic heart condition at the age of 46, his case still not cleared up, although—not untypically—his faith in the party persisted until the end.[23]

Other victims of the Stasi included Leo Bauer, a charismatic KPD leader in Hessen who had transferred to East Germany in 1947. Arrested on 23 August 1950 for his wartime connections with Field, he was apparently also destined for a show trial. He remained for two years in MfS custody, periodically interrogated and beaten by Soviet officers, culminating on 31 May 1951 in a 'confession'. But there was no trial. In December 1952 he was sentenced by a Soviet court martial to execution by firing squad for 'counter-revolutionary activity', but this was commuted to forced labour in Siberia after Stalin's death. Released alongside Müller in 1955, Bauer was almost dragged from the train at Frankfurt an der

---

[22] Kurt Müller, 'Ein historisches Dokument', *Aus Politik und Zeitgeschichte*, B 11/90 (9 Mar. 1990), 16–29; for the protocol of 23 Mar. 1950 see Lang, *Mielke*, 232–9.

[23] Karl Heinz Jahnke, *'... ich bin nie ein Parteifeind gewesen': Der tragische Weg der Kommunisten Fritz und Lydia Sperling* (Bonn, 1993), 81–108.

TABLE 13. Continuity and Discontinuity in the KPD Secretariat, 1948–1955[a]

Name	Year of birth	Location in 1945	1948	1949	1951	1953	1955
Paula Acker	1913	Switzerland	—		Recall to GDR		
Franz Ahrens	?	?				—	Gaol (FRG)
Jupp Angenfort	?	USSR	—				
Alb. Buchmann	1894	Germany (KZ)	—		Recall to GDR		
Erika Buchmann	1902	Germany (KZ)		—			
Hugo Ehrlich	1903	GB		—	Purged		
Kurt Erlebach	1922	USSR		—			—
Walter Fisch	1910	Switzerland		—	Purged	—	—
Franz Geittner	?	?	—				
Gust. Gundelach	1888	USSR	—			—	
Erich Jungmann	1907	Mexico		—	Purged		
Otto Kloock	1911	USSR			—	Purged	
Ilse Kötting	?	?					
Jupp Ledwohn	1907	Germany	—				Gaol (FRG)
Adel. Lißmann	?	?		—			

TABLE 13. *(cont'd)*

Name	Year of birth	Location in 1945	1948	1949	1951	1953	1955
Willi Mohn	1905	?			—		—
Ludwig Müller	?	?			—		—
Kurt Müller	1903	Germany (KZ)	—		Gaol (GDR)		
Oskar Müller	1896	Germany (KZ)	—		Purged		
Oskar Neumann	?	USSR	—		Gaol (FRG)	—	Gaol (FRG)
Fritz Nickolay	1909	France	—		Recall to GDR		
Otto Niebergall	1904	France	—			Gaol (FRG)	—
Hermann Nuding	1902	France	—	Purged			
Hugo Paul	1905	Germany (KZ)	—	Purged			
Walter Poth	?	?			—		
Gertrud Rast	1897	Germany (KZ)	—				
Max Reimann	1898	Germany (KZ)	—				
Fritz Rische	1914	Germany (KZ)	—				Gaol (FRG)
Max Schäfer	1913	Germany (KZ)	—		—		—
Herm. Schirmer	1897	Germany (KZ)	—				
Fritz Sperling	1911	Switzerland	—		Gaol (GDR)		
Grete Thiele	1913	Germany	—			—	

[a] Report on Herne Conf., 7 May 1948, SAPMO-BA, NY 4036/644; Westkomm., 1 Aug. 1949, SAPMO-BA, DY 30/IV 2/2.022/126; 1st KPD-PV, 5 Mar. 1951, SAPMO-BA, I 11/301/17; AdsD, Ostbüro, 0397a; Dok. IM-NRW Nr.: 37; Report, 29 Dec. 1955, SAPMO-BA, I 11/401/10.

Oder by East German officials, a fate prevented only by his physical resistance and the intervention of the accompanying Red Army officer.[24]

Last, but by no means completing the list of victims, was Willi Prinz, chairman of the Hamburg KPD, arrested in February 1951. He was interrogated on his links with Kurt Müller and the Neumann Group, and, since he had been a POW in Egypt until 1947, accused of collaboration with British and French intelligence. He had also allegedly sabotaged unity of action with the SPD; suppressed the Ohne uns! movement; and fostered an anti-party faction in Hamburg. Confronted with Müller's 'confession', he was also accused of supporting the 'special German road to socialism', now vilified as the Titoist road. Although not beaten, the same nocturnal interrogations and sleep deprivation occurred, culminating in Prinz's nervous breakdown in summer 1953. When released on 28 April 1954 he was to be posted to the SED in Leipzig, but claimed he was able to abscond to West Berlin, before telling his story to the western media.[25]

Although the purges had started in the upper echelons, they were complemented by a bureaucratic restructuring of the whole party apparatus. The targets were clearly leaders of pre-1933 vintage, who allegedly filled 95–8% of party posts. Parallel to the Ideological Resolution of December 1949, the principles of the 'Preparation and Implementation of the Re-election of the Leaderships' were published, a process which was to drag on until spring 1951.[26] Each level was to reselect its leaders, but only those 'politically clear and loyal to the party . . . without any wavering towards the politics of the Soviet Union, People's Democracies, and the German Democratic Republic'.[27]

Frustrated by the slow pace of reselection and the persistence of local loyalties, however, Berlin decided to circumvent formal party democracy and intervene directly. On 10 February 1951, at an all-night session of the KPD Executive at Löwenberg, about 20 miles from East Berlin, Reimann—apparently without warning—proceeded to replace almost all the regional western leaders in the space of a few hours. Some were accused of opportunism, others of being security risks *vis-à-vis* western intelligence. Willi Prinz, who was driven away in Stasi custody immediately afterwards, was confronted with his former links with the Neumann

---

[24] Peter Brandt *et al.*, *Karrieren eines Außenseiters* (West Berlin and Bonn, 1983), 99–103 and 185–219.

[25] *Schleswig-Holsteinische Volkszeitung*, Sept. 1954 *et seq.*

[26] 19th Westkomm., 13 Oct. 1949, SAPMO-BA, NY 4182/867; Staritz, 'Kommunistische Partei Deutschlands', 1793.

[27] Quoted by Gudrun Schädel, 'Die KPD in Nordrhein-Westfalen von 1945–1956', Ph.D. Thesis (Ruhr University of Bochum, 1973), 122.

TABLE 14. *Survivors of the KPD's 'Lightning Purges', 1951*[a]

Land	Secretariat	Executive
South Baden	1/ 6	2/15
Württemberg-Baden	1/ 9	11/32
Württemberg-Hohenzollern	0/ 5	0/16
Bavaria	3/10	7/26
Bremen	1/ 5	?/13
Hamburg	1/ 8	5/25
Hessen	2/ 7	8/27
Lower Saxony	0/ 8	2/29
North Rhine-Westphalia	1/10	3/39
Rhineland-Pfalz	1/ 6	?/18
Schleswig-Holstein	0/ 7	?/22
Saar	1/ 7	?/ ?

[a] Reselected leaders/total: SAPMO-BA, I 11/401/10; BAK, B 118/168. Ostbüro reports differ marginally; see AdsD, Ostbüro 0397a.

Group—in his words, 'this affair [which] sticks to you and you can never get rid of'. After stilted attempts at a self-critique, in which he admitted that '[t]he party is always right, even if subjectively one believes one has done no wrong', Reimann was dismissive: 'You cannot fool anyone with these speeches . . . [T]he fact that you are afraid is the best proof that you have not made an inner break'.[28]

Thus, the supposedly democratic reselection process leading up to the KPD's Munich Convention of 3–4 March 1951 (in fact held for con-spiratorial reasons in the GDR at Weimar), was entirely subverted. As well as affecting leading personalities, the so-called 'lightning purges' meant an almost wholesale turn-around of the KPD leadership, as Table 14 shows. Although the figures are not quite complete, it is safe to assume that between 80–5% of the 'old' leadership in the *Länder* disappeared in 1951.

With such a multitude of sins, it is difficult to discern a single set of motives for the purges. Were Weimar skeletons brought out of the closet to settle old scores or as ammunition in the Cold War? All that Mielke

[28] New chairmen with predecessors in brackets: Württ.-Baden—Weber (Leibbrand); Württ. -Hohenz.—Bechtle (W. Acker); Bremen—Gautier (Knigge); Hamburg—Fink (Prinz); Schleswig-H.—Meyn (Weigle); Hessen—Weigle from S-H (O. Müller); Lower Saxony—Zscherpe (Berliner); Saar—Körner (Nickolay). Rhineland-Pfalz and South Baden stayed open; Bavaria unchanged (Schirmer); and NRW's chairman, Paul, had already been replaced by Ledwohn in Dec. 1949; see 19th KPD-PV, 10 Feb. 1951, SAPMO-BA, I 11/301/16.

would tell the SED Central Committee in this respect was that 'it would not be right here to separate the things from back then, from the things today'.[29] Purges of popular local leaders for purported transgressions in the Third Reich may have been designed to create artificial tests of loyalty to Berlin, but these often backfired when comrades resigned in sympathy with absurdly accused colleagues.[30] What does seem certain is that the purges were part of a systematic restructuring of the KPD, transforming it into a new-type party. The West Commission urged local parties to replace 'wavering and tired comrades' with the young, who were praised for speaking 'fanatically about their work and struggle against party enemies and against the resistance from old comrades'.[31] British observers also noted that *Altkommunisten* were being systematically replaced by:

mainly younger men to a large extent Antifa-trained, whose lack of experience of the pre-war working class movement and traditions makes them more amenable to the unthinking discipline now imposed in the name of 'democratic centralism'.[32]

Deviation: Communist Splinter Groups

Such potent medicine was in danger of producing its own 'party enemies', or, at the very least, of reviving some of the KPD's earlier factions. At the end of Weimar there had been about 22,000 leftists in seven splinter groups in the middle-ground between KPD and SPD. The 3,000-strong Communist Party Opposition (KPO), formed in 1928 by rightist Communists disenchanted with the social fascist line, failed, however, to recruit leftist Social Democrats, who went instead to the 17,000-strong Socialist Workers' Party (SAP). The SPD was also generally more successful at reintegrating dissidents, with more KPO members gravitating towards the SPD than back to the KPD after 1933, although in 1945 the KPD did reabsorb some residual oppositionists.[33]

While on a visit from the USA, Ruth Fischer, *grande dame* of the Weimar KPD and well versed in factional politics, advised Schumacher to exploit the

---

[29] SED-ZK, 24 Aug. 1950, in Weber, 'Schauprozeßvorbereitungen', 443.

[30] For instance Franz Heitgres, one-time Hamburg Senator for Restitution and Refugees and chairman of the zonal VVN, who was expelled in Mar. 1954, prompting five others to leave; see Ralph Giordano, *Die Partei hat immer recht* (Cologne and Berlin, 1961), 95–110; Manfred Grieger et al., *Stalins Schatten* (Neuss, 1989), 178.

[31] Fuhrmann, 3 May 1950, SAPMO-BA, I 10/401/1. See also Herbert Mayer, 'Durchsetzt von Parteifeinden, Agenten, Verbrechern . . . ?: Zu den Parteisäuberungen in der KPD (1948–1952) und der Mitwirkung der SED', *Hefte zur DDR-Geschichte*, 29 (1995).

[32] Acting HC to FO, 2 May 1951, PRO, FO 371/93449.

[33] Jan Foitzik, *Zwischen den Fronten* (Bonn, 1986), 241 and 243; ID/EUCOM, 9 Mar. 1949, BAK, Z 45 F, 7–32–3/5–6.

potential pool of disaffected Communists with a strong left wing, or even a separate party to the left of the SPD. By then there were reportedly two loose minority factions inside the KPD: one rightist, made up largely of older Communists, placing German interests first; the other leftist, Trotskyite, and internationalist. Trotskyites and ex-KPO supporters were unhappy with the party's national and alliance politics, as well as pro-Soviet subservience, advocating instead a return to classic Marxist politics and revolutionary socialism. Actual resignations had remained below 100, however, limited to small and unstable groupings, the least minute of which was Bremen's Radical Socialist Party.[34] Apparently Tyulpanov and the SMAD were prepared to give more rein to the pro-German faction, which wanted a strong German state and 'liberal' Communism, but, as US intelligence concluded: 'The Western KPD simply has no possibility of extricating itself from identification with and dependence upon the USSR without splitting.'[35]

A direct descendant of the KPO was the Workers' Politics Group (GAP). Ex-KPO functionaries in the KPD, concentrated in Hamburg, Stuttgart, and Salzgitter, had maintained contact after 1945, while their old leaders, Brandler and Thalheimer, furnished literature from their Cuban exile. (Brandler returned in 1949 after his colleague's death.) In 1947 informal GAP discussion circles were formed, leading to expulsions in Solingen and Hamburg, where about 35 members of the Brandler Group had been active, including the Red *Bürgermeister* of Geesthacht, August Ziehl, expelled in 1949. That year the GAP published its 'Open Words to Communists', criticizing the KPD for subservience to Soviet foreign policy, and condemning co-operation with *all* occupation powers, East or West. From 1949–50 it recruited a small number of disaffected Communists, but remained highly localized and reliant on strong personalities. In Salzgitter, for instance, the works council chairman, Erich Söchtig, had taken about 120 KPD members with him by 1952. Another prominent ex-KPO leader, Heinrich Galm, had founded his own Workers' Party in Offenbach in 1945, outstripping the town's KPD but unable to break out of local politics with its labourist programme to integrate the *Mittelstand*. The party collapsed in 1954.[36]

[34] CIC Region VI, 9 Jan. 1948, in *Confidential (1945–1949)*, 40. 30–33; ID/EUCOM, 9 Mar. 1949, BAK, Z 45 F, 7–32–3/5–6.

[35] POLAD to State Dept., 30 Dec. 1947, BAK, Z 45 F, POLAD 32/12.

[36] Klaus Peter Wittemann, *Kommunistische Politik in Westdeutschland nach 1945: Der Ansatz der Gruppe Arbeiterpolitik* (Hannover, 1977); Bernd Klemm, *Die Arbeiter-Partei (Sozialistische Einheitspartei) Hessen 1945–1954* (Hannover, 1980).

A later abortive attempt was made to rally Trotskyites and Titoists, as well as disaffected and expelled KPD functionaries, under an umbrella party, the Independent Workers' Party of Germany (UAPD). On 24–5 March 1951 the UAPD was founded at Worms by Fischer, Boepple, Schappe, and Latzke, all high-ranking KPD resignees, and 144 other anti-Stalinist Communists, along with Wolfgang Leonhard and the Trotskyite International Communists of Germany. Yet in the late summer the Trotskyites were manœuvred out, and at the year's end Yugoslav financing via Leonhard dried up, leading to the party's dissolution in 1952. In fact, the UAPD never attracted significant numbers—at most 5–800 in the whole of West Germany.[37]

The KPD devoted large resources to combating these groups, including a special instructor, Harry Schmidt, who by early 1950 was investigating a whole catalogue of 'party enemies', from the Bremen Workers' Party under ex-Social Democrat Döll; to the Dortmund Independent KPD, led by an ex-Liberal, Bender; to Galm's Offenbach Workers' Party; Penk's Worms Socialist Union; Scholz's Bonn UAPD; the entire Salzgitter *Kreis* leadership; and the anonymous originators of the Hamburg KPO's 'Cadre Letters'.[38] The fate of the UAPD in 1951–2 was symptomatic, however, of intra-group divisions preventing coalescence into a serious opposition. The activists involved were also naive, to say the least, in thinking that a non-Stalinist Communist alternative would be any more attractive in the eyes of the West German electorate than the KPD itself. The polarizing logic of the Cold War always penalized the middle way.[39]

Diversification: KPD Mass and Auxiliary Organizations

As anti-Communism became more rampant, with even a hint of pink likely to deter most West Germans, the KPD itself had to adopt an increasingly low profile, pursuing its political goals by more indirect means. As

---

[37] Peter Kulemann, *Die Linke in Westdeutschland nach 1945: Die erste Nachkriegszeit, zwischen sozialdemokratischer Integration und dem Stalinismus der KPD—das Scheitern der 'Titoistischen' Unabhängigen Arbeiterpartei UAP 1950* (Hannover and Frankfurt am Main, 1978), 73 and 93–7; Düsseldorf Consulate to State Dept., 26 Aug. 1953, in *Confidential (1950–1954)*, 29. 383–402.

[38] POLAD to State Dept., 11 Aug. 1949, in *Confidential (1945–1949)*, 15. 188–9; ID/EUCOM, 6 Apr. 1950, in *Confidential (1950–1954)*, 28. 542–48.

[39] Siegfried Heimann, 'Zum Scheitern linker Sammlungsbewegungen zwischen SPD und KPD/SED nach 1945: Die Beispiele USPD und UAPD', in Rolf Ebbighausen and Friedrich Tiemann (eds.), *Das Ende der Arbeiterbewegung in Deutschland?* (Opladen, 1984), 301–22.

Stalin himself had advised, instead of the frontal assault favoured by the Teutons, the party should 'mask [its] struggle'.[40] Organizations such as the National Front thus began 'incrementally to take over the tasks of mass agitation and mass leadership from our party organizations which can thus concentrate chiefly on their cadre tasks'.[41] The KPD's peripheral organizations fell into two categories: on the one hand, ancillary 'mass organizations', integral to the party and more or less openly Communist, including youth, women's, and pro-Soviet groups run by the Secretariat; on the other, avowedly non-partisan, single-interest groups headed by non-Communist personalities, but administered and financed behind the scenes by party secretaries, and dubbed 'front organizations' by the authorities.

Chief among the post-war mass organizations was the Free German Youth (FDJ). Its Weimar predecessor, the KJVD, with perhaps 40,000 members in 1932, had not disguised its partisanship, but the FDJ claimed to be a neutral umbrella organization. Founded on 7 March 1946 in the SBZ, its first 'Parliament' in June included western delegates and thirty seats on the FDJ's Central Council in East Berlin. The FDJ chairman in the SBZ, Erich Honecker, also toured the western zones in May 1948, immediately after which a Liaison Bureau was instituted in Frankfurt. Upon the creation of the FRG, the western FDJ set up its own Central Bureau in Frankfurt (later Düsseldorf), but was effectively still run by the Central Council's western department under Heinz Lippmann. This group of up to seventy-five functionaries in East Berlin accounted for the lion's share of the Central Council's budget, for instance in 1956 4.6 out of 11.3 million marks, with 2.5 million earmarked for operations in West Germany. In September 1953 these funds proved too much of a temptation for Lippmann, however, when he defected to the West and led a brief but spectacular playboy lifestyle at the party's expense, before turning evidence against the KPD and FDJ.[42] Before the ban in 1956, however, the FDJ had sucessfully laid down a Stalinist cadre reservoir for the future, the so-called 'FDJ generation', including Herbert Mies, who went on to lead the DKP as an unwavering enemy of reform Communism and a friend of Honecker's GDR.

[40] Pieck's notes of Stalin meeting, 18 Dec. 1948, in *Wilhelm Pieck*, ed. Rolf Badstübner and Wilfried Loth (Berlin, 1994), 267.

[41] 'Alle Kommunisten in die Nationale Front!', n.d. [1950], ZI6, Sammlung Becker, Ordner 8.5/9.

[42] Michael Herms, 'Zur "Westarbeit" der FDJ', *Jahresbericht des Instituts für zeitgeschichtliche Jugendforschung*, 2 (1992), 59–60; id., 'Zur Westarbeit der FDJ 1953 bis 1956', *Jahresbericht des Instituts für zeitgeschichtliche Jugendforschung*, 3 (1993), 117–37; 50th Westkomm., 5 June 1950, SAPMO-BA, NY 4182/867.

Unlike the eastern FDJ, the 'friends' in the West, unable to convince others of their non-partisanship, found themselves competing against a host of other youth organizations. Thus, although by March 1948 the FDJ numbered 26,753 in the British Zone; 7,590 in the American; and 3,500 in the French—respectable compared with Weimar—this was a poor showing against the 85,000 SPD 'Falcons'; million-strong trade union youth; 300,000 Evangelicals; 800,000 Catholics; and the 1.5 million in youth sports clubs.[43] Negotiations between the FDJ and other western zones youth groups became deadlocked in November 1947, and finally, in October 1949, the Communists were excluded from the new Federal Youth Ring for refusing to accept the Basic Law, followed by creeping marginalization at regional level.[44]

FDJ membership in the West, offering all-night cross-country hikes to outwit the Federal Border Police in order to reach the two FDJ Germany Jamborees (*Deutschlandtreffen*) in East Berlin, combined patriotism with anti-authoritarianism. After the first such Whitsuntide Jamboree in June 1950, attended by 27,000 West Germans, Federal police attempted to close the border, corralling 10,000 young Communists in a field at Herrnburg in a futile two-day attempt to take names and addresses. At least 35,000 West Germans officially attended the August 1951 Third World Festival Games of Youth and Students for Peace in Berlin, in defiance of border closures, which led to one *FDJ'ler* drowning while swimming the Elbe. In the intervening twelve months clashes with the police had become increasingly violent, leaving injured on both sides. On 17 June 1951 there was what can only be described as a pitched battle, after 2,000 *FDJ'ler* were bussed to the Petersberg, the seat of the Allied High Commission overlooking Bonn. Demonstrators ignored police orders to remove their blue shirts, leading to scuffles and eighty arrests. Soon afterwards the organization was formally proscribed, but continued underground. The climax of FDJ–police clashes occurred on 11 May 1952, when a 30,000-strong Youth Caravan converged on Essen, provoking police baton charges in which KPD *Landtag* deputy Helga Dickel was knocked unconscious and 145 were arrested. When stone-throwing demonstrators failed to disperse, police fired into them, killing a young blueshirt, Philipp

[43] Report, n.d., Jugendarchiv/Institut für zeitgeschichtliche Jugendforschung, A 9.161; FO Research Dept., 3 June 1948, PRO, FO 371/70479.

[44] Manfred Kappeler, 'Jugendverbände im Ost-West-Konflikt: Die Beziehungen zwischen Jugendverbänden in den Westzonen und der FDJ in der Gründungsphase des Bundesjugendringes', in Helga Gotschlich (ed.), *'Links und links und Schritt gehalten . . .': Die FDJ: Konzepte—Abläufe—Grenzen* (Berlin, 1994), 32–57.

Müller, who was buried with full party honours and duly canonized as a martyr to remilitarization.[45]

Another prominent KPD mass organization was the Democratic Women's League of Germany (DFD). Founded in the SBZ in 1947, it was banned in the West until 1950, when it claimed 22,000 members. The SPD treated DFD membership as an expulsion matter, and the entire organization was ultimately banned in 1957. Maternal instincts predestined women in DFD eyes for peace work, whereas more overtly political activities, such as protests at the lenient sentencing of the Nazi matriarch, Gertrud Scholtz-Klink, were left to the party. Nevertheless, pioneering campaigns for equal pay for equal work should not be dismissed lightly, nor the difficulties for women in a male-dominated party which on occasion even frowned upon female members smoking in meetings.[46]

Similarly, the Society for German–Soviet Friendship (GfDSF) was very much an East German invention, subsequently exported to the West. Founded in the SBZ in June 1947, it was upgraded to a mass organization in 1949, attaining 655,203 members. Extended to the FRG in 1950 and co-ordinated by a western department under the eastern DSF's deputy leader, Hamacher, with over a dozen instructors, it was banned as early as 1953 by some *Länder* as a Communist front. Indeed, internally it was described as a mere 'appendage of the Western Department'. Besides, western membership was only 13,094 by 1951, drawing its leadership mainly from graduates of the *Antifa* schools in Soviet POW camps.[47]

Moving on to the KPD's 'non-political' auxiliary organizations, one must again ask how much neutrality was possible in the polarized atmosphere of the Cold War. Much has been made of the workers' parties' penumbral *Vorfeldorganisationen* in the Weimar Republic and earlier.

---

[45] Michael Herms, 'Zur Stalinisierung der West-FDJ 1949 bis 1952', in Gotschlich (ed.), *'Links und links'*, 107–10; *Gemeinsames Ministerialblatt*, 2/17 (29 June 1951), 149–51; Chef der Polizei (Knoche), 'Bericht über die Vorgänge am 11.5.1952 in Essen anläßlich des Westdeutschen Treffens der jungen Generation', 26 May 1952, NRW HStA, NW 34/9, fos. 201–15. See also Wolfgang Bartels and Bundesvorstand der SDAJ Arbeiterjugend (eds.), *Philipp Müller: 11. Mai 1952 in Essen: Polizeimord an einem jungen Arbeiter* (Dortmund, 1977), 76 ff.; Walther Pollatschek, *Philipp Müller: Held der Nation* (East Berlin, 1952).

[46] DFD/Büro Westdeutschland, 25 May 1950, BAK, B 118/132/6322; KPD-PV/ Frauensek. to SPD and DGB, 28 Nov. 1949, BAK, B 118/134/6670; see various DFD literature, including 'Hilfe, Mutter, Hilfe!' depicting a small girl with bombs raining down around her, BAK, B 118/133/6450.

[47] Thomas Schönknecht, 'Gesellschaft für Deutsch-Sowjetische Freundschaft', in Martin Broszat and Hermann Weber (eds.), *SBZ-Handbuch* (Munich, 1989), 741; 55th Westkomm., 8 June 1950, SAPMO-BA, NY 4182/867; GfDSF-ZV/Westabt., report on Jan.–Aug. 1951 and 'Gesamtbericht', n.d. [1951], SAPMO-BA, DSF-Zentralvorstand, A 111.

They helped to establish a working-class milieu, and, some would argue, a relatively neutral forum for workers of different persuasions to defy more confrontational high politics.[48] After 1945 there was an added problem in that the occupation authorities were not prepared to license such a plethora of competing political and confessional societies. To take the example of sports clubs, there was no revival of the Weimar KPD's *Rot-Sport*. There is some evidence, however, that, in provincial areas of Hessen, workers' sports clubs and football teams were refounded as inclusive bodies, tolerant of the Communists. Yet, this was perhaps more a question of limited resources and village culture than political defiance. In urban areas, most leisure activities were becoming increasingly professionalized, moving in the case of football from a participation to a spectator sport. Although the legendary Ruhr football team Schalke 04 offered its sporting services to the KPD in 1945, it went on to epitomize the more general commercialization of the game. With post-1945 labour histories still in their infancy, it is in any case too early to reach firm conclusions on the reasons for the breakdown of workers' culture. Based on a pioneering microstudy of a Bremen workers' district, Joachim Oltmann has nevertheless argued that even personal contacts were not enough to withstand the global politics of the Cold War. Communists may have been members of apolitical garden allotment societies, but their discipline over the issues of national unity and remilitarization always ended by isolating them from the rest of the labour movement.[49]

It would seem, therefore, that the high politics of the Cold War were capable of penetrating the remains of the working-class milieu, especially in the conurbations. The Association of Persecutees of the Nazi Regime (VVN) may be taken as a problematic example of a non-partisan body overtaken by outside events. It claimed genuine above-party status, but had an in-built Communist majority, of about 55% in 1948, reflecting the anti-Communist bias of Nazi persecution. Founded in the SBZ in February 1947, but only formally in January 1948, it was one of the few cases where the KPD did not simply copy the SED. There had been initiatives in the US Zone as early as August 1945, and in October 1946

---

[48] Klaus-Michael Mallmann, 'Milieu, Radikalismus und lokale Gesellschaft: Zur Sozialgeschichte des Kommunismus in der Weimarer Republik', *Geschichte und Gesellschaft*, 21 (1995), 5–31.

[49] Frank Deppe *et al.*, 'Lokales Milieu und große Politik zur Zeit des Kalten Krieges 1945–1960 am Beispiel ausgewählter hessischer Arbeiterwohngemeinden', in Peter Assion (ed.), *Transformationen der Arbeiterkultur* (Marburg, 1986), 198–219; Schabrod, 15 Aug. 1945, SAPMO-BA, I 10/23/8; Joachim Oltmann, *Kalter Krieg und Kommunale Integration* (Marburg, 1987), 121–69.

a VVN was founded in NRW, followed by a four-zone constituent conference in Frankfurt's Paulskirche on 15–17 March 1947. In February 1953, however, following the 1950–1 purges of western émigrés, the granting of full civil rights to ex-NSDAP members in 1952, and the anti-Zionist campaign during the Slansky trial, the association was dissolved as an embarrassment in the GDR.[50]

In the West, anti-Communism rapidly broke up the anti-fascist consensus even among fascism's victims, leading to breakaway groups. By January 1947 the VVN in NRW was confronted with a Community of Racially and Politically Persecuted Christians, and in March with an SPD boycott, reinforced by the 1948 convention's resolution banning concurrent SPD and VVN membership.[51] (A year later, however, there were still allegedly 17,000 SPD members defying this order.) In 1950 a further non-Communist rival, the League of Persecutees of the Nazi Regime, was set up, with both breakaways accusing the VVN of being a KPD front. Despite claims to the contrary, it is clear that the Communists *did* attempt to control the VVN. In late 1949 the West Commission wished to harness it to the national and peace struggle, although on a tight rein to prevent it 'from being absorbed organizationally and politically in uncontrollable "peace cartels" or "peace rings"'.[52] Events then came to a head in September 1950, when the VVN was branded 'unconstitutional' by the government, and in several *Länder* temporarily banned, although attempts after 1951 to seek a national ban prompted an international outcry and ultimately miscarried.

Although the VVN successfully defended itself against the accusation of being a Communist front, other groups could not evade the charge of being indirectly organized and financed by the party. The absolute numbers of such bodies fluctuated and there was, of course, the danger of the authorities labelling any pacifist organization crypto-Communist. In some cases, non-Communist initiatives were slowly annexed to the Communist cause. For instance, the Democratic Cultural League of Germany started off as a series of genuinely pluralistic bodies, which during the course of 1950–1 were centralized under the auspices of the Communist Johann Fladung, becoming increasingly a KPD mouthpiece. In May 1952 the Americans counted 54 such 'infiltrated organizations', making a distinction

[50] HICOG to State Dept., 27 Dec. 1950, in *Confidential (1950–1954)*, 28. 848–73; Jan Foitzik, 'Vereinigung der Verfolgten des Naziregimes (VVN)', in Broszat and Weber (eds.), *SBZ-Handbuch*, 750.

[51] RWIS, 'Political Summary No. 10', 17 June 1947, PRO, FO 1005/1722.

[52] Westkomm., 2 Dec. 1949, SAPMO-BA, NY 4182/867.

between these and 155 'front organizations', which had been Communist inspired from the outset.[53]

The majority of front organizations proper were single-interest groups, indefatigably arranging congresses for various social target groups such as students, housewives, or farmers. Their titles were usually of a pacifist or nationalist nature, and clearly in the venerable tradition of the bourgeois *Verein* rather than the workers' club. The non-Communist personalities recruited included the Catholic writer, Reinhold Schneider, and retired Major-General Karl Hentschel, as well as the eccentric 1930s racing driver, Manfred von Brauchitsch, who also headed the 1951 Committee for Unity and Freedom in German Sport, partly for pecuniary reasons. The party secretly seconded cadres to these organizations for the chore of administering and financing them, but was at great pains to demonstrate a cross-party spectrum. In trials against their organizers, however, evidence was produced that they were often receiving funds from their East German counterparts, and from 1951 all the KPD's mass and auxiliary organizations, except the VVN, were successively banned.[54]

The party attempted to compensate for its dwindling organizational possibilities by stepping up its publicistic ventures, although, like the mass organizations, newspapers were also vulnerable to bans (see the following chapter). From mid-1948 the party's Socialist Information Service functioned as a central news agency, superseded in 1951 by The Daily Argument.[55] In 1949 *Freies Volk* was promoted to 'central organ', the Executive's mouthpiece on matters of policy, with a circulation of 80,000, but falling to 48,000 by 1955. The leadership also published a theoretical periodical, *Wissen und Tat*, and a functionaries' organ, *Unser Weg*, dealing with practical agitation and propaganda.

As part of the new-type party, following a purge of the various editorial boards in 1951, a new-type press emerged. A perennial problem, however, was its inaccessibility to readers put off by its turgid prose, jargon, and politicization of all coverage. One attempt to bridge the gap was through Soviet-inspired amateur 'people's correspondents', who reported on local factory and pacifist initiatives. Yet sub-editors must soon have tired of correcting the spelling of endless sentimental blank verse (for example:

    [53] Schädel, 'KPD', 192–6; HICOG to State Dept., 5 May 1952, in *Confidential (1950–1954)*, 28. 249–73.
    [54] KPD-PV/*Sek.*, 5 Apr. 1951, BAK, B 118/135/7092–93; Willy Haas, *Abschied vom Paradies, das keines war: Bericht einer Wandlung* (Böblingen, 1988), 170–4; 'Stellenbesetzung' [HAfVB], n.d. [1951], BAK, B 118/137/7137–38.
    [55] Unless otherwise stated, Christa Hempel-Küter, *Die KPD-Presse in den Westzonen von 1945 bis 1956* (Frankfurt am Main, 1993).

'Da buhlet jetzt um unsere Gunst | Nicht nur der Sport, nein auch die Kunst. Gewünscht wird, daß auch noch geschrieben | Wie es steht in den Betrieben').[56] A central *Pressefest* in Solingen in September 1954, attracting a reported 50,000 visitors, went some way to popularizing the press. Yet after regional editors had suggested that *Freies Volk* be reserved for official propaganda, while they themselves became 'people's newspapers', KPD press chief, Max Schäfer, insisted in November 1955 that the press remain a transmission belt of the party line. Declining circulation figures speak for themselves: 691,500 in 1947; 563,700 in 1949; and only 332,000 in 1955.[57]

Just as the new-type press seemed to be concentrating more on internal propaganda than external agitation, party schools offered another means of servicing the burgeoning functionary corps. Younger members had always been seen as a long-term solution to the problems of plugging the gaps left by Nazi decimation, and, from 1948, of creating a more pliable new-type functionary. From 1946 evening classes were on offer, as well as a limited number of full-time fortnightly courses at three schools in the Ruhr. In 1947 general members' schooling was also introduced, soon supported by the Executive's monthly *Bildungshefte*. Finally, in 1950, following the SED's lead, the KPD instituted a Party Curriculum, including a one-year *Politische Grundschule* for basic party formations, as well as study circles. Yet attendance seems to have been low. In 1950, for instance, it was estimated that only about 15% of members were attending regular evening classes.[58]

Undaunted, in 1948 the new KPD Executive acquired a central school at Bad Wildungen in Hessen, but failed to renew its lease in June 1951. Its replacement at Rengsdorf closed in 1954 when forced to submit lists of pupils to the authorities. From mid-1949 the Wilhelm-Florin-Schule at Heidenoldendorf near Detmold trained functionaries, but closed in mid-1953 when the British built a training ground next door. The FDJ also ran a central school in Hirsau in Württemberg-Baden from 1947, transferred to the KPD after the FDJ ban in 1951. Under the impact of such official obstructionism, therefore, schools in the GDR became the favoured option. Ever since 1946 KPD functionaries had been able to attend the SED's Karl-Marx-Parteihochschule and other institutions, taking up about 10% of places. From 1953, however, the KPD went over

[56] Hempel-Küter, *KPD-Presse*, 95–105.
[57] Heinz-Dietrich Fischer, *Parteien und Presse in Deutschland seit 1945* (Bremen, 1971), 448, 461, and 500.
[58] Hans Kluth, *Die KPD in der Bundesrepublik* (Cologne and Opladen, 1959), 90–5.

to separate schooling at three special-purpose schools in the East German countryside. One of the aims of these establishments was clearly to phase out the KPD's *Altkommunisten* by training mainly younger KPD functionaries, who, after three-month courses, were duly installed in the West.

A quicker expedient was to import reliable 'Soviet' cadres direct from POW camps in the USSR. Returnees (*Heimkehrer*) were seen as more amenable to the Cominform line and immune to some of the local '*Kreis* Kings' in the West. From April–May 1942 regular *Antifa* courses had been started at certain Soviet POW camps run by the Red Army's Political Main Administration, and from 1946 by the NKVD and Interior Ministry. By 1947 there were 3 central schools at Krasnogorsk, Ogre, and Talitsa; as well as approximately 50 regional schools offering three-month courses; and a further 120 camp schools running four/six-week courses, schooling a total of about 50,000 POWs, many of whom were repatriated to the SBZ by 1949 as functionaries of the Society for German-Soviet Friendship (GfDSF).[59]

A number of these men were also returned to the West, prominent in their leather *Wehrmacht* greatcoats. The West Commission saw them as a potential cadre reservoir, and in November 1949 had indeed approached the CPSU for an overview of *Antifa* pupils and their qualifications 'for the purpose of assessing their suitability for the West'. Recruitment was to begin direct at Frankfurt an der Oder by the GfDSF. Via this route, five returnees eventually reached the KPD Executive itself, including Kloock (Cadre), Angenfort (FDJ), Neumann (Agitprop), as well as instructors and cadre workers. Moreover, on occasion returnees were even used as straight replacements for party enemies during the 1948–51 purges described above.[60]

It is difficult to quantify the overall numbers of *Heimkehrer* employed in the West. Yet, by the end of 1949, 2,848 *Antifa* graduates had returned to the British Zone; 1,726 to the American; and 684 to the French. At the turn of 1949–50 two Federal conferences were then held to encourage rejuvenation of the party with these 'comrade returnees'. Nevertheless, the *Länder* appeared reluctant, with a reported take-up rate in NRW of only 15% in April 1950. One ex-POW estimated that only about 1%

[59] Jan Foitzik, 'Sowjetische Militäradministration in Deutschland (SMAD)', in *SBZ-Handbuch*, 35–6.

[60] POLAD to State Dept., 13 Apr. 1948, BAK, Z 45 F, POLAD 32/2–5; 19th Westkomm., 13 Oct. 1949, 24th Westkomm., 24 Nov. 1949, 26th Westkomm., 5 Dec. 1949, SAPMO-BA, NY 4182/867; BAK, B 118/142/8153; Dickhut, *Was geschah danach?*, 56.

of ordinary POWs (as opposed to *Antifa* pupils) retained any Communist convictions whatsoever, and only half of those became party activists. As for the *Antifa* graduates proper, after surveillance of one batch of 90 from Ogre camp, the North Rhine-Westphalian interior ministry concluded that only 23 could be counted as 'agitators'. For the rest, *Antifa* training was probably little more than a fast ticket home.[61]

The Cadre Party, 1951–1956

In its remaining years—partly from conspiratorial necessity and partly from ideological design—the party developed a self-perpetuating, top-heavy bureaucratic superstructure. The fundamental Leninist principle of KPD organization was that of democratic centralism, as laid down in its statutes of 1921 and 1925, echoing the Comintern statute of 1920. The March 1951 statute was almost identical with that of 1925, barring a reference to the Comintern, and was one word short of the SED's 1950 constitution. Although all upper party echelons were technically electable by, and accountable to, lower levels, the most important practical principle was the binding nature of resolutions from above, and the subordination of the minority to the majority. From 1951 there were collective leadership elections only, creating an executive *en bloc*, from which a chair was nominated. Secretariats were installed by the next highest body (and not elected from below). The KPD Executive determined the delegates to the Party Convention which elected it, as well as making electoral 'suggestions'. Indeed, only in 1946, 1947, and 1949 had there been elected *Land* conventions, and the delegates for the 1951 and 1954 national conventions were chosen instead by nominated delegates' conferences. It goes without saying that party factions were forbidden.

Nomenclature became the operative principle whereby the leadership could predispose the subordinate party to its line by its cadre policy, and thus protect itself from any grass-roots stirrings. The SED had introduced the system in October 1949, and in August 1951 it was adopted by the KPD, bypassing the statute of the previous March.[62] It is thus nonsense to claim that the suspension of internal party democracy was

---

[61] Kurt Libera, 'Zur Entwicklung der antifaschistischen Bewegung unter den deutschen Kriegsgefangenen in der UdSSR nach dem Sieg über den Hitlerfaschismus (1945–1950)', Ph.D. thesis (Institut für Gesellschaftswissenschaften beim ZK der SED, East Berlin, 1968), ii. 118–19; Stuttgart Cons. to SD, 14 July 1947, in *Confidential (1945–1949)*, 39. 918–34; Dok. IM-NRW Nr.: 285, 30 Aug. 1949; Schmidt interview, 9 Aug. 1989.

[62] KPD-PV/*Sek.*, 7 Aug. 1951, BAK, B 118/135/7057.

merely a reaction to the government indictment in November of that year. From then on, all cadre transfers between Executive, *Land*, and *Kreis* leaderships were subject to confirmation by their respective secretariats (themselves all indirectly elected full-time functionaries). Even positions officially electable only by members' and delegates' conferences fell under *nomenklatura*. The central Vetting Commission thus enjoyed a *de facto* veto over the Secretariat and Executive, the Party Control Commission and its regional groupings, as well as the *Land* executives, as far down as the political secretaries of 22 *Schwerpunktkreise* and 24 *Schwerpunkt* factory groups.[63]

The larger the apparatus grew, the more apathetic the membership became, and the more frantic the leadership. The SPD estimated in 1952 that for every Social Democratic functionary there were 1,500 members; the ratio for the KPD was nearer 1 : 75.[64] (During 1952 there is some evidence, however, that the apparatus began to shrink again in anticipation of a ban.[65]) By 1954 even the Americans regarded the party as 'over-organized, and many of its members devote a large share of their time to serving on committees'.[66] Yet ordinary members' meetings were dogged by low attendance. In *the* party stronghold at Solingen, only 15% of rank-and-file members were turning out in 1950 (often prevented by their wives!). Only a minority of *Parteiaktiv* members—supposedly the cream of the local parties—bothered to discuss the 'Building of Socialism' in 1952. One explanation proffered by Ralph Giordano, then a young party member himself, for this decline in activism, which may not be far from the truth, was the competing claims of the new leisure culture. Above all, television was becoming the focus of evening entertainment in the 1950s, robbing the party of an important social function and encouraging an armchair membership.[67]

Many *Kreise* became single-handed operations, existing only on paper and constantly having to be bailed out by instructors from the *Land* leadership. Some *Kreis* secretaries were interchanged as many as seven times a year, and, in a survey in 1954, the average age of local leaders—many of them graduates of party schools—was revealed to be 24.[68] They were

[63] Kluth, *KPD in der Bundesrepublik*, 61–4.
[64] SPD-PV, 'Rundschreiben Nr. 35/52', 7 Apr. 1952, AdsD, *NL* Schmid 1500.
[65] 'Informationen des BfV', 31 Aug. 1952, BAK, B 106/15886.
[66] HICOG to State Dept., 10 Aug. 1954, in *Confidential (1950–1954)*, 29. 525–46.
[67] Dok. IM-NRW Nr.: 1, 21 Sept. 1950; Kluth, *KPD in der Bundesrepublik*, 66; Giordano, *Partei*, 230–1.
[68] *KPD 1945–1968*, i. 61–2.

chosen for their Marxist–Leninist orthodoxy, often bolstered by *Wehrmacht* discipline, rather than their organizational skills or shop-floor experience, causing scepticism from old hands. As one newcomer recalled: 'Schoolboy political *Schwärmereien* and revolutionary romanticism, pledged to improve the world, were not what they wanted.'[69]

The party leadership on the eve of the ban had thus changed out of all recognition from the party of the *Stunde Null*. Of the original hundred members of the NRW leadership in 1947, only three remained in 1956.[70] This does not mean, of course, that the men and women themselves had disappeared. In the Ruhr conurbations, at least, *Altkommunisten* remained the mainstay well into the 1950s.[71] Elsewhere, other old-timers continued to influence newcomers from the sidelines, such as the eccentric Folkert P., uncrowned '*Kreis* King' of Bremerhaven, who, despite holding no official posts, 'talks everybody else into the ground at executives and meetings'. When visited by a national executive investigator, he accused him of behaving worse than the Gestapo and pulled no punches in diagnosing the dire state of the party:

No wonder that they lost [the recent elections] when we are pursuing a nationalist instead of a socialist policy. . . . Comrade Herbert Warnke [the GDR's union leader] should come over here once in a while to relearn the class struggle. . . . We used to learn that piece-work kills ['Akkord ist Mord'] and cannot go along with what they are doing over there with Hennecke [the GDR's Stakhanov] etc. . . . Once the bureaucrats over there call the shots over here, then it's all over for us old Communists . . .[72]

In the early years, until 1949 at any rate, it had still not been too late for most opportunist KPD members to 'realize the error of their ways'. They could excuse short-term motives for joining, an emotional need to identify with the anti-fascists of 1945, which soon cooled once it became clear that the SBZ was not a 'workers' paradise'. Yet many of the objects of this early empathy, martyr figures who had suffered unspeakably for the Communist cause at the hands of the Nazis, found it less easy to turn their backs on the party. For Heinrich Schmitt, Denazification Minister

[69] Klaus Weigle, 'Vom Sturmgrenadier zum KPD-Landesvorsitzenden', *Demokratische Geschichte*, 7 (1992), 220.

[70] Agatz, Herzner, and Schabrod: report on Solingen Convention (14–16 May 1947), SAPMO-BA, NY 4036/646; Dok. IM-NRW Nr.: 48, 1 Aug. 1956.

[71] For a collective biography of the Bochum party in 1952 see my original thesis, 'The German Communist Party (KPD) in the Western Zones and in Western Germany, 1945–1956', D.Phil. (Oxford University, 1993), 118–21.

[72] Berliner, 25 Oct. 1951, BAK, B 118/219/102804.

of Bavaria, the KPD's 'slavish imitation' of SED policy tipped the balance in what was clearly a heart-rending decision:

The final separation from a party to which one has sacrificed all one's spare time, one's career, one's family, one's health and, within penitentiary walls, ten of one's best years, is not easy and should not be confused with resignation from a bowling club.[73]

Another resignee, this time from Bremen, expressed it in almost Freudian terms: 'I feel toward the KPD as a man feels toward his first sweetheart. Even though I know that she has become a whore, I find it hard to leave her for another so quickly.'[74] At the same time, many other core members were quite prepared to accept political martyrdom. Once the screws of 'ideological consolidation' were tightened on the party after 1949, it was too late for many functionaries to contemplate resigning. KPD membership had long since turned them into social pariahs in the West. In a period of relatively high unemployment, ex-Communists were unlikely to be high on most employers' lists. After his party expulsion in 1953, the ill-fated Kurt Lichtenstein, one-time SED confidant and KPD press chief, had to work for three years as an unskilled chemicals worker, door-to-door washing-machine salesman, and driver of a travelling cheese van. His continued fascination with Communism nevertheless proved fatal. While photographing the East German border in October 1961, after finding employment as a journalist again, he was mysteriously shot dead by East German border guards.[75]

Although the MfS was probably not involved in this incident, as it had been in the arrests of other KPD leaders, selective terror also helped to intimidate dissenters into silence. Some of those insistent enough to break away, founded their own non-Stalinist Communist parties, but these dwindled into obscurity even more rapidly than the KPD itself. There was no room for an alternative Communist party in the West German political spectrum, and from 1951 it became clear that the government wished to remove the Communist option altogether. The increasingly embattled position of the West German Communists encouraged their 'negative integration' inside a form of political ghetto, and thus perhaps prolonged the organizational coherence of a party otherwise doomed by centrifugal forces.

---

[73] Heinrich Schmitt, ex-Denazification Minister of Bavaria in OMG Bavaria, 'Trend Report', 17 Nov. 1947, PA Staritz.

[74] OMG Bremen/ICD, 21 May 1946, ZI6, Sammlung Brandt, Ordner 10.

[75] Lichtenstein to Kurt Müller, 23 Oct. 1955, NRW HStA, RWN 239/5; Zunder, *Erschossen in Zicherie*, 117–37.

Destalinization

Before moving from Communism to anti-Communism, one footnote should be added to the history of the post-war KPD: namely the role of destalinization. At long last there seemed to be some possibility of a genuine reform of the Stalinist machine, or at least a change of pilot. Already, soon after the death of Stalin in March 1953, there were faint signs of liberalization. In June Reimann appeared for the first time to stop using 1952's vocabulary of revolutionary 'overthrow'. A further conciliatory gesture was the decision to hold the second, and final, KPD Convention inside West Germany. Unlike the 1951 'Munich' Convention (which had actually met in Weimar), the Hamburg gathering of 28–30 December 1954 really did meet in Thälmann's birthplace. Still, 23 of the 537 delegates, including Reimann and 4 other Secretariat members, stayed away because of outstanding arrest warrants or actual prison sentences. As a concession to collective leadership, and probably in view of the banning trial taking place in Karlsruhe, Max Reimann was no longer to be 'Chairman' but 'First Secretary'.[76]

There was, of course, no serious reform discussion until after Khrushchev's 'secret speech' at the 20th Party Congress of the CPSU in February 1956. Even then, it was dealt with by the SED in cavalier fashion. On 4 March Ulbricht made his notorious understatement: 'Stalin does not belong to the classics of Marxism.' The cult of personality was criticized on 17 March, but at the end of April the Politburo pleaded not guilty, and denied Soviet-style mass repression. About 500 KPD functionaries were informed of Khrushchev's speech at special conferences, but most rank-and-file members first read of it in the non-Communist press.[77] Only on 18 March did the KPD Executive publish a reform document, 'It Must and Can Be Different', recanting 1952's slogans:

such as revolutionary overthrow of the Adenauer regime, because they do not correspond to the situation and conditions in West Germany and are impeding the establishment of the united front of the working class, as well as the *Sammlung* of progressive and nationally minded forces.[78]

[76] *FV*, 18 June 1953, 1; Michael Klein, *Antifaschistische Demokratie* (West Berlin, 1986), 203–4; *KPD 1945–1968*, i. 63.

[77] Berni Kelb, 'Hornhaut auf der Seele oder Wie der XX. Parteitag erledigt wurde', in Reinhard Crusius and Manfred Wilke (eds.), *Entstalinisierung: Der XX. Parteitag der KPdSU und seine Folgen* (Frankfurt am Main, 1977), 456–69; Grieger *et al.*, *Stalins Schatten*, 197; Valentin Senger, *Kurzer Frühling* (Frankfurt am Main, 1987), 251–61.

[78] KPD-PV, 18 Mar. 1956, *FV*, 23 Mar. 1956, 5.

The leadership embraced the concept of peaceful coexistence and non-violent transition to socialism, as well as a 'united front from above', stating that it had been operating 'from the outset on the terrain of constitutional basic rights and freedoms'. In *Wissen und Tat* Reimann explained that, 'in consideration of the level of maturity of the class constellations' in the FRG, 1952's Programme had been counterproductive to labour and democratic interests.[79] In late April Fisch also conceded that, although the general thrust of policy against Adenauer and western integration had been correct, the 'revolutionary overthrow' slogan had been wrong. With an eye on the *Bundesverfassungsgericht*, then deliberating on the party's constitutionality, he declared that:

The KPD aspires to change political relations in a peaceful manner. For precisely that reason it insists on respect for fundamental democratic and parliamentary rights. The KPD has never planned, prepared nor propagated acts of violence ... There was and never has been either an intention or preparation to infringe or remove the constitutional order in the Federal Republic.[80]

In some ways the KPD leadership was 'saved by the bell', banned before an internal party discussion could look for scapegoats for the disastrous policies of the past decade. Yet, it would be an exaggeration to think that 1956 was a missed opportunity for reform. In May the Secretariat told a disorientated rank and file that any questioning of Berlin and Moscow, as the KPD's acknowledged moral and political leaders, would be treated as 'slanders and anti-party subversion',[81] and even the limited freedom of speech within the SED evaporated after the Hungarian uprising in October. In the long term, East Berlin was to remain even more orthodox than Moscow, setting its face against reform, until forced by events in 1989–90. The KPD itself, and later the DKP, also suffered from a chronic lack of internal party democracy. The DKP's unregenerate 'concrete faction' under Herbert Mies was in fact to hold out even longer than its patron Erich Honecker.[82] The embattled position of the West German Communists, reaching new heights during the banning years of 1956–68, arguably helped to preserve even more perfectly the Stalinist system of organized paranoia. Since it is this study's underlying thesis that West German Communism would indeed be unintelligible without reference to the hostile forces at work upon it, it is to the phenomenon of anti-Communism that I now wish to turn in Part II.

---

[79] Siegfried Heimann, 'Die Deutsche Kommunistische Partei', in Richard Stöss (ed.), *Parteien-Handbuch* (Opladen, 1983), i. 917.
[80] *FV*, 28–29 Apr. 1956, 4.   [81] Heimann, 'Deutsche Kommunistische Partei', 918.
[82] Manfred Wilke *et al.*, *DKP* (Cologne, 1990), 195–246.

PART II

Anti-Communism in West Germany

7

Containing Communism

Anglo-American Policy towards the KPD, 1945–1950

ANTI-COMMUNISM has long been central to the historiography of the Cold War and the occupation of Germany. The traditionalist school of Cold War historians, writing mainly in the 1950s, tended to portray the battle against Communism, particularly by the United States, as a principled stand against inherent Soviet expansionism. This global quarantine programme, beginning publicly in 1947, and remaining US State Department orthodoxy until 1953, became known as the policy of 'containment'. Under American leadership, the moral high ground of freedom and democracy was successfully defended against the probing attacks of totalitarian world Communism. This, at any rate, was the self-proclaimed goal of the Truman Doctrine in March 1947, and to a lesser extent of the Marshall Plan in June, designed to overcome European economic nationalism, but also to immunize western Europe against Communism.[1]

In response to this largely reactive and somewhat idealized interpretation, in the late 1960s and 1970s revisionist historians, prompted by America's 'loss of innocence' following the débâcles of McCarthyism and Vietnam, began a critical re-examination of containment policy. Challenging previous justifications, they believed that anti-Communism had become an end in itself, often based on irrational fears. These had even blinded the West to legitimate Soviet security interests. Behind the hysteria, however, more hard-nosed economic motives were also discerned, in the form of a dollar imperialism seeking outlets for America's overextended wartime production capacity. The aggressive prime mover in the outbreak of the Cold War, according to the new argument, was thus to be sought not so much in the Kremlin as within the Truman administration

---

[1] It was succeeded in 1953 by John Foster Dulles's more proactive policy of 'roll-back'; see David Reynolds (ed.), *The Origins of the Cold War in Europe: International Perspectives* (New Haven and London, 1994).

itself. In the case of West Germany it was also alleged that, in order to create a stable anti-Communist bulwark, the initial anti-fascist reforming impulse of 1945 had been perverted by western military government into a capitalist restoration.[2]

In the 1980s, however, a so-called 'post-revisionist synthesis' began to emerge, arguing that the blame for the outbreak of the Cold War should be more evenly spread, and pleading for a differentiation of the bipolar model. Regional actors—in this case, the post-war European governments—were no longer to be seen as mere extensions of their respective super-power patrons. It is thus now generally accepted that, in the case of Germany, Britain played a crucial pace-making role in 1946 in bringing the United States around to a more confrontational stance in 1947.[3] At the same time, it should be noted that some critics have seen post-revisionism as little more than a disguised swing of the Cold War pendulum back towards traditionalism. As I have already hinted in my introduction, my own findings may act as a damper to some of these tendencies, although, as is the case with most detailed research, reality becomes only more complex with deepening knowledge.

Post-revisionism's plea for greater differentiation is, nevertheless, fundamentally correct. To pursue it to its logical conclusion, however, one needs to go beyond the diplomatic arena and to take into account the domestic politics of German anti-Communism. Even on the basis of the evidence already presented on the behaviour of the Social Democrats under Kurt Schumacher, as well as the non-Communist parliamentary factions and trade unions, it is clear that there was a strong indigenous hostility to the KPD in West Germany. The object of the final two chapters is therefore to enlarge this picture by tracing, firstly, Anglo-American attitudes to German Communism on the ground, as opposed to at the negotiating table, in the shape of local military government; secondly, to examine popular receptivity to anti-Communism among the West German general public, and, more specifically, the role of the Federal authorities in Bonn. In so doing, it is perhaps possible to understand better a phenomenon which was to become the defining feature of West German political culture well into the 1960s, and which has indeed enjoyed somewhat of a revival in the 1990s after the collapse of East German Communism.

---

[2] See, for instance, Ernst-Ulrich Huster *et al.*, *Determinanten der westdeutschen Restauration 1945–1949* (Frankfurt am Main, 1972).

[3] See John L. Gaddis, 'The Emerging Post-Revisionist Synthesis on the Origins of the Cold War', *Diplomatic History*, 7 (1983); for Britain's role, Anne Deighton, *The Impossible Peace: Britain, the Division of Germany, and the Origins of the Cold War* (Oxford, 1990).

In dealing with military government containment policy, it is necessary first of all to warn against regarding the Allied occupation regimes as too much of a monolithic mass. There were, for instance, clear differences—behind closed doors—between the metropolitan bureaucracies in Washington, Whitehall, and Paris, and military government on the spot in each of the occupation zones. Moreover, even within the separate layers of an occupation regime, one can detect various strains of anti-Communism which reflect different missions and objectives, as well as differing personal political sympathies. It is therefore perfectly possible to discover traditionalists and revisionists existing side by side within the military government hierarchy.

Although this chapter will concentrate on the British and American occupiers, whose combined zones accounted for around 90% of West German Communists, the French Zone deserves a few words by way of comparison. Here, too, there were political frictions within military government. It was well known at the time that the Gaullist governor, Koenig, did not see eye to eye with his more leftist deputy, Laffon, who indeed resigned in 1947. Nor should one forget that, as a legacy of the Resistance, the occupation power itself contained a number of Communists, until purged at the turn of 1947–8. Initial relations between the KPD and French front-line units appeared good, but reportedly deteriorated once these were replaced by occupation troops. Subsequently, a case could be made for the French Zone being the harshest environment for the KPD. France was second only to the Soviets in wishing to seal off her zone behind what her western partners only half-jokingly dubbed the 'silk curtain', and in extreme instances troublesome German Communists were simply deported into other zones.[4]

Turning to the Anglo-American occupiers, there were similar, if less pronounced, strains between leftists and conservatives. Austen Albu, sent to oversee political affairs in the British Zone in 1946, represented the Bevinite right wing of the Labour Party, but clearly regarded his colleague, Christopher Steel, as part of the Foreign Office establishment. Yet differences remained ones of means rather than ends, and the two in fact co-operated closely over the containment of the SED. More often than not, frictions were between the political and security interests of military government. Those responsible for day-to-day politics in the British

---

[4] Baden-Baden Consulate to State Dept., 18 Feb. 1948, BAK, Z 45 F, POLAD 825–14; Karl Kunde, *Die Odyssee eines Arbeiters* (Stuttgart, 1985), 122; see also Edgar Wolfrum, *Französische Besatzungspolitik und deutsche Sozialdemokratie: Politische Neuansätze in der 'vergessenen' Zone bis zur Bildung des Südweststaates 1945–1952* (Düsseldorf, 1991).

Zone, in the Control Commission's (CCG) Political Division, appeared relatively sanguine about the Communists. In stark contrast they noted that 'Counter-Intelligence naturally tend to be anti-Communist and to regard them as a potential subversive body. The ordinary Military Government official shies at the very mention of the name.'[5] Similar differences of opinion were evident in the Office of Military Government, United States (OMGUS). When its Counter Intelligence Corps started loyalty checks and undercover investigations into KPD subversion in autumn 1947, it seemed to Civil Administration Division (CAD) that innocuous evidence was being 'magnified into visions of streets running with blood' by local intelligence units. CAD, on the other hand, dismissed claims that the KPD/SED were capable of seizing political control of all of Germany as 'absolute rot'.[6]

It has also been argued that, on the other side of the Atlantic, the career diplomats at the State Department differed in their 'rational, goal-orientated attitude from the irrational, primarily ideological fear' of Communism and Socialism which had taken root among the American military, business world, and Congress, and which soon escalated to the hysterical red-baiting of the McCarthy era.[7] Nor should one assume that an anti-Communist stance automatically translated into the most conservative policy option available. If fear of Communist gains was genuine, then there was a temptation to head off what were seen to be radical KPD demands with moderate reforms. Thus, for instance, some Americans were prepared to compromise on their liberal capitalist beliefs and even entertained limited socialization plans, after German trade union leaders had warned that otherwise workers might be driven into the arms of the Communists. Importantly, for these officials, anti-Communism was a rational means to combat a larger economic malaise, but not an end in itself. This is not to deny that there were also plenty of ideological anti-Communists, for whom fighting the KPD was more akin to a religious crusade.

During the war the western Allies had already begun contingency planning for the potential threat posed by a post-war KPD. A common concern was that its underground network might enable it to steal an

---

[5] Annan to Steel, 27 Aug. 1945, PRO, FO 1049/70. More generally, Noel Annan, *Changing Enemies: The Defeat and Regeneration of Germany* (London, 1995), 187–212.

[6] Campbell to Rodes, 24 Sept. 1947, BAK, Z 45 F, ODI 7/20–3/10.

[7] Dörte Winkler, 'Die amerikanische Sozialisierungspolitik in Deutschland 1945–1948', in Heinrich A. Winkler (ed.), *Politische Weichenstellungen im Nachkriegsdeutschland 1945–1953* (Göttingen, 1979), 107.

organizational march on the other parties, especially the SPD. Whitehall forecasters predicted widespread proletarianization following Allied strategic bombing, but were open-minded as to whether German Communists would toe the Moscow line. The American Office of Strategic Services (OSS) anticipated KPD agitation in the western zones, but not such as to endanger inter-Allied relations. A collaborationist trend was expected, and indeed borne out, as the KPD promoted itself as a respectable 'collar-and-tie' party, loyal to every occupation power. As has already been seen in Chapter 3, the Communists went to great lengths to present a moderate programme, and since 1935 had been geared to a reformist, non-revolutionary alliance strategy. Self-restraint was not always easy for western members. Yet when, for instance, Hugo Paul, soon to be the KPD's North Rhine-Westphalian leader, threatened at the 1946 SED Merger Convention to boycott British directives at odds with Potsdam, he was conspicuously rebuked from the podium by Pieck and Ulbricht.[8]

As mentioned earlier, recent writing on the origins of the Cold War, above all that of Anne Deighton, has stressed the pace-setting role of the British in 1946. It does seem that Whitehall, as opposed to its local representatives in Germany, was prone to exaggerate Communist influence in the western zones, despite ever-mounting evidence to the contrary. Naturally, with very little to go on in 1945, initial predictions used Weimar precedent as a barometer of potential support, tilted perhaps over-generously in favour of a left-wing backlash against Nazism. Yet even in their Ruhr heartlands, where the Communists had outpolled all the other parties in 1932, the KPD was still expected to capture a minority of the electorate.[9] Later, when individual *Landtag* results became known, a national Communist election victory was all but ruled out. The British Political Adviser in Germany, Sir William Strang, then estimated that a combined SED/KPD vote of 6.8 million (KPD 1.7) would be swamped by a 22.2 million anti-Communist vote (including the non-Communist parties in the SBZ).[10]

---

[8] Morris memo. (No. 2), 22 Jan. 1945, BAK, Z 45 F, POLAD 34–2; 'Will Germany "go Communist" after the War?', 11 Sept. 1944, PRO, FO 1049/70; OSS report, 10 July 1944, PA Staritz; US War Dept., 'Policy Toward Revival of Old Parties and Establishment of New Parties in Germany', 22 July 1944, PA Staritz; CCG, 'Intelligence Review No. 8', Apr. 1946, PRO, FO 371/55365.

[9] It was estimated that in Westphalia the *Zentrum* would attract 40%, the SPD 30%, and the KPD 20%: Strang to Eden, 11 July 1945, PRO, FO 371/46933; 21 Army Gp. WPIS, 18 Aug. 1945, PRO, FO 371/46934.

[10] Strang's figures in Beam memo., 30 Oct. 1947, in *Foreign Relations of the United States, 1947* (Washington, DC, 1972), ii. 692–4.

Pre-emption of the parliamentary democratic process by Communist subversion was, however, another legitimate concern, based on widespread preconceptions that overt Communist strategy was always belied by a covert hidden agenda. The KPD/SPD fusion campaign in the SBZ in early 1946 fitted this pattern and clearly gave Whitehall a jolt.[11] Soon after it had become clear that there was no stopping an eastern merger, Con O'Neill alerted the Foreign Secretary, Ernest Bevin:

I feel it is much better for us to cut our losses in Berlin and the Russian Zone— which after all are not primarily our concern—and let the Social Democrat Party there cut its own throat if it wants to. As a corollary to this, we should give Schumacher his head in our own Zone.[12]

The Political Adviser even seemed resigned to recognition of some form of SED west of the Elbe, and by March Bevin was justifying forestalling the central administration envisaged by Potsdam, with fears of a Communist political offensive westwards. In the long run he was pessimistic that the non-Communist western parties could resist Soviet-sponsored German Communism, and the food crisis and economic chaos would only play into the hands of the 'totalitarians'.[13] At a crucial Foreign Office meeting on 3 April 1946, Bevin, his Permanent Under-Secretary, Sargent, and Hynd, the 'Germany Minister', discussed the possibility of a separate West Germany, the stark alternative to which Sargent claimed was 'Communism on the Rhine'.[14] Thus, the perceived Communist threat had soon reached such proportions that it was even being used to justify steps towards the division of Germany.

Bevin, of course, only ever once set foot inside the British Zone, in May 1949. Military government officers on the ground were better placed to judge, and tended to look beyond the KPD's high level of organization and activity and discount a serious threat. Thus, in December 1945 the Political Division's deputy head, Noel Annan, had reported that 'the KPD is the most powerful party in the eastern zone and least powerful in western Germany'.[15] Yet Annan later recollected with mild embarrassment

---

[11] Falk Pingel, ' "Die Russen am Rhein?": Zur Wende der britischen Besatzungspolitik im Frühjahr 1946', *VfZ*, 30 (1982), 98–116.

[12] O'Neill memo., 21 Feb. 1946, PRO, FO 371/55362.

[13] Strang to C-in-C/FO, 1 Mar. 1946, PRO, FO 371/55362; Bevin to Committee on German Industry, 11 Mar. 1946, in *Die Ruhrfrage 1945/46*, ed. Rolf Steininger (Düsseldorf, 1988), 545–60, here 557–8.

[14] Deighton, *Impossible Peace*, 71–3.

[15] Anthony Glees, *Exile Politics during the Second World War* (Oxford, 1982), 209. This picture of a weak KPD was repeated a year later: Steel to Bevin, 23 Dec. 1946, PRO, FO 1049/336.

the panicked proposals even he made in response to the SBZ merger in April 1946, including various concessions on co-determination, land reform, socialization, and 'progressive social change' in order to head off Communist propaganda. Increased levels of industry, regardless of quadripartite disagreement, and discouragement of French claims to western territories would be further ways of weakening Communism.[16]

Nevertheless, Annan soon reverted to his initial prognosis of a weak KPD. Despite his isolation as a self-confessed Labour sympathizer in a Conservative-dominated military establishment, he was not alone in resisting Whitehall's conspiracy theories. After Hynd pleaded for Control Commission backing for SPD and CDU action against the KPD, and in July London authorized criticism of Soviet policy in the zonal media, the Deputy Military Governor, Robertson, complied only against his better judgement.[17] When Sargent proposed the drastic course of removing all Communists from public office, the Military Governor himself, Douglas, preferred propaganda backed up by economic rehabilitation: 'Moreover, we believe that many German Communists are Germans first and Communists afterwards.'[18] Even within the Labour cabinet Bevin's views were not accepted unquestioningly. When he claimed that 'the balance of advantage seems to lie with the Russians', and that 'Communism already has its addicts in western Germany and the liberal attitudes of the occupying authorities in the west would allow them a free hand', Bevan and Shinwell both dismissed this as alarmist exaggeration.[19]

Once it was clear that the campaign for a western SED had come to a standstill in mid-1946, and the autumn local elections proved such a disaster for the KPD, it is difficult to construct a scenario in which the western Communists might have posed a serious threat. Of course, they could, and should, not be divorced from their comrades in the SBZ, who dominated the zonal infrastructure there well before an East German state was formed, and who pinned great hopes on controlling the old Reich capital. Yet, with the denial of a central administration based in Berlin, options for expanding influence beyond the Elbe were extremely limited. Furthermore, a conventional military attack by the Red Army had all but been discounted by the western powers. Nor does new knowledge of SED/KPD consultations in 1946, or the intensive military government

---

[16] Annan, 16 Apr. 1946, PRO, FO 371/55364; Annan interview, 14 July 1992.

[17] Pingel, ' "Russen am Rhein?" ', 107 and 112.

[18] Douglas to Bevin, 28 May 1946, in *Ruhrfrage*, 830–4. Bevin's comment: 'I'm not so sure; we always make this mistake.'

[19] 3 May 1946, in Deighton, *Impossible Peace*, 75–6.

investigations into KPD strike activity over the following winter, discussed in earlier chapters, reveal a concerted plan of action.

One must assume, if Whitehall's anti-Communist conspiracy theories could not be based rationally on reports from the field, that they were also ideologically, or even tactically, motivated. Much of Bevin's mistrust of Communists went back to bitter domestic union conflicts in the early 1920s. This no-nonsense Labour anti-Communism found its complement in more fastidious Conservative fears. As already observed, Bevin's closest advisers included Sir Orme Sargent, who was almost routinely fearful of Communist 'avalanches' and had advocated a showdown with the Soviets over Central Europe as early as April 1945. Con O'Neill was another early advocate of containment policy. Anti-Communism also had its practical uses. One plus for Bevin of the new *Land* of North Rhine-Westphalia was that it would dilute a supposedly KPD-dominated Ruhr. It seems there was in fact no serious Foreign Office investigation into KPD strength until 1948, but the worst-case scenario was regularly trundled out as confirmation of the need to revive the Bizonal economy. Even in 1949, when a realistic red menace was almost nil, Bevin was still prepared to play the Communist card to win tactical diplomatic battles, this time in order to gain the French foreign minister's approval for the Basic Law.[20]

The American Military Governor, Lucius D. Clay, displayed more ambivalence over the KPD threat, caught in the crossfire between a War Department wishing to deal with the Soviets and a more hawkish State Department. In the period 1945–7 he appears not to have been virulently anti-Communist, and was concerned in spring 1946 chiefly by the SED/KPD's nationalist rhetoric, only in late 1947 to perform an almost 180-degree about-turn.[21] In the meantime, Clay's assessment of the red threat appeared to move with the seasons. In March 1946 food shortages meant 'no choice between becoming a Communist on 1500 calories and a believer in democracy on 1000 calories'. Proposed ration cuts would 'pave the road to a Communist Germany'.[22] Despite this alarmism, the War Department,

---

[20] John Farquharson, 'From Unity to Division: What Prompted Britain to Change its Policy in Germany in 1946?', *European History Quarterly*, 26 (1996), 81–123; Alan Bullock, *Ernest Bevin: Foreign Secretary 1945–1951* (London, 1983), 105–7 and 483–90; Peter Weiler, *British Labour and the Cold War* (Stanford, Calif., 1988), 191; Bevin to Overseas Reconstruction Committee, 11 June 1946, in *Ruhrfrage*, 871–5, here 874; Erich J. Hahn, 'U.S. Policy on a West German Constitution, 1947–1949', in Jeffry M. Diefendorf *et al.* (eds.), *American Policy and the Reconstruction of West Germany, 1945–1955* (Cambridge, 1993), 39.

[21] Wolfgang Krieger, *General Lucius D. Clay* (Stuttgart, 1987), 155–6.

[22] Clay to Echols and Petersen, 27 Mar. 1946, in *The Papers of General Lucius D. Clay: Germany 1945–1949*, ed. Jean Edward Smith (Bloomington, Ind., 1974), i. 183–5.

which controlled the OMGUS budget, seemed more interested in the practicalities of food distribution than Communism as such. Yet five months later Clay rejected OMGUS action on behalf of non-Communist parties, since there was 'little evidence of Communist gains'.[23] After the severe winter of 1946–7 he was at his most apocalyptic: 'I am not exaggerating the penetration and growth of communism in western Germany. It can win western Germany if we continue to play our cards the way we are.'[24] A Communist Germany would lead to a Communist Europe. Yet, since Clay usually linked his alarmism with calls for more humanitarian aid, he should probably be categorized as a rational anti-Communist who was also concerned not to let actions against the KPD upset quadripartite negotiations.

By this point, however, OMGUS was coming under increasing State-side pressure to step up anti-Communist measures of a more ideological nature. In April 1947 Matthew Woll of the American Federation of Labor urged tougher action against Communists in OMGUS and no more equal rights for the KPD. Then, in July, Congress began attacks on 'fellow travellers' in military government. One aid adviser even informed Clay that he had evidence of Communist sympathizers 'infecting' OMGUS and called for the elimination of Communism in Germany, barring it from public office. Denunciations of OMGUS personnel as fellow travellers were also taken up personally by FBI director, J. Edgar Hoover.[25] In summer 1947 OMGUS did in fact discuss revoking the KPD's authorization. It was already debarred from certain offices. However, it was feared that the SMAD might retaliate against the CDUD and LDPD in the SBZ, and such a policy would only martyrize the KPD and impede its monitoring. It was agreed, however, to interpret regulations to restrict Communists and 'rap them on the knuckles', suspending local organizations if necessary. Non-Communist parties might also legitimately be favoured with cars, petrol, newsprint, and office equipment.[26] At the same time, Joint Chiefs of Staff directive JCS 1067, the basic OMGUS policy

---

[23] Clay to War Dept., 20 Aug. 1946, in *Papers*, i. 256–8.

[24] Clay to Noce, 14 Apr. 1947, in *Papers*, i. 337–8.

[25] Woll to Acheson, 3 Apr. 1947, in *Confidential U.S. State Department Central Files: Germany—Internal Affairs 1945–1949*, ed. Paul Kesaris (Frederick, Md., 1985), 14. 853–4; David Caute, *The Great Fear: The Anti-Communist Purge under Truman and Eisenhower* (London, 1978), 294; Armstrong to Clay, 5 Oct. 1947, in *Konrad Adenauer und die CDU der britischen Besatzungszone 1946–1949: Dokumente zur Gründungsgeschichte der CDU Deutschlands*, ed. Konrad-Adenauer-Stiftung (Bonn, 1975), 465–77; Hoover to State Dept. (Neal), 31 Aug. 1948, BAK, Z 45 F, ODI 7/20–3/10.

[26] Murphy to Hickerson, 19 Aug. 1947, and Hickerson to Murphy, 21 Oct. 1947, in *FRUS, 1947*, ii. 882–4 and 891–3.

document, was amended in JCS 1779 to include a clause 'to provide Military Government with a sufficiently flexible authority to deal with the problem of the KPD as it might develop'.[27]

Red Tape Versus the Red Threat

Until then, Anglo-Allied sanctions were limited to bureaucratic obstruction, usually in response to Communist initiatives. One of the KPD's commonest subsequent accusations was that of discrimination in military government's party licensing policy. In spring 1945 a total ban on political activity was in force, but much depended on the discretion of the local commander and respective occupying power. Although there was much unnecessary red tape, with some British licensing even improvised on an *ad hoc* basis between the local CCG and Field Security Service detachments, there is no evidence of systematic Communist victimization. Inevitably, the traditionally highly centralized workers' parties were bound to feel more hardly done by than the more amorphous bourgeois parties. Yet restrictions applied to *all* early political activity.[28]

At first, political parties could only apply for authorization at local *Kreis* level. (In general, *Land*-level licensing occurred in late 1945, and zonally from early 1946.) Vetting in smaller towns and rural areas was certainly considerably delayed, sometimes dragging on into spring 1946. There were also great time-lags between local KPD applications. In most cases, however, only a few days separated the granting of KPD and SPD licences. By the end of 1945 24 KPD, 24 SPD, and 21 CDU *Kreise* had been legalized in Westphalia; and by March 1946 29 KPD, 27 CDU, and 26 SPD organizations in North Rhine Region.[29] Similarly, in the American Zone, by 1 November 1945 OMGUS had authorized 85 SPD, 73 KPD, 44 CDU/CSU, and ten FDP *Kreise*.[30] Admittedly, publicity and rallies were not permitted until late in 1945, and required special vetting, with

---

[27] Daniel E. Rogers, 'Transforming the German Party System: The United States and the Origins of Political Moderation, 1945–1949', *Journal of Modern History*, 65 (1993), 531–2.

[28] 'Augenzeugenbericht', n.d. [May 1945], SAPMO-BA, NY 4182/859; Stötzel, 28 July 1945, SAPMO-BA, I 10/23/8; CCG/Westphalia report, 1–31 Oct. 1945, PRO, FO 1013/661; Georg Wulffius, 'Probleme mit der KPD-Lizenz', in Michael Schröder (ed.), *Auf geht's: Rama dama!* (Cologne, 1984), 35–45.

[29] CCG/Westphalia, 1–31 Dec. 1945, PRO, FO 1013/661; North Rhine Region, Mar. 1946, PRO, FO 1013/726. As well as 18 FDP and 13 *Zentrum*.

[30] Laukhuff to Murphy, 19 Sept. 1947, BAK, Z 45 F, POLAD 460–6; F. Roy Willis, *The French in Germany 1945–1949* (Stanford, Calif., 1962), 191.

OMGUS demanding ten days' notice of speakers from other zones. Yet such restrictions applied across the board, and, in the KPD's Ruhr heartlands, local leaders had in fact been able to address meetings as early as August 1945.[31]

A western KPD was one thing; a western SED was quite another. The explicit problem of authorizing a West German SED appears not to have been discussed at the Allied Control Council, although this must have been at the backs of representatives' minds as they began general discussions on regulating all-German political parties in February 1946. A possible precedent was even set on 31 May, when the *Kommandatura* went as far as licensing the SED and SPD in all four sectors of Berlin. By then, of course, the West had as much of an interest in seeing the return of an eastern SPD, as the East had in establishing a western SED. Yet Anglo-American proposals soon encountered French objections, and, by May, Soviet evasion. Although Soviet negotiators revived their interest in 1947, an initiative on national parties by Molotov at the Moscow CFM foundered on French resistance. Indeed, the ACC did not discuss the matter after October 1947, by which time both the USA and Britain were blocking Soviet proposals, making inter-zonal political mergers contingent on progress on economic unity.[32]

Accordingly, it was left to individual zonal commanders to devise ways of containing the SED. The French simply applied a blanket ban on all new parties. The Americans and the British, on the other hand, did grant passes to top SED leaders to come and speak in their zones, but, when the SMAD failed to reciprocate, the British revoked theirs at the end of July 1946. Nevertheless, Ulbricht, Pieck, Grotewohl, and Dahlem continued to be able to tour the US Zone throughout 1947, and Dahlem even spoke at the People's Congress in Bremen as late as January 1948. Regarding merger, events in Berlin clearly provided the model. In a famous *Urabstimmung*, held on 31 March 1946, over 80% of Social Democrats in the western sectors voted against fusion with the Communists. In anticipation of such a result, Clay announced a few days beforehand that OMGUS would only countenance an SED in the US Zone if both SPD and KPD agreed by *Land*-level referendum to amalgamate. Referenda had to be invoked by approved mustering committees. The British adopted a localized version of American procedure, whereby, if a *Kreis*

---

[31] Hartmut Pietsch, *Militärregierung, Bürokratie und Sozialisierung* (Duisburg, 1978), 132.

[32] Dietrich Staritz, 'Parteien für ganz Deutschland?: Zu den Kontroversen über ein Parteiengesetz im Alliierten Kontrollrat 1946/47', *VfZ*, 32 (1984), 263-4.

referendum did not produce a majority in both parties within three months, any provisional committees were to be disbanded. There is no evidence that any such referendum ever took place. Moreover, after accepting local KPD-sponsored applications, the British Political Adviser had hinted that 'we could sit on these as long as we liked'.[33]

Thereafter, discussion of a western SED became more and more of a Cold War bargaining chip in a wider diplomatic game. Already in 1946 the British had toyed with the idea of permitting the KPD to change its name 'as a lever to extract permission from the Russians for the re-establishment of [the] SPD in their zone'.[34] During the second campaign for a western SED in spring 1947, the western Allies further explored the possibility of a reciprocal deal, despite meeting an apparent dead end on the issue at the Moscow CFM. Behind the scenes, the Americans were torn between permitting the KPD to rename itself, so as to expose the eastern SED as Communist all along, and holding on to the trump card of reciprocity. Nevertheless, by mid-May OMGUS appeared to have lost interest in Soviet offers of a revived eastern SPD in return for a western SED.[35] The British appeared less undecided. When, on 5 May 1947, Dahlem informed the CCG that the SMAD would 'welcome any approach made to them by Schumacher with a view to reorganizing the SPD in the Russian Zone', privately Political Division remained sceptical of this 'old red herring'.[36] Steel later believed it would not 'be at all in our interests for the SPD to be recognized in the Soviet Zone. The SPD themselves are of the same opinion.'[37] Meanwhile, military government sanctions against the *Arbeitsgemeinschaft* SED-KPD continued, despite SED complaints, and SED applications were received without comment and filed.[38] By July 1947, however, the British could justifiably claim that the 'campaign for the establishment of the Social[ist] Unity Party . . . has now been fought to a standstill'.[39]

---

[33] Strang to FO, 25 Apr. 1946, PRO, FO 1049/327; Annan to Regions, 18 July 1946, and Concomb to RIOs, 27 July 1946, PRO, FO 1049/2118; RIO Düsseldorf to Political Division, 19 Dec. 1947, PRO, FO 1049/782; Ulrich Hauth, *Die Politik von KPD und SED* (Frankfurt am Main, 1978), 128; Daniel E. Rogers, *Politics after Hitler* (Basingstoke, 1995), 80–6.

[34] Steel to Pol. Div., 18 July 1946, PRO, FO 1049/2118.

[35] Heath to State Dept., 15 Mar. 1947, in *FRUS, 1947*, ii. 856–8; Scammon-Bolton/ Dahlem-Gniffke meeting, 12 May 1947, SAPMO-BA, NY 4036/646.

[36] Steel to FO, 21 May 1947, PRO, FO 1049/914.

[37] Steel to Chaput de Saintonge, 12 Aug. 1947, PRO, FO 1049/2111.

[38] *Dokumente der SED*, ed. PV/ZK der SED (East Berlin, 1951), i. 176–9; RB Arnsberg to Regional Gov. Office, 14 July 1947, PRO, FO 1013/409.

[39] CCG Monthly Report No. 7, July 1947; see Pietsch, *Militärregierung*, 249.

Covert Operations against 'Project Happiness'[40]

In the public party-political arena it thus seems clear that the Anglo-Americans were satisfied that West German Communism presented little or no obvious threat. It was argued at the beginning of the chapter, however, that there were internal conflicts between the political and security wings of military government. Is there indeed any evidence of the clandestine KPD activity so eagerly sought by Allied intelligence? Although the files of Britain's Intelligence Division remain tantalizingly closed, penetration of the KPD by America's Counter Intelligence Corps (CIC) is relatively well documented. Moreover, the Americans appeared to be reasonably well informed on internal KPD affairs, as the West Commission's chief instructor for the US Zone found to his cost when he was picked up and interrogated by CIC in 1946.[41]

The first recorded American covert action against the KPD occurred in September 1946, when the Bremen CIC launched Operation SUNRISE to 'turn' local party members. These newly recruited informants nevertheless revealed little that was not already known. From 1946 the Americans also began collating lists of Communists, and routinely screened POWs returning from the USSR for Soviet-trained *Antifa* graduates. Despite KPD suspicions that 35,000 of its members were kept on an OMGUS detention list for use during an East–West conflict, actual arrests were few in number. (Five Bavarian party leaders were apprehended on their way back from a covert trip to the SBZ in 1946 and sentenced to four months in gaol for illegal border-crossing, but released early.) Otherwise military government turned a blind eye to KPD visits to East Berlin. From September 1947 CIC also began to monitor KPD contingency plans for going underground in the event of prohibition or a 'hot' war. Resignations of prominent Communists were seen as first steps towards a dormant membership, which would resurface in the police and civil administration, although, as will be seen below, these fears proved largely unfounded.[42]

---

[40] 'Project Happiness' was intelligence jargon for West German Communism; see Ian Sayer and Douglas Botting, *America's Secret Army: The Untold Story of the Counter Intelligence Corps* (London, 1989), 280.

[41] Fuhrmann, 7 Dec. 1946, SAPMO-BA, DY 30/IV 2/2.022/130.

[42] Tom Bower, *Klaus Barbie: Butcher of Lyons* (London, 1984), 134; anonymous report, 4 Aug. 1946, SAPMO-BA, NY 4182/861; Fisch memo., 29 July 1947, SAPMO-BA, NY 4036/646; Wilkinson to Murphy, 11 Oct. 1946, BAK, Z 45 F, POLAD 748–3; POLAD to State Dept., 10 Sept. 1947, BAK, Z 45 F, POLAD 32/12.

Early on in the occupation CIC's priority had in fact been to support denazification by tracing wanted war criminals, yet as the Cold War intensified, ever more resources were switched to countering left-wing subversion. So much so that by mid-1948 the KPD had become the Americans' 'primary intelligence target', despite its weakness, since fellow-travelling 'sympathizers' could allegedly always make up for deficiency in numbers. In 1949, for example, CIC investigated 4,356 left-wing cases of political subversion, but only 1,313 on the right. Furthermore, despite official restrictions, local units soon found the temptation to use ex-Gestapo personnel irresistible. The ex-head of the Munich Gestapo's Communist desk, Eugen Fischer, was thus employed by CIC to penetrate the Bavarian KPD, supported by Anton Mahler who had interrogated the White Rose conspirators, and as many as half the former Munich Gestapo may have been on CIC Region IV's payroll. In January 1949 former SS-*Standartenführer* Walter Huppenkothen, who in the final days of the war had personally supervised the judicial murders of such resistance leaders as Bonhoeffer, Canaris, and Oster, even furnished the Americans with a report on Gestapo methods and pitfalls in combatting the KPD.[43]

The most notorious use of a Nazi for his anti-Communist expertise was that of Klaus Barbie. Recruited and protected by CIC Munich in April 1947, without the knowledge of its headquarters, he gathered information on the Russian Intelligence Services, including links with the KPD and Communist activities in the French Zone. After interrogation by CIC headquarters over the winter of 1947–8, his first official target in August 1948 became the KPD.[44] From November his Augsburg-based network was 'seeking out as many old Gestapo and SS informants as possible, and especially those whose mission was KPD penetration under the Nazi regime'.[45] Indeed, on one occasion he even posed as a Communist to attend a local party meeting![46] Barbie

knows more about CIC targets, modus operandi, EEIs [essential elements of information], etc., than most CIC agents. SUBJECT also knows the identity of

---

[43] Conran at Mil. Attachés conf., 7 June 1948, BAK, Z 45 F, POLAD 798/4; 66th CIC Detachment, 'Annual Narrative Report', 31 Dec. 1949, in Erhard Dabringhaus, *Klaus Barbie* (Washington, DC, 1984), 62; Sayer and Botting, *Secret Army*, 331 and 353; ID/EUCOM, 30 Mar. 1949, BAK, Z 45 F, 7–32–3/5–6.

[44] Allan A. Ryan, *Klaus Barbie and the United States Government* (Frederick, Md., 1984), 13 and 15–18; CIC/Region IV to HQ EUCOM, Dec. 1947, ibid. 239–50; CIC/Region IV to HQ EUCOM, 23 Aug. 1948, ibid. 258–61.

[45] CIC/Region IV to HQ EUCOM, 19 Feb. 1949, in Ryan, *Barbie*, 281–3.

[46] Dabringhaus, *Klaus Barbie*, 81.

most KPD penetration sources used by this office, due to the fact that he either handled those sources . . . or because he recruited or turned such sources.[47]

Although it is clear that he was as contemptuous of the Americans' exaggeration of Communist subversion, as he was of their Nazi conspiracy theories, he succeeded in 1949 in penetrating Munich party headquarters and intercepting its correspondence with Frankfurt. In March 1951, however, after French pressure to have him extradited as a material witness in the trial against suspected collaborator René Hardy, the Americans spirited Barbie away to Bolivia down the so-called 'ratline', run by a Croatian priest at the Vatican, Monsignor Dragonovic. In their defence, however, Barbie's American superiors could point out that the British, French, and Soviet authorities were equally guilty of employing ex-Nazis.[48]

The KPD slipped further into the murky world of the cloak and dagger during the so-called 'Protocol M' affair of 1948. On 14 January of that year Nordwestdeutscher Rundfunk broadcast disclosures of an alleged Cominform plan to sabotage Marshall Aid in West Germany. Transport and metalworkers' strikes in the Ruhr, designed to disrupt food supplies and force acceptance of a KPD/SPD[!]-sponsored plebiscite on socialization by December 1947, were to be followed by general strikes in March 1948—all orchestrated by a so-called 'MA-Cadre'. Far-fetched as this was, it fell on fertile ground, particularly in view of the preceding wave of Communist-inspired strikes against Marshall Aid in France and Italy, as well as the Prague Coup in Czechoslovakia the following month. The non-Communist press gave widespread coverage to the affair, adding ever more lurid details to the KPD's takeover plan. Yet recently released evidence proves 'Protocol M' to have been a forgery. In April, at a meeting of the top British diplomatic leadership, it was reported that the document had first been published in the *Kurier* and *Telegraf* in Berlin, faked by a Social Democrat named Hahn, working as an American agent, and leaked by the US State Department. Whether 'Hahn' was SPD press chief, Fritz Heine, as the KPD subsequently claimed, remains unclear.[49]

---

[47] CIC/Region XII to HQ EUCOM, 11 May 1950, in Ryan, *Barbie*, 365–8.

[48] Bower, *Barbie*, 151 and 155–6; Christopher Simpson, *Blowback: America's Recruitment of Nazis and Its Effects on the Cold War* (London, 1988), 70; David Cesarani, *Justice Delayed* (London, 1992), 149–54; Mark Aarons and John Loftus, *Ratlines: How the Vatican's Nazi Networks Betrayed Western Intelligence to the Soviets* (London, 1991), 254.

[49] POLAD to State Dept., 12 Jan. 1948, BAK, Z 45 F, POLAD 32/2–5; Bevin/ Robertson/Steel/Kirkpatrick/Roberts meeting, 17 Apr. 1948, PRO, FO 371/70478; Willy Perk, *Besatzungsmacht gegen Pressefreiheit* (Frankfurt am Main, 1979), 52–3.

Also available are the minutes of a top-level meeting in East Berlin from the day before the 'Protocol M' affair broke, which place the KPD's legalism beyond reasonable doubt. Pieck certainly sounded confrontational when he said 'In the western zones on the other hand, where they speak of alleged democracy, we shall only be able to beat the reactionaries in armed struggles.' Ulbricht's subsequent intervention nevertheless shows the rhetorical nature of such outbursts:

We can talk as much as we like about dictatorship of the proletariat and armed struggle. If we do not have the masses behind us, it is pointless. We can only win over the masses in practical struggles, in the struggle for more bread . . .[50]

Not long afterwards, in February, Dahlem categorically warned against 'deviating from the legal line now'.[51] He had, however, arranged that no more internal materials, card indexes, or lists be kept at party offices, and that KPD members should break off contacts with western intelligence services. Meetings with military government would henceforth be in twos. By March, in a consultation in Moscow, Pieck confirmed the need for the KPD to prepare for illegality and build an illegal apparatus. None the less, this appears to have been a defensive measure in fear of a ban. A party intelligence organization of the order of the Weimar KPD's AM-Apparatus, or paramilitary wings such as the Red Front Fighters' League and the armed *Parteiselbstschutz*, were out of the question after 1945. (In any case, the late Weimar party had never entertained serious plans for a putsch, and the terroristic attacks of 1931 were in fact largely individual initiatives.) As an espionage agency the post-war party was too obvious and vulnerable, and, on the whole, any intelligence gathered was low-grade in order to avoid provoking sanctions.[52]

After the 'Protocol M' scare there were nevertheless prolonged Anglo-American investigations into the KPD's actual potential to wreak havoc. Hideouts and covert printing presses were occasionally discovered, but no weapons caches. The Kampfgruppe Marx, allegedly set up by the SED in 1948 as a fifth column in West Germany, turned out to be a complete fabrication. There had been isolated incidents of alleged sabotage, such as at Dunlop's Hanau plant, when, in August 1947, shortly after it had

---

[50] SED-ZS/KPD meeting, 13 Jan. 1948, SAPMO-BA, DY 30/IV 2/1.01/73.

[51] SED-ZS/KPD meeting, 10 Feb. 1948, SAPMO-BA, DY 30/IV 2/1.01/79; *Wilhelm Pieck*, ed. Rolf Badstubner and Wilfried Loth (Berlin, 1994), 195.

[52] Eve Rosenhaft, *Beating the Fascists?: The German Communists and Political Violence 1929–1933* (Cambridge, 1983); POLAD to State Dept., 3 Mar. 1948, in *Confidential (1945–1949)*, 40. 62–76.

stopped deliveries to the SBZ, its water pumps were disabled, halting production for eleven days. An American investigation linked the sabotage
directly to the KPD factory group. The British also began to monitor
the situation specifically for signs of KPD-inspired unrest, but could
find no definite plans for insurgency beyond isolated strikes. Minister
President Arnold of NRW was confident that any 'red threat' was being
kept in check by the mild winter, increased rations, and Marshall Aid.
Surveys of KPD influence in the Bizone's transport network[53] and police[54]
also concluded that the KPD was in no position to cause serious disruption. Internally, the party even suspected 'radical revolutionary' members
of being CIC *agents provocateurs*.[55]

As the erstwhile KPD leader in the Ruhr recalled in an interview with
the author in 1993, in view of recent British intervention against Greek
Communist insurgents, there was no doubt among German Communists
that force would have been met with force. The Americans also concluded that, '[u]nder conditions of occupation, actual Communist "*guerilla-
warfare*" or "*attempts to seize political control* of the 4 zones of Germany"
by the KPD-SED is *technically impossible*'.[56] By November 1948 the intelligence divisions of both the Americans and the British could find 'no
evidence . . . that any type of an illegal organization has been established
by the Party to date'.[57] Later on, a CIC 'deep-penetration' investigation
concluded that, although the KPD was committed to the downfall of
the Bonn government and Allied troop withdrawals, it did not have the
capacity to achieve this by violence, relying instead on attempted mass

[53] Communists with 'sympathizers' in brackets: railwaymen—1–2% (2–3%); inland
waterways—1% (3.5%); inland ports—2% (3%); dockworkers 9% (33%): POLAD to State
Dept., 30 Sept. 1948, in *Confidential (1945–1949)*, 40. 251–5.

[54] In Hamburg only 0.5% of officers were Communists. In July 1950 1.9% of police
in the US Zone were KPD members (Munich 0.4%, Frankfurt 0.6%, Stuttgart 2.5%,
Mannheim 12%!, Bremen 0.9%): Hamburg Consulate to State Dept., 10 May 1948;
HICOG to State Dept., 27 Dec. 1950, in *Confidential U.S. State Department Central
Files: Germany—Federal Republic of Germany. Internal Affairs 1950–1954*, ed. Paul Kesaris
(Frederick, Md., 1986), 28. 848–73; POLAD to State Dept., 3 Dec. 1948; ID/EUCOM,
8 June 1949, in *Confidential (1945–1949)*, 40. 149–50, 317–26, 511–13.

[55] ODDI/EUCOM, 31 Oct. 1947, in *Confidential (1945–1949)*, 40. 93; Dok. IM-NRW
Nr.: 21 (BfV), 11 July 1951; report, 11 Mar. 1948, PRO, FO 371/70478; Bremen Consulate
to State Dept., 23 Mar. 1948, in *Confidential (1945–1949)*, 14. 902–4; KPD-Wetzlar, n.d.
[late 1947], SAPMO-BA, DY 30/IV 2/10.01/4.

[56] Kallmann to Rodes, 24 Sept. 1947, BAK, Z 45 F, ODI 7/20–3/10. Ledwohn interview, 14 Sept. 1993.

[57] POLAD to State Dept., 15 Nov. 1948, in *Confidential (1945–1949)*, 40. 306. Two
years later this still seemed to be the case, with activities limited to decentralization of
files and a non-provocation policy—HICOG to State Dept., 21 Nov. 1950, in *Confidential
(1950–1954)*, 28. 781–93.

demonstrations and labour unrest.[58] It would thus seem that, even behind the scenes, the Anglo-Americans were agreed that the KPD had neither the will nor wherewithal to become a fifth column.

1947–1948: Military Government Takes the Offensive

Nevertheless, at the turn of 1947–8 there was a significant hardening of the Anglo-American occupation authorities' line towards the KPD. Policy had clearly been under review since the inconclusive end of the Moscow CFM in March–April 1947, but restraint had been exercised so as not to rock the quadripartite boat. The failure of the London CFM in November –December of the same year then removed many of these inhibitions. In the case of the British, the more draconian measures appear to have originated in Whitehall; in the US Zone the military governor had always been delegated more local authority, and Clay's anti-Communist initiatives were even regarded as premature in some quarters of Washington. Moreover, unlike the British campaign, OMGUS action seems not to have been part of a global pattern, since anti-Communist crackdowns in US-occupied South Korea and Japan followed more local timetables.[59]

On 25 October 1947 Clay ordered Information Control Division to take the propaganda offensive against Communism in what became known as Operation TALKBACK.[60] Three days later he announced at a press conference that under JCS directive 1067 US policy objectives had been to 'protect democracy and to resist communism'. In response to recent Soviet allegations of western remilitarization, he intended 'to defend the principles we believe and attack those in which we don't believe, and we certainly don't believe in communism in any manner, shape, form, or fashion'.[61] In a cable to the War Department he added: 'We are engaged in political warfare and we might as well recognize it now.'[62] Both the State and War Departments were incensed that Clay had acted on

---

[58] Sayer and Botting, *Secret Army*, 355.

[59] In American-occupied south Korea the crackdown on leftists had begun as early as Feb. 1946; in Japan not until mid-1950, see Bruce Cumings, *The Origins of the Korean War: Liberation and the Emergence of Separate Regimes 1945–1947* (Princeton, 1981), 200–1 and 250; Michael Schaller, *The American Occupation of Japan* (New York and Oxford, 1985), 267–8; see also Thomas Baumann, 'Das Verhältnis der KPD und der amerikanischen Besatzungsmacht in Deutschland 1945–1949', Ph.D. thesis (University of Mannheim, 1994), which I was unable to consult.

[60] Clay, *Decision in Germany*, 158.

[61] Jean Edward Smith, *Lucius D. Clay: An American Life* (New York, 1990), 443.

[62] Clay to Draper, 30 Oct. 1947, in *Papers*, i. 459–60.

his own initiative, but lent retrospective support. The party's response was predictable, accusing the Americans of reverting to 'arguments and slogans from the Goebbels era'. Significantly, this policy change had occurred before the London CFM, and, in the event of the conference's failure, Clay was already urging the formation of a West German government as an anti-Communist bulwark.[63]

Still, there had never been any intention of prohibiting the KPD, and Clay preferred instead merely to quarantine it from the rest of the population and expose it in the press. Yet, following the 'Protocol M' affair (itself possibly a by-product of Operation TALKBACK), OMGUS began discussing more proactive measures to neutralize Communists west of the Elbe. Fears were less of revolution from below than an orchestrated coup as had just occurred in Prague in February 1948. US Public Safety proposed bars on party membership for state officials and their removal should they advocate unconstitutional action, as well as modification of proportional representation in favour of a first-past-the-post electoral system, so as to exclude Communists.[64] A long-range policy document, 'How to Fight Communism', was circulated on a pro-democracy, rather than anti-Communist campaign, designed as a bridging action until Marshall Aid made itself felt. Significantly, a ban of the KPD was ruled out as placing OMGUS on the same moral plane as the SMAD. Yet it was proposed to prohibit US Zone participation in inter-zonal meetings including SBZ representatives; to give non-Communist parties air time on RIAS and Voice of America to broadcast to the SBZ; to encourage irredentist claims as far east as Königsberg; and to raise calorie levels from 1,550 to 2,200, with the balance imported from the USA, regardless of expense. OMGUS was 'in a state of war':

The fate of the Marshall Plan will determine who is to be the victor in the great ideological conflict of democracy versus totalitarianism. Unless the Germans can get enough to eat and decent homes to live in, no amount of fine words about the benefit of democracy and no amount of repression will prevent them from going over to Communism.[65]

A secret OMGUS Co-ordinating Committee, chaired by Civil Administration Division (CAD), and including Political Affairs, Manpower, Intelligence, Information Control, and Education, as well as Cultural Affairs

---

[63] Krieger, *Clay*, 303; Werner Müller, *Die KPD und die 'Einheit der Arbeiterklasse'* (Frankfurt am Main and New York, 1979), 366; Clay to Draper, 3 Nov. 1947, in Smith, *Clay*, 445.

[64] Public Safety Branch, 11 Mar. 1948, BAK, Z 45 F, CAD 3/154–2/11.

[65] 'How to Fight Communism', 25 Mar. 1948, BAK, Z 45 F, CAD 3/154–2/11.

divisions, was set up to advise OMGUS on its reserved powers to remove Communist officials. It recommended 'vigorous needling of the German officials' to 'clean their own house', using CIC as a liaison and monitor.[66] In this connection, the ministers-president in the US Zone had been sounded out on 8 April 1948 on the Communist danger in the police. Stock of Hessen had argued that, if Germans were to be given responsibility, they needed a political police, although Maier of Württemberg-Baden warned against bolstering anti-democratic forces by an anti-Communist drive: 'then the old Nazi types will say, "we told you so—the Communists are the danger".'[67] The request for a secret political police and an armed paramilitary also alarmed the Americans, redolent as it was of arguments used to set up the Prussian Gestapo, which had, of course, begun under the Weimar Republic and not the Third Reich.[68] Yet by May CAD was congratulating itself on its pragmatic dual programme of 'civil liberties with what Mr. Gladstone used to call "no damn nonsense" '.[69]

The timing of the Foreign Office's anti-Communist offensive in Germany was almost identical with that of the Americans, although there is little evidence of direct collaboration. Actions in the British Zone were also part of a global anti-Communist drive by Bevin, approved five days *before* the London CFM, but handled separately because of Germany's sensitivity. After the SED scare of 1946, anti-Communist measures had been consciously limited to surreptitiously helping the SPD, yet after the Moscow CFM in spring 1947 the policy of strict neutrality towards the Communists was placed under review. Accordingly, Bevin had expressed his concern at KPD activities, particularly in the unions and works councils, asking for a contingency plan of counter-measures. At the same time the Foreign Office had succeeded in bringing the CCG more directly under its control, leaving less room for liberal unorthodoxy. Lance Pope, head of Political Division's Hannover station, confided to one Communist, after an informal get-together, that he was being recalled to Britain for being a 'German-lover and a Communist-lover'. Nevertheless, public restraint was maintained so as not to prejudice the next round of diplomacy. After the London CFM's collapse in December, however, voices in Whitehall began

[66] Kallmann (ODI), 29 Apr. 1948, BAK, Z 45 F, ODI 7/20-1/11; OMGUS General Order, BAK, Z 45 F, CAD 17/254-1/4.

[67] Hays/Min. Presidents meeting, 8 Apr. 1948, *Akten zur Vorgeschichte*, ed. Walter Vogel *et al.*, iv (Munich and Vienna, 1983), 442-7.

[68] OMGUS Committee to Clay, 2 May 1948, BAK, Z 45 F, CAD 17/254-1/4; Litchfield to Hays, 13 Apr. 1948, BAK, Z 45 F, CAD 3/154-2/11.

[69] Scammon to CAD/Director, 19 May 1948, BAK, *NL* Pollock 66.

to press for positive action, suggesting that ameliorating the poor living conditions in which Communism might thrive, was not enough.[70]

Thus, on Christmas Eve 1947, the Foreign Office solicited the Military Governor for his views on a harder line with the KPD, including a purge of the police and higher education; measures against its 'penetration' of unions, works councils, and youth organizations; illegal border traffic; possible cuts in newsprint; and a propaganda offensive against malpractices in the SBZ.[71] Robertson remained cautious. He was wary of active repressive measures, since the Germans were 'fundamentally anti-Communist' and only a total economic collapse would change this. Legal constraints meant that:

we cannot, beyond a certain point, treat the K.P.D. more harshly than other parties. We have however been definitely more severe with their newspapers than the others. . . . The knowledge that we have set our face against the S.E.D. has prevented many Germans from joining its organizations in the west, and on the basis of existing ordinances, we ought to be able to keep S.E.D. activity within fairly harmless limits.

Moreover, OMGUS's anti-Communist Operation TALKBACK had 'largely misfired' and:

measures to counter Communist activity will, and should, become increasingly the responsibility of the German authorities. They are not likely to be backward in this matter and, in some cases, we may even have to exercise a restraining influence.[72]

The next day the cabinet nevertheless authorized action. Bevin argued that the Soviets were aiming at entire world domination, and thus an anti-Communist propaganda agency was required to defend the 'whole fabric of Western civilisation'. An attached paper on Germany warned of 'German Communist stooges' penetrating the western zones.[73] The terms he argued in were often more ideological than pragmatic, indeed those of a spiritual crusade headed by the Foreign Secretary. Whitehall in fact consistently pressed for harsher measures than those advocated by Robertson.

[70] Weiler, *British Labour*, 200–2 and 205; CCG/HQ to Pol. Div., 3 June 1947, PRO, FO 1051/415; Deighton, *Impossible Peace*, 129–30; Jungmann, 12 Aug. 1947, SAPMO-BA, NY 4036/646; Leishman, 21 Dec. 1947, PRO, FO 371/64540.

[71] FO to Mil. Governor, 24 Dec. 1947, PRO, FO 371/64540.

[72] Robertson to FO, 7 Jan. 1948, PRO, FO 371/70477.

[73] C.P. (48) 5 (Bevin), 5 Jan. 1948, PRO, CAB 129/23; Weiler, *British Labour*, 206; W. Scott Lucas and C. J. Morris, 'A Very British Crusade: The Information Research Department and the Beginning of the Cold War', in Richard J. Aldrich (ed.), *British Intelligence, Strategy and the Cold War, 1945–51* (London and New York, 1992), 85–110.

Pat Dean, for example, saw no reason to restrain the German press, and favoured a distinctly hard line:

In fact we can behave rather more like the Russians and the SED behave in the Soviet Zone to the other parties and make membership of the Communist party an uncomfortable and unpleasant experience.[74]

On 16 January Bevin cabled Berlin that since economic improvement would be slow, 'we must hold the communists at bay on the one hand by publicity and on the other by repressive measures'. Publicity was to include revision of the charter of the newspaper *Die Welt* and a supply of 'suitable material' for broadcasting by Nordwestdeutscher Rundfunk, so that they might both follow an anti-Communist lead. Repressive measures could include reduction of paper supplies and suspension of newspapers, the banning of public meetings, and the requisition of buildings, with 'Protocol M' cited as proof of the need to act.[75]

It was not until April, however, that a top secret Basic Directive on Combatting Communist Propaganda was promulgated by the head of the CCG's Political Division, Steel, to the Regional Commissioners, to be passed on by word of mouth only. It did make the proviso, however, that anti-Communist action was not to degenerate into sterile negative publicity, but should be coupled with positive propaganda aimed at the centre-left, in order to rebuild democracy in West Germany. In the meantime Intelligence Division and Public Safety had begun purging the Hamburg police of Communists, and on 9 February Robertson convened the Regional Commissioners to press for 'sharp action', after amending legislation accordingly. The unions were also provided with extra paper to combat Communists in works council elections, which were postponed until the summer for 'psychological reasons'.[76]

London also pushed Berlin into banning the planned Solingen People's Congress (see Chapter 4), and on 20 January 1948, after the Bremen congress, OMGUS prohibited further such events as a 'deception', extending this veto in March to all local 'People's Committees'. Within days of the April 1948 resolution to change the KPD's name to Socialist People's Party, OMGUS also demanded that the party reapply for its licence and refrain from the new name. For the part of the CCG, Bishop, governor

[74] Dean, 9 Jan. 1948, PRO, FO 371/70477.

[75] FO to Robertson, 16 Jan. 1948, PRO, FO 371/70477.

[76] Directive of 2 Apr. 1948, PRO, FO 371/70478; RIO Hamburg (Ramsbotham), 5 Feb. 1948, PRO, FO 371/70478; Garran to Dean, 19 Mar. 1948, PRO, FO 371/70478.

of NRW, requested details of the party's 'new policy', but, until author-ization, forbade the name SVD. Despite a KPD petition to his superior, arguing that the Lower Saxon State Party had been allowed to alter its name to 'Deutsche Partei', Robertson definitively rejected the name-change on 7 June 1948, demanding clear labelling as a Communist party, since 'the word "socialist" has also been misused more than once in recent German history'.[77] The French, too, rigorously banned both the congresses and the change of identity. The only divergence in western Allied pol-icy in spring 1948 was over the *Volksbegehren* on national unity, which the French and Americans prohibited, while the British relied on counter-propaganda.[78]

The KPD's particular Achilles' heel in the Anglo-American offensive proved to be its press. In the British Zone party-political newspapers had been licensed in spring 1946, but in the case of the Ruhr KPD's *Westdeutsches Volks-Echo*, only after a suspiciously long period of paper-shuffling by Information Service Control Division. Initially, newsprint contingents were based on 1932 elections, but in August 1946 the CCG started reallocating paper to the detriment of the KPD. 'Closet readers' joked that, with dire paper shortages, the KPD press had indeed served a valuable function, but of a biological rather than ideological nature. Catholic priests were less impressed, threatening to deny Christian burial to some KPD readers. The ultimate sanction was suspension by the mili-tary government censor, who proved especially sensitive to reporting on coal productivity, food shortages, and socialization. Whitehall also declared an interest in silencing the Communists during the period of delicate nego-tiations for a West German state in the spring of 1948, 'when things of great moment may be anticipated, on which their comments could be nothing but harmful'.[79] This may help to explain the escalating nature of bans on the *WVE*. After being suspended for a month in June 1947, this rose to six weeks in March 1948, and on 4 May the paper was banned indefinitely, in this case for anti-American propaganda.[80]

---

[77] FO to Bercomb, 19 Jan. 1948, PRO, FO 1049/1205; OMG Bavaria, 23 Jan. 1948, PA Staritz; AG SED-KPD, 11 Mar. 1948, AdsD, *NL* Gniffke 33; CAD/Wiesbaden to Fisch, 1 May 1948, PA Staritz; Hans Kluth, *Die KPD in der Bundesrepublik* (Cologne and Opladen, 1959), 28; 'SVD'-PV to Robertson, 15 May 1948, AdsD, *NL* Gniffke 45; Robertson to Reimann, 7 June 1948, PRO, FO 1049/1211.

[78] Rogers, *Politics after Hitler*, 86–93; Bercomb to Regions, 5 May 1948, PRO, FO 1006/195.

[79] FO to Berlin, 30 Apr. 1948, PRO, FO 371/70779.

[80] Perk, *Besatzungsmacht, passim*; Helmuth Warnke, *'Bloß keine Fahnen'* (Hamburg, 1988), 77; Annan/KPD meeting, 31 July 1946, AdsD, *NL* Gniffke 31.

The Americans were initially chary of allowing any party papers. Only in February 1946 was the Hessen KPD granted an ersatz weekly information sheet with a circulation of 15,000–20,000. Otherwise, the party had to make do with collaboration on 'group newspapers'. By September 1947, however, it had representatives on only three out of forty-eight editorial boards in the US Zone, commanding 4.8% of the newsprint. The exception to the rule was the *Frankfurter Rundschau*, which at one point had four KPD licensees out of seven, but Wilhelm Gerst forfeited his licence in October 1946; Otto Grossmann soon left for another paper; Emil Carlebach lost the confidence of OMGUS in August 1947; and in November Arno Rudert was expelled from the KPD. Communist licensees came and went on three other newspapers: one was dropped for absenteeism; one for extremism; the other was expelled from the party.[81] The only KPD licensee in the French Zone was dropped from the Konstanz *Südkurier* in September 1948, and from mid-1947 the French authorities also began repeated bannings of the KPD's *Neue Zeit* in the Saar, which was suspended for 40 of the 96 months of its existence. Overall, between 1946–55 the KPD press suffered 141 separate bans, peaking in 1950 and 1951, when individual newspapers were suspended for 1,233 and 1,581 days respectively.[82]

In 1948 it was still felt that individual arrests of KPD leaders would only create martyrs. Yet, as has been seen, in January 1949 Reimann was imprisoned over the 'quisling affair' in the Parliamentary Council. In connection with Kurt Müller's arrest in 1950, described in the previous chapter, he was also denied parliamentary immunity for over a year, so that he was unable to appear in the *Bundestag* or at public meetings. Thus, between November 1950–July 1951, Reimann was hardly seen at all in West Germany. On one flying visit, however, accompanied by five bodyguards, he explained in hushed tones how a recorded 'live' speech was being played over the Berlin airwaves to throw off 'Adenauer's thugs'. The party indeed developed a consciously theatrical touch, spiriting the elusive KPD leader into darkened meetings while keeping the audience dazzled by a spotlight, only to behold Reimann as the house lights went up. From May 1954–September 1968 he was again a wanted man, so that the disembodied party chairman could only address the second Party Convention in December 1954 via a pre-recorded tape. Thus, without

[81] Harold Hurwitz, *Die Stunde Null der deutschen Presse: Die amerikanische Pressepolitik in Deutschland 1945–1949* (Cologne, 1972), 314–25.

[82] Frank Dingel, 'Die Kommunistische Partei Saar', in Richard Stöss (ed.), *Parteien-Handbuch* (Opladen, 1983), i. 1864; Christa Hempel-Küter, *Die KPD-Presse in den Westzonen von 1945 bis 1956* (Frankfurt am Main, 1993), 91 and 131–47.

denying the reality of KPD persecution, it is clear that the party was playing its victimization card for all it was worth.[83]

The Korean Crisis

> We do not need to venture to Korean latitudes, since evil lurks so near: what is going on in the eastern zone is enough for us. From there all manner of propaganda, sedition, and subversion is at work to bring down the Federal Republic. I believe we cannot stand by and watch. The rallying cry is not: Hannibal ante portas!, but, the Trojan horse is in our midst, and we must defend ourselves against it.[84]
>
> (Federal Justice Minister Dehler, 12 September 1950)

Analogies between divided Korea and divided Germany may have been more apparent than real, and the causes of the far eastern conflict more complex than reported in the western press, yet the North Korean invasion on 25 June 1950 was bound to create panic in West Germany. The Americans indeed noted a certain fickleness of popular opinion during the initial setbacks, until UN forces went on to the offensive later in the year. Reports of KPD intimidation and increased contributions to party coffers, as 'reinsurance' against an appearance by the Red Army, were nevertheless difficult to substantiate. As is frequently the case in moments of uncertainty, however, illusion was more persuasive than reality, and the Korean crisis proved crucial in upping the ante against the West German Communists.

The Americans and British became especially alarmed when the SED's 3rd Party Convention in July 1950 called for 'national resistance' in the FRG. This slogan earned the KPD designation as an 'official security threat'. A US court martial accordingly imposed an exemplary four-year gaol sentence on one FDJ member, Walter Zauner, for walling up a detonation chamber on a Regensburg bridge, and landings by Communist and other youths on Heligoland to protest at RAF target practice there resulted in 99 arrests and sentences totalling 357 years.[85] Within days of the outbreak of the Korean crisis the Allied High Commission had also

[83] Dok. IM-NRW Nr.: 88; Düsseldorf Consulate to State Dept., 18 July 1951, in *Confidential (1950–1954)*, 28. 70–2; Deutschland-Union-Dienst, 3 Jan. 1955.

[84] Jens Ulrich Klocksin, *Kommunisten im Parlament* (2nd edn.; Bonn, 1994), 273.

[85] HICOG to State Dept., 12 Oct. 1950, in *Confidential (1950–1954)*, 28. 731–45; McCloy to State Dept., 29 July 1950, in *Confidential (1950–1954)*, 28. 589; UKHC to *Land* Commissioners, 9 Aug. 1950, PRO, FO 1013/1907; *KPD 1945–1968: Dokumente*, ed. Günter Judick *et al.* (Neuss, 1989), i. 37.

decided on contingency measures against the KPD press, should it incite to resistance or sabotage. In early August *Freies Volk* was suspended for three months for the article 'Now It's Tanks and Poison Gas instead of Cigarettes | Bonn as Go-Between in US Arms Trade', and, all in all, twelve out of sixteen papers received the same treatment for pictures of the KPD poster 'Korea for the Koreans! Germany for the Germans! Ami Go Home!'. Ersatz papers and printing works soon suffered the same fate, so that between August and November 1950 there was an almost complete blackout of the West German Communist press.[86]

In response, the KPD launched a massive postering campaign over the summer, but, of the more than 50,000 posters put up by late August, over 40,000 were immediately taken down by police in a series of nocturnal running battles with the FDJ; 504 persons were detained and 89 sentenced to terms of six to eight months in the British Zone alone, whereas the Americans were slightly more lenient with two to four month sentences for 'Ami Go Home' posters. On 8 August, in one single swoop, British Public Safety in Herne confiscated 3 million leaflets accusing the Americans of intending to use the atomic bomb and recruit 25 German 'mercenary' divisions. All in all, therefore, Operation POSTER was deemed a victory for the authorities.[87]

The FDJ agitators were to become the target of another Allied–German action, Operation RALLY. On the day of the outbreak of the Korean War a Committee of Young Peace Fighters had been formed, calling for a 'Day of the 100,000 Young Peace Fighters' in Dortmund on 1 October 1950. Although outdoor rallies were prohibited by *Land* interior ministers in mid-August, there was every indication that the organizers intended to flout a ban. US Secretary of State, Dean Acheson, thus requested his High Commissioner in Germany, John J. McCloy, who had taken over from Clay the previous year, to combat the rally with counter-attractions, backed up by German police and, as a last resort, military personnel. The High Commissioner complied, applying pressure on the *Länder* to hamper the KPD and authorizing the use of 'psychological warfare'.[88]

---

[86] AHC Sub-Committee/Info. and Cult. Affairs, 29 June 1950, PRO, FO 1013/1907; Dietrich Staritz, 'Kommunistische Partei Deutschlands', in Stöss (ed.), *Parteien-Handbuch*, 1802.

[87] 'KPD Poster Campaign Statistics up to 23 Aug. 1950', PRO, FO 1049/2118; Chief Magistrate South Circuit to Legal Adviser, 6 Apr. 1951, PRO, FO 1060/609; Kirkpatrick to FO, 9 Aug. 1950, PRO, FO 1013/1907.

[88] Acheson to HICOG, 23 Aug. 1950, in *Confidential (1950–1954)*, 28. 625–6; McCloy to State Dept., 29 Aug. 1950, *FRUS, 1950*, iv. 712–13; Kai Bird, *The Chairman: John J. McCloy—the Making of the American Establishment* (New York, 1992), 356–7.

The British, under *Land* Commissioner Bishop in NRW, were becoming equally active in Operation RALLY. On 19 September Public Safety searched the KPD's recently completed national headquarters in Düsseldorf and on 26 September took the drastic step of requisitioning it as a British barracks, supposedly in order to stiffen German morale in the face of the impending FDJ inundation. After penetrating a cordon of 2,000 demonstrators, military personnel evicted passive resisters from the cellar, who stoically continued to sing the *Internationale* while being manhandled out. In addition, the next day the NRW *Landtag* followed a CDU motion to bar the KPD from forming a parliamentary faction.[89]

Nevertheless, FDJ attempts on 24 September to disrupt President Heuss's speech to young miners in Bochum had proved a damp squib, resulting only in ten bus loads of FDJ members being escorted to the East German border. Yet the authorities were taking no chances for 1 October: 2,000 revolvers were issued to the police, who were also trained by an American military team in the use of tear gas. Additional British and Belgian troops were placed on stand-by. In the Ruhr the 'almost wholesale detention of active FDJ and KPD officials' led to 781 'preventive' arrests, leaving the police somewhat disappointed that there had been no 'major clash to test their mettle'.[90] Elsewhere there were more serious disturbances on 1 October, between 2,500–3,000 Communists and police clashing on the Reeperbahn in Hamburg for instance; 130 arrests were made after stone-throwing and assaults on several policemen, and subsequently Hamburg's ex-chairman, Dettmann, was arrested along with 30 other leaders for incitement to riot. On the same day 170 arrests were made in Schleswig-Holstein, 77 in Lower Saxony, and 'athletic competitors' suspected of being *FDJ'ler* were turned back at the east–west border. None the less, Operation RALLY had exceeded all official expectations and highlighted how weak the Communists really were by late 1950, when they were definitively thrown back on to the defensive.[91]

The Korean crisis should be seen as another important turning-point, as the western Allies began to delegate responsibility for internal security to the Federal authorities. As already seen, the British military governor had warned nearly three years earlier that the Germans were not likely to be backward in their anti-Communism and might have to be restrained. The hysteria created by the Korean War after 1950 only reinforced the

[89] Stewart to Land Commissioner, 10 Oct. 1950, PRO, FO 1013/2067; Rhinfalen to Britcomb, 25 Sept. 1950, PRO, FO 1013/2061.

[90] Stewart to Land Commissioner, 10 Oct. 1950, PRO, FO 1013/2067.

[91] Hamburg Consulate to State Dept., 2 Oct. 1950, in *Confidential (1950–1954)*, 28. 713–4.

position of the hard-liners, just as the 'Protocol M' scare had done in 1948. Earlier liberal qualms about reviving latent German anti-Communism were now suppressed. The new latitude in the summer of 1950 was many a petty German bureaucrat's dream come true, with one municipality even contriving for the fire brigade to drill noisily in the main square during a KPD public meeting. In addition, from September Communists were denied the use of all public buildings in NRW.[92]

The crisis also prompted a fundamental rethink by OMGUS's successor, the US High Commission for Germany (HICOG), on policy towards the Communist party. It appeared to mark the victory of those arguing for the KPD to be treated as a security threat rather than a political problem, despite all the unverifiable assumptions that this entailed. For the first time, the Americans began seriously to entertain the possibility of a ban:

The argument that the KPD should not be suppressed because such action 'would drive it underground and make it harder to control and follow' is largely fallacious. The KPD, like other CP's in the non-Communist world, is comparable to an iceberg: its overt and legal superstructure is visible but its covert organization and operations are not. The KPD must be assumed already to be underground in large part and this apparatus must be assumed to be directed at subverting the Western program in Germany as well as the Federal Republic.[93]

The Allies were to rally the West German authorities to 'emasculate' the KPD, and legal suppression was deemed justifiable, but only should the KPD resort to 'outright sabotage and violent resistance'. KPD printing works and meetings were to be targeted, as well as GDR literature, and, as has been seen above in Operations POSTER and RALLY, this policy proved highly effective. More interestingly perhaps in terms of explaining the psychology behind the mood change, the document also suggested that anti-Communist action would enhance the western powers' prestige and encourage 'disenchanted segments' in East Germany, thus going beyond 'purely defensive or containing action'. In fact, this already sounded much more like John Foster Dulles's later concept of 'roll-back' than Clay's essentially defensive measures, and marked a departure from pragmatic to ideological anti-Communism. As the document also recognized, once outright repression had been launched, there would be no going back.

---

[92] 'Daily NRW Public Safety Sitrep', 17 July 1950, PRO, FO 1013/2037; Gudrun Schädel, 'Die Kommunistische Partei Deutschlands in Nordrhein-Westfalen von 1945–1956', Ph.D. thesis (Ruhr University of Bochum, 1973), 201–3; Manfred Demmer, 'Repressionen vor dem KPD-Verbot', in Marx-Engels-Stiftung (ed.), *Altlasten der politischen Justiz* (Wuppertal, 1991), 57–65.

[93] 'HICOG Policy vis-à-vis KPD and Affiliated Front Organizations', 30 Aug. 1950, in *Confidential (1950–1954)*, 28. 648–53.

8

Rolling Back the KPD

Communism on Trial in the Federal Republic, 1950–1956

ANTI-COMMUNISM has been described as both the 'legitimatory ideology' and 'state doctrine' of the early Federal Republic.[1] Contemporary explanations of the phenomenon naturally tended to follow the battle lines of the Cold War. Professional East German anti-Communist watchers, notably Leo Stern, accused West German 'NATO historians' of using anti-Communism to legitimize rearmament and later to undermine coexistence with the eastern bloc. Gerhard Ritter in particular, the doyen of West German Rankean historiography, but also Hans Rothfels, were singled out for rehabilitating militaristic values and invoking them in the defence against Communism, thus distracting attention from the expansionist aims of imperialism and militarism. Not surprisingly, the East Germans were especially sensitive to the West's theory of totalitarianism, which placed them on the same moral plane as the Nazis. Cold War anti-Communists had admittedly become more sophisticated than their Hitlerite predecessors, but, according to Stern, represented the same vested interests. A whole catalogue of international anti-Communist scholarly organizations was thus allegedly being funded by the 'finance oligarchy of Wall Street'. Yet, besides being an ideological weapon in the arsenal of the Federal Republic's 'clerico-militarist dictatorship', West German anti-Communism was symptomatic of the general crisis of bourgeois ideology, a last ditch attempt to paper over the socio-economic contradictions of capitalism. Besides fostering a latent war psychosis for foreign policy purposes, anti-Communist hysteria was also designed to disorientate West German workers and engender resignation over domestic social reform. Yet the overall thrust of these East German arguments seems to have been to legitimate the Communist project. The virulence of anti-Communism

---

[1] Christoph Kleßmann, *Die doppelte Staatsgründung* (4th edn., Bonn, 1986), 251; Hermann Weber, *Geschichte der DDR* (Munich, 1985), 328.

was thus taken as an indication of the desperate plight of capitalism, in the death throes of its 'third stage', and helpless in the long run against the march of socialism.[2]

Scholarly treatments in the Federal Republic of anti-Communism as a phenomenon in its own right did not occur until the late 1960s, when the anti-authoritarian student movement subjected West Germany to a critical reappraisal. One of the classic short critiques of the social effects of anti-Communism was formulated by Werner Hofmann. In it he postulated three theses. Firstly, that anti-Communists were guilty of projecting their own conceptual world on to that of the opponent; secondly, that anti-Communism distorted the social question into a political one; and finally, that domestic conflict was thereby transferred into the sphere of foreign policy. Hofmann also criticized many of the school textbooks of the 1950s and 1960s for failing to deal with Marxism as a set of ideas, but rather as a perverted power-political prop for the Kremlin oligarchy, or as an ersatz religion. Moreover, anti-Communism, in Hofmann's view, was used to discredit German Communists as 'alien' (*landfremd*) and thereby claim exclusive national authenticity for anti-Communists. The longevity of anti-Communism had allowed it to develop a dynamic of its own, far removed from the original spiritual confrontation, and the social disciplinary aspects which had once been a useful by-product, had now become central, justifying the retention of the parent ideology even when the Communist threat was receding. Eugen Kogon, a Catholic who survived Buchenwald with the help of Communist concentration camp inmates, was another rare critic of anti-Communism, taking to task Adenauer's failure to acknowledge Soviet interests, thereby upsetting east–west relations. For Kogon too, anti-Communism had lost its defensive rationale and had in fact become an offensive weapon of foreign policy.[3]

The rejection of Communism provided a lowest common denominator for groups as disparate as Social and Christian Democrats, Catholics and Protestants, conservative and radical right. It was thus an important factor in establishing the political consensus so evidently lacking under Weimar. For Bonn's political élites, the very *raison d'être* of the infant West German state was to act as a bulwark against Soviet expansionism.

---

[2] Leo Stern, *Der Antikommunismus als politische Hauptdoktrin des deutschen Imperialismus* (East Berlin, 1963); id. (ed.), *Der Antikommunismus in Theorie und Praxis des deutschen Imperialismus: Zur Auseinandersetzung mit der imperialistischen Geschichtsschreibung* (Halle-Wittenberg, 1963).

[3] Werner Hofmann, *Stalinismus und Antikommunismus* (Frankfurt am Main, 1967), 129–69; Eugen Kogon, 'Die Funktion des Antikommunismus in der Bundesrepublik Deutschland', in *Anatomie des Antikommunismus* (Olten and Freiburg im Breisgau, 1969), 190–205.

Although in the 1950s the American High Commission was not in the business of dictating policy to Bonn, the concurrent McCarthyite witch-hunts in the United States can only have encouraged those in the Federal Republic seeking a radical solution to the Communist problem. Nevertheless, it required a combination of political will from above, and public approval from below—however apathetically expressed—to achieve the final demise of the KPD. As will become clear in this final chapter, anti-Communism did indeed enjoy widespread acceptance in society at large. When, for instance, the public in the British Zone was asked what Communism brought to mind, the majority of associations were negative: 'enslavement of the masses', 'dictatorship', or simply 'the whole idea'.[4] Likewise, 71% of those questioned in the US Zone thought Communism was something entirely bad, a view fostered by:

the stand of the Church, the reports of the soldiers and appearance and tales of returned prisoners of war, Soviet policy as executed in its zone and fresh memories of Nazism's anti-Bolshevistic crusade.[5]

Popular Anti-Communism

Although Thomas Mann famously referred to anti-Communism as the 'basic folly of our epoch', it was in fact a complex phenomenon which tapped several long-running currents of popular prejudice. Bourgeois anti-Marxism dated back to at least 1848, when Marx and Engels's famous red spectre began to haunt Europe from the opening lines of the *Communist Party Manifesto*, and had been further institutionalized in Bismarck's Anti-Socialist Laws of 1878–90. Even after the laws were allowed to lapse, however, the Marxist Social Democrats were still regarded as 'enemies of the Reich', and their patriotic rallying to the nation's cause in 1914 was soon eclipsed by the myth of the 'stab in the back' in 1918. In 1919 the newly founded KPD in many ways supplanted the SPD as middle-class Germany's chief *Bürgerschreck*. Symbolically, the General Secretariat for the Study and Combatting of Bolshevism took over the role of the pre-war Reich Association against Social Democracy, although both workers' parties were usually lumped together as 'Marxists'. The

---

[4] PORO Report No. 271a (3,500 in the British Zone, Oct.–Nov. 1948), PRO, FO 1005/1869. About half could think of nothing good at all, and over a third were of no opinion.

[5] Conran at Military Attachés' conference, 7 June 1948, BAK, Z 45 F, POLAD 798/4; OMGUS Report No. 74, 27 Oct. 1947, in Anna J. Merritt and Richard L. Merritt (eds.), *Public Opinion in Occupied Germany: The OMGUS Surveys, 1945–1949* (Urbana, Ill., 1970), 179.

series of abortive putsches from 1919–23 branded the KPD for most observers, including the Majority Social Democrats who were especially keen to avoid the taint of Bolshevism, as a conspiratorial group of political desperadoes. The ultra-lefist turn in 1928 to the policy of 'social fascism' merely sealed the Communists' pariah status in Weimar society. Moreover, these political barriers were reinforced by cultural prejudices in what amounted to an anti-Communist folklore, more reliant on stereotype than reality. Thus, for instance, the *Freikorps* added new, red-baiting lyrics to traditional marching songs during the street-fighting after November 1918. The churches also preached against the sinfulness of Bolshevism. One boy's parents even substituted the old bedtime bogeyman with the threat of abduction by the dead KPD founder, Rosa Luxemburg, now demonized as a political 'wicked witch of the East', prowling the night with a dagger clenched between her teeth.[6]

What is more, the Bolshevik revolution of October 1917 added a new anti-Russian edge to anti-Marxism, dredging up ancient memories of the *Drang nach Osten* of the medieval German knights, and, more recently, in the Napoleonic, Crimean, and First World wars, fears of the might of the Tsarist army and the 'unculture' and despotism of the barbaric Asiatic hordes. Since the late nineteenth century, however, this largely liberal aversion to Tsarist autocracy had been overlaid by the social Darwinist anti-Slavism of *völkisch* lobby groups such as the Pan-German League. The latter's imagery of Germans as 'outposts amidst the flood' of resurgent Slavdom also prefigured the frequently recurring metaphor of the Federal Republic as an anti-Communist bulwark.[7] Moreover, during the First World War anti-Marxism took on disturbingly anti-Semitic overtones, when the extreme left in particular was portrayed as a vehicle for Jewish intellectuals. Thus, by the time the Nazis appeared on the scene, political anti-Communism had been acquiring an increasingly racial tinge.

Nazi anti-Communist propaganda was co-ordinated by a so-called General Association of Anti-Communist Organizations, better known as the Antikomintern. Under the direction of Eberhard Taubert at Goebbels's Propaganda Ministry, it specialized in brochures, radio broadcasts, public

---

[6] Christine Peyton, 'Bedeutung und Bedeutungswandel des Antikommunismus in der Konstituierungsphase der Bundesrepublik Deutschland 1945–1949', diploma (Otto Suhr Institute/Free University of Berlin, 1978), 59; Schmidt interview, 9 Aug. 1989.

[7] Roger Chickering, *We Men Who Feel Most German: A Cultural Study of the Pan-German League, 1886–1914* (London, 1984), 74–101; Wolfram Wette, 'Rußlandbilder der Deutschen im 20. Jahrhundert', *1999*, 4 (1995), 38–64.

lectures, and occasional mobile exhibitions. Since domestic Communism had been crushed, however, fears had to be projected outwards on to Republican Spain and the Soviet Union. Atrocity propaganda in the press and cinema provided an emotive collage of starving peasants, desecrated churches, and execution victims, identifying the Soviet Union as Communism incarnate: primitive, anarchic, and God-forsaken. Particularly after 1936, when Goebbels proclaimed Germany's anti-Bolshevist 'world mission', it became clear that anti-Communism was being manipulated to prepare the home population for a supposedly pre-emptive war, with Hitler cast in the role of saviour. Most importantly, political anti-Marxism and racial anti-Semitism were consciously interwoven. Yet while the NSDAP saw its unique strength in its racial fundamentalism, many ordinary Germans probably still supported it for its more conventional political stand against Bolshevism, at least during the rise to power. This is not to deny that certain social groups, such as the young who underwent their primary socialization in the Third Reich, were not more receptive to racism. Perhaps even those who grew up within the Weimar labour movement were prone to lose faith in the Soviet Union, always mockingly referred to by Nazi propaganda as the 'workers' paradise'. During service on the eastern front, it has been argued that *Wehrmacht* soldiers of *all* classes adopted fascist racial stereotypes. This is borne out by later opinion surveys, when 31% of those polled in the US Zone thought that less than half the Soviet population could read or write, with another 36% placing the figure at only about half.[8]

Not surprisingly, anti-Communism has not escaped more systematic psychological interpretation, as a form of collective paranoia, emotionally receptive to conspiracy theories and vigilantism. Borrowing from Adorno's work on the authoritarian personality, it has been argued that family hierarchies and repressed libidinal instincts predisposed many Germans to be particularly hostile to anti-authoritarianism as a form of quasi-sexual deviance. (This, of course, ignores the highly authoritarian nature of ruling Communist parties!) Another psychoanalytical approach explains this hostility as the retrospective projection of guilt for the treatment of Russian and German Communists before 1945 on to the victims themselves, as

---

[8] Z. A. B. Zeman, *Nazi Propaganda* (London, 1964), 83–103; Jutta Sywottek, *Mobilmachung für den totalen Krieg: Die propagandistische Vorbereitung der deutschen Bevölkerung auf den Zweiten Weltkrieg* (Opladen, 1975), 104–20; Ian Kershaw, *The 'Hitler Myth': Image and Reality in the Third Reich* (Oxford and New York, 1987), 254; Omer Bartov, *Hitler's Army: Soldiers, Nazis, and War in the Third Reich* (New York and Oxford, 1991), ch. 4; OMGUS Report No. 113, 15 Apr. 1948, in Merritt and Merritt, *OMGUS Surveys*, 228–9.

part of an ego-defence mechanism. Barbarous and inhuman behaviour was thereby transferred by the perpetrators to the victims, in order to justify, or rather disguise, the violence and moral repugnance of their own actions. However intriguing these insights of 'psychohistory' may be, they must, of course, be qualified as empirically unverifiable *ex post facto* and of dubious value for entire social groups.[9]

It is also tempting to see post-war anti-Communism as a psychological compensation for repressed anti-Semitism, now of course taboo after the revelations of the Holocaust. Indeed, both interpretations appear to employ a similar mechanism of 'negative integration' to gloss over mutual differences by focusing on an 'out-group'. Nevertheless, anti-Communists were probably only being true to type. Ultimately, of course, it would be futile to try to disentangle racial from political factors entirely, since they formed part of an inseparable complex of ideological *Feindbilder*, or hate-figures. Anti-Semitism, which certainly did not disappear in 1945, was, nevertheless, publicly discouraged by the victorious powers, while anti-Communism was officially sanctioned in the global fight against the Soviet threat.[10] It is the contention here, therefore, that political anti-Communism was always the more reliable and widespread of the two prejudices, and, in the special circumstances of the Cold War, was more capable of uniting previously hostile social groups. Most strikingly, this meant that even the proletarian Social Democratic and bourgeois Christian Democratic camps were prepared to enter into a basic anti-Communist consensus.

Chapter 2 explored how the West German SPD's strong latent antipathy to Communism was rapidly revived by the eastern party's effective annexation to the KPD in 1946. The Social Democrats' anti-Communism was thus first-hand and predominantly political. Clerical or Christian anti-Communism, on the other hand, originated more obliquely in a critique of the godlessness of totalitarianism, initially aimed more at National Socialism than Communism. Under Hitler, according to Catholic writers in particular, collectivist and materialist profanity had reached its destructive zenith.[11] Protestants were also quick to echo these sentiments, in spite

---

[9] Alexander and Margarete Mitscherlich, *Die Unfähigkeit zu trauern: Grundlagen kollektiven Verhaltens* (2nd edn.; Munich, 1977); also Peyton, 'Antikommunismus', 14–16.

[10] In Dec. 1946 American pollsters still noted 18% 'intense anti-Semites' and 21% 'anti-Semites', as opposed to 'racists', 'nationalists', and those with 'little bias'. Similar social groups appear to have been anti-Semitic as were anti-Communist, in other words, the less well educated, the rural, and women, although Catholics were less likely to be anti-Semitic than Protestants; see OMGUS Report No. 49, 3 Mar. 1947 and No. 122, 22 May 1948 in Merritt and Merritt, *OMGUS Surveys*, 146–8 and 239–40.

[11] The following on clerical and intellectual anti-Communism is deeply indebted to Jost Hermand, *Kultur im Wiederaufbau: Die Bundesrepublik Deutschland 1945–1965* (Munich, 1986), 77–88 and 234–44.

—or perhaps because—of their greater complicity with the Nazi regime. In search of a new spirituality, religiously inspired writers such as Alfred Andersch and Fritz Werner pleaded for a more cosmopolitan 'New Europe'. Yet, at the turn of 1946–7, a circle of intellectuals close to the CDU/CSU invested this rediscovered occidentalism, hitherto a symbol of moral regeneration, with a more politically conservative bias. This was directed not so much at the Nazi past, as at contemporary Communism in the East and even 'Christian Socialist' reformers within their own camp. Writers such as Otto Heuschele or Romano Guardini liked to cite Novalis's dictum that 'The Occident will be Christian, or it will not be at all'. T. S. Eliot's Christian Europeanism and Arnold J. Toynbee's 1947 *Civilisation on Trial* were also invoked in the 'return to God'. Yet, as the *Kölnische Rundschau* proved on 1 October 1946, Christian anti-Communism had also learned much of its political vocabulary from the recent German past:

We are the forward bulwark dividing the *Weltanschauungen*. Should we be over-run by Communism, then Europe would be left at its mercy. If the western world wants to secure its *Lebensraum*, then it must help to secure Germany, since for better or worse we are linked with the world of the Occident.[12]

The Christian stress on individual conscience also provided a convenient foundation for the nascent counter-ideology to Communism of democratic freedom, but was conceived very much as a freedom *from* Communism, rather than *for* civil liberties.[13] Equality, according to neo-Thomist theologians, was before God rather than before the law. Religion also lent many of the crusading metaphors to the vocabulary of this period, thanks largely to the pugnacious aphorisms of Martin Luther. Yet Catholics and Protestants alike came out firmly against Communism. At Whitsuntide 1947 the Catholic Cardinal Preysing of Berlin condemned the Soviet Union for withholding German POWs, as well as interning political opponents in former concentration camps and ignoring parental rights in educational matters. He was strongly supported by the Protestant Bishop Dibelius.[14] Religious periodicals such as *Neues Abendland* also came out firmly against pacifism, and in 1955 Cardinal Frings admonished Catholics actively to defend their fatherland. Two years later Dibelius, by then chairman of the Council of the Evangelical Church, even used the

---

[12] Hermand, *Kultur im Wiederaufbau*, 83.

[13] William D. Graf, 'Anti-Communism in the Federal Republic of Germany', *The Socialist Register*, 21 (1984), 178.

[14] Hermann-Josef Rupieper, *Die Wurzeln der westdeutschen Nachkriegsdemokratie: Der amerikanische Beitrag 1945–1952* (Opladen, 1993), 352.

horrifying argument that, 'if for example a single hydrogen bomb killed a million people, those affected would attain eternal life all the more quickly'.[15] The Manicheanism inherent in some Christian thinking was consequently being projected on to the politics of the Cold War, reaching one of its clearest articulations in 1953, when Erik von Kuehnelt-Leddhin spoke of the 'party of Satan' in the East and the 'party of God' in the West. Thus, what had started as an anti-fascist impulse had been distorted by the exigencies and opportunities of the Cold War into something quite different.

The bridge in this transition had been the common atheism of Hitler and Stalin. Although, depending upon one's theological stance, Christian anti-Communism may be seen as more irrational than rational, this equation of Nazism and Communism in the 1950s as 'totalitarian' also appealed to many secular thinkers and was an important cornerstone of what might be termed 'intellectual anti-Communism'. Political scientists such as Hannah Arendt in her 1951 *Origins of Totalitarianism*, as well as Neumann and Friedrich, were early proponents of totalitarian theory. The only apparent antidote was pro-westernism. Karl Jaspers, in his *Freiheit und Wiedervereinigung* of 1960, described a world divided between aggressive Soviet Communism and peace-loving western democracy, praising Adenauer for his pursuit of the integration of the Federal Republic into the West. It was important for such writers that anti-Communism did not stop half-way in some form of neutralist 'third way', but committed itself to the West. Historians such as Peter Rassow also looked to the past to justify contemporary geopolitics, and rewrote the German 'special path' or *Sonderweg* in the process. In his *Die geschichtliche Einheit des Abendlandes* of 1960, Rassow cited a long lineage of some rather unlikely 'great Germans' who were now presented as 'great Europeans': Charlemagne, Otto I, Prince Eugen, Metternich, Gentz, Novalis, Naumann, Stresemann, and finally Adenauer. Gerhard Ritter and Hans Rothfels even portrayed Luther, Friedrich II, and Bismarck as great proto-Europeans. Moreover, well into the 1960s, scholarly institutes of orientology, or *Ostforschung*, traced spurious lines of historical continuity between the culture-building of the medieval orders of Teutonic knights and irredentist claims on the lost eastern territories beyond the Oder-Neisse.[16]

---

[15] Hermand, *Kultur im Wiederaufbau*, 243.

[16] The veterans' journal *Der Stahlhelm* exhibited such signs of cultural imperialism; see Michael Burleigh, *Germany Turns Eastwards: A Study of* Ostforschung *in the Third Reich* (Cambridge, 1988), 313–18.

American anti-Communists soon realized the importance of fostering an educated German public opinion against Communism, using respected writers, many of them anti-Nazi exiles, to justify a common front against the Soviet Union. For instance, the CIA sponsored Melvin J. Lasky's journal, *Der Monat*, whose first editorial in 1948 pondered 'The Fate of the West', and in which Frank Borkenau later warned of a *homo sovieticus* threatening to replace the West's cherished values of freedom and democracy with eastern despotism and slavery. The stand against this barbarization predictably entailed support for the Marshall Plan and NATO, as well as Wendell Willkie's 'One World' concept. Other examples of political journalism displayed rather more alarmingly atavistic tendencies in the name of anti-Communism. Winfried Martini in 1954 was even prepared to countenance an authoritarian state along the lines of Salazar's Portugal, sacrificing liberty for security, and Hans Grimm wrote of West Germany as the last 'rampart of the Occident against the East and against the Communism surging in from Asia', requiring the Germans to increase their birth rate to avoid inundation.[17] It was thus important that anti-Communism had some intellectual as well as emotive appeal, however tendentious the scholarly rationale of totalitarian theory may have been. Nor should it be forgotten that the West German process of renouncing the *Sonderweg* to embrace 'western' values within a 'United States of Europe' was hardly a quantum paradigm shift. It involved selective retention of German peculiarities, as well as tactical acquiescence in western novelties, which probably took decades rather than years to internalize. In the interim it served the quite short-term purpose of repressing the immediate political past.

Such intellectual anti-Communism soon filtered down to the popular press and mass literature of the Cold War. One only needs to glance at the tabloid newspapers of the western zones and early Federal Republic, especially after mid-1947 when reporting restrictions were relaxed, to realize what a gift the SBZ was for journalists. SED leaders were portrayed as 'un-German' marionettes whose strings were being pulled by Moscow. The SMAD's despoliation of the Soviet Zone represented the true face of Communism.[18] Most graphic of all were the illustrated weeklies. One photo-story in *Stern* magazine, for instance, depicting post-war Dresden, implied that the primitive living conditions there were more the result of the 'conquerors from Asia' than of wartime destruction. Visual propaganda

---

[17] Hermand, *Kultur im Wiederaufbau*, 240.
[18] Based on *Neue Illustrierte* and *Stern*; see Peyton, 'Antikommunismus', 83–99.

also made heavy use of the ironic caption, a technique pioneered by Goebbels, conveying a mixture of pathos and scorn. Indeed, western anti-Communist propaganda which focused on the human interest stories of the Cold War seems to have had far more impact than reporting on the high politics of the disintegrating quadripartite alliance. Above all, the Berlin Blockade made the headlines. Reports on POW camps in the Soviet Union were also common, but failed to put the plight of German prisoners into context. This media bombardment was supplemented by a whole flood of 'grey literature', ranging from pseudo-scholarly information brochures to sensationalist pulp fiction, whose titles alone give some flavour of their quality: *Red Spring Tide, Soviets Win with Spies, The Satanic Plan, The Trojan Herd*, and *Brainwash*.[19] Anti-Communism was apparently also rife in that most ephemeral of genres, the lavatory graffito. The men's toilets at Stuttgart railway station in 1948 were covered with scrawlings such as 'Long live the NSDAP—*So Ends Deutschland!*' (a novel acronym for the SED), and 'Better 12 years of Nazi tyranny than 3 years of being free!'.[20]

The imagery of political posters is also revealing of the psychological appeal of anti-Communism. One CSU poster of 1949 shows a lurid, slant-eyed Asiatic giant reaching out from the East across the map of Europe towards the blue-and-white diamonds of Bavaria, with the motto 'No— That's Why: CSU'. In the same series, the same face peers at western Europe through a shield planted in the earth bearing the letters 'SPD', but cracked down the middle (an implicit reference to the SPD's failure to resist the SED in the SBZ), followed by the words 'The Rescue: CDU'. An FDP poster from 1953 repeats this smear on the Social Democrats, showing the new SPD leader at a plough behind which a skeleton in Red Army uniform casts star-shaped seeds: 'Where Ollenhauer ploughs, Moscow sows!' Other, more specifically anti-Communist interest groups also borrowed from the clichés of the past. The Storm Troop against Bolshevist Subversion issued a poster with a trail of cowed silhouettes, hammers-and-sickles stencilled on their backs, snaking towards an eastern horizon, above the legend 'Defenceless, You Will Become a Soviet Slave'.[21]

As already observed, refugees and expellees from the East formed an almost uniformly anti-Communist group in society, accounting for one

[19] Hermand, *Kultur im Wiederaufbau*, 241.

[20] Instructor's report on a trip to Stuttgart between 7–12 July 1948; report of 2 Aug. 1948, SAPMO-BA, DY 30/IV 2/10.02/64, fos. 58–61 and 69–74.

[21] Hermand, *Kultur im Wiederaufbau*, 64–5 and 256–7.

in six of the West German population. They were one of the most important transmitters of anti-Communist propaganda, and thus merit closer
consideration. Often preferring to see their upheaval in terms of inherent Communist vindictiveness, rather than as a backlash to Nazi wartime
resettlement policy, expellees found an easy scapegoat in the KPD. At a
KPD conference for expellees in Hessen in October 1947, Leo Bauer tried
to grasp the nettle by pointing out the joint responsibility of the Anglo-
Americans at Yalta and Potsdam for the expulsions, but to little effect.
Most expellees and refugees continued to blame the Communists. In 1953,
one East German refugee from Thuringia even entered the NRW *Landtag*
with a truncheon in his briefcase, holding Reimann personally responsible
for his plight and threatening to 'knock the Communist deputies dead one
by one'.[22]

Highly conscious of its vulnerability on the refugee issue, the party
made determined efforts among what it rather euphemistically called
'new citizens'. An early example was Karl Hefter, who became a vigorous
but short-lived KPD State Commissar for Refugees in Bavaria in late
1945, before falling victim to an interior ministry unwilling to create an
autonomous refugee administration. The party also tried in vain to profile
itself with legislative proposals aimed at integrating refugees through work
creation schemes, legal equality, land reform, and generous equalization-
of-burdens payments. Yet KPD activities at the refugee camps were doomed
to remain defensive public relations exercises rather than offensive recruiting drives, despite the authorities' fears that the camps would become a
breeding ground for Communism. At one seemingly typical election for
camp representatives in southern Bavaria, the KPD came a poor third,
and in Hessen in 1948 received only 1% of votes.[23] Although the Bavarian
party fielded about twenty refugee candidates for the 1949 *Bundestag*, it
could attract only one prominent maverick refugee leader, Egon Hermann,
an ex-Nazi who had organized hunger strikes at Dachau in 1948. In fact,
the KPD fared consistently badly in Bavarian areas of high refugee dens-
ity, unlike radical rightist groups such as the Economic Reconstruction
Union.[24]

---

[22] Fritz S. on 24 Feb. 1953, NRW HStA, NW 179/1033; OMG/Hessen, 6 Nov. 1947,
in *Confidential U.S. State Department Central Files: Germany—Internal Affairs 1945–1949*,
ed. Paul Kesaris (Frederick, Md., 1985), 40. 8–10.
[23] SPD 714, CSU 583, KPD 109 votes: Munich Consulate to State Dept., 16 Oct. 1947,
PA Staritz; Morris memo. (No. 356), 25 May 1948, BAK, Z 45 F, POLAD 798–6.
[24] Munich Consulate to State Dept., 26 July 1949, in *Confidential (1945–1949)*, 15. 169–
72; Ian D. Connor, 'The Bavarian Government and the Refugee Problem 1945–50',
European History Quarterly, 16 (1986), 131–53; see also Franz J. Bauer, *Flüchtlinge und*

The refugees soon organized themselves politically, first of all into the so-called *Landsmannschaften*, which acted as cultural bodies to keep alive memories of the lost *Heimat*. From 1953 those covering East Germany were then united under the umbrella of a General Association of Refugees from the Soviet Zone.[25] Perhaps more cohesive as a political lobby, however, was the Bloc of Homeland Expellees and Dispossessed Persons (BHE), representing those from the eastern territories, which even entered the 1953 *Bundestag* with a respectable 5.9% of the vote. Conspiracy theories abounded among its members that the expulsions were part of a Machiavellian scheme by Stalin to import a social time bomb into West Germany. As one Bonn deputy put it, a 'Satanic plan by the Kremlin of enormous and momentous extent', designed to engender 'a social status-slide linked with *Vermassung*, proletarianization, radicalization, and thus laying the seedbed of any Bolshevist plan for world domination'.[26] Although the BHE occasionally threatened that its members might themselves veer leftwards if their needs were not met, privately they boasted of being practically immune to Communism. As the BHE chairman later said in 1960:

If there are no more Communists today, it has less to do with the brochures and speeches of those armchair, book-learned students of Bolshevism, than with those hundreds of thousands of us who, over the years, have stared into the face of terror in the old homeland.[27]

Another anti-Communist transmission belt to the West was provided by POWs returning from the USSR. Their poor physical state of health, and tales of conditions there, further reinforced western prejudices against Communism, despite the Germans' own appalling record on Soviet POWs. A local KPD member witnessed the return of fifty POWs at Hannover in October 1946: upon disembarking from the train, they immediately launched into their erstwhile captors with a mixture of pity and contempt. One returning POW in spring 1949 was Reimann's own son, Josef,

---

Flüchtlingspolitik in Bayern 1945–1950 (Stuttgart, 1982), 49–60, and Helmut Grieser, *Die ausgebliebene Radikalisierung: Zur Sozialgeschichte der Kieler Flüchtlingslager im Spannungsfeld von sozialdemokratischer Landespolitik und Stadtverwaltung 1945–1950* (Wiesbaden, 1980).

[25] Helge Heidemeyer, *Flucht und Zuwanderung aus der SBZ/DDR 1945/1949–1961: Die Flüchtlingspolitik der Bundesrepublik Deutschland bis zum Bau der Berliner Mauer* (Düsseldorf, 1994), 315–30.

[26] Dr Johannes Strosche in Franz Neumann, *Der Block der Heimatvertriebenen und Entrechteten 1950–1960: Ein Beitrag zur Geschichte und Struktur einer politischen Interessenpartei* (Meisenheim am Glan, 1968), 394.

[27] Frank Seiboth speech, 6 Mar. 1960, ibid. 395 n. 75.

who upon arrival promptly denounced Communism, and his father, after his experiences in the USSR. The other parties naturally leaped on such tales as ready-made anti-Communist propaganda. Although, as early as autumn 1945, the Hessen KPD had tried to defuse the issue with proposals to exchange German Nazis for anti-fascist POWs, these were ignored, as were counter-claims of inhuman treatment of POWs in western camps. Huge posters at the 1946 KPD/SED rallies in the West even called on the Allies to 'Free the prisoners-of-war for reconstruction!', yet by 1947 it was impossible to argue away as battlefield casualties over a million Germans who had died in Soviet captivity.[28]

After 1949 public anti-Communist prejudice was further institutionalized under the aegis of the state. The Federal Ministry of All-German Affairs became the main exponent of anti-Communist propaganda, referring to Communists in one publication, penned by Dr Eberhard Taubert, as 'stubborn and inventive as insects . . . They must be stamped out on sight'.[29] 'Dr Anti', already familiar as the inspiration behind the Nazi Antikomintern, had been approached in spring 1946 by British intelligence for information on Communist infiltration techniques, but in 1947 found employment with the Americans in CIC. In 1948 he even revamped his 1944 memorandum, 'The Anti-Bolshevist Work of the German Propaganda Ministry', for the Gehlen Organization, the forerunner of West Germany's Federal Intelligence Service, and later liaised with the SPD's *Ostbüro*. Until 1953 the All-German Ministry regularly used the services of Taubert's People's League for Peace and Freedom (Volksbund für Frieden und Freiheit), whose market value rose especially during the Korean War, when it was allegedly offered 7 million DM by the Americans for anti-Communist contract work. In 1951 it went from freelancing to regular work for the Interior and All-German Ministries, receiving an annual subsidy of 600,000 DM. Taubert continued to use graphic artists from Goebbels's Propaganda Ministry, who—not insignificantly—still chose to work in the colours red, white, and black. Imagery borrowed from the recent past revived the Mongol-featured Soviet commissar, who in one picture is seen opening a set of trapdoors in the iron curtain to smuggle in the booty of eastward-bound dismantled plant,

[28] Murphy to State Dept., 31 Oct. 1947, in *Confidential (1945–1949)*, 39. 943–7; Pawlowski, 17 Oct. 1946, SAPMO-BA, NY 4182/862; Hamburg Consulate to State Dept., 29 Mar. 1949, in *Confidential (1945–1949)*, 15. 111; SED-ZS/KPD meeting, 18 Dec. 1946, SAPMO-BA, DY 30/IV 2/1.01/30; *WVE*, 23 July 1946, 1.

[29] Bundesministerium für gesamtdeutsche Fragen (ed.), 'Augen auf! Kommunismus durch die Hintertür', (Bonn, n.d.) in Michael Klein, *Antifaschistische Demokratie und nationaler Befreiungskampf* (2nd edn.; West Berlin, 1986), 149.

while releasing packs of westward-bound rats from another. A second illustration, this time playing on fears of collective *Vermassung*, shows a series of paths leading to six doorways under the signs 'Peace', 'Security', 'Unity', 'Freedom', 'Democracy', and 'Self-Determination'. The avuncular figure of Wilhelm Pieck stretches out a welcoming hand, but on the other side the paths merge and the individuals are marshalled by a giant Stalin into battalions labelled 'People's Police' and 'Forced Labour'. The moral of the piece: 'Under the Soviet star words and concepts lose their meaning. They are abused for mendacious propaganda platitudes behind which lurks a gruesome reality.' Taubert also allegedly designed the CDU's notorious 1953 *Bundestag* election poster, 'All Roads of Marxism Lead to Moscow: That's Why CDU', which was, of course, also an ulterior attack on the SPD. The viewer's gaze is drawn along a plane of converging red paths to a foreshortened horizon, over which stares a sinister pair of giant, unblinking eyes, luminous under the peak of a Red Army cap.[30]

The League also provided rent-a-crowds to disrupt official visits from the GDR and blacklists of fellow travellers, sent out under the name of the Action Committee against the Fifth Column, whose mocking slogan was 'Smash the Stalinists wherever you meet them!'.[31] There were countless other such anti-Communist organizations, including the Combat League for the Securing of Democracy, the Working Group for European Politics, Freedom in Action, Liberation Committee for the Victims of Totalitarian Oppression, and the Storm Troop against Bolshevist Subversion, to name but a few.[32] There were, nevertheless, relatively few documented clashes between organized anti-Communists and the KPD. On 12 September 1952, however, the CDU, FDP, League of German Youth, and Europa-Union bussed 300 eastern refugees to a KPD meeting in Bremen with the clear intention of breaking it up. A mêlée ensued, reminiscent of Weimar 'hall brawls', which wrecked 14 windows, 4 doors, 3 tables, and 67 chairs in the establishment concerned! KPD rallies became prime targets, including one at Rheine in NRW in August 1953 when, as a party paper reported, the *Land* chairman, Ledwohn, was blinded in one eye: 'Half an hour before the beginning of the meeting the fascist

---

[30] *Spiegel*, 9/34 (1955), 11–13; Klaus Körner, 'Erst in Goebbels', dann in Adenauers Diensten', *Die Zeit* (24 Aug. 1990), 37–8; id., 'Kalter Krieg und kleine Schriften', *Aus dem Antiquariat*, 9 (1991), 1–7.

[31] A parody of the 1920s social fascist slogan 'Smash the fascists wherever you meet them!'.

[32] Hermand, *Kultur im Wiederaufbau*, 241.

bandits smashed up the podium, demolished the loudspeaker vans and burned the workers' red flags while singing the German anthem.'[33] The American-sponsored League of German Youth (BDJ) also became notorious for roughing up Communists and vandalizing their offices, and in 1952 it was revealed that, in the event of a Soviet attack, it even had plans to assassinate KPD and SPD leaders as part of the CIA-financed GLADIO 'stay-behind' network.[34]

More often, clashes were with the police. In February 1953 the worst rioting in Munich since Weimar occurred at the Winterbahn when police attempted to break up a KPD rally of about 6,000 Communists. After Reimann had threatened local Social Democratic leaders with reprisals for conniving in the division of Germany, two detectives tried to close the meeting, but were thrown into the street. When riot police then appeared on the scene to clear the venue, the doors were barricaded. After scuffles, during which a KPD brass band stoically played 'Brüder zur Sonne, zur Freiheit!', the gathering was dispersed, and a planned torchlight procession fizzled out under the attentions of police water cannon, blocking traffic in the city centre for an hour.[35]

How much of all this rubbed off on the public at large? Opinion surveys offer the most easily quantifiable insights into popular anti-Communism in West Germany. OMGUS conducted regular questionnaires, periodically asking residents in south Germany, if forced to choose between living under Communism or National Socialism, which they would prefer. In the first survey of November 1945 35% chose Communism, 19% Nazism, 22% neither, and 24% were of no opinion. Yet the rapidity with which the Communist option declined, suggests that it had been a tactical response, possibly hedging various bets while the westward extent of Soviet influence remained uncertain. The 'Communists' thus appear to have defected first to the 'neither' camp, and then to the 'pro-Nazis'. By November 1946, by which time it had become clear that the Americans intended to stay in western Germany, pro-Communism had dropped to around 9%, whereas 17% still admitted to a preference for Nazism, with 66% 'neithers'; by February 1949 only 2% chose Communism, whereas a staggering 43% identified with Nazism, 52% with neither, and 3% were

---

[33] *Volksecho*, 10 Aug. 1953, quoted by Jens Ulrich Klocksin, *Kommunisten im Parlament* (2nd edn.; Bonn, 1994), 298–9.

[34] Bremen Consulate to State Dept., 19 Sept. 1952, in *Confidential U.S. State Department Central Files: Germany—Federal Republic of Germany. Internal Affairs 1950–1954*, ed. Paul Kesaris (Frederick, Md., 1986), 28. 303–5; Leo A. Müller, *Gladio—Das Erbe des Kalten Krieges* (Reinbek bei Hamburg, 1991), 127–34.

[35] Bundespressinf/BMI telex, 21 Feb. 1953, BAK, B 106/15886.

TABLE 15. *Anti-Communist Public Opinion in the British Zone, February 1948*[a]

Question: 'If forced to choose, would you (a) choose Communism or National Socialism, or (b) if neither, which form of government would you disapprove of least?'

Age	Sex	Pro-Communist (a) %	Pro-Communist (b) %	Pro-Nazi (a) %	Pro-Nazi (b) %	Neither to (a) and (b) %	No opinion %	Size of sample
17–24	Male	7	5	38	23	21	6	146
	Female	4	1	37	28	22	8	155
25–32	Male	3	4	32	34	20	7	246
	Female	2	6	26	34	24	8	293
33–40	Male	5	5	24	32	28	7	354
	Female	4	5	24	31	23	13	366
41–8	Male	6	6	20	29	30	10	325
	Female	5	6	17	38	24	10	278
49–56	Male	6	7	18	27	36	6	281
	Female	3	5	20	36	26	10	228
Over 56	Male	7	5	18	29	36	5	299
	Female	1	4	21	30	30	14	207
Total								3,178

[a] PORO Special Report No. 164, 'German Choice of Communism or National Socialism', Feb. 1948, PRO, FO 1005/1869. (I have slightly reformulated the original question.)

of no opinion. Subsequent HICOG polls traced the downward slide of pro-Communists who, by July 1956, had reached just 1%.[36]

Similar results were produced in the British Zone, as evidenced by a February 1948 poll of over 3,000 Germans (see Table 15). Although, depending on region, between a half and two-thirds initially rejected both alternatives, among the minority prepared to commit themselves, around five times as many chose Nazism as Communism. When the 'neithers' were pressed for an answer ('which form of government would they approve of least'), around six times as many saw Nazism as the lesser evil to Communism. Overall, women were more resistant to Communism than men, and those who had not yet reached adulthood in 1933 were significantly more pro-Nazi. It was also telling that approval of Communism among those listed as without political affiliation (well over a third of the sample), reached only 8% among men, and 5% among women. This evidence clearly contradicts fears that the material privation of the years 1946–8 might have turned the West German population Communist. If anything, the opposite tendency was the case, manifested in a nostalgia for the relative abundance and artificial security of National Socialism.

Even more detailed information on the attitudes and social background of anti-Communists is provided in a HICOG poll of October 1950.[37] The first question the sample of 2,000 was asked was what they thought the KPD's current line actually was: 48% could think of nothing at all; and of those who thought they did know, most believed it was socio-economic (equality and higher living standards—16%; socialization and anti-capitalism—11%) rather than nationalist (4%) or pacifist (4%). Almost no one had received any Communist literature (2%), or knew of anyone who had, and very few had experienced any KPD activity at first hand (7%). Just a small minority believed that numbers of fellow travellers were rising (15%), and only 8% that the KPD was expanding its official support. Only 19% agreed that the chances of West Germany falling under Communist domination had increased, even since the Korean War. The remarkable thing about this survey, however, is that, far from being rabidly anti-Communist (only 2% favoured the same methods as Hitler), most of those questioned appeared relatively sanguine, or even indifferent, about

---

[36] Merritt and Merritt, *OMGUS Surveys*, 33, 55, 163, and 295; Charles H. Sheldon, 'Public Opinion and High Courts: Communist Party Cases in Four Constitutional Systems', *The Western Political Quarterly*, 20 (1967), 350–2.

[37] Reactions Analysis Staff, Office of Public Affairs, HICOG, 'Report No. 59, Series No. 2', in HICOG to State Dept., 7 Feb. 1951, in *Confidential (1950–1954)*, 28. 441–78. All the figures given are for the US Zone only.

TABLE 16. *Anti-Communist Public Opinion in the Former American Zone, October 1950*[a]

	Question: 'Has the number of convinced Communists increased?'				Question: 'Would you personally prohibit the KPD?'		
	More %	Less %	Same %	No opinion %	Yes %	No %	No opinion %
Area							
Bavaria	—	—	—	—	65	29	6
Hessen	—	—	—	—	51	33	16
Württemberg-Baden	—	—	—	—	54	38	8
US ZONE	8	39	27	26	59	32	9
Berlin	7	63	18	12	69	29	2
Bremen	9	36	32	23	61	31	8
Educational level							
Elementary school	8	38	25	29	64	26	10
Secondary school	13	38	34	15	42	52	6
College/university	10	46	32	12	28	72	0
Socio-economic status							
Upper class	11	46	35	8	46	54	0
Middle class	9	42	30	19	56	38	6
Lower class	7	36	23	34	64	24	12

Occupation:							
Professional	12	35	36	17	38	59	3
Business/managerial	11	36	31	22	61	35	4
Office-worker	6	48	30	16	42	52	6
Skilled labour	8	43	30	19	57	34	9
Semi-skilled labour	7	32	27	34	61	26	13
Farmers/farm labour	10	34	25	31	71	21	8
Housewives	5	45	16	34	73	18	9
Students/pensioners	8	42	18	32	63	24	13
Sex							
Male	9	49	27	15	51	43	6
Female	8	30	26	36	66	23	11
Income (per month)							
0–199 DM	9	33	21	37	63	24	13
200–399 DM	7	45	31	17	58	37	5
400+ DM	12	41	33	14	50	47	3
Age							
Under 30 years	—	—	—	—	57	36	7
30–50 years	—	—	—	—	56	35	9
Over 50 years	—	—	—	—	65	26	9
Town size							
0–4,999 population	—	—	—	—	66	25	9
5,000–24,999	—	—	—	—	55	37	8
25,000–99,999	—	—	—	—	60	37	3
100,000–249,999	—	—	—	—	42	45	13
250,000 and over	—	—	—	—	45	46	9

TABLE 16. *(cont'd)*

	Question: 'Has the number of convinced Communists increased?'				Question: 'Would you personally prohibit the KPD?'		
	More %	Less %	Same %	No opinion %	Yes %	No %	No opinion %
Party preference							
CDU/CSU	7	41	26	26	74	22	4
SPD	10	50	26	14	54	43	3
FDP	4	52	36	8	47	48	5
Bavarian Party	11	33	32	24	78	18	4
Religion							
Catholic	—	—	—	—	64	29	7
Protestant	—	—	—	—	55	35	10

a Reactions Analysis Staff, Office of Public Affairs, HICOG, 'Report No. 59, Series No. 2', in HICOG to SD, 7 Feb. 1951, in *Confidential (1950–1954)*, 28. 441–78.

Communist influence, but were still prepared to go along with anti-Communist measures. Thus, when answering the question, 'Do you believe that the number of really convinced Communists in West Germany has increased or decreased recently, or has it remained the same?', only 8% thought it had increased, 39% that it had decreased, 27% that it had remained constant, and 26% ventured no opinion. Few volunteered banning as an option, but when asked, 'If you personally had to decide, would you prohibit the Communist party in West Germany or not?', 59% were in favour, with 32% against, and only 9% 'don't knows'. The social breakdown of respondents on these two issues is reproduced in Table 16. Those least likely to advocate banning were urban Protestant males in the educated, upper-income bracket, in other words, categories 'motivated by an intellectual regard for civil liberties'. On the other hand, two-thirds of women and inhabitants of towns under 5,000, and three-quarters of CDU/CSU supporters favoured a ban. It was also significant that a social group such as 'semi-skilled labour', the most likely Communist clientele, opted by 61% to ban the party (ironically exactly the same proportion as 'business and managerial'!). The report concluded by saying that:

The majority view that the Communist party should be outlawed is based apparently not on weakness but on strength vis-a-vis Communism and Communists. Analysis of the relationship of the issue of banning the party to other attitudes on Communist activity shows that it is precisely the people who disparage Communist effectiveness in Western Germany who favor outlawing the party. Conversely, people who believe [the] KPD has influence are much less inclined to advocate banning it. Thus it is permissible to say that the majority wishes to ban [the] KPD because it is regarded as a nuisance, not as a threat to West German security.[38]

Political Justice in the Federal Republic

It is at this point that I would like to return to the practice of anti-Communism in West Germany, this time under the auspices of the Federal authorities, culminating in the trial and ban of the KPD. Part of the rationale for the Anglo-American hard line during the Korean crisis had been to prepare the West German authorities before delegating responsibility to them. Even at the time, however, there were qualms in some Allied quarters about the alacrity with which the Germans were responding. It must be made clear from the outset, however, that Federal repressive measures can in no sense be equated with Nazi persecution. The Federal

[38] Ibid. 28. 477.

Republic remained a constititional state whose *Verfassungsschutz* did not become a law unto itself, unlike the Gestapo. Nor can West Germany's treatment of political opponents bear comparison with the massive surveillance undertaken in East Germany by the equally notorious Stasi. What I would argue is permissible, however, is to measure the Federal Republic's performance against the very high standards it set itself in the Basic Law of 1949. As well as admonishing the political parties to heed the 'free democratic basic order', the constitution guaranteed equality before the law, freedom of opinion, and freedom of association. The more meaningful question, therefore, is to ask how far the Federal Republic lived up to its own liberal-democratic ideals in the 1950s. This is, of course, a sensitive area, open to critical interpretation, especially when dealing with the spirit as well as the letter of the law.

One of the first liberal critics to pose some of these difficult questions in the early 1960s was Otto Kirchheimer. In his *Political Justice: The Use of Legal Procedure for Political Ends*, he advanced a largely functional theory of 'political justice', whereby even courts, claiming to be adhering to the letter of the law, could unwittingly be serving political ends. He went on to demonstrate this by various historical examples, as well as by recent practice in both East and West Germany.[39] Kirchheimer has since influenced a generation of what might loosely be termed 'left-liberal' historians and political scientists. Strictly constitutional historians might find such an approach problematic, but it would be equally misleading to believe that justice occurs in a vacuum. Even the supreme constitutional instance, the *Bundesverfassungsgericht*, was painfully aware of the political nature of its decisions. Moreover, in the late 1960s the Federal government itself, under the influence of Willy Brandt, undertook a sweeping reform of the penal code, which would suggest that all had not been well.

One of the Adenauer coalition's first actions in relation to the KPD was the 'Resolution on the Political Activity of Members of the Civil Service against the Democratic Order' of 19 September 1950. It aimed at removing from public service officials, employees, and workers promoting 'national resistance', and was in many ways a forerunner of the notorious *Berufsverbote* of the early 1970s. In it 13 organizations were listed, 11 Communist and 2 neo-Nazi, membership of which was prohibited in local government, the police, post offices, and schools, although it is unknown how many individuals were ultimately affected. (The KPD's

---

[39] Otto Kirchheimer, *Political Justice: The Use of Legal Procedure for Political Ends* (Princeton, 1961).

two restitution lawyers, Marcel Frenkel in Düsseldorf, and Alphonse Kahn in Rhineland-Pfalz, were certainly among them.[40]) Although a Federal resolution was not legally binding, all *Land* governments except Württemberg-Hohenzollern followed suit. On 27 February 1951 Bonn also suspended government contracts with enterprises supporting 'anti-constitutional' organizations (those defined as such by itself), as a deterrent to firms advertising in the KPD press. Then, on 24 April 1951, the government promulgated a further batch of resolutions, banning as anti-constitutional the FDJ, VVN, and the *Volksbefragung*, inspired by the SED, in Bonn's words, 'to render the population of the Federal territory ripe for an attempted Communist coup'.[41] Nevertheless, the FDJ ban had to be repeated in June for legal reasons, and, as has been seen, the VVN contested the decision and eventually won, much to the embarrassment of the Federal government.

Nobody was more aware than Bonn, therefore, of the need for a systematic penal code to replace improvised and often unconstitutional government resolutions. In February 1950 the SPD *Bundestag* faction had introduced a bill targeted primarily at the far right, but by the time the government had whipped the amended *Strafrechtsänderungsgesetz* through on 11 July 1951—hence its nickname of 'Blitz Law'—it had become a weapon against the extreme left. The Korean crisis had been instrumental in causing this shift, and, as Minister of Justice Dehler disarmingly conceded, 'We must sacrifice one freedom in order to guarantee liberty.'[42] The new treasonable crime of 'endangering the state' (*Staatsgefährdung*) was defined as the attempt to bring the state 'under foreign dominion'. Whether consciously or unconsciously, 'combative democracy' ('streitbare Demokratie') revived the proactive terminology of the Nazi jurists Gürtner and Freisler—often verbatim!—arguing for the state's defences to be pushed as far forward as possible. Under the new law it was therefore unnecessary to prove violent action, merely intent. The only body competent to determine whether the KPD's intentions were *de jure* incompatible with the 'free democratic basic order', was the *Bundesverfassungsgericht*, which as yet only existed on paper in mid-1951. Nevertheless, the government had unilaterally declared the KPD to be unconstitutional in 1950, inferring this from its plebiscitary politics and implicit intention to import the

---

[40] Dismissed in Oct. 1950 and May 1951 respectively; see Marfred Grieger *et al.*, *Stalins Schatten* (Neuss, 1989), 159; NRW HStA, NW 284/12.

[41] Alexander von Brünneck, *Politische Justiz* (Frankfurt am Main, 1978), 54–7 and 62–3.

[42] Lutz Lehmann, *Legal und Opportun: Politische Justiz in der Bundesrepublik* (West Berlin, 1966), 41.

GDR's political system to the FRG. Special political 'penal chambers' at the *Oberlandesgerichte* were backed up by the investigative resources of the *Verfassungsschutz* and executive powers of the Criminal Police's political commissariats. Despite continuing legal uncertainties, in individual cases simple KPD membership or association became the *de facto* criterion for prosecution. Even strikes were interpreted by some courts as 'violence' under the terms of the legislation, and one judge actually took into account previous convictions under the Nazis.[43]

The law was implemented primarily against individual leaders since it was still legally problematic to proscribe whole organizations, but in many cases only a shell was left by the time of a ban. The *Bundesgerichtshof* thus presided over four high treason trials against Communist leaders, all for disseminating the November 1952 Programme advocating the 'overthrow of the Adenauer government'. In May 1954 Reichel and Beyer, KPD *Kreis* secretaries at Salzgitter, were gaoled for 3 years and 18 months respectively. In June 1955 FDJ Chairman, Josef Angenfort, received 5 years' penal servitude, and Wolfgang Seiffert 4 years' imprisonment. Two Secretariat members, Rische and Ledwohn, were sentenced to $3\frac{1}{2}$ years in July 1956, whereas Richard Scheringer was pardoned after a lesser conviction. Finally, in June 1958, Walter Fisch received 3 years, having evaded arrest since May 1954.[44]

There were also a number of trials, for conspiracy, of ringleaders of Communist organizations. Serious subversion was not at stake, but in the period 1953–6 there was a spate of actions against FDJ leaders for activities as banal as leafleting and reading FDJ literature. In August 1954 the three leaders of the Main Committee for *Volksbefragung*, Oskar Neumann, Karl Dickel, and Emil Bechtle, were sentenced by the *Bundesgerichtshof* to up to three years' imprisonment for disobedience against the state, although the first two had already absconded to the GDR. The leaders of various 'front' organizations such as the German Workers' Committee against the Remilitarization of Germany, Socialist Action, Central Council for the Protection of Democratic Rights, Society of German–Soviet Friendship, and National Front, as well as members of East German organizations, were likewise prosecuted. Indeed, *all* the KPD's auxiliaries were brought to court and 80 were successfully proscribed

[43] Reinhard Schiffers, 'Grundlegung des strafrechtlichen Staatsschutzes in der Bundesrepublik Deutschland 1949–1951', *VfZ*, 38 (1990), 597–602; Ingo Müller, *Furchtbare Juristen: Die unbewältigte Vergangenheit unserer Justiz* (Munich, 1987), 233–5; Brünneck, *Politische Justiz*, 82–3.

[44] UKHC to FO, 4 Sept. 1954, PRO, FO 371/109757; Brünneck, *Politische Justiz*, 93–5.

by the administrative courts between 1951 and 1958. A notorious instance of retrospective justice, later overturned by the *Bundesverfassungsgericht*, even occurred with a string of trials *after* the 1956 ban for KPD activity *before* 1956. Nor was the *Verfassungsschutz* averse to using *agents provocateurs*. In 1953 the majority of 'party' instructors of NRW's National Front were thus revealed to be undercover agents, including its secretary.[45]

Critics of this form of persecution for one's convictions (*Gesinnungsstrafrecht*) have also pointed to the high levels of continuity of personnel within the judiciary between the Third Reich and Federal Republic. In 1948 30% of Court Presidents and 80–90% of *Land* Court Directors and Counsellors in the British Zone were ex-NSDAP members.[46] Prominent 'tainted' personnel later included President of the Federal Office for *Verfassungsschutz* (BfV), Schrübbers; the Federal Attorney-General, Fränkel; and President of the *Bundesgerichthof*'s Third Senate, Kanter, all forced into early retirement by compromised pasts.[47] Paulheinz Baldus, who had worked in the Führer Chancellery in 1939, was also instrumental in anti-Communist cases. The list of individual instances of political rehabilitation of the judiciary, often involving nominal changes or minor relocations, is almost endless. Despite similar doubts about the probity of the *Bundesverfassungsgericht* itself, however, Ingo Müller highlights it as one of the few exceptions to the rule.[48]

It would be a mistake, therefore, to assume that *all* Federal authorities were awash with ex-Nazis. Since most German anti-Communist intelligence experts were *too* politically compromised, the BfV, set up in 1950, was forced to build up many of its operations from scratch and was plagued by teething troubles. Adenauer was reluctant to use it at all—convinced of KPD infiltration!—and in July 1954, of course, its head, Otto John, did indeed 'defect' to the GDR for 18 months. BfV officials, acutely aware of their vulnerable democratic credentials, copied US anti-Communist methods, and the first head of the NRW *Verfassungsschutz* was in fact a Jewish Social Democratic émigré, returned from the USA. Nevertheless, there were so many judges of Nazi vintage still passing sentence in the FRG that it is very difficult to talk of an unprejudiced judiciary in the

---

[45] Brünneck, *Politische Justiz*, 113–4 and 145–50; Klein, *Antifaschistische Demokratie*, 105–6.
[46] Müller, *Furchtbare Juristen*, 205.   [47] Brünneck, *Politische Justiz*, 228–9.
[48] Müller, *Furchtbare Juristen*, 205–19; Bernt Engelmann, *Rechtsverfall, Justizterror und das schwere Erbe* (Cologne, 1989), ii. 283–95; Robert Steigerwald, 'Antikommunismus— Anmerkungen zu einem Thema', in Marx–Engels-Stiftung (ed.), *Altlasten der politischen Justiz* (Wuppertal, 1991), 43; Diether Posser, *Anwalt im kalten Krieg: Ein Stück deutscher Geschichte in politischen Prozessen 1951–1968* (Munich, 1991), 109–82; Rolf Gössner, *Die vergessenen Justizopfer des kalten Kriegs* (Hamburg, 1994).

1950s and 1960s, and it was only amid the later atmosphere of liberal change that the *Strafrechtsänderungsgesetz* was repealed in 1968, ending a period of political justice which did not reflect credit upon the Federal Republic's legal system.[49]

In the balance between political investigations against the left and right, the latter probably accounted for only a couple of per cent of cases in this period. A cautious estimate of the number of investigations of individual Communists between 1951–68 is 125,000, about a third of which occurred while the party was still legal, leading to a total of 6,000–7,000 prison sentences. Of the 46,476 political investigations carried out from 1953–8, the vast majority against Communists, only 1,905, or less than one in 25, led to convictions. Since half of criminal prosecutions resulted in conviction, the charge can be levelled of a scatter-gun system of political justice, more reliant on police custody than court sentences to keep Communists off the streets. Furthermore, besides affecting real or suspected Communists, 'endangering of the state' could be interpreted to criminalize even family contacts with the GDR or any political thinking which happened to coincide with, or did not explicitly condemn, Communist propaganda, including pacifism and national unification without the eastern territories.[50]

Perhaps the saddest chapter in the history of official West German anti-Communism was the disqualification of some Communists from restitution (*Wiedergutmachung*) for Nazi persecution. From as early as mid-1950 the CDU had applied pressure to exclude the KPD from compensation proceedings in NRW, where the head of restitution, Dr Marcel Frenkel, was a Communist. In 1953 the *Bundesergänzungsgesetz* envisaged loss of compensation for anyone who 'has abetted the National Socialist or any other dictatorship' or 'combats the free democratic basic order'. Several courts interpreted this to include Communists, who allegedly wished to replace one totalitarian system with another, and in a few grotesque cases were penalized for resistance in the Third Reich, and in one instance for participation in the Munich Soviet of 1919! Other pettifogging measures included withholding passports and driving licences from convicted Communists. The *Bundesentschädigungsgesetz* of June 1956 still

---

[49] HICOG to State Dept., 10 Aug. 1954, in *Confidential (1950–1954)*, 29. 525–46; AHC, 22 Mar. 1950, *Akten zur auswärtigen Politik der Bundesrepublik Deutschland: Adenauer und die Hohen Kommissare*, i. *1949–1951*, ed. Hans-Peter Schwarz (Munich, 1989), 152.

[50] Brünneck, *Politische Justiz*, 237 and 241–2; Lehmann cited by Dietrich Staritz, 'Die Kommunistische Partei Deutschlands', in Richard Stöss (ed.), *Parteien–Handbuch* (Opladen, 1983), 1746.

backdated attacks on the 'free democratic basic order' to May 1949 (until this practice was overturned in 1961), and many Communists indeed had their compensation revoked. These men and women were then forced to repay large sums, sometimes running into tens of thousands of marks, from what had often been their only livelihood.[51]

The Banning Trial

A ban of the KPD had been discussed within months of the founding of the FRG and thus cannot be attributed wholly to the Korean War scare. Adenauer made his position plain in December 1949:

If we were to set certain legal requirements with regard to the founding of parties, these would probably end up with having to suspend the Communist Party. For the Communist Party is utterly bent on national treason.[52]

The Chancellor continued to complain of personal vilification by the Communists, such as the slogan 'Adenauer must fall, so that Germany can live', as well as FDJ ditties celebrating the septuagenarian's supposedly imminent demise. Although an internal KPD threat does not appear to have dominated his thinking, he was always prepared to exploit alarmist reports, for instance at the time of the ratification of the Paris treaties, making the fanciful claim that several directors of large concerns were closet Communists.[53]

Justice Minister Dehler was more open, publicly advocating a KPD ban in May 1950, and only waiting for the *Bundesverfassungsgericht* to become operational before indictment. At the same time Walter Menzel, Interior Minister of NRW, tried in vain for a *Land* government decree outlawing the KPD, a move Bonn still viewed as unconstitutional. A few days later a conference of *Land* interior ministers, chaired by the Federal Minister, Gustav Heinemann, also rejected banning in favour of effective

---

[51] Willi Dickhut, *Was geschah danach?* (Essen, 1990), 43; Gotthard Jasper, 'Die disqualifizierten Opfer', in Ludolf Herbst and Constantin Goschler (eds.), *Wiedergutmachung in der Bundesrepublik Deutschlend* (Munich, 1989), 363–4; Posser, *Anwalt im kalten Krieg*, 234.

[52] AHC, 8 Dec. 1949, in *Akten zur auswärtigen Politik*, i. 51.

[53] 234th Bundeskabinett, 11 July 1952, in *Die Kabinettsprotokolle der Bundesregierung*, v. *1952*, ed. Kai von Jena (Boppard am Rhein, 1989), 450; Bundeskabinett, 10 June 1952, in *Im Zentrum der Macht: Das Tagebuch von Staatssekretär Lenz 1951–1953*, ed. Klaus Gotto et al. (Düsseldorf, 1989), 359–60.

counter-propaganda.[54] Heinemann would almost certainly have opposed a ban, and indeed defended Communists in later trials, but after his resignation over rearmament in October 1950 was replaced by hardliner Robert Lehr, whom the British High Commissioner later described as 'obsessed by a Communist internal threat'.[55] Indeed, Lehr was soon informing his subordinates that, since the FRG was the 'weakest link in the European defence front against Communism', they should resort to every available legal and executive counter-measure.[56]

The impetus for actual indictment was nonetheless somewhat oblique, originating, like the *Strafrechtsänderungsgesetz*, in planned moves against the radical right. As internal correspondence reveals, the government feared public disapproval of unilateral action against the far right, and thus felt the need for compensatory action against the left. As Lehr reported to Adenauer on 1 May 1951, the desired restrictions on the neo-Nazi Socialist Reich Party (SRP) were being balanced by recent prohibitions of Communist organizations: 'We cannot be accused of one-sidedly doing something against the SRP.'[57] After the Lower Saxon *Landtag* election five days later, in which the SRP won an alarming 11%, Adenauer moved in cabinet to start collecting incriminating material for use against the SRP before the nascent supreme court, the *Bundesverfassungsgericht*. The Housing Minister, Eberhard Wildermuth (FDP), then asked 'whether the KPD might not be treated in the same way'.[58] This double indictment duly crystallized in discussions between the Interior and Justice ministries in July, during which Dehler felt that prospects for a successful ban of the SRP were poor, but indictment of the KPD would be more hopeful and a 'psychological relief' for the court. Lehr, too, had become convinced several months earlier that the KPD should be banned and had already authorized a draft indictment.[59]

Evidence of transatlantic McCarthyism is circumstantial, but it was at precisely this juncture that the US Supreme Court upheld the indictment of the CPUSA leadership, heralding a wave of FBI arrests on 20 June. The next day HICOG's Political and Economic Projects Committee reported that German 'Commie penetration' was not deemed

---

[54] *Kurier*, 2 May 1950; 64th Bundeskabinett, 9 May 1950, and 66th Bundeskabinett, 16 May 1950, in *Kabinettsprotokolle*, ii. 371 and 393.

[55] Kirkpatrick to FO, 23 Mar. 1953, PRO, FO 371/103939.

[56] Lehr to Flecken (MI-NRW), 5 July 1951, BAK, B 106/15886.

[57] BMI to Adenauer, 1 May 1951, BAK, B 106/15530.

[58] 146th Bundeskabinett, 8 May 1951, in *Kabinettsprotokolle*, iv. 356.

[59] Dehler to Lehr, 16 July 1951, BAK, B 106/15541; Lehr to Dehler, 2 Aug. 1951, BAK, B 106/15541.

serious but that 'appropriate pressures sh[ou]ld be maintained to urge FEDREP to enact legislation necessary to proceed with [the] constitutional ouster program'. Allied and German security agencies would thus provide evidence for the constitutional dismissal of German Communists in sensitive areas such as railways and post offices. On 12 June the Americans' Bonn liaison office had also raised the question of whether, in proceeding against the SRP, the government might not logically do the same against the KPD. PEPCO, however, did not believe the situation justified this draconian course. Banning the KPD would merely accentuate its underground apparatus, and a case against the SRP would stick better under the Basic Law. It was agreed, nevertheless, to sound out the Interior and All-German Affairs ministries on their attitudes towards a KPD ban.[60]

Whereas the Americans appear to have been content to leave matters to the Germans, the British were becoming more alarmed at the turn of events. In May the Acting British High Commissioner, Ward, had reported no need 'to proceed further now in the direction of suppression, as the communist movement in Western Germany has at present but little hold on the population'.[61] The High Commission had indeed been perturbed by the German authorities' new-found zeal:

Germans tend to extremes; and there is something a little ominous in the exuberance with which officials and the police, often with scanty legal authority, are taking the offensive against the KPD.[62]

Ward had already advised Adenauer that the contemplated ban would be a mistake. Other voices in Whitehall argued that compensatory action for the SRP ban was necessary for Adenauer to hold together his parliamentary coalition. (It does seem, on the basis of the cabinet meetings discussed below, that the Deutsche Partei, whose constituency members were drifting steadily rightwards, and upon which the CDU and FDP depended for a majority, did press for parallel action against the KPD.) Little is known of France's attitude, but since on 4 June the French High Commissioner had baulked at press bans, for domestic electoral reasons, or so the Americans inferred, it seems unlikely that he would have subscribed to a ban of the party itself. The SPD, for its part, opposed a proscription which would only mask the KPD's lack of electoral support and upset

---

[60] Hays to State Dept., 21 June 1951, in *Confidential (1950–1954)*, 29. 33–5.
[61] Acting HC to FO, 2 May 1951, PRO, FO 371/93449.
[62] Ward to Morrison, 30 July 1951, PRO, FO 371/93449.

negotiations on reunification. Even British intelligence and the *Verfassungsschutz* counselled against banning, since such action would only hamper surveillance. It thus seems that the decision to go ahead was emphatically political.[63]

Even within the ruling CDU/CSU and the coalition cabinet, however, unanimity was not forthcoming. Ernst Lemmer, on the CDU's Christian Socialist wing, later decried the indictment as the use of 'the heaviest judicial artillery against a flock of wind-tossed political sparrows'.[64] After agreeing to consider a double indictment in October, some cabinet ministers, such as the Deutsche Partei's faction chairman, Mühlenfeld, advocated inclusion of the KPD, whereas Minister of Labour Storch (CDU) warned of Communists becoming less visible after a ban.[65] Later that month, the British High Commissioner, Kirkpatrick, relayed London's concern about the repercussions of a KPD ban for all-German elections and the GDR's bloc parties. Adenauer refused to be drawn, explaining that the cabinet was insisting on a double indictment, and was prepared to assume full responsibility in the expectation of SPD resistance, ending with the words, 'This is a highly political matter'.[66] Kirkpatrick detected cabinet splits, however, and even Ritter von Lex, the secretary of state in the Interior Ministry who later conducted the prosecution, was not happy about indicting the KPD. At the CDU executive on 29 October von Brentano, Bach, and Strickrodt were in favour, but Zimmer called it 'punching water', since the KPD had already begun to melt into front organizations. The next day in cabinet, while Adenauer insisted that the SRP be indicted as a liability with the western Allies, von Merkatz of the DP demanded the KPD's indictment too. Thus, on 16 November, the cabinet finally took the plunge of a double indictment of the SRP and KPD, discounting the dangers of a Communist ban for future reunification. At a press conference afterwards Lehr called on workers and employers to search their ranks for 'enemies of the constitution'. Then, on 22 November

---

[63] Richards, 27 Aug. 1951, PRO, FO 371/93361; *Süddeutsche Zeitung*, 21 Nov. 1951; McCloy to State Dept., 5 June 1951, in *Foreign Relations of the United States, 1951*, iii/2. 1773–4; UKHC to FO, 21 Nov. 1951, PRO, FO 371/93368; Düsseldorf Consulate to State Dept., 17 Oct. 1952, in *Confidential (1950–1954)*, 29. 306–8.

[64] *Frankfurter Allgemeine Zeitung*, 9 June 1953.

[65] 178th Bundeskabinett, 9 Oct. 1951, and 179th Bundeskabinett, 12 Oct. 1951, in *Kabinettsprotokolle*, iv. 692 and 698.

[66] AHC, 25 Oct. 1951, in *Akten zur auswärtigen Politik*, i. 558. Later, Adenauer confided that a ban would provide a basis for emergency legislation on censorship, ostensibly required for monitoring Communists; see Hoyer Millar to Eden, 14 Jan. 1955, PRO, FO 1056/347.

1951, a few days after indicting the SRP, the Federal government also formally petitioned Karlsruhe to test the KPD for unconstitutionality.[67] The Communist party, in long anticipation of this day, responded swiftly. Conspiratorial contingency plans, including a 'second tier' parallel to the legal party, were put into action, activating secret 'triumvirates' in the *Länder* to oversee clandestine three-member cells in the *Kreise*. Ernst Schmidt, for instance, dropped out of the NRW leadership to head the Bavarian triumvirate, detaching inconspicuous threesomes from regular party *Kreise* and preparing primitive illegal printing facilities.[68] The authorities also acted. On 31 January 1952 raids took place on SRP and KPD premises, looking in the latter's case for Secretariat and Party Control Commission reports and correspondence with the SED. Yet the KPD, unlike the SRP, was not fully unprepared for the swoop, so that the exercise had to be repeated on 12 July 1952, when a number of its cadre files were located in caches around Düsseldorf.[69] In fact, by the time of the trial, the BfV and western intelligence had, in the words of HICOG, 'thoroughly penetrated' a party 'riddled with agents':

The KPD is under the observation of more hostile agencies probably than any other political party in the world. Much of the mail of its members is surreptitiously examined by western officials, and many of their phone calls are tapped. Although it has not gone underground, the repeated harassment by the government in the form of arrests and long detentions of important leaders . . . confiscations, and attacks by anti-communist refugees, etc., on communist meetings have brought the party to a position where to all intents and purposes it is operating as an underground party.[70]

Whereas proscription of the SRP was achieved within a year, the KPD trial was far more drawn out, prompting Lehr to comment bitterly, 'We need a law against the *Bundesverfassungsgericht* for dealing with things so dilatorily'.[71] Proceedings in Karlsruhe before the court's First Senate were

---

[67] Kirkpatrick to Roberts, 30 Oct. 1951, PRO, FO 371/93366; *Adenauer: 'Es mußte alles neu gemacht werden': Die Protokolle des CDU-Bundesvorstandes 1950–1953*, ed. Günter Buchstab (Stuttgart, 1986), 92–3; Bundeskabinett, 30 Oct. 1951, in *Im Zentrum der Macht*, 156–8; 186th Bundeskabinett, 16 Nov. 1951, in *Kabinettsprotokolle*, iv. 765; BBC monitoring service, 16 Nov. 1951, PRO, FO 371/93368.

[68] Dickhut, *Was geschah danach?*, 81; *KPD 1945–1968: Dokumente* ed. Günter Judick *et al.* (Neuss, 1989), i. 82.; Schmidt interview, 9 Aug. 1989.

[69] Sondersitzung, 31 Jan. 1952, in *Kabinettsprotokolle*, v. 84 and 87–8; Informationen des BfV, 31 Aug. 1952, BAK, B 106/15886.

[70] HICOG to State Dept., 10 Aug. 1954, in *Confidential (1950–1954)*, 29. 525–46.

[71] Kabinett, 20 May 1952, in *Im Zentrum der Macht*, 337.

originally scheduled for 8 June 1953, but were delayed at the KPD's request and not opened until 23 November 1954. Shortly beforehand, however, the President of the First Senate, Wintrich, caused speculation about Karlsruhe's tacit disapproval, by formally requesting Bonn to confirm its wish to proceed and thus offering an escape route.[72] By then, however, there was no turning back and the government pressed its case.

In its original petition the government had claimed that the KPD was unconstitutional according to Article 21 of the Basic Law, which prohibits:

Parties which, by their aims or the conduct of their supporters, are intent upon infringing or removing the free democratic basic order, or endanger the existence, of the Federal Republic.

The KPD, although an unelectable 'splinter party', infringed the Basic Law, according to the government, by its lack of internal democracy, revolutionary pursuit of the dictatorship of the proletariat, 'national resistance', and *Volksbefragung* against remilitarization, as well as the intended extension to the FRG of the political system of the 'so-called GDR'.[73]

Chief counsel Ritter von Lex elaborated the government's case that the KPD was a threat to the political pluralism of the FRG by seeking to impose the East German bloc system. Unlike the Weimar constitution, however, which had 'delivered weapons into the hands of the very enemies of democracy', the Basic Law defended a 'free democratic basic order and thus a normative (*wertgebunden*) democracy'. Rather than any concrete evidence of treasonable activities (such as putsches or political violence), he argued that Article 21's phrase 'are intent upon' ('darauf ausgehen') did not require that 'the intentions harboured can be realized in the foreseeable future', or stipulate any 'already existing planning'. Instead, the KPD's doctrine and implicit hidden aims were at stake. This meant that a great deal of the trial was devoted to quotations from the Marxist-Leninist-Stalinist classics, including Marx's *Critique of Political Economy* and Lenin's *Left-Wing Communism: An Infantile Disorder*. In effect, a *Weltanschauung* as well as a party was being put in the dock. The semantics of the party's strategy and tactics, and the relationship between long-term and short-term goals, were thus scrutinized in various textual criticisms. Of course, specific programmatic statements also played a part in government evidence, such as the 1948 phrase 'revolutionary mass

---

[72] Brünneck, *Politische Justiz*, 117.
[73] *KPD-Prozeß*, ed. Gerd Pfeiffer and Hans-Georg Strickert (Karlsruhe, 1955), i. 2–21.

struggle'; 1950's 'national resistance'; and above all the phrase 'overthrow of the Adenauer regime' from the 1952 Programme for the National Reunification of Germany (despite the latter's publication a year after the indictment). The KPD's role was adduced to be that of a 'dependent sub-division of the Socialist Unity Party' and the West Commission, which were using the various mass and front organizations as 'transmission belts' to the West. National unity was a bait to 'force the totalitarian system of rule already realized in the Soviet zone' on to West Germany.[74]

Half-way through the trial the Interior Minister's personal assistant, Krause, confided to a HICOG official that 'it had not been wholly wise to bring the case' since many people thought 'there was no danger from the KPD, that the voters had in effect "outlawed" the KPD by turning it out of the Bundestag at the polls'. A ban would only succeed in martyrizing the party.[75] Indeed, Ulbricht had immediately seen the impending trial as a golden opportunity for a negative publicity campaign. Communist propaganda went on to compare events in Karlsruhe with the Nazis' *Reichstag* fire trial, which had, of course, resulted in the acquittal of Dimitrov and the humiliation of the prosecution.[76] Von Lex apparently also admired the 'ability and impudence of the KPD lawyers'.[77]

The KPD defence consisted of seven men, led by Professor Kröger, Dean of the Law Faculty at the Humboldt University in East Berlin, supported by Rische, Ledwohn, Renner, and Fisch for the KPD Executive. Since the first two were already in custody, they were brought up from the cells to each day's proceedings. Fisch, a wanted man since May, was granted safe conduct.[78] The party opened its defence by questioning the impartiality of the judges and claiming that the trial was inherently political, a 'medieval inquisition and witch-hunt'.[79] It also drew attention to the great contradiction underlying proceedings: 'Why then, if the KPD is supposed to be as weak and ineffective as the Federal government claims —why then this entire banning trial?'[80] Although the timing of the trial had supposedly been determined by the 'orchestrators in Washington', Dulles and Murphy, more sinister parallels were drawn with the *Reichstag* fire trial. Furthermore:

---

[74] *KPD-Prozeß*, i. 132–54.
[75] HICOG to State Dept., 23 Dec. 1954, in *Confidential (1950–1954)*, 29. 641–3.
[76] Ulbricht to Verner, 21 Nov. 1951, SAPMO-BA, NY 4182/868; BfV/Abt. III to BMI/BMJ/BVerfG, 19 Feb. 1952, BAK, B 106/15544.
[77] Hoyer Millar to Eden, 14 Jan. 1955, PRO, FO 1056/347.
[78] BVerfG to Böhmer, 9 Nov. 1954, BAK, B 118/14.   [79] *KPD-Prozeß*, i. 87.
[80] *KPD-Prozeß*, i. 183.

Ten years after the highly ignominious end of the Hitler system, which pinned anti-Communism on its colours, we are expected to discuss a petition springing from the same anti-Communism with which Hitler was temporarily able to deceive mankind . . .

    President: I must most emphatically reject any such inferred and unsubstantiated motive.[81]

The defence persisted in its claim that the government was seeking to make an example of the KPD, to set 'a precedent to terrorize in future all right-thinking and peace-loving people without legal constraints'.[82] Nevertheless, the Communists asserted the citizen's right of resistance against the state in defence of the Basic Law's freedom of expression. The Communists also denied that their hostility to the Adenauer government meant a more fundamental attack on the 'free democratic basic order'. At the same time, every opportunity was taken to demonstrate the KPD's patriotic credentials, since, as the KPD's lawyers pointed out, the Basic Law also made reunification a goal of the West German body politic. Furthermore, since the KPD had been licensed on the basis of Potsdam by three of the occupying powers, its banning would only impede reunification. As for the government's claim that the KPD was a revolutionary organization, Fisch replied that: 'There is not a single KPD document which calls for the commission of acts of violence or recommends the principled use of violence.'[83]

    Summing up for the prosecution, Ritter von Lex, besides repeating the government's arguments, also fired a shot across the bows of the general politics of class conflict:

As far as sorting out social differences and social tensions goes, this occurs here [in the Federal Republic] by the free means of parliamentary legislation, understanding between social partners, tariff negotiations, and welfare provisions. We consider it a serious infringement of the free democratic basic order to want to impose economic and social equality by the illiberal, anti-constitutional means of revolutionary class struggle. This goes especially for the mass strike as a means of revolutionary class struggle.[84]

Closing on a perhaps unwise biological metaphor, given the Nazis' fondness for them, von Lex decried the KPD as 'a dangerous source of infection for the body of our people, sending poisonous substances into the bloodstream of the Federal Republic's state and social organism'.[85]

---

[81] *KPD-Prozeß*, i. 171.   [82] *KPD-Prozeß*, i. 172.   [83] *KPD-Prozeß*, ii. 62.
[84] *KPD-Prozeß*, iii. 112.   [85] *KPD-Prozeß*, iii. 116.

The defence contested the imputation that general or political strikes were unconstitutional, even though the right to strike was not explicitly guaranteed in the Basic Law. The trial had the function of an anti-Communist show trial—'a model trial according to the methods of the McCarran Report and the wishes of the McCarthy circle'.[86] Reminding the court of the government chief counsel's judicial activities during the Third Reich, 'the KPD considers it an honour to be defamed and insulted by State Secretary Ritter von Lex'.[87] Fritz Rische then delivered the party's defiant peroration:

The trial of the Adenauer government against the KPD is a blow against the unity of Germany, an attempt on the peace of our people, and an attack on the labour movement. . . . Hitler came and went, but the Communists remained. The Adenauers come and go, but the Communists will remain. . . . Long live the struggle of the German people and long live a united and independent Germany of democracy and peace. Long live the German working class and its Communist Party of Germany![88]

Overall, the trial had lasted for fifty-one days, until 14 July 1955. In spite of KPD applications on 14 March and 5 April 1956 for a resumption of proceedings on the basis of programmatic changes after Khrushchev's 'secret speech', the court was already deliberating its verdict. It took over a year. The slow pace appears to have had political rather than constitutional motives. It was, of course, at precisely this time that Adenauer was resuming diplomatic relations with Moscow, including negotiations for the release of the last German POWs in the Soviet Union. The announcement of a ban might have upset such talks. Nevertheless, by spring 1956 the Interior Ministry was putting pressure on the court to reach a verdict, and once and for all to end the 'fatal weakening of the position of our state in the east–west confrontation so decisive for our whole people'.[89] By any standards, this would seem an unwarranted interference by the executive in the judiciary. Yet the government did not shy away from using a technicality to precipitate a decision, when it conspicuously transferred competence for party prohibitions from the court's First to its Second Senate, to be effective from 1 September.

Thus, on 17 August 1956, the long-awaited verdict was announced, declaring the KPD to be unconstitutional, dissolving it, and forbidding ersatz organizations. Beforehand, the President made some attempt to distance the court from the government: 'The Constitutional Court cannot

[86] *KPD-Prozeß*, iii. 293. [87] *KPD-Prozeß*, iii. 305. [88] *KPD-Prozeß*, iii. 306.
[89] BMI to BVerfG, 25 May 1956, BAK, B 106/56600.

initiate proceedings of its own accord. . . . therefore considerations of political opportunism are not permissible.' The court explicitly stated that a
party could be deemed anti-constitutional 'even if by human judgement
there is no prospect of it realizing its anti-constitutional intentions in the
foreseeable future'.[90] Marxism-Leninism was portrayed as a pseudo-
religious faith, aiming at a Communist social order via a dictatorship of
the proletariat, incompatible with the 'free democratic basic order', infringing its principles of equality, pluralism, opposition, responsible government, and separation of powers. The defence's objection that the KPD
had not currently been advocating dictatorship of the proletariat was rejected
on the grounds that a tactical acceptance of the Basic Law merely belied
a fundamental, irreconcilable hostility. Extra-parliamentary actions were
not ruled out as such, only when employed by an anti-constitutional force.
What had clinched the government's case was the KPD's 1952 Programme. The court closed with the admonitory words that, 'Precisely its
stance towards National Socialism should have led the KPD to respect a
system which grew out of the struggle against National Socialist ideas and
which desires to realize the basic values rejected by National Socialism.'[91]

Despite the experience of 1933 the KPD seems to have been inad-
equately prepared for illegality in 1956. By 22 August 2,398 offices and
apartments had been searched; 199 party headquarters, 33 printers, pub-
lishers, and newspapers closed down; 53 vehicles impounded; and 199
functionaries arrested. The top leaders fled to the GDR, joining Reimann
and others, who were already co-ordinating illegal work from the SED's
Karl-Liebknecht-Haus under conditions of virtual house arrest. Almost
immediately a Deutscher Freiheitssender 904 started transmitting from
near Magdeburg, offering a mixture of political commentary, cryptic
messages, and popular music. The KPD Executive became a Central
Committee, and an underground Party Convention in East Berlin in June
1957 re-elected Reimann as 1st Secretary of a new 11-strong Politbüro,
a privilege it had never enjoyed while still legal.[92]

Lower down the party there was almost complete inactivity. On
17 August there had been only one protest demonstration of about 300
in Munich, whereas in 'red' Hamburg the news was greeted with apathy.
The SPD and DGB expressed as little regret at the ban as they had at
the indictment. In the *Kreise* the conspiratorially trained triumvirates
took over pentagons of residual members, but many couriers and even

[90] *KPD-Prozeß*, iii. 613.   [91] *KPD-Prozeß*, iii. 581–746.
[92] BfV to BMI, 7 Sept. 1956, BAK, B 106/15889; Hans Kluth, *Die KPD in der
Bundesrepublik* (Cologne and Opladen, 1959), 122.

top leaders were arrested by the Federal authorities. Literature such as *Wissen und Tat* continued to be smuggled in under ingeniously innocuous covers, but in October 1957 the distribution apparatus was broken up. A petition by the illegal KPD that year to the European Commission on Human Rights, complaining at violation of the freedoms of speech and association, was also thrown out on the grounds that an organization seeking to remove these rights could not itself invoke them.[93]

By a strange quirk of fate, the Nazi and Federal bans were of almost exactly equal duration. So, for that matter, were Bismarck's Anti-Socialist Laws. All lasted for twelve years. During that period, despite KPD protestations to the contrary, the party all but disappeared from public consciousness. Among those politically active on the New Left in the mid-1960s, it was becoming apparent that the pseudo-military discipline of the old Communists had little in common with the anarchic anti-authoritarianism of the student movement. Even for kindred spirits such as Ulrike Meinhof, who indeed briefly joined the illegal KPD, there was no reconciliation with Lenin's dictum that terrorism is counter-productive. Campaigns to re-legalize the KPD fell on deaf ears, and only under a political amnesty inspired by Willy Brandt was a Deutsche Kommunistische Partei (DKP) permitted to constitute itself on 25 September 1968. And, even then, only after explicitly renouncing revolution as a political means. The underground KPD itself endured nominally until 1971, when it was finally dissolved and Reimann made honorary DKP chairman, thereby pronouncing the old party officially and definitively dead.[94]

---

[93] Georg Fülberth, *KPD und DKP 1945–1990* (Heilbronn, 1990), 91; Ralph Giordano, *Die Partei hat Immer recht* (Cologne and Berlin, 1961), 236–7; Ursula Straka, 'SPD, DGB und KPD-Verbot—Eine Untersuchung der Positionen von Sozialdemokratischer Partei und Deutschem Gewerkschaftsbund zum Antrag auf Verbot der KPD 1951 und zur Urteilsverkündung 1956', diploma (University of Erlangen-Nürnberg, 1978); Kluth, *KPD in der Bundesrepublik*, 119 and 121.

[94] Manfred Wilke *et al.*, *DKP* (Cologne, 1990), 71–6.

Conclusion
Germany's Cold Civil War

THE history of the KPD after 1945 was a catalogue of failures. Yet the party did not disintegrate nor break with Moscow, and in 1989 the West German Communists in Düsseldorf resisted the blandishments of the 'renewers' for even longer than their comrades in East Berlin. As well as seeking answers to the demise of the KPD as a party, it is necessary also to explain the loyalty of individual cadres, apparently 'immune' to failure. One might begin by returning to the disaster analogy offered in the introduction, on the respective roles of human error, structural failure, and adverse environmental conditions.

If anybody can be regarded as the pilot of the KPD, albeit of the backseat variety, it must be the East German leader, Walter Ulbricht. Notoriously autocratic in his personal style of leadership, he determined the overall direction of the western party. Whether out of misplaced idealism or disguised cynicism, the SED leadership imposed on the non-ruling KPD a set of largely inappropriate policies, designed instead for a ruling Communist party like itself. Yet bloc politics, land reform, socialization, and denazification could not work in the West according to the eastern model. Without a monopoly of bureaucratic positions, the KPD could not hope to enact a similar administrative revolution from above.

The western party proved too weak to take over the controls for itself. Max Reimann was at best a dutiful co-pilot. Throughout, he owed his position to Ulbricht's patronage and the purges of potential challengers by East Berlin. According to American intelligence, whose views coincided surprisingly closely with those of his SED overseers, the KPD leader was acknowledged as a 'very effective speaker, but is not considered a well-organized worker'.[1] Indeed, Reimann was by no means the intellectual equal of Thorez or Togliatti, apparently not even up to the task of writing his own speeches. The KPD suffered from a general dearth of

---

[1] ID/EUCOM, report of 16 Sept. 1949, BAK, Z 45 F, 7–32–3/5–6; Schirdewan interview, 24 Aug. 1990.

top-rank cadres, who, with few exceptions, had made their careers in the Soviet Zone. (Nazi decimation had, of course, played a significant role too.)

At a further remove, the KPD was also very much influenced by the will of Joseph Stalin, both in terms of the Stalinist culture inherited from Weimar, but also by the generalissimo's personal interest in the German question. Although evidence is only circumstantial, the programmatic emphasis on nationalism, but also pacifism, would appear to have been pet projects of the Soviet leader. In meetings with SED functionaries in Moscow, Stalin clearly set great store by the supposedly irresistible allure of national reunification for the German public. In fact, the brand of romanticized, emancipatory nationalism championed by the Communists, citing the anti-colonial independence movements in the developing world, sat uneasily with recent memories of the oppressive, racial nationalism of the Nazis. Moreover, because nationalism was not a class-specific creed, it proved unpopular with many cadres raised on class struggle, and the KPD's addressees were put off by the party's repeated identification with the GDR and its 'second fatherland', the Soviet Union. For these, and many other reasons, West Germany's Communists found it impossible to recruit the 'national neutralist' right to their cause. By overplaying the historical continuity between Versailles and Potsdam, and miscalculating on a right-wing backlash, the KPD was committing a fundamental error of judgement.

Moving from leadership mistakes to party structures, by which I mean above all the rank and file, it can be seen that ordinary members were sent off on a number of hopeless and often contradictory courses. The resulting disorientation more often than not ended in attempts to navigate by instinct. The Third Reich had indeed left many grass-roots Communists traumatized and incorrigibly 'sectarian', suspicious of alliance politics. Yet, however understandable the emotional appeal of direct action, the leadership was probably correct to suppress local militancy. Rioting or strikes would have done little against the economic paralysis of 1946–8, and could conceivably have led to bloodshed. Nevertheless, more pragmatic frontism was continually impeded by grass-roots foot-dragging. Moreover, despite initial promises not to repeat the mistakes of Weimar, even the KPD leadership displayed frustration and gradually slipped back into ultra-leftist rhetoric. Especially after 1949, rightist SPD and DGB leaders were attacked as aiding and abetting a militarist and fascist revival, but the strategy backfired just as badly as it had done twenty years before.

All the same, one must be wary of the leadership's own diagnosis of the party's structural weakness. There is certainly something to be said for the fact that in the early years the western party was not a model of democratic centralism. But nor were the more successful Social or Christian Democrats! As argued at the end of Chapter 6, however, the KPD soon became overorganized. As was also seen in the numerous electoral post-mortems in Chapter 3, the party's 'organizational fetishism' tended to interpret political shortcomings as failures of discipline. On the contrary, the core support of the post-war KPD, often dating back to Weimar, proved remarkably resilient as a cadre party. Where the post-war KPD did remain unstable, however, was as a mass party. Despite the leadership's attempts to transform it into a 'Sozialistische Volkspartei Deutschlands' in 1948, it conspicuously failed to become a cross-class people's party. A glance at its social composition shows that it never made significant inroads into the peasantry or *Mittelstand*, let alone the intelligentsia. To even the casual observer, the KPD still bore far too many resemblances to what Sigmund Neumann called the Weimar 'absolutist party of integration', which, of course, included the now discredited NSDAP. The rituals of mass mobilization and uniformed youth were out of place in a post-fascist society reclaiming the private sphere.

I do not wish to suggest that West German Communist success was impossible and the KPD's demise in some way preordained. The French and Italian Communists proved that there could be such a thing as a moderately successful post-war western European Communist party. Clearly, one key to the French and Italian Communists' superior performance was their leading role in the wartime resistance. The KPD had nothing comparable to build upon. More controversially, it might be argued that French and Italian society was less modern than in the Federal Republic, and offered more scope for clientelist politics. The PCI, besides its bastions in the 'red triangle' of Milan-Turin-Genoa, also established a subculture of *Case del Popolo* in the small towns and rural hinterland of central Italy. Perhaps more intellectual in origin, the French PCF also integrated members inside an all-encompassing 'counter-society' (Kriegel). Such associational networks may have been a feature of the German labour movement until the 1920s, but even then the Communists had not been able to compete effectively with the Social Democrats and the German welfare state. Thereafter, the Nazis had gone a long way to destroying the bases for such 'communities of solidarity'. The final socio-economic nail in the KPD's coffin was the sustained economic upturn of the 1950s, which continued to rationalize and depoliticize the West German workforce.

Although the KPD was more exposed on the geopolitical front line, PCI and PCF were ultimately buffeted by the same Cold War winds.

They, too, adopted a similarly cautious, parliamentary strategy. Togliatti's *svolta di Salerno* and 'progressive democracy' held the PCI to the same gradualist, étatist course as 'anti-fascist democracy', and he too sacrificed socio-political demands for the sake of 'national liberation' and a doomed alliance with the Christian Democrats. PCI and PCF militancy was the exception to the rule. Nor should it be forgotten that, despite their greater strength, both PCF and PCI were also excluded from government in 1947, as were KPD ministers in 1948.

The relationship between state marginalization and self-ghettoization is a complex one. Some critics have interpreted the latter as a symptom of the former. Undoubtedly, state surveillance helped to produce a semi-underground cadre party, but so too did Communist ideology. Vestigial class-based *Lagerdenken*, or 'camp mentality', from Weimar, reinforced by Zhdanov's geopolitical fortress mentality, made the KPD particularly susceptible to sectarianism. The historian is, of course, always wise after the event, but should not forget that in the Cold War illusion and mis-perception were often more important in determining courses of action than 'objective' reality. Agents were feared under every bed, and, in the case of the KPD, not without cause. Yet the Communist leadership deliber-ately personalized the enemy, often speaking in the collective singular of 'the adversary', be it military government, CDU or SPD, recrudescent imperialism, or international finance capital. From 1948 the party was in a state of permanent vigilance. Such conspiracy theories were a key reason why so few West German Communists entertained serious hopes of severing their ties with their East German patrons, who offered at least some comfort in a hostile world. The bleak alternatives for any *heimat-lose Linke* and the intimidation accompanying the party's cadrification, effectively deterred larger-scale defections of core support. I would there-fore make a special plea not to regard Communist apparatchiks simply as political automata, but also as individuals with psychological frailties and an unbroken personal history of persecution and pariahdom. There was also a high degree of personal politics involved in what I have earlier termed the 'emperor's new clothes syndrome'. Subordinates often told superiors what they thought they wanted to hear, and thus helped to dis-tort the party's perception of reality.

The Communist mind-set thereby contributed to the KPD's pre-dicament, but at the same time shielded it from an acceptance of failure. Ideologically the party could justify its minority position as a self-selecting Marxist-Leninist *avant-garde*, and the supportive proletarian internationalism of the 1920s was to some extent resurrected after 1947 in the Cominform. As part of the world Communist movement, domestic defeats could be reckoned against global victories such as China. There was a danger, however, of slipping into a sacrificial role as the Cold War's 'internationalist martyrs', a role prepared by Nazi persecution, and of thinking in moral rather than political categories. Whatever the level of blame pertaining to the KPD for its own downfall, its own mistakes could be reinterpreted—all too readily—as consequences of victimization.

Anti-Communism is an equally, if not more, complex phenomenon, if only by virtue of its diversity. With regard to Anglo-American policy, the historian of the western Allied occupation should not take at face value claims made by contemporaries about a growing Communist groundswell, so crucial to arguments for an economic rehabilitation of the western zones. In the light of my findings on the intelligence community's dismissal of a serious Communist threat, the alarmism evinced by Whitehall and Washington seems misdirected and indeed misleading. A revival of pro-fascist sentiment was far more evident. Anti-Communism was nevertheless a useful lubricant for unjamming the diplomatic machinery, in which a purported security threat could be used to override political or economic objections.

As for the infant Bonn Republic, infinitely more democratic, but no less artificial than its East German antagonist, it proved unwilling to tolerate even verbal Communist attacks on its national sovereignty. As seen in Chapter 4, the KPD did not tire of questioning West Germany's claim to sole representation of the German nation, and championed instead the GDR. I would argue, therefore, that the specific post-war factor reviving latent German anti-Communist tendencies was the threat from a rival East German state. The Russian menace had become real, with Red Army troops now stationed on German soil. For many observers, including conservative historians such as Ernst Nolte, the KPD and its sympathizers had in fact become a political fifth column, 'the "Party of the GDR" in the Federal Republic'.[2]

The evidence adduced over the course of the book has shown that much of this was true. The KPD's strategy was decided in Moscow and its tactics in East Berlin. Nor is it my intention to suggest that anti-Communist critiques were mere phantoms. Systematic rapes by Red Army troops well after the liberation, the internment of political opponents in former concentration camps, and dismantling of capital equipment on an unprecedented scale, did all occur—East Germany *was* a dictatorship. The KPD

---

[2] Ernst Nolte, *Deutschland und der kalte Krieg* (Munich, 1974), 426.

thus seriously damaged itself by identifying with the political upheavals there. It was to some extent, therefore, a perpetrator by association. Yet West German Communists could always justify such complicity with reference to their own current predicament and a millenarian commitment to future social justice. In a series of fifty OMGUS interviews with rank-and-file KPD members in late 1947, most respondents were certainly aware of the existence of labour camps in the USSR, although few had personal experience of the SBZ, but accepted what they saw as short-term evils for the sake of the long-term good.[3]

Nevertheless, whereas the wrongs of the Communist system continue to be exposed by post-Cold War historians, anti-Communism has often evaded serious criticism. Its fixation with the East produced a form of political tunnel vision which tended to place the entire blame for Germany's division on the 'other side'. American pollsters noted of German respondents that, despite ignorance about Russians, 'when in doubt, they tend to select the "fact" least favorable to Russia'.[4] This created two major blindspots among anti-Communists: firstly, an unwillingness to consider the Nazi contribution, through a failed war of predation, to the national predicament; secondly, an inability to differentiate between an external and an internal threat. Self-defence against East German Communism thus slipped into active persecution of West German Communists. By the 1950s in particular, when the FRG was proving demonstrably more stable than the GDR, this was a clear case of overreaction.

Many of the counter-measures involved affected non-Communists as badly as Communists. Personal visits to the East often became the subject of police investigation, and mail from the GDR was frequently returned to sender by the Federal post office. There was also an underlying paternalistic authoritarianism in government measures which took decisions on matters of political conscience out of the hands of its citizens. For instance, East Germany's 'Happy Holidays for Children' scheme, although clearly also a GDR publicity exercise, was proscribed by Bonn, leading to many a coach load of West German youngsters being turned back at the East German border by Federal customs officers.[5] Such measures not only played into the hands of SED propagandists, but also contradicted Bonn's avowed policy of maintaining family and personal ties between

---

[3] ID/Director, 20 Jan. 1948, PA Staritz.

[4] Anna J. Merritt and Richard L. Merritt, *Public Opinion in Occupied Germany: The OMGUS Surveys, 1945–1949* (Urbana, Ill., 1970), 55.

[5] Leaflet 'Frohe Ferien', Jugendarchiv/Institut für zeitgeschichtliche Jugendforschung, A 2.757/I.

the two Germanys (although the East German government was, of course, far more culpable on this count, especially after the building of the Berlin Wall).

As well as being a cure which was in danger of killing the patient, anti-Communism also proved not always to be about the KPD, nor, for that matter, even about Communism. Deploying the red threat was a useful tactic in budgetary battles and institutional empire-building. It has already been noted how West Germans were prepared to play up the Communist danger in order to secure Marshall Aid. During 1947–8 74% of German respondents in the American Zone believed the chief purpose of the Marshall Plan was to help keep western Europe from turning Communist (as opposed to American altruism or the creation of a market for American dumping).[6] The Communist menace also served to justify the build-up of a secret police force, the *Verfassungsschutz*.[7] One plan by the Federal Centre of Home Affairs (later the Federal Centre of Political Education) in April 1956 stated that, 'The countering of the Communist offensive, which is being waged with diverse methods, is the *raison d'être* of the Federal Republic': 'general enlightenment', 'scholarly research', and 'immunization of certain groups of persons and areas' would require an annual subsidy of 55 million DM.[8]

Anti-Communism also had useful knock-on effects in stigmatizing the peace movement in the 1950s, leaving no room for neutralism or a third way: unless non-Communists became actively anti-Communist, they were little better than stooges of Communist expansionism. The SPD and trade unions, and anything vaguely socialist and at odds with NATO, could therefore be tarred by the ruling CDU/CSU-led coalition with the same anti-Communist brush. In a 1956 conversation with US Secretary of State Dulles, for example, Adenauer drew the American's attention to the SPD's reformist programme, which opposed NATO and espoused *détente*. Dulles asked if this meant the effective 'Communization of all of Germany?', to which Adenauer disingenuously replied that, 'this was exactly what it meant'.[9] The ulterior target of the Chancellor's anti-Communism was therefore clearly the more real threat of the SPD.

[6] OMGUS Report No. 149, 10 Dec. 1948, in Merritt and Merritt, *OMGUS Surveys*, 270.

[7] Request for subsidy for LfV S-H, IM/S-H to BMI, 29 Aug. 1950, BAK, B 106/63038.

[8] Wendorff memo., Apr. 1956, BAK, B 106/15829.

[9] Dulles/Adenauer meeting, 14 June 1956, in *Foreign Relations of the United States, 1955–57*, xxvi. 125.

By shifting the emphasis from denazification to anti-Communism Adenauer could also offer a quid pro quo to a conservative national opposition sceptical of western integration. The awkward transition could be somewhat eased by conflating Nazism with Communism as part of the same totalitarian impulse. Yet the danger of this form of *Vergangenheitsbewältigung* was that, once the anti-Communist pillar of Nazi ideology had been revived for the purposes of the Cold War, its other sustaining forces would be, if not condoned, then at least repressed. This leaves serious question marks about the selectivity of the Allies' re-education programme, open to accusations of hypocrisy and double standards, and helps to explain many West Germans' lip-service to denazification.

Any ideology which defines itself almost wholly negatively, in terms of its enemy, can easily lose sight of what it is trying to defend. The Stalinist dictatorship in East Germany took institutionalized paranoia to absurd lengths, with correspondingly dire consequences for perceived enemies within. Nevertheless, West Germany was not free from this friend/foe mentality either. Anti-Communist persecution in West Germany reached alarming proportions in the 1950s and early 1960s, seeking out scapegoats for injustices behind the iron curtain. Yet, as I have argued above, the real test is not how West Germany compared with East Germany, but how it lived up to its own self-proclaimed standards. A constitutional state which claimed the moral high ground of freedom and democracy would have further to fall if compromising these principles. Although the Basic Law called for the protection of the 'free democratic basic order', all too often West German government officials spoke among themselves of defending the 'state order'.[10] On this reading, anti-Communism was invoked not so much to guarantee individual civil liberties as to protect the machinery of government. Although the general public may have been receptive to anti-Communism, and thus created a hostile environment for the party, it was the state which provided the final lethal force.

The peculiarity of the Cold War in Germany was that it was at once an international and an internal conflict. For this reason, I speak of Germany's 'cold civil war'. The two halves of Germany never became truly separate states, and, throughout this period, neither renounced the claim to represent the whole nation. The east–west border remained remarkably permeable until 1961. At the same time, the two Germanys were worlds

---

[10] See for instance BMI to Staatssekretär des Innern im Bundeskanzleramt, 'Kabinettssache! 15.9.50: Betr. Politische Betätigung von Angehörigen des öffentlichen Dienstes gegen die demokratische Staatsordnung', 14 Sept. 1950, BAK, B 106/6748.

apart as frontline members of opposing superpower blocs. The result of this tension between togetherness and apartness was often a blurring of the line between enemies within and enemies without.

The interplay between the external and internal led both to the super-imposition of international conflicts onto domestic problems, but also to long-standing internal class antagonisms being raised to the level of diplomatic confrontations. Thus, for the German Communists, their declared enemies, the Junkers and monopoly capitalists, were allegedly using the Cold War to wage a revanchist class war. The most effective socialist defence against the 'imperialists', or so it was argued, was to use labour unity to achieve national unity, and thus defeat the enemy from above and below. For western military government, too, diplomatic and domestic policy in Germany were intimately connected. The KPD was seen to be trying to pre-empt, or at least to force, the diplomatic process by fomenting disorder in the debilitated western zones. Yet, while hope of a solution continued, the occupation powers treated the West German Communists with caution, for fear of upsetting negotiations. Once a quadripartite break had been made in late 1947, however, Allied inhibitions about imposing domestic sanctions on the KPD inside their respective zones all but disappeared.

In the cold civil war, superpower conflicts could all too easily be manipulated against internal enemies. Many political salvoes, ostensibly fired at the Cold War opponent, were designed to have at least a collateral impact on certain sections of the home population. I have already argued above that West German anti-Communism had a number of ulterior domestic targets, such as the SPD and the peace movement. On the other side of the Elbe, too, many of the national unification efforts by the East German Communists, as well as trying to embarrass Adenauer, were also intended to neutralize a potential opposition within East Germany. Party and press bombarded 'wavering' sections of society, above all the intelligentsia and *Mittelstand*, with evidence of the SED's patriotic credentials (not very convincingly, it might be added). The KPD also played an important part in this cold war propaganda battle, not as victor but as victim, helping to justify the East's own hard line against enemies within.

By arguing for the concept of a cold civil war, I do not wish to suggest that both parties to the conflict should bear an equal burden of war guilt. The West German leadership's actions enjoyed far greater popular support than did offensives in East Germany, where a powerful if subdued anti-Communism persisted. Nor do I wish to enter into debates about who started hostilities. Yet once the Cold War was under way, and despite all claims to the contrary, neither side remained merely reactive. Moscow and Washington, London and Paris, Berlin and Bonn, all became prime movers. Only such a critical application of the post-revisionist synthesis can properly explain the mutually reinforcing, upward spiral of confrontation, which has so far been insufficiently catered for by more one-sided traditionalist and revisionist models. Communism and anti-Communism may have been diametrically opposed subjectively, but at a deeper level were inextricably linked within a dialectical system of conflict.

Finally, a few historiographical afterthoughts. For too long, Cold War history has been diplomatic history. It has, moreover, been one of the great conceits of some Anglo-American diplomatic historians to think that one can write the history of post-war Germany without exploring German sources or literature. As a result, accounts have become bogged down in policy-making and contingency-planning at the expense of policy implementation on the ground. Nevertheless, in order to understand the effects as well as causes of the Cold War in Germany, the historian must venture away from the high politics of the negotiating table, to the domestic middle politics of the parliaments and courts, and the low politics of the factories and streets. It was, after all, here, on the home fronts of both East and West Germany, that one will find the casualties of the cold civil war. This is not an excuse for a victim-based history, but a plea for a broader socio-cultural sweep to what must, at heart, remain a political phenomenon. The interaction of politics, society, and culture can only enrich the history of the Cold War.

At the same time, German labour histories have been finding it equally difficult to strike a happy medium between high and low politics. The work of Mallmann on the Weimar KPD represents a belated but welcome move by German social historians away from the functionary corps and towards the grass roots.[11] Although the present study is pitched at the national level, it should be clear from some of my local findings that the post-war rank and file, too, were quite capable of sabotaging the party line. (One must, of course, also recognize that the political positions were reversed: whereas the Weimar grass roots were criticized for opportunism, after 1945 they were accused of sectarianism.) It would thus be disappointing if, given the wealth of new material available on post-war Communism, future studies were to relapse into the same sort of personalization and institutionalization of KPD cadre politics which has

---

[11] Klaus-Michael Mallmann, 'Milieu, Radikalismus und lokale Gesellschaft', *Geschichte und Gesellschaft*, 21 (1995), 5–31.

bedevilled the diplomatic school of Cold War history. Yet, just as I would urge the latter to open up more towards the socio-cultural, I would also warn labour historians against drifting too far from the political. The socio-cultural reconstruction of the milieu cannot become an end in itself. Indeed, since the cold civil war patently nationalized—and internationalized—the domestic cleavages between Communists and anti-Communists, the way ahead must surely lie in a synthesis of Cold War political history and labour social history. I hope that what stands above is at least a step in the right direction.

BIOGRAPHICAL APPENDIX[1]

AGATZ, WILLI (1904–57), born in Essen, miner, 1920 Socialist Workers' Youth, 1922 Communist Youth Association, 1924 KPD, disciplined during 1923 Ruhr occupation and 1930 miners' strike, 1928 works council chairman at Ludwig colliery, 1930–3 Member of *Reichstag*, 1931 secretary of Revolutionary Trade Union Opposition (RGO) in Ruhr, 1932–3 1st chairman of United Association of German Miners, 1933–4 RGO Organization Leader, 1934–9 hard labour and KZ Sachsenhausen, 1943 Penal Battalion 999, 1945–May 1946 Soviet POW (*Antifa* instructor), 1946 Miners' Union works council secretary, Nov. 1946–Dec. 1948 deputy chairman of Miners' Union in Bizone, 1947 Member of NRW *Landtag*, 1949–53 Member of *Bundestag*, Aug. 1950 expulsion from Miners' Union, 1950 mining desk on KPD's NRW secretariat and later on national executive, died in an East Berlin sanatorium.

BAUER, LEOPOLD (Leo) (1912–72), born in Tarnopol (Russia), 1928 SPD, Socialist Workers' Party, 1931 KPD, 1932–3 university, then worked for party's counter-intelligence, 1933 arrested before going underground, then to Prague, Paris, and Spain, working for various refugee agencies, 1939 interned in France before moving in 1940 to Switzerland to liaise with PCF and Marseille KPD, 1942 contact with Noel Field and US intelligence, Oct. 1942 arrested by Swiss for espionage, acquitted, but interned until 1944, headed Free Germany movement in western Switzerland, 1945–6 freelance on *Frankfurter Rundschau*, deputy chairman of Hessen KPD, 1946–9 charismatic KPD faction chairman of Hessen *Landtag*, editor of *Wissen und Tat*, Oct. 1947 hospitalized by car crash in SBZ where he remained on party orders, 1949 director of Deutschlandsender radio, 23 Aug. 1950 arrested in Field Affair and Dec. 1952 sentenced to death by Soviet court martial (commuted to twenty-five years' hard labour), Jan. 1953 moved to Siberia but Oct. 1955 released to FRG, joined SPD, 1961 editor on *Stern* and 1968 of *Neue Gesellschaft*, also adviser to Willy Brandt.

DETTMANN, FRIEDRICH (Fiete) (1897–1970), born in Hamburg, metalworker, 1911 Socialist Workers' Youth, 1917 Independent Social Democrats, 1917–19 British POW, 1920 KPD, 1923 editor on *Hamburger Volkszeitung*, 1924 convicted of illegal Communist activity, 1924–33 Member of Hamburg Senate, 1929 head of North German Workers' Protection League (ersatz for Red Front Fighters' League), until 1933 with KPD Wasserkante in Hamburg, Oct. 1933 to Denmark,

---

[1] For biographies of all the post-war KPD's leading functionaries, see my original thesis, 'The German Communist Party (KPD) in the Western Zones and in Western Germany, 1945–1956', D.Phil. thesis (University of Oxford, 1993), 245–50.

where arrested and deported to USSR, working on Comintern's Central Europe desk, Sept. 1934 sent to Leipzig, 1935 arrested and imprisoned until 1945, June 1945–May 1946 chairman of Wasserkante KPD, 1945–8 Senator for Health in Hamburg, 1946–51 Member of Hamburg Senate, 1951 removed to minor posts in GDR.

FISCH, WALTER (1910–66), born in Heidelberg, business trainee then miner, 1928 Communist Youth Association (KJVD), 1930 KPD, until 1933 KJVD chairman in Hessen, 1933 Organization Leader of underground Hessen KPD, arrested, 1933 led Swiss KPD until deportation in 1935, to Prague as Red Aid worker, 1938 illegal return to Switzerland but interned in 1939, 1944 on local Free Germany leadership, 1945 chairman of Hessen KPD, Dec. 1946–9 Member of Hessen *Landtag*, Apr. 1946–Jan. 1949 on SED executive, but critical of eastern interference, 1947 KPD chairman of US Zone, Apr. 1948–51 deputy national chairman, credited as one of party's few thinkers, 1949–53 Member of *Bundestag*, Nov. 1949 'neutralized' during anti-Titoist campaign, 1954–5 KPD defendant at banning trial, Feb. 1958–June 1959 imprisoned in FRG.

HARIG, PAUL (1900–?), born in Nivilingen (Saar), metalworker, 1920 unionized, 1923 KPD, 1925 works councillor at Klöckner's Hagen-Haspe steelworks, Nov. 1928 involved in Ruhr metalworkers' strike (sacked in Mar. 1929 and later expelled from Metalworkers' Union), then Revolutionary Trade Union Opposition leader at Hagen-Haspe, 1933 to Saar, 1935 return, arrest, and two years' imprisonment, after 1945 on KPD's NRW leadership, works council chairman at Hagen-Haspe, town councillor, 1946 local representative of IG Metall and 1947 of DGB, as well as sitting on supervisory board at Hagen-Haspe, 1947 on Bizonal IG Metall advisory board, 1949 Member of *Bundestag*, 1950 expelled from IG Metall and sacked from Haspe, 1968 DKP.

LEDWOHN, JOSEF (Jupp) (1907–), born in Rünthe (Westphalia), electrical fitter, 1922 Socialist Workers' Youth, 1926 SPD, 1927 KPD, 1929 KPD Political Leader in Ahlen, arrested Feb. 1933, sentenced to 3½ years' hard labour, upon release worked in Stettin and Essen, maintaining loose illegal contacts, exempted from war service, 1945 helped to refound KPD in Ahlen and Essen, 1947 chairman of Ruhr KPD, 1947–54 Member of NRW *Landtag*, Sept. 1947–Jan. 1949 member of SED executive and from Apr. 1948 of KPD Executive, 1949–56 KPD chairman of NRW, 1954–7 imprisoned in FRG for disseminating 1952's National Programme, thereafter active for underground KPD, 1968 DKP.

LICHTENSTEIN, KURT (1911–61), born in Berlin into a Jewish family (parents and sister died in Holocaust), toolmaker, Socialist Workers' Youth, 1928 Communist Youth Association (KJVD), 1931 KPD, 1933 to USSR, 1934 KJVD instructor in Saar, 1935 coordinated illegal border-crossings into Germany from France, accused of conciliationism (*Versöhnlertum*), 1936–39 International Brigadist in Spain, wounded but expelled from KPD for one year for alleged cowardice, 1939–41 interned in France before escaping to join resistance, 1944 returned to Germany disguised as French forced labourer, 1946 on KPD's Ruhr and British Zonal leaderships, deputy editor of *Westdeutsches Volks-Echo*, then 1947 editor of *Freiheit* and 1948 of *Neue Volkszeitung*, 1946–50 on KPD's NRW leadership, 1947–50 Member of NRW *Landtag*, Aug. 1950 stripped of functions including editorship of *NVZ* for involvement with Kurt Müller, Apr. 1953 KPD expulsion, 1954 SPD, odd jobs then journalism, 12 Oct. 1961 shot dead near Wolfsburg by East German border guards while collecting material on the Wall.

MÜLLER, KURT (Kutschi) (1903–90), born in Berlin, toolmaker, 1919 Communist Youth Association (KJVD), 1920 KPD, 1927–8 Communist Youth International (CYI) trade union desk in Moscow, 1928–31 union secretary then chairman of KJVD Central Committee in Germany, 1931 candidate for Comintern's Executive Committee, 1931–2 CYI secretary in Moscow, 1932 ostracized as adherent of Neumann, 1933–4 banished to Gorki car works, 1934 sent to head resistance in Baden but arrested in Sept., 1934–40 solitary confinement at Kassel penitentiary, 1940–5 KZ Sachsenhausen, 1945–8 KPD chairman of Lower Saxony and 1946–8 Member of *Landtag*, Apr. 1946–Jan. 1949 on SED party executive, Apr. 1948–May 1950 deputy chairman of national KPD, 1948–9 Economic Council, 1949–50 Member of *Bundestag*, 22 Mar. 1950 arrested by MfS as alleged western agent for abortive show trial in GDR, interrogated until Mar. 1953 before receiving twenty-five years' hard labour in Siberia, Oct. 1955 released to FRG, 1957 SPD, 1960–85 researcher for Friedrich-Ebert-Stiftung in Bonn.

NIEBERGALL, OTTO (1904–77), born in Kusel (Pfalz), metalworker/miner, 1918 Socialist Workers' Youth in Saarbrücken, 1924–35 leader of Saar KPD, 1935 Saar-Pfalz Section Leader based in Lorraine, 1936 to Spain, 1937–40 Rhineland Section Leader based in Brussels, 1940 to France where interned before escaping to join KPD's Toulouse leadership, 1942 led KPD's Western Leadership in Paris, responsible for Agitprop against German occupation troops, Oct. 1943–5 headed Committee for Free Germany in the West, 1945 returned to Saar, 1946–7 and 1953–7 town councillor in Saarbrücken, 1947 chairman of KPD in French Zone, 1947 expelled from Saar by French authorities, 1947–Jan. 1949 member of SED executive and from Apr. 1948 of KPD Executive, 1948 KPD chairman of Rhineland-Pfalz, 1949–53 Member of *Bundestag*, 1949 led purges as head of KPD's Party Control Commission, 1968 chairman of DKP in Rhineland-Pfalz.

NUDING, HERMANN (1902–66), born in Oberurbach (Württemberg), tanner, 1918 unionized and 1919 led KPD in his native town, 1920 on Communist Youth Association (KJVD) leadership in Württemberg, 1923–5 worked for International Workers' Aid in USA, then headed Württemberg KJVD, graduating to its Central Committee in 1925, 1927–8 attended Comintern's Lenin School in Moscow, 1929 Political Leader of Hagen KPD, Central Committee instructor in

Upper Silesia, 1930 Political Leader at Chemnitz, 1932 Organization Leader at Berlin-Brandenburg under Ulbricht, 1933–4 arrested, 1934 to Czechoslovakia, then USSR, until 1935 on Comintern's Central Europe desk, organized ersatz 'Military'-Apparatus before apparently falling out with Ulbricht, 1939–40 interned in France, working as farmhand before joining resistance, 1944–5 on Committee for Free Germany in the West, 1945 deputy leader of Württemberg-Baden KPD and Member of *Landtag* until 1950, 1946 on SED executive, 1948 opposed renaming KPD 'SVD' and defended autonomy from SED, 1949–Apr. 1951 Member of *Bundestag*, 1949–July 1950 Labour and Social Affairs desk on KPD secretariat, 1950 demoted for 'opportunism' and expelled in Feb. 1951.

PAUL, HUGO (1905–62), born in Hagen (Westphalia), fitter, 1923 KPD, 1928 on KPD's Lower Rhine leadership, 1931 union official, 1932 Member of *Reichstag* and *Landtag*, sub-district leader of Hagen KPD, June 1933 arrested and imprisoned for twelve years (including 3 1/2 at KZ Sachsenhausen), 1945–6 chairman of Lower Rhine KPD, Apr. 1946–Sept. 1947 SED executive, 1946 on British Zonal Leadership, 1946–50 Member of NRW *Landtag*, 1946–8 Minister of Reconstruction in NRW until dismissed, Apr. 1948 on KPD Executive, 1948–9 KPD chairman of NRW (Dec. 1949 removed for 'insufficient vigilance' in anti-Tito campaign), Feb. 1950 on Executive's Labour and Social Affairs desk, 1949–53 Member of *Bundestag*, Nov. 1951 tried in FRG for 'resistance against the state', after ban member of illegal KPD leadership.

PRINZ, WILLI (1909–?), born in Cologne, 1927 KPD, 1930 under Kurt Müller at Communist Youth International in Moscow, then Communist Youth Association leader in Middle Rhine, 1932 deposed as member of Neumann Group, after 1933 underground in Trier, then Saar, before illegal work in France and Netherlands, 1941 arrested, extradited, and imprisoned (including periods in KZ Sachsenhausen and Penal Battalion 999), British POW in Egypt, 1947 returned to Germany, 1947 on KPD's French Zonal Leadership, deputy chairman of Rhineland-Pfalz, then from Sept. 1949–Feb. 1951 of Hamburg, Member of Hamburg Senate, Feb. 1951 arrested in GDR by MfS, imprisoned until Apr. 1954, released but defected to West.

REIMANN, MAX (1898–1977), born in Elbing (East Prussia), shipyard worker then miner, joined Socialist Workers' Youth, 1914–18 soldier and Spartacist, 1919 KPD, from 1920 Ruhr miner, 1932 deputy leader of Revolutionary Trade Union Organization (RGO) in Ruhr, 1933 headed illegal RGO in Ruhr and Lower Rhine, 1933–4 to Saar, 1935 attended 7th Comintern world congress, until 1939 on KPD Central Committee's Foreign Secretariat, Apr. 1939 arrested on Czech–German border, sentenced to three years in Dortmund prison, before being transferred to KZ Sachsenhausen in 1942, Sept. 1945–May 1947 chairman of Ruhr KPD and from 1947–8 of NRW, Apr. 1946–Jan. 1949 on SED executive, 1946 headed KPD's British Zonal Leadership and from Apr. 1948 national party chairman, 1946–7 on British Zonal Advisory Council, 1947–8 Economic Council and 1948–9 Parliamentary Council, 1947–54 Member of NRW *Landtag* and 1949–53 of *Bundestag*, 1949 gaoled by British for three months for describing Germans working with military government as 'quislings', 1954 moved to GDR where *de facto* member of SED Politburo, after 1956 ban led underground KPD, 1969 returned to FRG and from 1971 honorary chairman of DKP.

RENNER, HEINZ (1892–1964), born in Lückenburg (Moselle), dentist, 1910 Social Democratic students' movement, 1913 SPD, 1914–18 army (badly wounded), 1919 USPD, then KPD, 1920–3 branch chairman in Essen, 1923–33 *Gauleiter* of International League of Victims of War and Work in Rhineland-Westphalia, 1922–33 faction chairman of Essen city council, from 1924 Member of Rhine Province *Landtag*, 1933 to Saar, then 1935 France, active for International Workers' Aid, 1936–7 in Britain to raise money for Spain, 1937–9 on KPD's Paris leadership, 1939 interned but Mar. 1943 extradited and imprisoned in Germany until Apr. 1945, after liberation rebuilt KPD Essen, Feb.–Oct. 1946 *Oberbürgermeister* of Essen, Aug.–Dec. 1946 Minister of Social Affairs in NRW and June 1947–Feb. 1948 Minister of Transport (dismissed), 1947–54 Member of NRW *Landtag*, 1948–9 Parliamentary Council, 1949–53 Member of *Bundestag*, a faction chairman famed for his biting wit, 1949–56 on national KPD Executive, 1958 unsuccessful independent *Bundestag* candidate.

RISCHE, FRIEDRICH (Fritz) (1914–), born in Bochum, metalworker, Communist Youth Association, 1932 KPD, 1933–45 multiple arrests and police surveillance during underground work in Ruhr, 1945 helped to refound local KPD, 1946 deputy editor of *Westdeutsches Volks-Echo*, 1948 spokesman on Economic Council, 1949–53 Member of *Bundestag*, 1951 Labour and Social Affairs desk on national executive, deputy chairman of Baden-Württemberg KPD, member of Programme Commission for 1952's National Liberation Programme, early 1954 arrested in FRG and sentenced in 1956 to 3¹/₂ years' imprisonment, after 1968 active in DKP, responsible for economic and social policy.

SPERLING, FRITZ (1911–58), born in Algringen (Lorraine), clerk, Socialist Workers' Youth, then 1931 Communist Youth Association (KJVD) functionary, 1932 KPD, 1933–5 after temporary arrest coordinated underground KJVD in Rhine-Ruhr region, 1935 to Amsterdam, 1935–7 attended Comintern's Lenin School in Moscow, 1937–9 Central Committee instructor conducting trips to Germany from Switzerland, 1941–4 arrested in Zurich and interned, contacts with Noel Field, 1946–8 KPD chairman of Bavaria, 1946–Jan. 1949 on SED executive, 1947 member of KPD's US Zonal Leadership, Apr. 1948 Cadre Secretary of KPD Executive, May 1950 deputy national chairman, Oct. 1950 moved to GDR for heart treatment, 26 Feb. 1951 arrested by MfS in Field Affair and 1954 sentenced to seven years' hard labour, 1956 released, partially rehabilitated, but died of heart condition.

BIBLIOGRAPHY

A Archival Sources

Archiv der sozialen Demokratie, Friedrich-Ebert-Stiftung, Bonn-Bad Godesberg (AdsD)

    Bezirk Westliches Westfalen

    NL Rudolf Dux

    NL Erich Gniffke

    NL Carlo Schmid

    NL Kurt Schumacher

    Ostbüro-Archiv

Archivsammlung-Ernst-Schmidt, Ruhrland-Museum, Essen (AES)

    Materials 1945–6

    19–396 *NL* Heinz Renner

Bergbau-Archiv beim Deutschen Bergbaumuseum, Bochum

    Bestand 54 Schachtanlage Sachsen, Hamm-Heesen

Bundesarchiv Koblenz (BAK)

    B 106   Bundesministerium des Innern

    B 118   Kommunistische Partei Deutschlands

    NL James Pollock

    Z 45 F   CAD—Civil Administration Division

    (OMGUS) ODI—Office of the Director of Intelligence

               POLAD—Political Advisor (Murphy)

    ZSg 1/65   KPD Publications

Deutscher Gewerkschaftsbund-Archiv, Hans-Böckler-Stiftung, Bonn-Bad Godesberg (DGB-Archiv)

    Bestand 11 DGB-Bundesvorstand

    NL Hans Böckler

    NL Matthias Föcher

    NL Hans Gottfurcht

Industriegewerkschaft Bergbau und Energie, Aktenarchiv, Bochum (IGBE)

    A (Org)   Akten

    DIV.   Diverses

    V4   Vorstandssitzungen

    NL Weeke

Innenministerium Nordrhein-Westfalen, Düsseldorf (IM-NRW)

Stiftung Archiv der Parteien und Massenorganisationen der DDR im Bundesarchiv, Berlin (SAPMO-BA)

    Kommunistische Partei Deutschlands—Westzonen/BRD

I 10/3   Parteivorstand
I 10/4   Abteilungen des PV/ZK
I 10/5   Zonenleitungen
I 10/23   Bezirksleitung Ruhrgebiet
I 10/28   Landesleitung Nordrhein-Westfalen
Kommunistische Partei Deutschlands—Westzonen/BRD (S)
I 11/3   Parteivorstand/Zentralkomitee
I 11/4   Abteilungen des PV/ZK
I 11/5   Zonenleitungen
I 11/23   Bezirksleitung Ruhrgebiet
Sozialistische Einheitspartei Deutschlands—Zentralkomitee
    DY 30/IV 2/1   Sessions of the SED Parteivorstand
    DY 30/IV 2/1.01   Consultations of the SED Parteivorstand
    DY 30/IV 2/2.022   Büro Merker
    DY 30/IV 2/10.01   Arbeitsgemeinschaft SED-KPD
    DY 30/IV 2/10.02   Westkommission beim PB des ZK der SED
Freie Deutsche Jugend—Zentralrat
Gesellschaft für Deutsch-Sowjetische Freundschaft—Zentralvorstand
    Nachlässe
    NY 4036   Wilhelm Pieck
    NY 4090   Otto Grotewohl
    NY 4142   Hermann Nuding
    NY 4182   Walter Ulbricht
Mannheimer Zentrum für Europäische Sozialforschung
    Arbeitsbereich IV—DDR-Geschichte, Universität Mannheim
        Privatarchiv (PA) Staritz
Modern Records Centre, University of Warwick (MRC)
    MSS 292/943   Trades Union Congress Archive—'Germany'
Nachlaß Kurt Müller, Dingelsdorf (courtesy of Dr Paul Müller)
Nordrhein-Westfälisches Hauptstaatsarchiv, Düsseldorf (NRW HStA)
    NW 106   Innenministerium NRW
    NW 110   Innenministerium NRW
    NW 179   Ministerpräsident—Staatskanzlei
    NW 284
    NL Peter Clark
    NL Kurt Lichtenstein
Otto-Suhr-Institut/Archiv und Dokumentation, Freie Universität
    Berlin
    DW 215   Press clippings on the KPD
Public Record Office, Kew (PRO)
    CAB 129   Cabinet Papers
    FO 371   General Correspondence
    Control Commission for Germany (British Element)

FO 1005 Allied Control Authority/Records Library
FO 1006 Regional Commissioner for Schleswig-Holstein
FO 1013 Regional Commissioner for Nordrhein-Westfalen
FO 1014 Regional Commissioner for Hansestadt Hamburg
FO 1030 Military Government Headquarters
FO 1049 Political Division
FO 1051 Manpower Division
FO 1056 Public Relations and Information Services Control Group
FO 1060 Legal Division
Zentralinstitut für sozialwissenschaftliche Forschungen, Freie Universität Berlin
(ZI6)
   Sammlung Michael Becker
   Sammlung Peter Brandt
Interviews
   Lord Annan, 14 July 1992
   Josef Ledwohn, 14 Sept. 1993
   Karl Schirdewan, 24 Aug. 1990
   Dr Ernst Schmidt, 9 Aug. 1989

B. Printed Sources

PRIMARY SOURCES

(*a*) Contemporary KPD Printed Sources

Freies Volk (central organ, 1949–56).
Unser Weg (functionaries' periodical, 1951–6).
Westdeutsches Volks-Echo (Ruhr organ, 1946–8).
Wissen und Tat (theoretical journal, 1946–56).

(*b*) Published Collections of Documents

Adenauer: 'Es mußte alles neu gemacht werden': Die Protokolle des CDU-Bundesvor-standes 1950–1953, ed. Günter Buchstab (Stuttgart, 1986).
Akten zur auswärtigen Politik der Bundesrepublik Deutschland: Adenauer und die Hohen Kommissare, i. *1949–1951*, ed. Hans-Peter Schwarz (Munich, 1989).
Akten zur Vorgeschichte der Bundesrepublik Deutschland 1945–1949, ed. Christoph Weisz *et al.*, iv (Munich and Vienna, 1983).
Auf dem Weg zur SED: Die Sozialdemokratie und die Bildung einer Einheitspartei in den Ländern der SBZ, ed. Andreas Malycha (Bonn, 1995).
Die Auseinandersetzung um die Länderverfassungen in Hessen und Bayern 1946—Dokumente, ed. Institut für Marxistische Studien und Forschungen (Frankfurt am Main, 1978).
Confidential U.S. State Department Central Files: Germany—Internal Affairs 1945–1949, ed. Paul Kesaris (Frederick, Md., 1985), microfilm reels 14. 838–944; 15. 1–219; 39. 905–48; 40. 1–571.

Confidential U.S. State Department Central Files: Germany—Federal Republic of Germany. Internal Affairs 1950–1954, ed. Paul Kesaris (Frederick, Md., 1986), microfilm reels 28. 432–941; 29. 1–643.

Dokumente der Kommunistischen Partei Deutschlands 1945–1956, ed. ZK der KPD (East Berlin, 1965).

Dokumente der Sozialistischen Einheitspartei Deutschlands: Beschlüsse und Erklärungen des Zentralsekretariats und des Parteivorstandes, ed. PV/ZK der SED (East Berlin, 1951 et seq.).

Dokumente und Materialien zur Geschichte der deutschen Arbeiterbewegung, series III, i. *Mai 1945–April 1946*, ed. Institut für Marxismus-Leninismus beim ZK der SED (East Berlin, 1959).

Dokumente zur Geschichte der kommunistischen Bewegung in Deutschland: Reihe 1945/1946, iii. *Protokoll der Reichsberatung der KPD 8./9. Januar 1946*, ed. Günter Benser and Hans-Joachim Krusch (Munich, 1995).

'Edith Ede' schreibt an 'xkx Jan'—aus geheimen akten, ed. Kurt Zentner (Bonn, 1956).

Einheitsdrang oder Zwangsvereinigung?: Die Sechziger-Konferenzen von KPD und SPD 1945 und 1946, ed. Hans-Joachim Krusch and Andreas Malycha (Berlin, 1990).

Foreign Relations of the United States (FRUS), *1945*, iii; *1947*, ii; *1949*, iii; *1950*, iv; *1951*, iii/pt. 2; *1955–57*, xxvi (Washington, DC, 1968/1972/1974/1980/1981/1992).

Der Freiheit eine Straße: Dortmund 1945, ed. IG Metall, Verwaltungsstelle Dortmund (Kösching, 1985).

Gewerkschaften in Politik, Wirtschaft und Gesellschaft 1945–1949 (*Quellen zur Geschichte der deutschen Arbeiterbewegung im 20. Jahrhundert*, vii), ed. Siegfried Mielke and Peter Rütters (Cologne, 1991).

Herrnstadt, Rudolf, *Das Herrnstadt-Dokument: Das Politbüro der SED und die Geschichte des 17. Juni 1953*, ed. Nadja Stulz-Herrnstadt (Reinbek bei Hamburg, 1990).

Im Zentrum der Macht: Das Tagebuch von Staatssekretär Lenz 1951–1953, ed. Klaus Gotto et al. (Düsseldorf, 1989).

Die Kabinettsprotokolle der Bundesregierung, ii. *1950*, ed. Ulrich Enders and Konrad Reiser; iv. *1951*, ed. Ursula Hüllbüsch; v. *1952*, ed. Kai von Jena (Boppard am Rhein, 1984/1988/1989).

Konrad Adenauer und die CDU der britischen Besatzungszone 1946–1949: Dokumente zur Gründungsgeschichte der CDU Deutschlands, ed. Konrad-Adenauer-Stiftung (Bonn, 1975).

KPD 1945–1968: Dokumente, ed. Günter Judick et al. (2 vols.; Neuss, 1989).

KPD-Prozeß: Dokumentarwerk zu dem Verfahren über den Antrag der Bundesregierung zur Feststellung der Verfassungswidrigkeit der Kommunistischen Partei Deutschlands vor dem Ersten Senat des Bundesverfassungsgerichts, ed. Gerd Pfeiffer and Hans-Georg Strickert (3 vols.; Karlsruhe, 1955/6).

Organisatorischer Aufbau der Gewerkschaften 1945–1949 (*Quellen zur Geschichte der deutschen Arbeiterbewegung im 20. Jahrhundert*, vi), ed. Siegfried Mielke *et al.* (Cologne, 1987).

The Papers of General Lucius D. Clay: Germany 1945–1949, ed. Jean Edward Smith (2 vols.; Bloomington, Ind., 1974).

Parteiensystem zwischen Demokratie und Volksdemokratie: Dokumente und Materialien zum Funktionswandel der Parteien und Massenorganisationen in der SBZ/DDR 1945–1950, ed. Hermann Weber (Cologne, 1982).

Protokoll der Verhandlungen des Parteitages der Sozialdemokratischen Partei Deutschlands vom 29. Juni bis 2. Juli 1947 in Nürnberg (reprint; West Berlin and Bonn-Bad Godesberg, 1976).

Protokoll der Verhandlungen des III. Parteitages der Sozialistischen Einheitspartei Deutschlands 20. bis 24. Juli 1950 in der Werner-Seelenbinder-Halle zu Berlin (2 vols.; East Berlin, 1951).

Protokoll der Verhandlungen der II. Parteikonferenz der Sozialistischen Einheitspartei Deutschlands 9. bis 12. Juli 1952 in der Werner-Seelenbinder-Halle zu Berlin (East Berlin, 1952).

Die Ruhrfrage 1945/46 und die Entstehung des Landes Nordrhein-Westfalen: Britische, französische und amerikanische Akten (*Quellen zur Geschichte des Parlamentarismus und der politischen Parteien*, 4th series/iv), ed. Rolf Steininger (Düsseldorf, 1988).

Statistisches Jahrbuch für die Bundesrepublik Deutschland, ed. Statistisches Bundesamt (Stuttgart and Cologne, 1952 *et seq.*).

Verhandlungen des Deutschen Bundestages: I. Wahlperiode 1949: Stenographische Berichte (17 vols.; Bonn, 1950/3).

4 Jahre Bundestag: Handbuch der Bundestagsfraktion der KPD, ed. Bundestagsfraktion der KPD (Oppau, n.d. [1953]).

Wilhelm Pieck—Aufzeichnungen zur Deutschlandpolitik 1945–1953, ed. Rolf Badstübner and Wilfried Loth (Berlin, 1994).

SECONDARY SOURCES

AARONS, MARK, and LOFTUS, JOHN, *Ratlines: How the Vatican's Nazi Networks Betrayed Western Intelligence to the Soviets* (London, 1991).

ABENDROTH, WOLFGANG, 'Das KPD-Verbotsurteil des Bundesverfassungsgerichts: Ein Beitrag zum Problem der richterlichen Interpretation von Rechtsgrundsätzen der Verfassung im demokratischen Staat', *Zeitschrift für Politik*, 3 (1956), 305–27.

—— *et al.* (eds.), *KPD-Verbot oder Mit Kommunisten leben* (Reinbek bei Hamburg, 1968).

AHRENS, FRANZ, *et al.*, *Streiflichter aus dem Leben eines Kommunisten: Franz Ahrens über Max Reimann* (Hamburg, 1968).

ANNAN, NOEL, *Changing Enemies: The Defeat and Regeneration of Germany* (London, 1995).

Archiv der Stadt Salzgitter (ed.), *Die Demontage der Reichswerke (1945–1951)* (Salzgitter, 1990).

AZZOLA, AXEL, and CRÖSSMANN, JÜRGEN, '30 Jahre Verbot der KPD', *Demokratie und Recht*, 14 (1986), 266–81.

BADSTÜBNER, ROLF, and THOMAS, SIEGFRIED, *Restauration und Spaltung: Entstehung und Entwicklung der BRD 1945–1955* (Cologne, 1975).

BAHNE, SIEGFRIED, *Die KPD und das Ende von Weimar: Das Scheitern einer Politik 1932–1935* (Frankfurt am Main and New York, 1976).

—— 'Die KPD vom Sozialfaschismus zur Blockpolitik', in Winfried Becker (ed.), *Die Kapitulation von 1945 und der demokratische Neubeginn* (Cologne and Vienna, 1987), 335–51.

BALZER, FRIEDRICH-MARTIN (ed.), *Ärgernis und Zeichen: Erwin Eckert—Sozialistischer Revolutionär aus christlichem Glauben* (Bonn, 1993).

BARTELS, WOLFGANG, and Bundesvorstand der Sozialistischen Deutschen Arbeiterjugend (eds.), *Philipp Müller: 11. Mai 1952 in Essen: Polizeimord an einem jungen Arbeiter* (Dortmund, 1977).

BARTOV, OMER, 'The Missing Years: German Workers, German Soldiers', *German History*, 8 (1990), 46–65.

—— *Hitler's Army: Soldiers, Nazis, and War in the Third Reich* (New York and Oxford, 1991).

BAUER, FRANZ J., *Flüchtlinge und Flüchtlingspolitik in Bayern 1945–1950* (Stuttgart, 1982).

BAUMANN, THOMAS, 'Das Verhältnis der KPD und der amerikanischen Besatzungsmacht in Deutschland 1945–1949', Ph.D. thesis (University of Mannheim, 1994).

BEHAN, THOMAS, '"Riding the Tiger": The Italian Communist Party and the Working Class of the Porta Romana Area of Milan, 1943–48', *The Italianist*, 10 (1990), 111–50.

BEHRENDT, ALBERT, *Die Interzonenkonferenzen der deutschen Gewerkschaften: Der Kampf des Freien Deutschen Gewerkschaftsbundes um eine fortschrittliche, gesamtdeutsche Gewerkschaftspolitik auf den Interzonenkonferenzen der deutschen Gewerkschaften* (East Berlin, 1959).

BENDER, KLAUS, *Deutschland, einig Vaterland?: Die Volkskongreßbewegung für deutsche Einheit und einen gerechten Frieden in der Deutschlandpolitik der Sozialistischen Einheitspartei Deutschlands* (Frankfurt am Main, 1992).

BENSER, GÜNTER, *Die KPD im Jahre der Befreiung: Vorbereitung und Aufbau der legalen kommunistischen Massenpartei (Jahreswende 1944/1945 bis Herbst 1945)* (East Berlin, 1985).

BERGMANN, KARL HANS, *Die Bewegung 'Freies Deutschland' in der Schweiz 1943–1945* (Munich, 1974).

BERRY, WALLACE W., 'A History and Case Study of the Communist Party of Germany (KPD) 1945–1969', Ph.D. thesis (Stanford University, Calif., 1971).

BETTIEN, ARNOLD, *Arbeitskampf im Kalten Krieg: Hessische Metallarbeiter gegen Lohndiktat und Restauration* (Marburg, 1983).

BEYER, HANS-CHRISTOFFER, 'Die verfassungspolitischen Auseinandersetzungen um die Sozialisierung in Hessen 1946', Ph.D. thesis (University of Marburg, 1977).

BILLSTEIN, REINHOLD, *Das entscheidende Jahr: Sozialdemokratie und Kommunistische Partei in Köln 1945/46* (Cologne, 1988).

BIRD, KAI, *The Chairman: John J. McCloy—the Making of the American Establishment* (New York, 1992).

BODENSIECK, HEINRICH, et al., *Die Deutschlandfrage von der staatlichen Teilung Deutschlands bis zum Tode Stalins* (Berlin, 1993).

BOFHLING, REBECCA, 'German Municipal Self-Government and the Personnel Policies of the Local US Military Government in Three Major Cities of the Zone of Occupation: Frankfurt, Munich, Stuttgart', *Archiv für Sozialgeschichte*, 25 (1985), 333–83.

BOHN, WILLI, *Einer von vielen: Ein Leben für Frieden und Freiheit* (Frankfurt am Main, 1981).

BORSDORF, ULRICH, 'Speck oder Sozialisierung?: Produktionskampagnen im Ruhrbergbau 1945–1947', in Hans Mommsen et al. (eds.), *Glück auf, Kameraden!: Die Bergarbeiter und ihre Organisation in Deutschland* (Cologne, 1979), 345–66.

BOWER, TOM, *Klaus Barbie: Butcher of Lyons* (London, 1984).

BRANDT, PETER, *Antifaschismus und Arbeiterbewegung: Aufbau—Ausprägung—Politik in Bremen 1945/46* (Hamburg, 1976).

——et al., *Karrieren eines Außenseiters: Leo Bauer zwischen Kommunismus und Sozialdemokratie 1912 bis 1972* (West Berlin and Bonn, 1983).

BRAUNTHAL, JULIUS, *History of the International* (3 vols.; London, 1980).

BROSZAT, MARTIN, and WEBER, HERMANN (eds.), *SBZ-Handbuch: Staatliche Verwaltungen, Parteien, gesellschaftliche Organisationen und ihre Führungskräfte in der Sowjetischen Besatzungszone Deutschlands 1945–1949* (Munich, 1989).

BRÜCHER, THOMAS, 'Die Gewerkschaftspolitik der KPD im Bergbau und in der Metallindustrie des Ruhrgebiets in den Jahren 1945–1949', diploma (Ruhr University of Bochum, 1976).

BRÜNNECK, ALEXANDER VON, *Politische Justiz gegen Kommunisten in der Bundesrepublik Deutschland 1949–1968* (Frankfurt am Main, 1978).

BULLOCK, ALAN, *Ernest Bevin: Foreign Secretary 1945–1951* (London, 1983).

BURLEIGH, MICHAEL, *Germany Turns Eastwards: A Study of Ostforschung in the Third Reich* (Cambridge, 1988).

BURNS, ROB, and WILL, WILFRIED VAN DER, *Protest and Democracy in West Germany: Extra-Parliamentary Opposition and the Democratic Agenda* (Basingstoke, 1988).

CARACCIOLO, LUCIO, 'Der Untergang der Sozialdemokratie in der sowjetischen Besatzungszone: Otto Grotewohl und die "Einheit der Arbeiterklasse" 1945/46', *VfZ*, 36 (1988), 281–318.

CARLEBACH, EMIL, *Zensur ohne Schere: Die Gründerjahre der 'Frankfurter Rundschau' 1945/47: Ein unbekanntes Kapitel Nachkriegsgeschichte* (Frankfurt am Main, 1985).

CAUTE, DAVID, *The Great Fear: The Anti-Communist Purge under Truman and Eisenhower* (London, 1978).

CESARANI, DAVID, *Justice Delayed* (London, 1992).

CHICKERING, ROGER, *We Men Who Feel Most German: A Cultural Study of the Pan-German League, 1886–1914* (London, 1984).

CHRISTIER, HOLGER, *Sozialdemokratie und Kommunismus: Die Politik der SPD und der KPD in Hamburg 1945–1949* (Hamburg, 1975).

CLARKE, MICHAEL, 'Die Gewerkschaftspolitik der KPD 1945–1951, dargestellt am Beispiel des "Industrieverbandes Bergbau/Industriegewerkschaft Bergbau" im Ruhrgebiet', diploma (Ruhr University of Bochum, 1982).

CLAUDIN, FERNANDO, *The Communist Movement: From Comintern to Cominform* (London, 1975).

CLAY, LUCIUS D., *Decision in Germany* (London, 1950).

CONNOR, IAN D., 'The Bavarian Government and the Refugee Problem 1945–50', *European History Quarterly*, 16 (1986), 131–53.

CRÜGER, HERBERT, *Verschwiegene Zeiten: Vom geheimen Apparat der KPD ins Gefängnis der Staatssicherheit* (Berlin, 1990).

CUMINGS, BRUCE, *The Origins of the Korean War: Liberation and the Emergence of Separate Regimes 1945–1947* (Princeton, 1981).

DABRINGHAUS, ERHARD, *Klaus Barbie: The Shocking Story of How the U.S. Used this Nazi War Criminal as an Intelligence Agent* (Washington, DC, 1984).

DEIGHTON, ANNE, *The Impossible Peace: Britain, the Division of Germany, and the Origins of the Cold War* (Oxford, 1990).

DEPPE, FRANK, *et al.*, 'Lokales Milieu und große Politik zur Zeit des Kalten Krieges 1945–1960 am Beispiel ausgewählter hessischer Arbeiterwohngemeinden', in Peter Assion (ed.), *Transformationen der Arbeiterkultur* (Marburg, 1986), 198–219.

DICKHUT, WILLI, *So war's damals . . . : Tatsachenbericht eines Solinger Arbeiters 1926–1948* (Stuttgart, 1979).

—— *Was geschah danach?: Zweiter Tatsachenbericht eines Solinger Arbeiters ab 1949* (Essen, 1990).

DIEFENDORF, JEFFRY M., *In the Wake of War: The Reconstruction of German Cities after World War II* (New York, 1993).

DIETRICH, WERNER, *Sozialdemokraten und Kommunisten in den Metallgewerkschaften Nordbadens 1945–1949* (Frankfurt am Main, 1990).

DI LORETO, PIETRO, *Togliatti e la 'doppiezza': Il Pci tra democrazia e insurrezione (1944–49)* (Bologna, 1991).

DINGEL, FRANK, 'Die Kommunistische Partei Saar', in Richard Stöss (ed.), *Parteien-Handbuch: Die Parteien der Bundesrepublik Deutschland 1945–1980*, ii (Opladen, 1983), 1852–79.

DI SCALA, SPENCER M., *Renewing Italian Socialism: Nenni to Craxi* (New York and Oxford, 1988).

DISKANT, JAMES, 'Scarcity, Survival and Local Activism: Miners and Steelworkers, Dortmund, 1945–8', *Journal of Contemporary History*, 24 (1989), 547–73.

DOUGLAS, WILLIAM A., 'The KPD against Rearmament: The Role of the West German Communist Party in the Soviet Campaign against West German Rearmament, 1949–1953', Ph.D. thesis (Princeton University, 1964).

DOWE, DIETER, and Friedrich-Ebert-Stiftung (eds.), *Kurt Müller (1903–1990) zum Gedenken* (Bonn, 1991).

DUHNKE, HORST, *Die KPD von 1933 bis 1945* (Cologne, 1972).

DUPEUX, LOUIS, *'Nationalbolschewismus' in Deutschland 1919–1933: Kommunistische Strategie und konservative Dynamik* (Munich, 1985).

EBERLE, EUGEN, and GROHMANN, PETER, *Die schlaflosen Nächte des Eugen E.: Erinnerungen eines neuen schwäbischen Jacobiners* (Stuttgart, 1982).

EDINGER, LEWIS J., *Kurt Schumacher: A Study in Personality and Political Behavior* (Stanford, Calif., 1965).

EISENBERG, CAROLYN, 'Working-Class Politics and the Cold War: American Intervention in the German Labor Movement, 1945–49', *Diplomatic History*, 7 (1983), 283–306.

EISNER, FREYA, *Das Verhältnis der KPD zu den Gewerkschaften in der Weimarer Republik* (Cologne and Frankfurt am Main, 1977).

ENGELMANN, BERNT, *Rechtsverfall, Justizterror und das schwere Erbe: Ein Beitrag zur Geschichte der deutschen Strafjustiz von 1919 bis heute* (2 vols.; Cologne, 1989).

FABIAN, RUTH, and COULMAS, CORINNA, *Die deutsche Emigration in Frankreich nach 1933* (Munich, 1978).

FARQUHARSON, JOHN, 'From Unity to Division: What Prompted Britain to Change its Policy in Germany in 1946?', *European History Quarterly*, 26 (1996), 81–123.

FAULHABER, MAX, *'Aufgegeben haben wir nie . . .': Erinnerungen aus einem Leben in der Arbeiterbewegung* (Marburg, 1988).

FICHTER, MICHAEL, *Besatzungsmacht und Gewerkschaften: Zur Entwicklung und Anwendung der US-Gewerkschaftspolitik in Deutschland 1944–1948* (Opladen, 1982).

—— 'Aufbau und Neuordnung: Betriebsräte zwischen Klassensolidarität und Betriebsloyalität', in Martin Broszat *et al.* (eds.), *Von Stalingrad zur Währungsreform: Zur Sozialgeschichte des Umbruchs in Deutschland* (Munich, 1988), 469–549.

—— *Einheit und Organisation: Der Deutsche Gewerkschaftsbund im Aufbau 1945 bis 1949* (Cologne, 1990).

—— 'HICOG and the Unions in West Germany', in Jeffry M. Diefendorf *et al.* (eds.), *American Policy and the Reconstruction of West Germany, 1945–1955* (Cambridge, 1993), 257–80.

FICHTER, TILMAN, and EBERLE, EUGEN, *Kampf um Bosch* (Berlin, 1974).

FILITOV, ALEXEI, 'The Soviet Policy and Early Years of Two German States, 1949–1961' (unpublished paper delivered at CWIHP conference, 28–30 June 1994).

FISCH, GERHARD, and KRAUSE, FRITZ, *SPD und KPD 1945/46: Einheitsbestrebungen der Arbeiterparteien: Dargestellt an Beispielen aus Südhessen* (Frankfurt am Main, 1978).

FISCHER, GEORG, *Vom aufrechten Gang eines Sozialisten: Ein Parteiarbeiter erzählt* (West Berlin and Bonn, 1979).

FISCHER, HEINZ-DIETRICH, *Parteien und Presse in Deutschland seit 1945* (Bremen, 1971).

Först, Walter, *Geschichte Nordrhein-Westfalens* (2 vols.; Cologne and Berlin, 1970).

Foitzik, Jan, *Zwischen den Fronten: Zur Politik, Organisation und Funktion linker politischer Kleinorganisationen im Widerstand 1933 bis 1939/40 unter besonderer Berücksichtigung des Exils* (Bonn, 1986).

—— 'Revolution und Demokratie: Zu den Sofort- und Übergangsplanungen des sozialdemokratischen Exils für Deutschland 1943–1945', *IWK*, 24 (1988), 308–42.

—— 'Die Kommunistische Partei Deutschlands und der Hitler-Stalin-Pakt: Die Erklärung des Zentralkomitees vom 25. August 1939 im Wortlaut', *VfZ*, 37 (1989), 499–514.

—— 'Die Bildung des Kominform-Büros 1947 im Lichte neuer Quellen', *Zeitschrift für Geschichtswissenschaft*, 40 (1992), 1109–26.

Friedrich, Thomas, 'Antworten der SED-Führung auf Fragen Stalins 1948', *BzG*, 33 (1991), 364–73.

—— 'Das Kominform und die SED', *BzG*, 33 (1991), 322–35.

Fülberth, Georg, *KPD und DKP 1945–1990: Zwei kommunistische Parteien in der vierten Periode kapitalistischer Entwicklung* (Heilbronn, 1990).

Gaddis, John L., 'The Emerging Post-Revisionist Synthesis on the Origins of the Cold War', *Diplomatic History*, 7 (1983), 171–204.

Geary, Dick, *European Labour Protest 1848–1939* (London, 1981).

Gieseking, Erwin, and Pfannenschwarz, Karl (eds.), *Urteil—KPD-Verbot aufheben: Politisches und Rechtliches zum Verbot der KPD. Protokoll des öffentlichen Hearings über die Problematik des KPD-Verbots mit Gästen aus der Bundesrepublik und aus dem Ausland am 5. Juni 1971 in der Mercator-Halle in Duisburg* (Cologne, 1971).

Gillingham, John, 'The "Deproletarianization" of German Society: Vocational Training in the Third Reich', *Journal of Social History*, 19 (1986), 423–32.

Giordano, Ralph, *Die Partei hat immer recht* (Cologne and Berlin, 1961).

Glees, Anthony, *Exile Politics during the Second World War: The German Social Democrats in Britain* (Oxford, 1982).

Gniffke, Erich W., *Jahre mit Ulbricht* (Cologne, 1966).

Goch, Stefan, *Sozialdemokratische Arbeiterbewegung und Arbeiterkultur im Ruhrgebiet: Eine Untersuchung am Beispiel Gelsenkirchen 1848–1975* (Düsseldorf, 1990).

Gössner, Rolf, *Die vergessenen Justizopfer des kalten Kriegs: Über den unterschiedlichen Umgang mit der deutschen Geschichte in Ost und West* (Hamburg, 1994).

Graf, William D., 'Anti-Communism in the Federal Republic of Germany', *The Socialist Register*, 21 (1984), 164–213.

Grafe, Peter, 'Der Kommunist im Ost-West-Konflikt: Erinnerungen von Ernst Schmidt', in id. et al. (eds.), *Der Lokomotive in voller Fahrt die Räder wechseln: Geschichte und Geschichten aus Nordrhein-Westfalen* (West Berlin and Bonn, 1987), 96–103.

Graml, Hermann, 'Die Legende von der verpaßten Gelegenheit: Zur sowjetischen Notenkampagne des Jahres 1952', *VfZ*, 29 (1981), 307–41.

GREINER-PETTER, ELKE, 'Antifaschistisch-demokratische Aktivitäten der KPD in den Landtagen Hessens und Nordrhein-Westfalens 1946–1948', Ph.D. thesis (Humboldt University, East Berlin, 1986).

GRIEGER, MANFRED, et al., *Stalins Schatten: Stalin und die westeuropäischen Kommunisten* (Neuss, 1989).

GRIESER, HELMUT, *Die ausgebliebene Radikalisierung: Zur Sozialgeschichte der Kieler Flüchtlingslager im Spannungsfeld von sozialdemokratischer Landespolitik und Stadtverwaltung 1945–1950* (Wiesbaden, 1980).

HAAS, WILLY, *Abschied vom Paradies, das keines war: Bericht einer Wandlung* (Böblingen, 1988).

HARIG, PAUL, *Arbeiter—Gewerkschafter—Kommunist* (Frankfurt am Main, 1973).

HARTMANN, GOTTFRIED, 'Die Arbeit der KPD im Parlamentarischen Rat', diploma (University of Marburg, 1978).

HARTNAGEL, THOMAS, and SYWOTTEK, ARNOLD, 'KPD, SED und der Marshall-Plan', in Othmar Haberl and Lutz Niethammer (eds.), *Der Marshall-Plan und die europäische Linke* (Frankfurt am Main, 1986), 231–62.

HAUMANN, HEIKO, *'Der Fall Max Faulhaber': Gewerkschaften und Kommunisten—ein Beispiel aus Südbaden 1949–1952* (Marburg, 1987).

HAUTH, ULRICH, *Die Politik von KPD und SED gegenüber der westdeutschen Sozialdemokratie (1945–1948)* (Frankfurt am Main, 1978).

HEIDEMEYER, HELGE, *Flucht und Zuwanderung aus der SBZ/DDR 1945/1949–1961: Die Flüchtlingspolitik der Bundesrepublik Deutschland bis zum Bau der Berliner Mauer* (Düsseldorf, 1994).

HEIMANN, SIEGFRIED, 'Die Deutsche Kommunistische Partei', in Richard Stöss (ed.), *Parteien-Handbuch: Die Parteien der Bundesrepublik Deutschland 1945–1980*, i (Opladen, 1983), 901–81.

—— 'Zum Scheitern linker Sammlungsbewegungen zwischen SPD und KPD/SED nach 1945: Die Beispiele USPD und UAPD', in Rolf Ebbighausen and Friedrich Tiemann (eds.), *Das Ende der Arbeiterbewegung in Deutschland?* (Opladen, 1984), 301–22.

HEMPEL-KÜTER, CHRISTA, *Die KPD-Presse in den Westzonen von 1945 bis 1956: Historische Einführung, Bibliographie und Standortverzeichnis* (Frankfurt am Main, 1993).

HERBERT, ULRICH, *Fremdarbeiter: Politik und Praxis des 'Ausländer-Einsatzes' in der Kriegswirtschaft des Dritten Reiches* (West Berlin and Bonn, 1985).

HERLEMANN, BEATRIX, *Die Emigration als Kampfposten: Die Anleitung des kommunistischen Widerstandes in Deutschland aus Frankreich, Belgien und den Niederlanden* (Königstein im Taunus, 1982).

—— *Auf verlorenem Posten: Kommunistischer Widerstand im Zweiten Weltkrieg: Die Knöchel-Organisation* (Bonn, 1986).

HERMAND, JOST, *Kultur im Wiederaufbau: Die Bundesrepublik Deutschland 1945–1965* (Munich, 1986).

HERMS, MICHAEL, 'Zur "Westarbeit" der FDJ', *Jahresbericht des Instituts für zeitgeschichtliche Jugendforschung*, 2 (1992), 41–63.

CHT, *Antifaschistische Aktion 1945: Die 'Stunde Null' in Braunschweig* n, 1978).

HAEL, 'Eine deutsche Chance?: Die innerdeutsche Diskussion um den lbrief vom November 1950' (unpublished paper delivered at CWIHP e, 28–30 June 1994).

HANS-ALBERT, *Zur Rechtsprechung des Bundesverfassungsgerichts zu den Parteien* (Munich, 1982).

WOLFGANG, *Die Revolution entläßt ihre Kinder* (Cologne and West 955).

RT, 'Zur Entwicklung der antifaschistischen Bewegung unter den Kriegsgefangenen in der UdSSR nach dem Sieg über den Hitler- us (1945–1950)', Ph.D. thesis (2 vols.; Institut für Gesellschaftswis- ten beim ZK der SED, East Berlin, 1968).

RNER, 'German Political Refugees in the United States during the World War', in Anthony Nicholls and Erich Matthias (eds.), *German cy and the Triumph of Hitler: Essays in Recent German History* (London,

LFRIED, 'Die französische Linke und die "Einheit der Arbeiterklasse" 947', in Dietrich Staritz and Hermann Weber (eds.), *Einheitsfront— artei: Kommunisten und Sozialdemokraten in Ost- und Westeuropa 1944– Cologne, 1989).

ins ungeliebtes Kind: Warum Moskau die DDR nicht wollte* (Berlin, 1994).

SCOTT, and MORRIS, C. J., 'A Very British Crusade: The Information Department and the Beginning of the Cold War', in Richard J. Aldrich British Intelligence, Strategy and the Cold War, 1945–51* (London and ork, 1992), 85–110.

NE, DENIS, *International Labour and the Origins of the Cold War* (Oxford,

NN, KLAUS-MICHAEL, 'Milieu, Radikalismus und lokale Gesellschaft: Zur geschichte des Kommunismus in der Weimarer Republik', *Geschichte und chaft*, 21 (1995), 5–31.

A, ANDREAS, '"Hier stehe ich, ich kann nicht anders!": Rede Otto wohls am 11. November 1945', *BzG*, 34 (1992), 167–84.

HATZ, GERHARD, and SEIDER, JOSEF, *Zum Kampf der KPD im Ruhrgebiet Einigung der Arbeiterklasse und die Entmachtung der Monopolherren 1945– East Berlin, 1962).

EK, INGE, *Arbeiterbewegung nach dem Krieg (1945–1948): Am Beispiel heid, Solingen, Wuppertal* (Frankfurt am Main and New York, 1983).

TIMOTHY, *Arbeiterklasse und Volksgemeinschaft: Dokumente und Mater- zur deutschen Arbeiterpolitik 1936–1939* (Opladen, 1975).

HARTMUT, 'Das Verbot politischer Parteien—Zur Problematik des Art. os. 2 GG', *Archiv des öffentlichen Rechts* (1971), 203–36.

HERBERT, 'Nur eine Wahlniederlage?: Zum Verhältnis zwischen SED und in den Jahren 1948/49', *Hefte zur DDR-Geschichte*, 12 (1993), 29–46.

—— 'Zur Westarbeit der FDJ 1953 bis 1956', *Jahresbericht des Instituts für zeit- geschichtliche Jugendforschung*, 3 (1993), 117–37.

—— 'Zur Stalinisierung der West-FDJ 1949 bis 1952', in Helga Gotschlich (ed.), *'Links und links und Schritt gehalten...': Die FDJ: Konzepte—Abläufe— Grenzen* (Berlin, 1994), 97–113.

HEYDEN, ULRICH-WILHELM, 'Die Politik der KPD in Westdeutschland 1945– 1948/49 unter besonderer Berücksichtigung Hamburgs anhand der Berichterstat- tung und Kommentierung in der "Hamburger Volkszeitung"', MA thesis (University of Hamburg, 1990).

—— 'Säuberungen in der KPD 1948 bis 1951', in Wolfgang Maderthaner *et al.* (eds.), *'Ich habe den Tod verdient': Schauprozesse und politische Verfolgung in Mittel- und Osteuropa 1945–1956* (Vienna, 1991), 139–58.

HODOS, GEORG H., *Show Trials: Stalinist Purges in Eastern Europe 1948–1954* (New York, 1987).

HÖGL, GÜNTHER, 'Die Reorganisation der sozialistischen Arbeiterbewegung in Dortmund unter der Britischen Besatzungsherrschaft 1945–1949', *Beiträge zur Geschichte Dortmunds und der Grafschaft Mark*, 76/7 (1984/5), 13–78.

HOFMANN, WERNER, *Stalinismus und Antikommunismus: Zur Soziologie des Ost-West- Konflikts* (Frankfurt am Main, 1967).

HOFSCHEN, HEINZ-GERD, 'Werftarbeiterstreik, Gewerkschaftsausschlüsse und die Absetzung des Betriebsrates der AG "Weser" 1953', *1999*, 2 (1990), 36–59.

HOROWITZ, DANIEL L., *The Italian Labor Movement* (Cambridge, Mass., 1963).

HÜTTENBERGER, PETER, *Nordrhein-Westfalen und die Entstehung seiner parlament- arischen Demokratie* (Siegburg, 1973).

HUND, WULF D., 'Die Sozialistische Freie Gewerkschaft', *Marxistische Studien*, 8 (1985), 165–95.

HURWITZ, HAROLD, *Die Stunde Null der deutschen Presse: Die amerikanische Pressepol- itik in Deutschland 1945–1949* (Cologne, 1972).

—— *Die Anfänge des Widerstands* (2 vols.; Cologne, 1990).

HUSTER, ERNST-ULRICH, *et al.*, *Determinanten der westdeutschen Restauration 1945–1949* (Frankfurt am Main, 1972).

Institut für Marxismus-Leninismus beim ZK der SED (ed.), *Geschichte der deutschen Arbeiterbewegung* (8 vols.; East Berlin, 1966).

—— (ed.), *Vereint sind wir alles: Erinnerungen an die Gründung der SED* (East Berlin, 1966).

JAHNKE, KARL HEINZ, 'Gegen die Allmacht der Staatssicherheit: Bericht von Fritz Sperling aus dem Gefängnis, März 1956', *BzG*, 33 (1991), 789–803.

—— '... ich bin nie ein Parteifeind gewesen': Der tragische Weg der Kommunisten Fritz und Lydia Sperling* (Bonn, 1993).

JASPER, GOTTHARD, 'Die disqualifizierten Opfer: Der Kalte Krieg und die Entschädig- ung für Kommunisten', in Ludolf Herbst and Constantin Goschler (eds.), *Wiedergutmachung in der Bundesrepublik Deutschland* (Munich, 1989), 361–84.

KADEN, ALBRECHT, *Einheit oder Freiheit: Die Wiedergründung der SPD 1945/46* (Bonn, 1964).

KALBITZ, RAINER, 'Gewerkschaftsausschlüsse in den 50er Jahren', in Otto Jacobi et al. (eds.), *Gewerkschaftspolitik in der Krise—Kritisches Gewerkschaftsjahrbuch 1977/78* (Berlin, 1978), 159–65.

—— *Aussperrungen in der Bundesrepublik: Die vergessenen Konflikte* (Cologne and Frankfurt am Main, 1979).

KAPPELER, MANFRED, 'Jugendverbände im Ost-West-Konflikt: Die Beziehungen zwischen Jugendverbänden in den Westzonen und der FDJ in der Gründungsphase des Bundesjugendringes', in Helga Gotschlich (ed.), *'Links und links und Schritt gehalten . . .': Die FDJ: Konzepte—Abläufe—Grenzen* (Berlin, 1994), 32–57.

KELB, BERNI, 'Hornhaut auf der Seele oder Wie der XX. Parteitag erledigt wurde', in Reinhard Crusius and Manfred Wilke (eds.), *Entstalinisierung: Der XX. Parteitag der KPdSU und seine Folgen* (Frankfurt am Main, 1977), 456–69.

KERSHAW, IAN, *The 'Hitler Myth': Image and Reality in the Third Reich* (Oxford and New York, 1987).

KIRCHHEIMER, OTTO, *Political Justice: The Use of Legal Procedure for Political Ends* (Princeton, 1961).

KITTEL, MANFRED, 'Genesis einer Legende: Die Diskussion um die Stalin-Noten in der Bundesrepublik 1952–1958', *VfZ*, 41 (1993), 355–89.

KLEIN, MICHAEL, *Antifaschistische Demokratie und nationaler Befreiungskampf: Die nationale Politik der KPD 1945–1953* (2nd edn.; West Berlin, 1986).

KLEMM, BERND, *Die Arbeiter-Partei (Sozialistische Einheitspartei) Hessen 1945–1954: Entstehungsbedingungen, Geschichte und Programmatik einer dritten deutschen Arbeiterpartei nach dem Zweiten Weltkrieg* (Hannover, 1980).

KLESSMANN, CHRISTOPH, 'Betriebsräte und Gewerkschaften in Deutschland 1945–1952', in Heinrich August Winkler (ed.), *Politische Weichenstellungen im Nachkriegsdeutschland 1945–1953* (Göttingen, 1979), 44–73.

—— 'Betriebsparteigruppen und Einheitsgewerkschaft: Zur betrieblichen Arbeit der politischen Parteien in der Frühphase der westdeutschen Arbeiterbewegung 1945–1952', *VfZ*, 31 (1983), 272–307.

—— *Die doppelte Staatsgründung: Deutsche Geschichte 1945–1955* (4th edn.; Bonn, 1986).

—— 'Elemente der ideologischen und sozialpolitischen Integration der westdeutschen Arbeiterbewegung', in Ludolf Herbst (ed.), *Westdeutschland 1945–1955: Unterwerfung, Kontrolle, Integration* (Munich, 1986), 107–16.

—— and FRIEDEMANN, PETER, *Streiks und Hungermärsche im Ruhrgebiet 1946–1948* (Frankfurt am Main and New York, 1977).

KLOCKSIN, JENS ULRICH, *Kommunisten im Parlament: Die KPD in Regierungen und Parlamenten der westdeutschen Besatzungszonen und der Bundesrepublik Deutschland (1945–1956)* (2nd edn.; Bonn, 1994).

KLOTZBACH, KURT, *Der Weg zur Staatspartei: Programmatik, praktische Politik und Organisation der deutschen Sozialdemokratie 1945 bis 1965* (Berlin and Bonn, 1982).

KLUTH, HANS, *Die KPD in der Bundesrepubl[ik] . . . isation 1945–1956* (Cologne and Opladen . . .

KÖRNER, KLAUS, 'Erst in Goebbels', dann i[n] . . . Aug. 1990), 37–8.

—— 'Kalter Krieg und kleine Schriften', *A* . . .

KOGON, EUGEN, 'Die Funktion des Antiko[mmunismus in] Deutschland', in *Anatomie des Antikommu[nismus . . .]* Education Division des American Friends Se[rvice . . .] im Breisgau, 1969), 190–205.

KRAUSE, FRITZ, *Antimilitaristische Opposition [. . .* Main, 1971).

KRIEGER, WOLFGANG, *General Lucius D. Clay un[d . . .* 1945–1949* (Stuttgart, 1987).

KRUSCH, HANS-JOACHIM, 'Neuansatz und w[. . .* 1945/1946', *BzG*, 33 (1991), 615–27.

KUEHL, HERBERT, *Die Gewerkschaftspolitik der [. . .* der Parteimitglieder in betrieblichen Konfli[kten . . .] anhand des Hamburger Werftarbeiterstreiks vo[. . .*

KUHN, HERMANN, *Bruch mit dem Kommunismus* [. . .* von Ex-Kommunisten im geteilten Deutschland [. . .*

KULEMANN, PETER, *Die Linke in Westdeutschlan[d . . .* zeit, zwischen sozialdemokratischer Integration u[nd . . .] Scheitern der 'Titoistischen' Unabhängigen Arb[eiterpartei . . .] and Frankfurt am Main, 1978).

KUNDE, KARL, *Die Odyssee eines Arbeiters* (Stuttg[art . . .*

KUTSCHA, MARTIN, 'Das KPD-Verbot', in Udo [. . .* *Das lädierte Grundgesetz: Beiträge und Dokument[e . . .] 1976* (Cologne, 1977), 42–77.

LANG, JOCHEN VON, *Erich Mielke: Eine deutsche [. . .*

LAUSCHKE, KARL, ' "Der Dicke muß weg!": Be[. . .* Westfalenhütte', in Peter Grafe et al. (eds.), *D[. . .* Räder wechseln: Geschichte und Geschichten a[. . .] Berlin and Bonn, 1987), 86–95.

LEBER, GEORG, *Vom Frieden* (Stuttgart, 1979).

LEDWOHN, JOSEF, 'Nichts in der Geschichte ist wi[. . .* nisse aus dem Neubeginn 1945/1946', in Ma[. . .* deutschen Neuanfang 1945–1949: Tatsachen—P[. . .* Die Arbeiterbewegung und die Entstehung der beiden [. . .] 130–9.

LEHMANN, LUTZ, *Legal & Opportun: Politische Justi[z . . .* Berlin, 1966).

LEHNDORFF-FELSKO, ANGELIKA, and RISCHE, FRITZ, [. . .* bis 1956: Wie es dazu kam—sein Verlauf—die Folge[n . . .*

LEIN, ALB[. . .* (Götting[en . . .*

LEMKE, M[. . .* Grotew[ohl . . .* conferen[ce . . .*

LENNARTZ[. . .* *politisch[e . . .*

LEONHARD[. . .* Berlin, [. . .*

LIBERA, [. . .* deutsch[. . .* faschis[. . .* senscha[. . .*

LINK, W[. . .* Second[. . .* *Democr[. . .* 1971).

LOTH, W[. . .* 1943–[. . .* *Einhei[. . .* 1948 [. . .* —— St[. . .*

LUCAS, [. . .* Resea[rch . . .* (ed.), [. . .* New [. . .*

MACSHA[. . .* 1992)[. . .*

MALLMA[NN . . .* Sozia[. . .* *Gesel[. . .*

MALYCH[. . .* Grot[. . .*

MANNS[. . .* für d[. . .* 1947[. . .*

MARßO[. . .* Rem[. . .*

MASON[. . .* italie[. . .*

MAUER[. . .* 21 [. . .*

MAYER[. . .* KP[. . .*

——— 'Durchsetzt von Parteifeinden, Agenten, Verbrechern . . . ?: Zu den Parteisäuberungen in der KPD (1948–1952) und der Mitwirkung der SED', *Hefte zur DDR-Geschichte*, 29 (1995).

MEINERS, JOCHEN, *Die doppelte Deutschlandpolitik: Zur nationalen Politik der SED im Spiegel ihres Zentralorgans 'Neues Deutschland' 1946 bis 1952* (Frankfurt am Main, 1987).

MERRITT, ANNA J., and MERRITT, RICHARD L. (eds.), *Public Opinion in Occupied Germany: The OMGUS Surveys, 1945–1949* (Urbana, Ill., 1970).

——— and ——— (eds.), *Public Opinion in Semisovereign Germany: The HICOG Surveys, 1949–1955* (Urbana, Ill., 1980).

MERSON, ALLAN, *Communist Resistance in Nazi Germany* (London, 1985).

MEUTER, PAUL, *Lebenserinnerungen eines Solinger Kommunisten* (Solingen, 1992).

MEYER, BEATE, and SZODRZYNSKI, JOACHIM (eds.), *Vom Zweifeln und Weitermachen: Fragmente der Hamburger KPD-Geschichte* (Hamburg, 1988).

MILLER, JAMES E., *The United States and Italy, 1940–1950: The Politics and Diplomacy of Stabilization* (Chapel Hill, NC, and London, 1986).

MITSCHERLICH, ALEXANDER and MARGARETE, *Die Unfähigkeit zu trauern: Grundlagen kollektiven Verhaltens* (2nd edn.; Munich, 1977).

MORAW, FRANK, *Die Parole der 'Einheit' und die Sozialdemokratie* (2nd edn.; Bonn, 1990).

MÜHLHAUSEN, WALTER, *Hessen 1945–1950: Zur politischen Geschichte eines Landes in der Besatzungszeit* (Frankfurt am Main, 1985).

MÜLLER, GLORIA, *Mitbestimmung in der Nachkriegszeit: Britische Besatzungsmacht— Unternehmer—Gewerkschaften* (Düsseldorf, 1987).

MÜLLER, INGO, *Furchtbare Juristen: Die unbewältigte Vergangenheit unserer Justiz* (Munich, 1987).

MÜLLER, KARL-FRIEDRICH, *Das Jahr 1945 in Südbaden* (Frankfurt am Main, 1987).

MÜLLER, KURT, 'Ein historisches Dokument aus dem Jahre 1956: Brief an den DDR-Ministerpräsidenten Otto Grotewohl', *Aus Politik und Zeitgeschichte*, B 11/90 (9 Mar. 1990), 16–29.

MÜLLER, LEO A., *Gladio—das Erbe des Kalten Krieges: Der Nato-Geheimbund und sein deutscher Vorläufer* (Reinbek bei Hamburg, 1991).

MÜLLER, WALTER, 'Die Aktionsgemeinschaft zwischen KPD und SPD in München 1945/1946', *BzG*, 3: Sonderheft (1961), 117–38.

MÜLLER, WERNER, *Die KPD und die 'Einheit der Arbeiterklasse'* (Frankfurt am Main and New York, 1979).

——— *Lohnkampf, Massenstreik, Sowjetmacht: Ziele und Grenzen der 'Revolutionären Gewerkschafts-Opposition' (RGO) in Deutschland 1928 bis 1933* (Cologne, 1988).

MÜSSENER, HELMUT, *Exil in Schweden: Politische und kulturelle Emigration nach 1933* (Munich, 1974).

MUSCHKAU, MARTIN, *Entscheidende Jahre 1928–1948: Bericht eines Zeitzeugen* (Hannover, 1990).

NEUMANN, FRANZ, *Der Block der Heimatvertriebenen und Entrechteten 1950–1960: Ein Beitrag zur Geschichte und Struktur einer politischen Interessenpartei* (Meisenheim am Glan, 1968).

NIETHAMMER, LUTZ, et al. (eds.), *Arbeiterinitiative 1945: Antifaschistische Ausschüsse und Reorganisation der Arbeiterbewegung in Deutschland* (Wuppertal, 1976).

—— 'Rekonstruktion und Desintegration: Zum Verständnis der deutschen Arbeiterbewegung zwischen Krieg und Kaltem Krieg', in Heinrich August Winkler (ed.), *Politische Weichenstellungen im Nachkriegsdeutschland 1945–1953* (Göttingen, 1979), 26–43.

—— (ed.), *Lebensgeschichte und Sozialstruktur im Ruhrgebiet 1930 bis 1960*, i. *'Die Jahre weiß man nicht, wo man die heute hinsetzen soll': Faschismus-Erfahrungen im Ruhrgebiet*; ii. *'Hinterher merkt man, daß es richtig war, daß es schiefgegangen ist': Nachkriegs-Erfahrungen im Ruhrgebiet*; iii, with Alexander von Plato. *'Wir kriegen jetzt andere Zeiten': Auf der Suche nach der Erfahrung des Volkes in nachfaschistischen Ländern* (West Berlin and Bonn, 1983/1983/1985).

—— (ed.), *Der 'gesäuberte' Antifaschismus: Die SED und die roten Kapos von Buchenwald* (Berlin, 1994).

NOLTE, ERNST, *Deutschland und der kalte Krieg* (Munich, 1974).

OLTMANN, JOACHIM, *Kalter Krieg und kommunale Integration: Arbeiterbewegung im Stadtteil Bremen-Vegesack 1945–1956* (Marburg, 1987).

OPPENHEIMER, MAX, 'Aufgaben und Tätigkeit der Landesgruppe deutscher Gewerkschafter in Großbritannien: Ein Beitrag zur Vorbereitung der Einheitsgewerkschaft', *Exilforschung*, 5 (1987), 241–56.

OTTO, WILFRIEDE, 'Dokumente zur Auseinandersetzung in der SED 1953', *BzG*, 32 (1990), 655–72.

—— 'Sowjetische Deutschlandnote 1952. Stalin und die DDR: Bisher unveröffentlichte handschriftliche Notizen Wilhelm Piecks', *BzG*, 33 (1991), 374–89.

PAUL, ELFRIEDE, *Ein Sprechzimmer der Roten Kapelle* (East Berlin, 1981).

PERK, WILLY, *Besatzungsmacht gegen Pressefreiheit: Geschichte der Zeitung 'Westdeutsches Volksecho', 7. Mai 1946 bis 4. Mai 1948* (Frankfurt am Main, 1979).

PEUKERT, DETLEV, *Die KPD im Widerstand: Verfolgung und Untergrundarbeit an Rhein und Ruhr 1933 bis 1945* (Wuppertal, 1980).

—— and BAJOHR, FRANK, *Spuren des Widerstands: Die Bergarbeiterbewegung im Dritten Reich und im Exil* (Munich, 1987).

PEYTON, CHRISTINE, 'Bedeutung und Bedeutungswandel des Antikommunismus in der Konstituierungsphase der Bundesrepublik Deutschland 1945–1949', diploma (Otto Suhr Institute/Free University of Berlin, 1978).

PIETSCH, HARTMUT, *Militärregierung, Bürokratie und Sozialisierung: Zur Entwicklung des politischen Systems in den Städten des Ruhrgebietes 1945 bis 1948* (Duisburg, 1978).

PINGEL, FALK, ' "Die Russen am Rhein?": Zur Wende der britischen Besatzungspolitik im Frühjahr 1946', *VfZ*, 30 (1982), 98–116.

PIRKER, THEO, 'Das Ende der Arbeiterbewegung', in Rolf Ebbighausen et al. (eds.), *Das Ende der Arbeiterbewegung in Deutschland?: Ein Diskussionsband zum 60. Geburtstag von Theo Pirker* (Opladen, 1984).

PLATO, ALEXANDER VON, *'Der Verlierer geht nicht leer aus': Betriebsräte geben zu Protokoll* (West Berlin and Bonn, 1984).

POLLATSCHEK, WALTHER, *Philipp Müller: Held der Nation* (East Berlin, 1952).

POMMERIN, REINER, 'Die Zwangsvereinigung von KPD und SPD zur SED: Eine britische Analyse vom April 1946', *VfZ*, 36 (1988), 319–38.

POPALL, KÄTHE, *Ein schwieriges politisches Leben: Erzählte Geschichte*, ed. Alheit and Jörg Wollenberg (Fischerhude, 1985).

POSSER, DIETHER, *Anwalt im kalten Krieg: Ein Stück deutscher Geschichte in politischen Prozessen 1951–1968* (Munich, 1991).

POTTHOFF, HEINRICH (ed.), *Handbuch Politischer Institutionen und Organisationen 1945–1949* (Düsseldorf, 1983).

RECKERT, WILFRIED, 'Die "Zerschlagung des Titoismus" in der KPD', *LILI Korrespondenz*, 1 (1991), 33–51.

REIMANN, MAX (ed.), *Die KPD lebt und kämpft: Dokumente der Kommunistischen Partei Deutschlands 1956–1962* (East Berlin, 1963).

—— *Entscheidungen 1945–1956* (Frankfurt am Main, 1973).

—— *et al.* (eds.), *KPD-Verbot: Ursachen und Folgen 1956–71* (Frankfurt am Main, 1971).

REYNOLDS, DAVID (ed.), *The Origins of the Cold War in Europe: International Perspectives* (New Haven and London, 1994).

RICHTER, JAMES, 'Reexamining Soviet Policy towards Germany during the Beria Interregnum', *Cold War International History Project: Working Papers*, 3 (1992).

RIDDER, HELMUT, *Aktuelle Rechtsfragen des KPD-Verbots* (Neuwied and West Berlin, 1966).

RISCHE, FRITZ, 'Die KPD-Fraktion im 1. Deutschen Bundestag für die deutsche Einheit und den Abschluß eines Friedensvertrags', in Marx-Engels-Stiftung (ed.), *Zum deutschen Neuanfang 1945–1949: Tatsachen—Probleme—Ergebnisse—Irrwege: Die Arbeiterbewegung und die Entstehung der beiden deutschen Staaten* (Bonn, 1993), 58–73.

RITTER, GERHARD A., and NIEHUSS, MERITH, *Wahlen in der Bundesrepublik Deutschland: Bundestags- und Landtagswahlen 1946–1987* (Munich, 1987).

RÖDER, WERNER, *Die deutschen sozialistischen Exilgruppen in Großbritannien 1940–1945: Ein Beitrag zur Geschichte des Widerstandes gegen den Nationalsozialismus* (Hannover, 1968).

—— 'Zum Verhältnis von Exil und innerdeutschem Widerstand', *Exilforschung*, 5 (1987), 28–39.

ROGERS, DANIEL E., 'Transforming the German Party System: The United States and the Origins of Political Moderation, 1945–1949, *Journal of Modern History*, 65 (1993), 512–41.

—— *Politics after Hitler: The Western Allies and the German Party System* (Basingstoke, 1995).

ROHE, KARL, *Vom Revier zum Ruhrgebiet: Wahlen, Parteien, Politische Kultur* (Essen, 1986).

ROSEMAN, MARK, *Recasting the Ruhr, 1945–1958: Manpower, Economic Recovery and Labour Relations* (New York and Oxford, 1992).

ROSENHAFT, EVE, *Beating the Fascists?: The German Communists and Political Violence 1929–1933* (Cambridge, 1983).

Ross, George, *Workers and Communists in France: From Popular Front to Euro-communism* (Berkeley, 1982).

Runge, Erika (ed.), *Bottroper Protokolle* (Frankfurt am Main, 1968).

Rupieper, Hermann-Josef, *Die Wurzeln der westdeutschen Nachkriegsdemokratie: Der amerikanische Beitrag 1945–1952* (Opladen, 1993).

Rupp, Hans Karl, *Außerparlamentarische Opposition in der Ära Adenauer: Der Kampf gegen die Atombewaffnung in den fünfziger Jahren* (Cologne, 1970).

Ryan, Allan A., *Klaus Barbie and the United States Government: The Report, with Documentary Appendix, to the Attorney General of the United States* (Frederick, Md., 1984).

Sabarko, Boris, 'Das Kominformbüro—ein Rückblick', *BzG*, 32 (1990), 446–57.

Sassoon, Donald, *The Strategy of the Italian Communist Party: From the Resistance to the Historic Compromise* (London, 1981).

Sator, Klaus, 'Das kommunistische Exil und der deutsch-sowjetische Nichtangriffspakt', *Exilforschung*, 8 (1990), 29–45.

Sayer, Ian, and Botting, Douglas, *America's Secret Army: The Untold Story of the Counter Intelligence Corps* (London, 1989).

Schädel, Gudrun, 'Die Kommunistische Partei Deutschlands in Nordrhein-Westfalen von 1945–1956', Ph.D. thesis (Ruhr University of Bochum, 1973).

Schaller, Michael, *The American Occupation of Japan: The Origins of the Cold War in Asia* (New York and Oxford, 1985).

Scheringer, Richard, *Unter Soldaten, Bauern und Rebellen: Das große Los* (reprint; Cologne, 1988).

Scherstjanoi, Elke, ' "Wollen wir den Sozialismus?" Dokumente aus der Sitzung des Politbüros des ZK der SED am 6. Juni 1953', *BzG*, 33 (1991), 658–80.

Schiffers, Reinhard, 'Grundlegung des strafrechtlichen Staatsschutzes in der Bundesrepublik Deutschland 1949–1951', *VfZ*, 38 (1990), 589–607.

Schildt, Axel, and Sywottek, Arnold (eds.), *Modernisierung und Wiederaufbau: Die westdeutsche Gesellschaft der 50er Jahre* (Bonn, 1993).

Schirdewan, Karl, *Aufstand gegen Ulbricht: Im Kampf um politische Kurskorrektur, gegen stalinistische, dogmatische Politik* (Berlin, 1994).

Schleifstein, Josef, *Der Intellektuelle in der Partei: Gespräche* (Marburg, 1987).

Schmidt, Eberhard, *Die verhinderte Neuordnung 1945–1952: Zur Auseinandersetzung um die Demokratisierung der Wirtschaft in den westlichen Besatzungszonen und in der Bundesrepublik Deutschland* (Frankfurt am Main, 1970).

Schmidt, Ute, and Fichter, Tilman, *Der erzwungene Kapitalismus: Klassenkämpfe in den Westzonen 1945–1948* (West Berlin, 1971).

Schneider, Johannes, *KP im Untergrund: Kommunistische Untergrundarbeit in der Bundesrepublik* (Munich, 1963).

Schuster, Rudolf, 'Relegalisierung der KPD oder Illegalisierung der NPD?: Zur politischen und rechtlichen Problematik von Parteiverboten', *Zeitschrift für Politik*, 24 (1968), 413–29.

Schwabe, Klaus, 'German Policy Responses to the Marshall Plan', in Charles S. Maier (ed.), *The Marshall Plan and Germany: West German Development within the Framework of the European Recovery Program* (New York and Oxford, 1991), 225–81.

SEEGERT, CHRISTIAN, 'Betriebsfrieden im Kalten Krieg: Materialien zur Bedeutung von Betriebsverfassung und Arbeitsgerichten bei der Kommunistenverfolgung der 50er Jahre', *Marxistische Studien: Jahrbuch des IMSF*, 8 (1985), 224–57.

SEMJONOW, WLADIMIR S., *Von Stalin bis Gorbatschow: Ein halbes Jahrhundert in diplomatischer Mission 1939–1991* (Berlin, 1995).

SENGER, VALENTIN, *Kurzer Frühling* (Frankfurt am Main, 1987).

SHELDON, CHARLES H., 'Public Opinion and High Courts: Communist Party Cases in Four Constitutional Systems', *The Western Political Quarterly*, 20 (1967), 341–60.

SIEGFRIED, DETLEF, *Zwischen Einheitspartei und 'Bruderkampf': SPD und KPD in Schleswig-Holstein 1945/46* (Kiel, 1992).

SIMPSON, CHRISTOPHER, *Blowback: America's Recruitment of Nazis and Its Effect on the Cold War* (London, 1988).

SMITH, JEAN EDWARD, *Lucius D. Clay: An American Life* (New York, 1990).

SOMMER, GERALD, 'Streik im Hamburger Hafen: Arbeiterprotest, Gewerkschaften und KPD', *Ergebnisse*, 13 (1981).

SPONHEUER, BERND (ed.), *zeitGenossen: 17 Lebensbilder von Kommunist/inn/en* (Düsseldorf, 1988).

STARITZ, DIETRICH, 'KPD und Kalter Krieg bis 1950', in Bernhard Blanke *et al.* (eds.), *Die Linke im Rechtsstaat*, i. *Bedingungen sozialistischer Politik 1945–1965* (Berlin, 1976), 195–210.

—— 'Die Kommunistische Partei Deutschlands', in Richard Stöss (ed.), *Parteien-Handbuch: Die Parteien der Bundesrepublik Deutschland 1945–1980* (Opladen, 1983), 1663–1809.

—— 'Parteien für ganz Deutschland?: Zu den Kontroversen über ein Parteiengesetz im Alliierten Kontrollrat 1946/47', *VfZ*, 32 (1984), 240–68.

—— 'Die SED, Stalin und der "Aufbau des Sozialismus" in der DDR: Aus den Akten des Zentralen Parteiarchivs', *Deutschland-Archiv*, 24 (1991), 686–700.

—— 'Die SED, Stalin und die Gründung der DDR: Aus den Akten des Zentralen Parteiarchivs des Instituts für Geschichte der Arbeiterbewegung (ehemals Institut für Marxismus-Leninismus beim ZK der SED), *Aus Politik und Zeitgeschichte*, B 5/91 (25 Jan. 1991), 3–16.

—— 'The SED, Stalin, and the German Question: Interests and Decision-Making in the Light of New Sources', *German History*, 10 (1992), 274–89.

—— 'Zur Gründung der SED: Forschungsstand, Kontroversen, offene Fragen', in id., *Was war: Historische Studien zu Geschichte und Politik der DDR* (Berlin, 1994), 105–36.

—— and WEBER, HERMANN (eds.), *Einheitsfront—Einheitspartei: Kommunisten und Sozialdemokraten in Ost- und Westeuropa 1944–1948* (Cologne, 1989).

STEIGERWALD, ROBERT, 'Antikommunismus—Anmerkungen zu einem Thema', in Marx-Engels-Stiftung (ed.), *Altlasten der politischen Justiz: Politische Strafjustiz der Bundesrepublik Deutschland in den 50er und 60er Jahren—Wirkungen des Antikommunismus im kalten Krieg* (Wuppertal, 1991), 39–52.

STEININGER, ROLF, *The German Question: The Stalin Note of 1952 and the Problem of Reunification* (New York, 1990).

STERN, CAROLA, *Die SED: Ein Handbuch über Aufbau, Organisation und Funktion des Parteiapparates* (Cologne, n.d. [1954]).

STERN, LEO, *Der Antikommunismus als politische Hauptdoktrin des deutschen Imperialismus* (East Berlin, 1963).

—— (ed.), *Der Antikommunismus in Theorie und Praxis des deutschen Imperialismus: Zur Auseinandersetzung mit der imperialistischen Geschichtsschreibung* (Halle-Wittenberg, 1963).

STEVEN, STEWART, *Operation Splinter Factor* (London, 1974).

STÖCKIGT, ROLF, 'Ein Dokument von großer historischer Bedeutung vom Mai 1953', *BzG*, 32 (1990), 648–54.

STÖßEL, FRANK THOMAS, *Positionen und Strömungen in der KPD/SED 1945–1954* (2 vols.; Cologne, 1985).

STRAKA, URSULA, 'SPD, DGB und KPD-Verbot—Eine Untersuchung der Positionen von Sozialdemokratischer Partei und Deutschem Gewerkschaftsbund zum Antrag auf Verbot der KPD 1951 und zur Urteilsverkündung 1956', diploma (University of Erlangen-Nürnberg, 1978).

SUCKUT, SIEGFRIED, 'Die Entscheidung zur Gründung der DDR. Die Protokolle der Beratungen des SED-Parteivorstandes am 4. und 9. Oktober 1949', *VfZ*, 39 (1991), 125–75.

SYWOTTEK, ARNOLD, *Deutsche Volksdemokratie: Studien zur politischen Konzeption der KPD 1935–1946* (Düsseldorf, 1971).

—— 'Die Opposition der SPD und KPD gegen die westdeutsche Aufrüstung in der Tradition sozialdemokratischer und kommunistischer Friedenspolitik seit dem ersten Weltkrieg', in Wolfgang Huber and Johannes Schwerdtfeger (eds.), *Frieden, Gewalt, Sozialismus: Studien zur Geschichte der sozialistischen Arbeiterbewegung* (Stuttgart, 1976), 496–610.

SYWOTTEK, JUTTA, *Mobilmachung für den totalen Krieg: Die propagandistische Vorbereitung der deutschen Bevölkerung auf den Zweiten Weltkrieg* (Opladen, 1975)

TIERSKY, RONALD, *French Communism, 1920–1972* (New York and London, 1974).

TOPF, DR, *Kommunistische Betriebs- und Gewerkschaftsarbeit: Eine Abhandlung* (Düsseldorf, n.d. [1958]).

TOPPE, HILMAR, *Der Kommunismus in Deutschland* (Munich, 1961).

TORMIN, WALTER, *Der Traum von der Einheit: Der Schriftwechsel zwischen SPD und KPD in Hamburg über die Gründung einer Einheitspartei 1945/46 und ergänzende Dokumente* (Hamburg, 1990).

TRITTEL, GÜNTER J., *Hunger und Politik: Die Ernährungskrise in der Bizone (1945–1949)* (Frankfurt am Main and New York, 1990).

URBAN, JOAN BARTH, *Moscow and the Italian Communist Party: From Togliatti to Berlinguer* (London, 1986).

VOIGT, ANDREAS, 'Nach dem Verbot: Die kommunistische Politik in Westdeutschland 1956–1961, dargestellt anhand illegaler KPD-Publizistik', MA thesis (University of Hamburg, 1989).

VORHOLT, UDO, and ZAIB, VOLKER, *SED im Ruhrgebiet?: Einheitsfront-Politik im Nachkriegsdeutschland—eine regionale Studie* (Münster and Hamburg, 1994).

WALL, IRWIN M., *French Communism in the Era of Stalin: The Quest for Unity and Integration, 1945–1962* (Westport, Conn., and London, 1983).

WALTER, HANS-ALBERT, 'Das Pariser KPD-Sekretariat, der deutsch-sowjetische Nichtangriffsvertrag und die Internierung deutscher Emigranten in Frankreich zu Beginn des Zweiten Weltkriegs', *VfZ*, 36 (1988), 483–528.

WARNKE, HELMUTH, *'Bloß keine Fahnen': Auskünfte über schwierige Zeiten 1923–1954* (Hamburg, 1988).

WEBER, HERMANN, *Die Wandlung des deutschen Kommunismus: Die Stalinisierung der KPD in der Weimarer Republik* (2 vols.; Frankfurt am Main, 1969).

—— *Hauptfeind Sozialdemokratie: Strategie und Taktik der KPD 1929–1933* (Düsseldorf, 1982).

—— *Geschichte der DDR* (Munich, 1985).

—— 'Ursachen und Umfang der deutschen Emigration nach 1933 unter besonderer Berücksichtigung von SPD und KPD im Exil', *IWK*, 24 (1988), 2–16.

—— *'Weiße Flecken' in der Geschichte: Die KPD-Opfer der Stalinschen Säuberungen und ihre Rehabilitierung* (2nd edn.; Frankfurt am Main, 1990).

—— 'Schauprozeßvorbereitungen in der DDR', in id. and Dietrich Staritz (eds.), *Kommunisten verfolgen Kommunisten: Stalinistischer Terror und 'Säuberungen' in den kommunistischen Parteien Europas seit den dreißiger Jahren* (Berlin, 1993), 436–49.

—— and OLDENBURG, FRED, *25 Jahre SED: Chronik einer Partei* (Cologne, 1971).

WEIGLE, KLAUS, 'Vom Sturmgrenadier zum KPD-Landesvorsitzenden: Eine autobiographische Skizze (1946/50)', *Demokratische Geschichte*, 7 (1992), 213–41.

WEILER, PETER, *British Labour and the Cold War* (Stanford, Calif., 1988).

WENDLER, JÜRGEN, *Die Deutschlandpolitik der SED in den Jahren 1952 bis 1958: Publizistisches Erscheinungsbild und Hintergründe der Wiedervereinigungsrhetorik* (Cologne, Weimar, and Vienna, 1991).

WERNER, WOLFGANG FRANZ, *'Bleib übrig!': Deutsche Arbeiter in der nationalsozialistischen Kriegswirtschaft* (Düsseldorf, 1983).

WEST, NIGEL, *Secret War: The Story of SOE, Britain's Wartime Sabotage Organisation* (London, 1992).

WETTE, WOLFRAM, 'Rußlandbilder der Deutschen im 20. Jahrhundert', *1999*, 7 (1995), 38–64.

WETTIG, GERHARD, 'Die Deutschland-Note vom 10. März 1952 auf der Basis der diplomatischen Akten des russischen Außenministeriums', *Deutschland-Archiv*, 26 (1993), 786–805.

—— 'All-German Unity and East German Separation in Soviet Policy, 1947–1949' (unpublished paper delivered at CWIHP conference, 28–30 June 1994).

WETTIG, GERHARD, 'Die KPD als Instrument der sowjetischen Deutschland-Politik: Festlegungen 1949 und Implementierungen 1952', *Deutschland-Archiv*, 27 (1994), 816–29.

WILKE, MANFRED, *et al.*, *Die Deutsche Kommunistische Partei (DKP): Geschichte—Organisation—Politik* (Cologne, 1990).

WILLIS, F. ROY, *The French in Germany 1945–1949* (Stanford, Calif., 1962).

WINKLER, DÖRTE, 'Die amerikanische Sozialisierungspolitik in Deutschland 1945–1948', in Heinrich August Winkler (ed.), *Politische Weichenstellungen im Nachkriegsdeutschland 1945–1953* (Göttingen, 1979), 88–110.

WINKLER, HEINRICH AUGUST, *Der Weg in die Katastrophe: Arbeiter und Arbeiterbewegung in der Weimarer Republik 1930 bis 1933* (West Berlin and Bonn, 1987).

WISOTZKY, KLAUS, *Der Ruhrbergbau im Dritten Reich: Studien zur Sozialpolitik im Ruhrbergbau und zum sozialen Verhalten der Bergleute in den Jahren 1933 bis 1939* (Düsseldorf, 1983).

WITTEMANN, KLAUS PETER, *Kommunistische Politik in Westdeutschland nach 1945: Der Ansatz der Gruppe Arbeiterpolitik: Darstellung ihrer grundlegenden politischen Auffassungen und ihrer Entwicklung zwischen 1945 und 1952* (Hannover, 1977).

WOLFRUM, EDGAR, *Französische Besatzungspolitik und deutsche Sozialdemokratie: Politische Neuansätze in der 'vergessenen' Zone bis zur Bildung des Südweststaates 1945–1952* (Düsseldorf, 1991).

—— '"In der französischen Zone ist der Teufel los": Die Sozialistische Partei von 1946 und ihr überkommenes Zerrbild', *IWK*, 28 (1992), 39–51.

WOLLER, HANS, 'Germany in Transition from Stalingrad (1943) to Currency Reform (1948)', in Michael Ermarth (ed.), *America and the Shaping of German Society, 1945–1955* (Providence, RI and Oxford, 1993), 23–34.

WULFFIUS, GEORG, 'Probleme mit der KPD-Lizenz', in Michael Schröder (ed.), *Auf geht's: Rama dama! Frauen und Männer aus der Arbeiterbewegung berichten über Wiederaufbau und Neubeginn 1945 bis 1949* (Cologne, 1984), 34–45.

ZEMAN, Z. A. B., *Nazi Propaganda* (London, 1964).

ZUBOK, VLADISLAV, and PLESHAKOV, CONSTANTINE, *Inside the Kremlin's Cold War: From Stalin to Khrushchev* (Cambridge, Mass., and London, 1996).

ZUNDER, RAINER, *Erschossen in Zicherie: Vom Leben und Sterben des Journalisten Kurt Lichtenstein* (Berlin, 1994).

INDEX